W9-BFS-924

A WOMAN'S PLACE

Also by Norton Juster

The Phantom Tollbooth
The Dot and the Line
Alberic the Wise
Stark Naked
Otter Nonsense
As: A Surfeit of Similes

A WOMAN'S PLACE

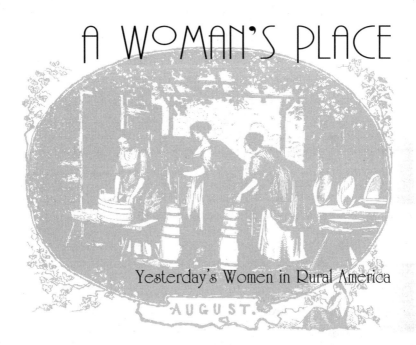

Yesterday's Women in Rural America

NORTON JUSTER

FULCRUM PUBLISHING
GOLDEN, COLORADO

FOR JEANNE

Copyright © 1996 Norton Juster
Cover image, "Woman Doing Wash" (WHi (X3) 50162), courtesy State Historical Society of Wisconsin

Book Design by Deborah Rich

All rights reserved. No part of this book may be reproduced or transmitted in any form or by any means, electronic or mechanical, including photocopying, recording, or by any information storage and retrieval system, without permission in writing from the publisher.

Library of Congress Cataloging-in-Publication Data

A woman's place : yesterday's women in rural America / [compiled
   by] Norton Juster.
        p.   cm.
     Originally published: So sweet to labor. New York : Viking, 1979.
     Includes bibliographical references.
     ISBN 1-55591-250-8 (pbk.)
     1. Rural women—United States—History—19th century.   I. Juster,
Norton, 1929–   .   II. Title.
HQ1419.S63   1996
305.4′0973′091734—dc20   96-3244
                                                                CIP

Printed in the United States of America
0   9   8   7   6   5   4   3   2   1

Fulcrum Publishing
350 Indiana Street, Suite 350
Golden, Colorado 80401-5093
(800) 992-2908
(303) 277-1623

ACKNOWLEDGMENTS

There are a number of people and institutions that have touched and affected the sense of this book. I would like to express my thanks to Carol Dubie and Laura Hartman for their research assistance, to Robert Lyon for his photographic help, to Frank Smith whose insight and poet's sensibility helped me to say more through saying less, to Lou Farnham for her sensitive criticism, to all the Cohens at the Argosy Bookstore for allowing me to rummage at will through their pictorial treasures, to my partner in architectural practice, Earl Pope, whose forbearance must by now be threadbare, to Hampshire College for its support in many ways (some of which, I must admit, they are not aware of), to the libraries, research institutions, state and local historical societies who were unfailingly helpful, and to the many anonymous pack rats (like myself) who save things in attics and occasionally become impatient with them.

And special thanks to Mrs. Constance C. Kuhn for permission to quote from *Grandmother Brown's Hundred Years* by Harriet Connor Brown. Beyond these, my special appreciation to my wife, Jeanne, who continually infuriated me by not understanding what I was sure I had made clear, and hadn't; and to Dolores Klaich, who took a mass of material, edited and shaped it, and through her care, understanding, and skill, made it happen.

Women govern us, let us try to render them perfect.

—Richard Brinsley Sheridan

The thirty-five years from the end of the Civil War to the turn of the century saw surge after surge of vigorous activity as the nation reached full manhood.

—from the foreword to *After the Civil War* by John S. Blay

Let all wives who are unhappy because of discontent accept admonition and compassion. Let "farmers' wives as a class" protect against the prevailing tone of condolence, and assert themselves to be healthfully nurtured, wholesomely fed, sufficiently cultured, becomingly attired, comely as well, and not apprehensive of insanity.

—letter from a farmer's wife in the *New York Post*, 1880

CONTENTS

INTRODUCTION

I came to this book by a circuitous route. It represents a journey of discovery for me on many levels, and the thought and research for it were a dominant part of my life for more than eight years. My interest, however, did not begin with the idea of doing a book about the life of rural women, nor, in fact, were my efforts focused on any disciplined investigation. They coalesced rather as a result of the circumstances and concerns of my life during the 1970s, and I think it is important to the recognition of whatever particular bias this book contains to understand how it evolved.

I am an architect, author, and until recently a teacher of environmental design. I was born in New York and lived most of my life there. My wife is a graphic designer from London. Strictly urban products, both of us. In 1969, we moved to an old farm in western Massachusetts, one of those rocky hillside farms that must have made the rich Ohio Valley look so inviting to the New England farmers. It hadn't been worked for fifty years or more—a nineteenth-century relic that lingered ghostlike into the twentieth century. Life there, for which my wife and I were largely unprepared, unfolded as a series of unexpected revelations.

First, the farm was not cared for by that invisible presence that always seemed to keep the rural landscape in order when we were passing through or visiting. Too many things weren't provided or just didn't happen, as they did in the city. Second, living on the farm jarred and conflicted with our sense of pace and place. Despite all modern means of communication, we had a strong feeling of removal—of not having everything and everyone accessible—and there was the attendant necessity of finding local occupation and involvement. The isolation contained and limited our lives in more ways than we were prepared for. Third, our sense of time and pace was substantially altered and the criteria by which we had previously measured them were no longer applicable. A much larger percentage of our time was taken up doing the things that simply had to be done to keep the place from coming down around our ears or disappearing back into the woods. At first this change was burdensome, then gradually it became an ordering influence on our time, and finally it established itself as a kind of inevitable, almost satisfying concomitant of life. Even though we did not attempt to farm it, the place made great demands, and it was not easy to understand how people managed to do all they did one hundred years before, nor to grasp what it meant in terms of their lives.

. . .

One result of the move was that it added great scope to my opportunities for collecting. I have always had a persistent itch for accumulating old things, mostly books, prints, tools, or objects that move or do something—machines, pieces of machines, or mechanical gadgets. I had never collected in any organized way but rather picked up what appealed to my eye or curiosity. In the city, it was easy to scavenge from an almost limitless supply of "rubbish," but difficult, unless you really worked at it, to direct your collecting to any coherent end. When we moved to the farm, I found my collecting becoming more focused. What was most readily available tended to be the paraphernalia of rural life, and what was affordable—on the occasions when we *had* to buy—tended to be those objects and/or periods not in popular demand. From barn sales, flea markets, auctions, and town dumps came an assortment of tools and objects. These acquisitions were not the exquisite hand-crafted eighteenth- and early nineteenth-century ones, but the later, semimechanized hybrids that fall between craft and machine. Along with them came a kind of literature much different from what I was used to seeing. There was always a box or two of old farm manuals and journals, home medical advisors with their incredible fold-back/peel-away anatomical drawings, domestic-economy tracts, guide books to morals and manners, housekeeping manuals, cookbooks, patent office reports, mechanics' receipt books, diaries, popular poetry anthologies, "ladies" books, catalogs, agricultural society annuals—all relegated by dealers to the junk category: "What am I bid for this box?" Most of it fell into the period between the Civil War and World War I and all of it seemed to relate to aspects of the life I was now leading, or at least being thrust into contact with.

In studying the material I had collected I was struck by the amount that people from this era knew and appalled at the amount they *had* to know. Understandably, much of what I found was no longer applicable or was just plain wrong; however, a large part was not only still useful but also strikingly germane to my new circumstances. The great collection of recipes, methods, formulas, cures, ideas, advice, facts, techniques, and intuitive and mystical knowledge offered essentially the strategy for a different kind of life, a life related to the one that I could still see in the decaying remains around me, or sense in my own daily tasks. Yet it was a life remote from my understanding of what it would mean to *have* to live it.

. . .

The "back-to-the-land" movement and the interest in alternative lifestyles that had become increasingly insistent themes in American life in the late 1960s touched my life only peripherally, but it had become a deep commitment for many people I knew or knew of. Their sense of disaffection seemed to be fueled by the perception that we were in danger of severing our connections to the essential processes and tasks that had always established the context of human existence. When we wanted something, it was there for us. Milk came from a container, water from the tap, relief from a small bottle, light from the electric company, clothing from the mall. Most of the time we didn't understand how it happened, but we'd come to depend on it. The disturbing consequence when things didn't work was the feeling of loss of personal command, or involvement in the circumstances of our living—i.e., the essential feeling that we could make do under any conditions and not stand helplessly in front of the broken machine.

It seemed, moreover, that in gaining technological mastery over the conditions of our lives, we had gone a long way toward diminishing the quality and meaning of life itself. In gradually removing from our concern most of the things that people previously had to do to live, we had left great amounts of time for other pursuits or diversions not directly concerned with necessity. For society in general this transition made possible a materially richer and more secure life than we could have imagined a hundred years ago. Along with it, however, a dilemma was suggested in which for many, the necessary had been replaced by the trivial, the real by the cosmetic and, increasingly, that cosmetic was applied onto a diminished sense of being.

The answer for some was to find a way to step back, drop out, or leave the mainstream, and seek to lead a more "rational" life; and, along with it, to reject much of the established social order as well as the technology that supported it. For many others the response was more passive but no less deeply felt—an intensified, painful, and disorienting nostalgia for an older, simpler time.

The desire to return to a more simple and "understandable" life has always been a durable idea. What intensified it during the 1960s (and still does to the present time) was the frightening pace with which the world had become incomprehensible and beyond our command. Fewer and fewer people remained completely confident in the machine's ability to fix the machine. Each round of "corrective" solutions seemed to reveal even larger problems and, like the roaches, these problems become more and more resistant to control.

What began to interest me was how well that idea of a more elemental life was understood and what the implications of such a choice were. How simple or "free" was the self-sufficient life? What conditions would it impose, and how free is any life when we really subject ourselves to the conditions self-sufficiency imposes? Can we really choose to know less than we know, or do less than we can do? I didn't know the answers, and I felt that a large number of those who had so joyously opted for or advocated such a life probably didn't either. In too much of the rhetoric there was a disquieting element of fantasy and flight. It seemed clear to me that if an alternative did lie in the return to a life as lived in another period of our history, some real understanding of what it meant to live at that time and under those conditions would be essential.

. . .

Any useful relationship to the past requires us to see it as it was and not as it is so often merchandised. Nostalgia, however, requires a soft focus. Its prerequisites are often a bad memory and a longing for something distant or lost (even if it was not we who lost it). That glowing picture of "the good old days," the image of an undefined or located "then" when things were better—people more concerned, the land understood and respected, and everyone knowing what to expect—has become a significant natural resource and one of our more spectacular growth industries. For upward of one hundred years we have been working it diligently and are now doing so at an increasingly frantic and profitable clip, reflected most poignantly today in the countless theme parks and historic village re-creations that have become such popular tourist destinations. As a form of emotional strip mining, the immediate returns may be satisfying, but the longer-range effects are perhaps less benign. We have begun to re-create our past with a vengeance—as it would please us and as we will have it. In our entertainment and politics, of course, we have always done so, but we've now begun to add further dimension and refinement so that the past becomes both a sanitized fantasy and a kind of surreal reproach to the present.

Interest in post–Civil War America seems particularly susceptible to poetic illusions—visions of flickering gaslight, overstuffed furniture, ample rooms, friendly clutter, Dickensian holiday meals, wholesome pleasures, snug towns, gingerbread cottages—both picturesque and kinky, the period has become a decorators' playground of the bizarre, a passport to lost elegance, an epochal conversation piece.

4

Our relationship to this period, even more than most, has been in the nature of a romantic rip-off, with little genuine understanding of the quality of life or its context. And, if this is true for the urban situation, it is even more so for rural life. For while conditions were somewhat less than elegant or comfortable for most people in the city, they were more often grim and hostile in the country. Yet it is here that we have really brought in a sentimental gusher. Even in the relatively settled and civilized East, rural life was, in large measure, lonely, demanding, and unsure—a life of grim necessity and little choice. Beyond the mountains to the Mississippi, the Northwest Territory and plains, life was, at each stage, a pioneering and colonizing venture of incredible tenuousness. With whatever satisfaction it offered, for most people rural living was a wearing, monotonous, isolated, and often soul-destroying existence.

. . .

With all this in mind, I decided to piece together, as a book, a picture of rural life that would reveal its demands set against the increasingly romanticized image. What particularly interested me were those things that defined the tasks and concerns of daily existence, what people had to do to live—i.e., how they made and maintained shelter, how they provided for the necessities of life, how they preserved and prepared the food they ate, and how they dealt with problems of health, illness, and general well-being.

The material I was collecting advised or instructed on virtually every practical aspect of rural life—from siting a house to placing a lightning rod, from manufacturing paint to ventilating a stable, from choosing a farm to sharpening an axe, draining a field, organizing spring-cleaning, making soap, preserving eggs, mixing a perpetual ink for tombstones, repairing stoves, preventing swallows from nesting, stewing a sheep's tongue, preparing a poultice or a six-course breakfast, what to do when someone swallowed a wasp, the value of earwax on wounds, gilding a picture frame, embalming a floral parasol, and constructing a harp. Collecting and organizing all this material became a fascinating and compulsive pastime, but its result was ultimately unsatisfactory, for while this flood of detail did convey a sense of what was done and how to do it, the sum of these tasks alone did not seem to illuminate the substance of daily living. It remained more a disembodied catalog than a resonant portrayal of life.

The specifics of man's work and world that I found were almost always directly and narrowly concerned with what he did and how he did it. A typical magazine of the time, *The American Agriculturist,* which was aimed primarily at men, would contain market reports, seasonal work schedules, innumerable articles on tools, techniques, horticultural advances, descriptions of farm operations, and a range of technical inquiries and answers. There might be also a page or two directed to the ladies or the children, but these were merely instructional or strictly informative, and what few letters there were stuck strictly to business. These were interesting, but they displayed little range and even less concern for the larger issues of life.

The literature that related particularly to woman's life and sphere, however, dealt with and defined the quality of rural life more humanly and inclusively. The publications for women, as detailed as the men's in their specifics, conveyed or revealed a much broader concern for the meaning and content of life. *The Household,* for example, would range not only through those subjects that were the special province of women—cleaning, mending, cooking, food preservation, care of children, etiquette, and so forth—but would offer also an impressive compass of articles on the home, its planning, furnishing, and its influence on healthy living. There were also articles on medicine, gardening, reading, educational opportunities and amusements, history, reminiscences, philosophy, and world affairs. In addition, there was a selection of poetry (pertinent if not profound), fiction, music scores and lyrics, and an extraordinary selection of letters on every imaginable subject, from inquiries for specific recipes or literary references to uninhibited and revealing accounts of lives and experiences. For woman's work and concerns were not only her life but also the armature of her family's life. Her attempts to define herself, rationalize her existence, mitigate her burdens, and maintain the continuity of home and family, as reflected in the material I found, made life during that time both accessible and compelling. My understanding of the period emerged primarily through the expression of *her* life; it provided the framework that made all the rest meaningful. Quite simply, understanding the rural life meant understanding the woman's life.

Woman's place during the late nineteenth century as portrayed in this literature was that of supporter and follower—the one who adapts and makes do. Her work was the anonymous background for someone else's "meaningful activity." Despite periodic efforts to give some status to homemaking, she had little sense of craft and little scope for self-esteem. She was effectively removed not only from participation in but also from an understanding of the complex forces and processes that controlled her life. The discontinuity, alienation, and despair that this implies were certainly dominant facts of woman's life then and remain, sadly, central facts for many women today. What has changed, of course, is that, in the years since World War II, it has become an increasingly compelling perception of life for everyone—a shared dilemma. This disquieting condition, if perhaps new to our collective conscious-ness in the 1960s and 1970s, had been, historically, the given condition of women's lives. What was emerging from the mass of material I had collected was not only a picture of the life of rural woman in the late nineteenth century but, clearly, a vivid illustration of a problem that has ceased to concern only women but defines an increasingly common human predicament.

My decision to address this problem was motivated, therefore, less by a desire to do a book about women than by the wish to respond to an issue best exempli-fied by a life imposed upon and led by women—a life and an era that, if perceived more realistically, might provide some insight into the costs of an irrational flight into the past.

. . .

This book attempts to witness the life of women in rural America during the decades following the Civil War—the life on the farms and in the remote villages and small towns where, in the 1870s and 1880s, the majority of the American people still lived. It is a record and an evocation of the content and circumstance of that life—in effect, a parade of the ordinary and the infinitesimal, of the daily job of coping and providing, of the strategies, rationales, and costs of being female and being human.

My aim has been to make the detail and quality of the rural woman's life accessible through the issues and questions that defined it. What were the de-mands, the satisfactions and discontents, disabilities and terrors of woman's sphere and woman's place? How did women see themselves, and how were they seen? What was it their special province to know and do?

I am not suggesting that there was a universal or homogeneous "woman's experience" then (or at any time) but rather that there were common and com-pelling themes that characterized their lives. I believe that these themes still influ-ence, modulate, and relate to contemporary life in many vital ways, for in the lives of the women at that time we can read the effort to preserve woman's traditional place in our society—an effort that remains with us today.

The writings gathered here are not the historically important feminist and intellectual thoughts of those years, which were little read when published, but today widely reprinted and an integral part of the examination of women's his-tory. Rather, they are examples of the popular literature of the time, mainstream fare culled mostly from high-circulation weekly or monthly newspapers, maga-zines, and popular books of the day; items, often uncataloged, that gather dust in the basements of state and county historical societies, university archives, and rarely consulted areas of major libraries. Intensely read in its day, this popular literature was more often than not taken as gospel by the women who read and wrote it, and it mirrors their lives in important detail.

For example, the monthly newspaper, *The Household,* which began its publishing life in 1868 with a circulation of 10,000, had 50,000 subscribers by 1870, and 70,000 by 1884. The thousands of letters *The Household* received from female readers attest to the excitement and involvement with which it was read, showing how important to their lives it had become. The following sample of reader response is taken from a June 1884 letter from a Missouri farm wife, who signs herself E. B., and from whom we will hear more in later pages:

DEAR HOUSEHOLD: If you only knew the enthusiasm, and could hear the expressions of delight with which "our" paper is welcomed every month at our house, it would provoke a smile at least. I do not know what to do when the magazine arrives, we all want to read it first, and I scarcely know how to settle the difficulty …. Something must be done, for when we are through reading it, it has to be "taken up tenderly, lifted with care," so dilapidated is its condition.

"Winter still lingers in the lap of spring," and from present indications will continue there for some time to come. The past winter was the coldest I ever experienced, the mercury often falling as low as 25° below zero. Ladies, you who live in the sunny south, just think of getting breakfast for a family of sixteen when the mercury is 32° below zero! Kitchen as cold as an iceberg, lard like marble, sausage ditto, coffee pot ditto, and in fact, everything that can freeze, in the same ice bound condition. I often felt while preparing breakfast that I would freeze too, but resisted the temptation to do so, when I remembered what an ignominious death it would be— to freeze to death over the cooking stove!

When we built our new kitchen I wanted it 14 x 14, but John wanted it larger, and many were the consultations held about its length, width and height, but they ended as usual by his having his own way (that is the only way I can manage him), and our kitchen is large enough to hold a meeting in, and when the mercury sinks on the lower line, the cooking stove gives out about as much heat as a lightning bug (that is a hyperbole, remember). The children soon discovered that one or two buckets of water accidentally (?) spilled upon the floor, transformed it into a most delightful skating rink, and I have perhaps practiced standing upon ice more the past winter, than I have since I was a girl.

Now, here is my letter growing long and not a word have I said to Helen Herbert, Pat, Maple Leaves, and many others who have given me words of sympathy and encouragement. Thanks, kind friends, rest assured your remarks shall ever be held in grateful remembrance ... .

While E. B. was busy turning her domestic travail into a joke in order to cope, and thanking her *Household* sisterhood for their sympathy and concern, a thousand miles away in Johnstown, New York, the feminist Elizabeth Cady Stanton, mother of seven, wrote in her diary of the same year, 1884:

AUGUST 28. On the 8th we held a woman's convention in the old Court House, where in the past my father [Judge Daniel Cady] argued more than one case. Several times during the sittings I wondered if his spirit was present ... . Of course such a gathering is but a drop in the great bucket of the United States. But it has always been my rule to "keep the pot aboiling"... . Miss [Susan B.] Anthony and I ... thought of what a great step in advance all this meant, happening in our sleepy old Johnstown, where my father once refused to have me visit him because of my radicalism. Tears came to my eyes as I thought of that dead past and this dawning future ... .

Susan B. Anthony's and Elizabeth Cady Stanton's important feminist newspaper, the weekly *Revolution,* begun in the same year as *The Household,* lasted only two and one-half years with a very modest circulation, at best.

If one hundred years from today one were to look back at the state of American women in the twentieth century by reading only feminist theory like that found, for example, in Shulamith Firestone's *Dialectic of Sex* (which has sold about 7,000 or 8,000 hardcover copies since it was published in 1970) and ignored books such as Marabel Morgan's *Total Woman* (which sold 400,000 hardcover copies in 1974 alone and was the largest seller of all nonfiction hardcover books for that year), it is obvious that the sense of our time would be distorted. The popular currents of the day are an essential component in understanding life as it was lived and commonly understood.

In the late nineteenth century, popular writings reflected the pressures that served to circumscribe and diminish the context of women's lives, at a time in American history when that context was being profoundly altered. What emerges from this material is the mass of custom, belief, and myth that had, through the first half of the nineteenth century, gradually but relentlessly solidified. The "Cult of Domesticity" had found its ideal medium in the rural environment, and it was here that these beliefs flourished and were embodied until they were seen to be fixed and inevitable. But we also find here the questions, protests, and cries of pain that evidenced an understanding that all was not right. Rural woman was not entirely unaware of what was going on beyond the confines of her kitchen. Both those who observed and those who experienced the burden of that life had begun, if only tentatively, to explore and question. Rarely, as attested here, did they reach what could be called the feminist root of the problem—that would have been too drastic and dangerous a step. As women sought whatever change or amelioration that seemed attainable and embraced whatever rationale offered solace, their growing awareness in most cases left them only with poignant aches, more questions, and few answers. The picture is a jarring counterpoint of image and reality, a picture that also consistently characterizes the time.

. . .

The rural condition, enduring and conservative, was, until the late nineteenth century, the common condition. We were still the "agrarian Eden," if not entirely in fact, then at least in common cognizance. While the demands of expansion and change were creating new opportunities in the cities, the rural world represented stability. Rural women were not, in most cases, women on the move, but the carriers and sustainers of tradition—perpetuators of the status quo—subject to (and in most cases supporters of) the full weight of held values and assigned roles. Rural life has always been the enduring American ideal. It is, despite all logic or evidence to the contrary, where we still seek our identity, indulge our longings, and evoke the qualities—honesty, simplicity, independence, self-sufficiency—that we choose to think describe us. In terms of how women were seen and how they saw themselves, it is the rural tradition, nurtured through the nineteenth century, that represents our most enduring image of their lives and consciousness.

But, though traditions linger, conditions do change, and from the close of the Civil War to the end of the century, the conditions that nurtured and supported that rural tradition were all but obliterated from American life. In the 1860s, rural America was still the core of the country's identity and wealth, but by the mid-1890s, what was left was an isolated and increasingly powerless vestige. In 1860, about 60 percent of American workers were on farms. By the turn of the century that figure had dropped below 40 percent. The population of the country doubled during this period, from 38,000,000 to 76,000,000, but the common experience became the city, the factory, the mill, the office. And along with this came the inevitable transformation in values and expectations that further isolated rural experience and tradition.

By the end of the Civil War, the context of life in the United States had been transformed. Those trends that had become visible earlier in the century—the move from country to city, from handcraft to machine production, from small comprehensible business entities to large-scale corporate enterprises, and from a pay-as-you-go morality to unprecedented financial manipulation and speculation—had become decisive in the life and identity of the country. From the late eighteenth century onward a parade of new inventions, ideas, processes, tools, and techniques came into daily life. Some were small and hardly noticed, others were more startling in effect or implication, but while no one was decisive in itself, each made some condition of life or consciousness different.

In terms of daily life, new building technology and the development of standardized building components made improved housing widely affordable and available. Advances in environmental controls and convenience (indoor plumbing and waste disposal, central heating, refrigeration, and the introduction of both gas and electric lighting) made possible the changes in form and arrangement that would so alter the American home and the life within it. The introduction of improved cooking ranges and stoves along with the flood of labor-saving "domestic machinery"—including the apple peelers, raisin pitters, egg beaters, carpet sweepers, and sewing and washing machines—had a profound effect on woman's work, and if it did not entirely relieve her burden, it certainly altered her outlook. The industrial production of essential commodities and the processing and distribution of staple foods made possible varied diets not dependent on seasonal supply. Food production itself was transformed by the new machinery and methods of cultivation called into being by the westward migration. Expanded networks of communication and transportation—rural free delivery, mail-order merchandising, mass-circulation magazines, the telephone, the typewriter, transcontinental railroad links, and the web of interurban and rural services—moved goods and ideas in a way that suggested for the first time the emergence of a truly national identity. It is a large and familiar catalog. One that can only be suggested here. Its significance lies in its cumulative effect. The transformation in life was subtle rather than sudden, a result of the gradual accrual of and piecemeal accommodation to the overwhelming weight of change. As the Tin Woodsman of

11

Oz discovered, things can be altered only so much before they become something entirely different.

In a perversely logical way, the Civil War punctuated and accelerated this change by tending, as wars do, to concentrate energies, mobilize technology, and suggest further directions for exploration and change. Equally important, the war left a residue of physical and moral exhaustion that allowed established forms and ways to be contested.

Movement, progress, and opportunity were the watchwords; the times did not simply offer them, but demanded they be embraced. Success was an obligation. Failure lay in nothing more than standing pat. Life was for the taking. The results, in almost all aspects of American life, were manifestly illogical, corrupt, or ugly. It was a period often described as sordid, debased, immoral, self-indulgent, and it was all these things. Yet in its excesses and in the movement and energy it released, there was the expression of a new American identity. What happened, for all its untidiness, was the emergence of a world we can, for the first time, recognize as our own, and out of whose mistakes, experiments, and often grotesque responses we now define our present existence and problems.

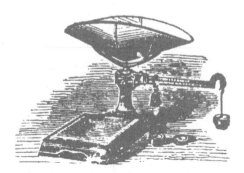

It was a watershed time, particularly for women, for the changing circumstances of life were suggesting for the first time, to any meaningful extent, the possibility of their participation in the processes and events that shaped their lives. In scrambling for a new order, needs arose for which no precedents existed, and those needs created a range of opportunities and responses that were not clearly or traditionally men's nor women's. Many doors were now ajar.

Running parallel to this, however, was the force of tradition, ever more passionately extolled and defended as it was increasingly threatened. We had taken a turn toward a new kind of life, and like the tail of the comet, the rural world trailed along, carrying with it its determined ways and values. While it was a time of change, it was also the last moment in our history when a persuasive claim could be made for that insistent concept of "women's place" or for the necessity of maintaining their domestic focus. And this, of course, was seen primarily in the context of rural demands and circumstance. But, more important, we must see much of the effort to fix woman's place as an attempt to mitigate the uncertainties and pressures of the time.

If "success," "exploitation," and "get up and go" were the themes that characterized the late nineteenth century, they brought with them a pervasive climate of instability and stress. Nervous debility or neurasthenia became known as "The American Disease." Dyspepsia was almost a birthright. Women and the stable family structure represented a desperately needed emotional anchor and refuge for the questing male—a connection to some consistent system of value and morality. The wave of sentimentality and idealization of home, mother, and family that washed over the time served that need then, and still distorts our sense of history today. Women at home provided the services and presence that remain the subject of the most enduring and romantic nostalgia. But the reality of those images exacted a cruel price. The rural woman had to perform the tasks and endure the burdens, but she was denied, in her narrowly circumscribed life, the essential ingredients necessary to create a logical rationale for that life—beyond embracing those sentimental, exploitive myths that kept her in her place.

Whatever good could attach to that demanding life would require some sense of a larger meaning and fulfillment. But what existed in most cases was a life tied to house and children, lacking opportunity for outside contacts, stimulation, or variety of experience, constant adaptation to the terms of life established by someone else, endless unacknowledged work, and little relief from relentless triviality. This isolated life ground down the health and spirit of vast numbers of women and, no doubt, accounts for the disproportionate reports of insanity and mental aberration among rural women at that time.

It is the persistent distorted image of woman's life and the domestic tradition as it was portrayed, accepted, confronted, and influenced by the emergence of wider possibility that I have tried to fix as the informing idea of this book.

The references I have used are not strictly limited to the period 1865–1895 but include some overlap at each end. Much early material, books especially, remained in use and had continuing influence (things reached the rural areas more slowly, and lingered longer), and many later publications carried forth ideas and methods that had already become widely accepted. I have, for the most part, limited the geographic scope of my concern to the line of consistent settlement extending from New England and the Middle Atlantic states across the mountains to the Ohio Valley, the upper

Mississippi, and the old Northwest Territory and central plains, eliminating from general consideration the far western frontier and the southern states. While much of the material I have used relates as much to them as to the other areas, I have not attempted to deal with the special conditions attached to pioneering or the slave culture, whose influences on women's lives were so singular.

The excerpts I have included are not necessarily by women. They do not try to represent a woman's viewpoint, but rather a view of women. Many of the writers and almost all the editors of magazines and books were men, and one can only guess at the extent to which they controlled what was published. Many axes are ground here—by both men and women—and yet there is much here that is direct and ingenuous in articles, stories, and especially the letters. I have included them not only for their content but also for their quality of expression and literacy, which for women of relatively little formal education is startlingly high.

I have tried to range widely in my sources in order to present what seemed to me to be representative of commonly held views and attitudes. Many of the subjects appeared and reappeared constantly, with some of the articles being reprinted several times in newspapers, books, and magazines. Many of the most widely read publications, of course, originated in the East and in the larger cities (even those directed to rural audiences or concerns), but by the 1880s, there were agricultural and home magazines and papers published in virtually every state.

In borrowing from certain publications, such as *The Household,* which I have used frequently, I return many times to the same writers and correspondents, who seem to address the important questions and who, for me, became representative witnesses to the times. Who "Olive Oldstyle" or "E. B." were, I don't know—sagacious, concerned women or an editor's useful invention (I hope not)—but the reader must recognize that there is room here too for some intrinsic, if not always obvious, bias.

I have tried also to include the various sides and shades of issues—opposing viewpoints and arguments—so that much of what appears here is contentious and contradictory. Insofar as possible, I have let the material speak for itself, intervening mainly to set the scene and provide whatever background, definition, or continuity I thought was necessary.

The book is organized into two parts. In part one, "Image and Identity," I try to establish the context of the rural woman's life, the roles she played, the themes that seemed most clearly to characterize her existence, and the way she is portrayed or chooses to portray herself—the accepted image of her life—the role she was assigned to play. In part two, "Burdens, Costs, Responses," I have attempted to present more the reality of that life, the growing awareness and discontent, the costs, some of the rationalizations used to maintain her place, the alternatives offered, and the reaction to them.

Paralleling the two parts is a continuous miscellany of method and task—the jobs women did, the things they had to know, the tools and methods they used, the rules they followed—in short, the art of homemaking and the science of housekeeping. Although I could present only the briefest sampling of this, my aim was to establish some sense of the detail of life as an inescapable part of its substance.

PART ONE
IMAGE AND IDENTITY

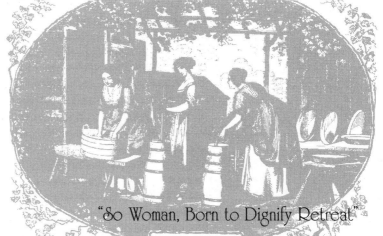

"So Woman, Born to Dignify Retreat"

AUGUST.

Lithograph on previous page:
Gleason's Pictorial, *Aug. 19, 1854.*
Courtesy: Argosy Bookstore, N.Y.C.

THE PROVINCE OF WOMAN

As some fair violet, loveliest of the glade,
Sheds its mild fragrance on the lonely shade,
Withdraws its modest head from public sight,
Nor courts the sun, nor seeks the glare of light:
Should some rude hand profanely dare intrude,
And bear its beauties from its native wood,
Exposed abroad its languid colors fly,
Its form decays, and all its odors die:
So woman, born to dignify retreat;
Unknown to flourish, and unseen be great;
To give domestic life its sweetest charm;
With softness polish, and with virtue warm;
Fearful of fame, unwilling to be known,
Should seek but Heaven's applause and her own.

—Hannah More

R ural woman's God-given role was that of dutiful daughter, wife, mother, and home-maker. The rationales used to justify and exalt that role held her in a determined embrace, and her acceptance of them further circumscribed and enshrined her place. Whatever power or status she held was based on her tacit acceptance of that identity, a catalog of limiting and disabling perceptions of character and aptitude.

She nurtured, sustained, and consoled. She maintained order and tranquillity and was the fixed point of reference in a chaotic and uncertain world. Tempering and mediating the shocks and demands of family life, she was the armature of well-being—dispensing hospitality; nursing the sick and hurt; serving up food, cheer, and love; providing moral and cultural guidance. Yet, as manager of the circumstances of life, she was all but powerless to control them. The "elevated" issues of taste, sentiment, virtue, and morality of which she was arbiter were almost always peripheral to the real imperatives of living. She functioned as alter ego and rationale for man's efforts and adventures, and as a refuge from them. Clearly, she had to be insulated from the world, for while she had a body, brain, and nervous system (so well suited to certain tasks), they were manifestly inferior to man's and could not be burdened with rigorous cares and pressures.

Every right-thinking person knew that the old ways were the right ways. Woman's duty was to perpetuate the race and care for her family. Life would come to her through her father, her husband, and her children. Her needs were minimal, her role supportive, and her rewards deferred. When it was all over, whatever the hardships and sacrifices, it would all have been worth it, for "Heaven's applauses" awaited.

19

The excerpts in this section present rural women as they were seen and, in large part, as they saw themselves—the roles in which they were accepted and from which they drew their own identity:

The wife as resource and material asset—contented bird—industrious, happy, decorative, deferential, and lovingly devious.

The mother, whose life was defined and filled by her children, whose aura filled and warmed the house, and whose example shaped the future as she encouraged learning and guided amusement. She was a well of strength and sacrifice, a gentle angel.

The daughter, innocent and true, who must be taught her woman's obligations and duties, be steered past the dangers of unguided choice, convinced of the blessedness of her destiny, and apprised of the precarious future that any deviation offered.

And the homemaker, the virtuoso of pot and pan, mop and brush, who conjured up ease and comfort from whatever was at hand, who was endlessly and cheerfully occupied, dependable, punctual, organized, and thorough—anticipating all needs and rising to all tests.

WIFE

A Farmer's Wife I'll Be

I'm a wild and laughing girl, just turned of sweet sixteen,
As full of mischief and of fun as ever you have seen;
And when I am a woman grown, no city beaux for me—
If e'er I marry in my life, a farmer's wife I'll be.

I love a country life, I love the joyous breeze,
I love to hear the singing birds along the lofty trees;
The lowing herds and bleating flocks make music sweet for me—
If e'er I marry in my life, a farmer's wife I'll be.

I love to feed the chickens, and I love to milk the cow,
I love to hear the farmer's boy a whistling at his plough;
And fields of corn and waving grain are pleasant sights to me—
If e'er I marry in my life, a farmer's wife I'll be.

I love to see the orchards where the golden apples grow,
I love to walk in meadows where the bright streamlets flow;
And flowery banks and shady woods have many charms for me—
If e'er I marry in my life, a farmer's wife I'll be.

Let other girls who love it best, enjoy the gloomy town,
'Mid dusty walls and dusty streets, to ramble up and down,
But flowery fields, and shady woods, and sunny skies for me—
If e'er I marry in my life, a farmer's wife I'll be.

—*New England Farmer*
OCTOBER 1854

Photo on previous page: Frame and Sod House, Custer, Co., 1888.
Solomon D. Butcher Collection, Nebraska State Historical Society.

THE FARMER'S WIFE

Bird-like she's up at day-dawn's blush,
In summer heats or winter snows—
Her veins with healthful blood aflush,
Her breath of balm, her cheek a rose.
In eyes—the kindest eyes on earth—
Are sparkles of a homely mirth;
All vanished is the brief eclipse!
Hark! to the sound of wedded lips,
And words of tender warmth that start
From out the husband's grateful heart!
O! well he knows how vain is life,
Unsweetened by the farmer's wife.

But lo! the height of pure delight
Comes with the evening's stainless joys,
When by the hearthstone spaces bright
Blend the glad tones of girls and boys;
Their voices rise in gleeful swells,
Their laughter rings like elfin bells,

Till with a look 'twixt smile and frown
The mother lay her infant down,
And at her firm, uplifted hand,
There's silence 'mid the jovial band;
Demure, arch humor's ambush in
The clear curves of her dimpled chin.
Ah! guileless creature, hale and good,
Ah! fount of wholesome womanhood,
Far from the world's unhallowed strife!
God's blessing on the farmer's wife.

I love to mark her matron charms,
Her fearless steps through household ways.
Her sun-burnt hands and buxom arms,
Her waist unbound by torturing stays;
Blithe as a bee, with busy care,
She's here, she's there, she's everywhere;
Long ere the clock has struck for noon
Home chords of toil are all in tune;
And from each richly bounteous hour
She drains its use, as bees a flower.
Apart from passion's pain and strife,
Peace gently girds the farmer's wife!

Homeward (his daily labors done)
    The stalwart farmer slowly plods,
From battling, between shade and sun,
    With sullen glebe and stubborn sods.
Her welcome on his spirit bowed
Is sunshine flashing on a cloud!
Her signal stills their harmless strife—
Love crowns with law the farmer's wife!

Ye dames in proud, palatial halls—
    Of lavish wiles and jeweled dress,
On whom, perchance, no infant calls,
    (For barren oft YOUR loveliness)—
Turn hitherward those languid eyes
And for a moment's pace be wise;
Your sister 'mid the country dew
Is three times nearer heaven than you,
And where the palms of Eden stir,
Dream not that he shall stand by her,
Though in your false, bewildering life,
Your folly scorned the farmer's wife!

—Paul Hamilton Hayne
Crown Jewels
1887

TO SELECT A GOOD WIFE

Choose a woman who has been inured to industry, and is not ashamed of it. Be sure she has a good constitution, good temper, and has not been accustomed to *"dashing"* without knowing the value of the means, is not fond of novels, and has no giddy and fashionable relations, and you need inquire no further—*she is a fortune.*

—*The Southern Cultivator*
MARCH 1844

LOVE LIGHTENS LABOR

A good wife rose from her bed one morn,
    And thought with a nervous dread
Of the piles of clothes to be washed, and more
    Than a dozen mouths to be fed.
There are meals to be got for the men in the field,
    And the children to fix away

WHAT FOLLOWS

in this marginal column throughout the book is a sampler of information, methods, formulas, beliefs, materials, recipes, and advice that suggests the range of daily practical concerns that, in large part, made up the content of the rural woman's life. Taken from many sources, these items represent only an infinitesimal part of the detail she had to be concerned with. What is not included could well fill another volume. The items presented, for the most part, are complete on each page; a few span facing pages.

NOTE

THE READER is cautioned that the recipes, medicines, home remedies, and other suggestions presented in this book have not been tested and are not recommended by the author.

To school, and the milk to be skimmed and churned;
And all to be done that day.

It had rained in the night, and all the wood
Was wet as it could be;
And there were pudding and pies to bake,
Besides a loaf of cake for tea.
The day was hot and her aching head
Throbbed wearily as she said,—
"If maidens but knew what good wives know,
They would be in no hurry to wed."

"Jennie, what do you think I told Ben Brown?"
Called the farmer from the well;
And a flash crept up to his bronzed brow,
And his eye half bashfully fell;
"It was this," he said, and coming near,
He smiled, and stooping down,
Kissed her cheek—" 'twas this, that you were the best
And dearest wife in town!"

The farmer went back to the field, and the wife,
In a smiling and absent way,
Sang snatches of tender little songs
She'd not sung for many a day.
And the pain in her head was gone, and the clothes
Were white as foam of the sea;
Her bread was light, and her butter was sweet,
And golden as it could be.

"Just think," the children all called, in a breath,
"Tom Wood has run off to sea!
He wouldn't, I know, if he only had
As happy a home as we."
The night came down, and the good wife smiled
To herself, as she softly said:
" 'Tis sweet to labor for those we love,
It is not strange that maids will wed!"

—*The Household*
VOL. I, 1868

THE GOOD WIFE

Wife is said to be the most agreeable and delightful name in
nature. A woman indeed ventures much when she assumes it,

RED INK—

Take of white wine vinegar one
quart, powdered Brazil wood two
ounces, and alum half an ounce;
infuse them together for ten days,
then let them gently simmer over a
slow fire, after which add a good
half ounce of gum arabic. When the
gum is dissolved, strain the mixture
and bottle it for use. Ink thus
prepared will keep its color for
many years.

CHAIR TIDIES

Chair tidies are both useful and ornamental, and may be made in a great variety of ways. A very pretty pattern is made by crocheting in afghan stitch two strips of white cotton and three of green worsted, five-eighths of a yard in length and three inches wide. Each strip is narrowed down to a point at both ends and terminates in a tassel. The white strips have a pretty running vine of green leaves, with rose buds, worked in cross stitch on each of them. The strips are crocheted together, green and white alternating, and the tidy is surrounded with a narrow green crocheted border.

for it is to her the final throw for happiness or unhappiness. Be she ever so good, so gifted, so true, so noble, she may marry a man who will disgrace her and make her unhappy; she has no security whatever against the most cruel fate.

And home must be her battle-ground. The man has the world before him, where to choose; therefore, an unhappy marriage is but one bitter drop in his full cup. With the wife, it is the whole draught. Let her weigh well the dangers of the future; even with prudence she may not escape misfortune.

It is well if she can always think her husband wise, whether he is or not. She is a happy woman who can make her husband always a hero. She is happiest who is humblest, and who takes a pleasure in looking up. ... A good wife, if it ever occurs to her that her husband is her inferior, conceals the fact religiously; many a witty wife has put good stories into her husband's lips—a forgivable deceit. Women have the talent of ready utterance to much greater perfection than men; they are quicker-witted; they have more ready tact. A wife's mind has traveled over the whole journey, and started home again, often before the husband has gone ten miles; but she has (or should have) the sense to keep silent until he has caught up with her. ... It is the glory of woman that she was sent into the world to live for others rather than herself, to live, yes, and to die for them. Let her never forget that she was sent here to make man better, to temper his greed, control his avarice, soften his temper, refine his grosser nature, and teach him that there is something better than success.

—Mrs. M. L. Rayne
What Can a Woman Do
1893

COOKING A HUSBAND

DEAR SISTERS—My conscience, hardened as it is, smites me sometimes when I think how little I give for the entertainment of our family, and how much I receive, so, when my brother handed me the following recipe, clipped from the Toledo Blade, I thought some of the sisters might like to use it. I cannot say from experience that it is a good one, for being a "belated sister" *he* is as yet uncaught.

"How to cook a husband. The first thing to be done is to catch him. Having done so the mode of cooking him, so as to make a good dish, is as follows: Many good husbands are spoiled in cooking. Some women keep them constantly in hot water, while others freeze them in conjugal coldness; some smother them in hatred and contention, and still others keep them in a pickle all their lives. These women always serve them up with tongue sauce. Now, it cannot be supposed that husbands will be tender and good, if treated in this way, but they are, on the contrary, very delicious when managed as follows:

Get a large jar, called the jar of carefulness (which all good wives have on hand), place your husband in it, and set him near the fire of conjugal love; let the fire be pretty hot, especially let it be clear, above all let the heat be constant, cover him over with affection and subjection; garnish him with the spices of pleasantry, and if you add kisses and other confections, let them be accompanied with a sufficient portion of secresy, mixed with prudence and moderation." Now, I advise all the women of THE HOUSEHOLD, both married and contemplating marriage to try this recipe, and realize how admirable a dish husbands are when properly cooked.

—Kathleen
The Household
VOL. XI, 1878

TALLOW, TO CLARIFY

Dissolve one pound of alum in one quart of water, add this to 100 pounds of tallow in a jacket kettle (a kettle set in a larger one, and the intervening space filled with water). This prevents burning the tallow. Boil three quarters of an hour and skim. Then add one pound of salt dissolved in a quart of water. Boil and skim. When well clarified the tallow should be nearly the color of water.

MAN THE COMMANDMENT, WOMAN THE OBEDIENT

Every family, as well as everything, must have its sovereign controller and head. What could an army, however courageous or well-appointed, do without a general; or a government, or any meeting or corporation, without its president, or the body without its legitimate head? Some one member of every family must of necessity assume its leadership. Obviously the husband is the natural head of the woman and family, the rightful author of what is to be done, and its "committee of ways and means," as well as the one especially "responsible," pecuniarily and generally. Unmistakably God in Nature has assigned this place to the husband and father. All civilized, even all savage and semi-barbarous nations, in all times, have acted on this human instinct. Proof that the father, not mother, is the natural family sovereign, is no more necessary than to prove that the sun gives light. All genuine men naturally assume the command, while all women willingly accord it, glad to be relieved from its concomitant responsibilities.

Hence, the female head is always flatter and lower at the crown than that of man. Hence genuine women can rarely love

TALLOW, TO HARDEN

I have used the following mixture with success: To one pound tallow take one fourth of a pound common rosin; melt them together, and mold the candles the usual way. This will give a candle of superior lighting power, and as hard as a wax candle; a vast improvement upon the common tallow candle, in all respects except color.

TO FATTEN TURKEYS

Every morning for a month, give them mashed potatoes mixed with buckwheat flour, barley or beans; take away what remains in the evening. After a month, add half a dozen balls made of barley flour, when they go to roost. Give them these eight days successively; turkeys thus fed are fat and good.

men to whom they cannot look up as superiors. Not so man, who, the stronger physically, bolder, more resolute, begins and leads off, while woman follows suit, and is his "help-mate"—a very expressive designation, yet significant of dependence. Men love those women best, other things being equal, who love to lean on both their arm and judgment, and who depend on them, instead of those who prefer to be independent.

Woman is man's "privy councillor." The husband should always consult his "intuitional" wife, provided she loves him. Everything between them should be coöperative and mutual, like their creative office. Yet, after all, man is the natural head of the household. Wives should indeed obey their husbands, yet husbands should "command" only in emergencies, and then always and only in tenderness and love. A stern, domineering, authoritative tone and bearing towards a wife, as if she were a serf, is anything but manly or conjugal. Neither should rule, but both should serve each other, and their dear little ones.

Accordingly, all matrimonial ceremonies in all ages, and among all peoples, oblige the bride to swear to obey and reverence her husband, yet never bind him to obey her. Paul also expresses this same principle, by imperiously commanding,—

"Wives, obey your husbands in all things;"

adding that "man is the head of the woman, as Christ is the head of the church."

Hence, also, all pattern women who are compelled to support a family by "keeping boarders," or store, or carrying on any millinery, or other business, must lean on some masculine adviser because loth to assume responsibilities. To give orders and head measures is not feminine. Or, if she ever wields sway, like "the Maid of Orleans," it is always by inspiring man. She governs through his affections far more effectually and absolutely, than by fear or force.

"But if woman is thus naturally obedient, what often renders her so blindly, so furiously wilful and obstinate that she is bent on carrying her points in spite of all difficulties and consequences?"

Because of her emotionality, not Firmness. This intensity of all her feelings renders her desires well nigh resistless, which creates persistency. What she wants at all, she craves with such a frenzy of desire that she compasses sea and land to gratify it.

This is sometimes necessary in order to overcome all "prudential considerations." Change her current of feeling or desire, and she yields readily.

—O. S. Fowler
Sexual Science
1875

A FABLE FOR THE TIMES

The following beautiful fable will attract attention by the truthful lesson it imparts:

"Oak," said the vine, "bend your trunk so that you may be support to me."

"My support," replied the oak, "is naturally yours, and you may depend on my strength to bear you up, but I am too solid to bend. Put your arms around me, my pretty vine, and I will manfully support and cherish you, if you have ambition to climb as high as the clouds. While I thus hold you up, you will ornament my rough trunk with your pretty green leaves and scarlet berries. They will be as frontlets to my head, as I stand in the forest, like a glorious warrior with all his plumes. We were made by the great Master to grow together, and that by our union the weak may be made strong, and the strong render aid to the weak."

"But I wish to grow independently," said the vine, "why cannot you twine around me, and let me grow up straight, and not be a mere dependent upon you."

"Nature," answered the oak, "did not design it. It is impossible that you should grow to my height alone, and if you try it, the winds and rains, if not your own weight, will bring you to the ground. Neither is it proper for you to run your arms hither and thither, for the trees will begin to say it is not my vine, it is a stranger, get thee gone: I will not cherish thee. By this time thou wilt be so entangled among the different branches that thou canst not get back to the oak; and nobody will admire or pity thee."

"Ah me!" said the vine, "let me escape from such a destiny"; and with this she twined herself around the oak, and both grew and flourished happily together.

—*The Household*
VOL III, 1870

DEAR HOUSEHOLD:—May I come into your home circle? I, like some of the other brides, live in Eastern Oregon among the

NERVOUS HEADACHE

One quart of cider, three tablespoonfuls of white mustard seed, three of burdock seed, a small horseradish root, well steeped together. To be kept in a bottle well corked; dose, a wine-glassful two or three times a day.

A ground mustard poultice applied to the back of the neck, between the shoulders, is good.

For an ordinary headache, take a shovelful of clean wood ashes; put them into clean cold water: when it has settled, drink the water; it may cause vomiting; if it does, the headache will be relieved the sooner.

For cold in the head nothing is better than powdered borax, sniffed up the nostrils.

foot hills, ten miles from town, and fifteen miles from timber, so I shall be glad to hear from others who have just started to build a home of their own. In one letter a bride said she was afraid to write for fear some one might say she was too young for a bride,

Immigrant Couple, Black River Falls, Wisconsin, 1890. State Historical Society of Wisconsin (WHi (V2) 89).

she was only nineteen. I am only eighteen, but if our husbands are satisfied with us, what should we care what others say? Is it not better for us to do and be as our companion wishes us than as others wish? I will close, hoping you will all find as much comfort in THE HOUSEHOLD as I do. I remain
Your truly,

Maude
—*The Household*
VOL. XXV, SEPTEMBER 1892

A Gentleman

"Are my biscuits light, John?" asks the charming young wife,
As she smiles on her husband; and he,
With emphasis answers, "They're lovely, my life,
As light as the foam of the sea."

"Is the steak cooked to suit you?" she gently inquires;
And he says, as he smilingly nods,
"It might have been cooked at celestial fires,
And is tender enough for the gods."

"And the coffee; that pleases you, too, does it, dear?"
She asked, overjoyed with his praise,
Which rather than strains of sweet music she'd hear.
"It couldn't be better," he says.

So she sits down beside him and with him partakes,
And the rigid, no doubt, will confess,
If there's wilful deceit in the answer John makes,
He's a gentleman, nevertheless.

—*The Household*
VOL. XXV, JUNE 1892

A TALE FOR WIVES

"Now this is what I call comfort," said Madge Harley, as she sat down by her neighbor's fire one evening; "here you are at your sewing with the kettle steaming on the hob and the tea things on the table, expecting every minute to hear your husband's step, and see his face look in at the door. Ah! if my husband was like yours, Janet!"

"He is like mine in many of his ways," said Janet, with a smile, "and if you will allow me to speak plainly, he would be still more like him if you took more pains to make him comfortable."

"What do you mean!" cried Madge; "our house is as clean as yours, I mend my husband's clothes and cook his dinner as carefully as any woman in the parish, and yet he never stays at home of an evening, while you two sit here by your cheerful fire night after night as happy as can be."

"As happy as can be on earth," her friend said gravely, "yes—and shall I tell you the secret of it, Madge?"

"I wish you would," said Madge with a deep sigh, "it's misery to live as I do now."

"Well, then," said Janet, speaking slowly and distinctly, "I let my husband see that I love him still, and that I learn every day to love him more. Love is the chain that binds him to his home. The world may call it folly, but the world is not my lawgiver!"

"And do you really think," exclaimed Madge in surprise, "that husbands care for that sort of thing?"

PIECE BAGS

Out of an old calico dress make three piece bags, and label each one of them with its written name upon a small square piece of white muslin, which must be sewn upon the side of the bag. One should be the "rag-bag," another the "white piece-bag," a third the "colored piece-bag,"—they will be found very useful.

31

"For love, do you mean?" asked Janet.

"Yes, they don't feel at all as we do, Janet, and it don't take many years of married life to make them think of a wife as a sort of maid of all work."

"A libel, Madge," said Mrs. Matson, laughing, "I won't allow you to sit in William's chair and talk so."

"No, because your husband is different, and values his wife's love, whilst John cares for me only as his housekeeper."

"I don't think that" said Janet, "although he said to my husband the other day that courting time was the happiest of a man's life. William reminded him that there is a greater happiness than that even on earth if men but give their hearts to Christ. I know John did after his opinion, but he went away still thinking of his courting time as of a joy too great to be exceeded."

"Dear fellow," cried Madge, smiling through her tears, "I do believe he was happy then. I remember I used to listen for him as I sat with my dear mother by the fire, longing for the happiness of seeing him."

"Just so," said Janet. "Do you feel like that now?"

Madge hesitated. "Well, no, not exactly."

"And why not?"

"Oh, I don't know," said Madge; "married people give up that sort of thing."

"Love, do you mean?" asked Janet a second time.

"No, but what people call the sentimental," said Mrs. Harley. "Longing to see your husband is a very proper sentiment," replied Janet.

"But some people are ridiculously foolish before others," reasoned Madge.

"This proves they want sense. I am not likely to approve of that, as William would soon tell you; all I want is that wives let their husbands know they are still loved."

"But men are so vain," said Madge, "that it is dangerous to show much attention."

Her friend looked up. "Oh! Madge, what are you saying? Have you then married with the notion that it is not good for John to believe you love him?"

"No, but it is not wise to show that you care too much for them."

"Say I and him; do not talk of husbands in general, but of yours in particular."

STOVES BLACKING

Blacking for stoves may be made with 1/2 a pound of black lead finely powdered, and (to make it stick) mix with it the whites of 3 eggs well beaten; then dilute it with sour beer or porter till it becomes as thin as shoe-blacking; after stirring it, set it over hot coals to simmer for 20 minutes; when cold it may be kept for use.

"He thinks quite enough of himself already, I assure you."

"Dear Madge," said Janet, smiling, "would it do you any harm to receive a little attention from your husband?"

"Of course not, I wish he'd try;" and Mrs. Harley laughed at the idea.

"Then you don' think enough of yourself already? and nothing would make you vain I suppose?"

Madge colored, and all the more when she perceived that William Matson had come in quietly, and was now standing behind her, listening to Janet's words; and to confess secretly that they were wise.

Hours passed before John Harley returned home. He was a man of good abilities and well to do in the world, and having married Madge because he truly loved her, he expected to have a happy home. But, partly because he was reserved and sensitive and partly because Madge feared to make him vain, they had grown cold toward each other; so cold that John began to think the alehouse a more comfortable place than his own home.

That night the rain fell in torrents; the wind howled, and it was not until the midnight hour arrived that Harley left the public house and hastened towards his cottage. He was wet through, when he at length crossed the threshold. He was, as he gruffly muttered, "used to that"; but he was not "used" to the tone and look with which his wife drew near to welcome him; nor to find warm clothes by the crackling fire and slippers on the hearth; nor to hear no reproach for the late hours, and neglect, and dirty footmarks, as he sat in his arm-chair. Some change had come to Madge he was very sure. She wore a dress he had bought for her years ago, with a linen collar round her neck, and had a cap trimmed with white ribbons on her head.

"You're smart, Madge," he exclaimed, at last when he stared at her for some little time in silence. "Who has been here worth dressing for to-night?"

"No one until you came," said Madge, half laughing.

"I? Nonsense, you didn't dress for *me*," cried John.

"You won't believe it, perhaps, but I *did*; I have been talking with Mrs. Matson this evening, and she has given me some very good advice. So now, John, what would you like for your supper?"

John, who wont to steal to the shelf at night and content himself with anything he could find, thought Madge's offer too excellent to be refused, and very soon a large bowl of hot chocolate

MILKING SHED, CARE AND KIND OF MILK-PAILS, ETC.

For summer dairying an open shed in which the cows can be tied and given a few mouthfuls of fresh green fodder after they are milked, and which should be cleanly scraped after each milking, is a very great advantage, which can also be utilized in winter for sheep or other stock. Then the milk can be drawn free from dust and dirt "flicked" by the switching of the cows' tails; as will happen with cows loose in a barn-yard. Moreover, the milk-pails should be of tin and not wood. An old wooden milk-pail can not be made clean by dint of any amount of scouring. Nor should the milk-pail be used for any other purpose; but as soon as the milk is strained, the pail should be washed with cold water, scalded, and turned bottom upward upon a bench or on a stone.

was steaming on the table. Then his wife sat down for a wonder at his side, and talked a little, and listened, and looked pleased, when at last, as if he couldn't help it, he said, "Dear old Madge!"

That was enough, her elbow somehow found way then to the arm of his great chair, and she sat quietly looking at the fire. After awhile John spoke again—

"Madge, dear, do you remember the old days when we used to sit side by side in your mother's kitchen?"

"Yes."

"I was a younger man then, Madge, and as they told me, handsome, now I am growing older, plainer, duller. *Then* you— *loved* me; do you love me still?"

She looked up into his face, and her eyes answered him. It was like looking back to old days to feel again his arm around her as her head lay upon his shoulder, and to hear once again those kind words meant for her ear alone.

She never once asked if this would make him "vain." She knew as if by instinct, that it was making him a wiser, a more thoughtful, more earnest-hearted man. And when, after a happy silence, he took down the Bible and read a chapter, as he had been wont to read to her and her mother in former times, she bowed her head and prayed.

Yes, prayed—for pardon, through the blood of Jesus Christ, for strength to fulfill every duty in the future, for the all-powerful influence of the Spirit, for blessings on her husband evermore.

She prayed not in vain.

—*The Household*
VOL. I, 1860

SECRECY, TACT, AND ARTIFICE NATURAL TO WOMAN

The female sex is generally accused of being "false" and "deceptive." This accusation rests on this shadow of truth, that man seeks safety in bold, manly defiance and encounter; while woman is ordained to seek it by art, intrigue, policy, artifice, and stratagems. Undoubtedly her "Maker" understood Himself when He created her thus reserved, discreet, guarded, self-governed, and politic. This attribute in her is equally valuable to him, by enabling her often to work with and for him, or rather working both cards; she employing shrewdness and tact, while he uses force. She may, indeed, pervert it to false appearances, even hypocrisy and duplicity; but usually Conscientiousness is larger in woman than in man, which generally does, and always should, prevent its wronging others, while it enables her to reach ends only attainable by tortuous measures. Hence men love female reserve and discretion much more than bluntness and abruptness.

—O. S. Fowler
Sexual Science
1875

A WOMAN'S WEAPON

"What is a woman's weapon?"
    I asked a charming girl.
She dropped her lashes shyly,
    And stroked a vagrant curl;
Then consciously she murmured—
    This rosebud newly cut—
"I have a strong suspicion
    Her weapon is a pout."

"What is a woman's weapon?"
    I asked a lover true.
He turned him to a maiden
    With eyes of heavenly blue
Her velvet lips were parted,
    All innocent of guile,
And eagerly he answered,
    "Her weapon is a smile."

"What is a woman'a weapon ?"
    I asked a poet, then.
With sudden inspiration
    He seized upon his pen.
"Oh, I could name a thousand,"
    He cried, in accents clear,
"But woman's surest weapon,
    I grant you, is a tear!"

—*The Household*
VOL. XXV, 1892

A HINT TO THE WIFE

Here is a hint for some well-meaning but misguided wives:
    When you have told your husband a thing once don't tell it to him again and again in rapid succession, under the impression that he will forget all about it if you don't.

This is one species of "nagging" that few men can bear unmoved.

If you say at the breakfast table, "John, we need some sugar," don't keep on saying it through the entire meal and while he is getting on his hat and overcoat, finally working him into a frenzy by calling out after him when he is at the gate, "Now *don't* forget that sugar."

Men sometimes feel like leaving home, and never coming back again, for no greater cause than this.

I know a woman who told her husband ten times to stop at the grocery and order two pounds of coffee, and the eleventh time she added, "and *don't* go and get two pounds of codfish, instead."

Before noon the groceryman arrived with two pounds of codfish.

The moral is plain. If she hadn't said anything about codfish he wouldn't have mixed it up with coffee, and would have sent up the right article.

—*The Household*
1892

To Whom It May Concern

Some one said the other evening—was it you or I, dear friends? for in these HOUSEHOLD talks of ours I often seem to myself to be your mouthpiece, giving utterance to your thoughts as well as to my own—some one said that woman's best work is that which is unseen by mortal eye. What if we consider that work a little to-night?

Harper's Weekly, March 22, 1873.
Courtesy: the Amherst College Library
(Amherst, Massachusetts).

In the first place—what is it? It is hard to define it, hard to put into words that which is in its very essence so intangible. As there are thoughts that are too vast for human speech, so is there work that is too nearly allied to the spiritual, too ethereal in its very nature, to be fitly defined by human tongue. But perhaps we may make an approximation towards it by saying that this work is the steady uplifting and upholding of a higher standard of living; it is the reaching forward and upward, both for ourselves and others, towards a loftier life.

Do you tell me that this is hard work? Do you say that the world, the flesh and the devil stand in the way, stretching out hindering hands, and opposing us with weapons sharper and keener than the blades of Damascus?

Yes, it is hard. But, sisters, it is work that belongs to us. It is work that, if not done by us, will never be done at all.

For man cannot do it—as far as the family is concerned. He may do it for the world. With lips and pen and eager, helpful hands he may do—and he does do—grand work for God and for humanity. But when he steps within the family circle, into woman's own peculiar domain, he is comparatively powerless. Without her aid, her countenance, her support, he can do little or nothing. I venture to say that there is hardly a man on the earth to-day—no matter what his hopes, his desires, his aspirations may be, who can long hold his household up to a lofty standard of living without the help and co-operation of his wife and daughters.

So, young men, you see that it behooves you, when you marry, to know what manner of woman she is whom you make the crowned queen of your hearts and homes.

For as a rule, and it is a rule that has few exceptions, woman creates the atmosphere of the home. Outside influences have their weight; adverse influences from within may change and modify. But after all home is for the most part what woman makes it; or what she allows it to be.

And it seems to some of us that she has enough to do for the present; and that it is not until the homes of America approach more nearly the ideal standard, that she needs to weep for new worlds to conquer.

—Mrs. Julia C. R. Dorr
The Household
VOL. V, 1872

SIMPLE AND EFFECTUAL CURE FOR THOSE WHO MAY ACCIDENTALLY HAVE SWALLOWED A WASP

Instantly, on the alarming accident taking place, put a teaspoon full of common salt in your mouth, which will not only kill the wasp, but at the same time heal the sting.

Those who have a home which they can make happy, will not sigh for contact with the outer world, to be permitted to wrestle and contend among its fierce trials and the fiercer spirits that struggle there for daily bread; or despise the peaceful path of domestic duty, which, although it has its trials, is yet in a great degree sheltered; or reject the gentle ties of wife, mother, sister, to study some learned profession, and rush into those haunts and paths already too crowded with the sterner sex. Such must be the lot, nevertheless, of many women, whom necessitous circumstances have forced into an unnatural position.

Our "model housewife" believes with us that we should endeavor a

> *"Well ordered home, man's best delight, to make;*
> *And by submissive wisdom, modest skill,*
> *With every gentle, care-eluding art,*
> *To raise the virtues, animate the bliss,*
> *And sweeten all the toils of human life;*
> *This is true female dignity and praise."*
> —The New Cyclopedia of Domestic Economy
> 1872

TO CLEAN A BROWN PORCELAIN KETTLE

Boil peeled potatoes in it. The porcelain will be rendered nearly as white as when new.

WOMAN ON THE FARM

MESSERS. EDITORS:—Having a high esteem for your valuable paper, I have been pleased to see several contributions in it, recently, from *ladies*. It will not be denied, I presume, that the "ladies" exert not a little influence in the world, by *words*, as well as *actions;* and perhaps nowhere have they used their influence more to bless or to blight, to encourage or discourage, to help or to hinder, than in agriculture.

That sickly sentimentality, so often a characteristic trait of some *would-be ladies*, causing them to speak so disparagingly of farmers and their wives, of farmers' sons and daughters, has driven many a young man from the old homestead, to seek a fortune where it is not to be found. Thus may woman's influence be exerted to blight, to mar, to deface the beauty of that employment to which her own attention should oftener be turned, and where she may, by her own efforts, help to "make the wilderness blossom as the rose."

The early institution of marriage is often quoted; let it also be remembered, that the *place* was a *garden* where it was instituted. It was *there* that she was appointed to be his "help-meet," while assisting him to "keep the garden, and to dress it."

Essential as is good *husbandry* to the success of the farmer *good wifery* is not less. To cultivate the beautiful is woman's peculiar province; and where can she better display her taste than in training the roses to the trellis, and arranging flowers of every tint and hue in such contrast, as to best please the observer? Yes, it is her highest prerogative *to please;* and where can she find and ampler field for her ambition, than the farm and rural occupations afford?

Is she young, and desirous of personal attractions? Whose cheeks can vie with the farmer's daughters for their rosy tints? Whose complexion so fair as hers who bathes in the early morning dew? Who, so happy and light-hearted as she who witnesses the morning dawn ushered in with songs of sweetest symphony? What wife so cheerful and happy as she, who offers to her husband, when he returns from toil, some luxury, the product of the farm, prepared by her own hands?

I know that we are called rustics, to whom "the lines have fallen in pleasant places"; and that our goodly heritage is thought by many to be semi-barbarous at least; but if the country is unsightly and destitute of beauty to some and the dwellers on the soil partake of its deformity, not so its flowers and fruits.

Where shall we find flowers in their beauty, fruits in their perfection, birds singing their merry songs of freedom, if not in the country? Our *ice-creams,* too, are no city invention, for where but in the country will you find the ingredients, in their freshness, their sweetness, and their richness?

It was not my intention in this article to draw comparisons unfavorable to the city; its elegance I would not affect to despise. But I do love the country; I love the farm, I love the motley groups of the farm-yard; the noisy cackle of the hen, and the infant-like bleat of the little lamb, are pleasant sounds in the ears of the farmer's child.

Yes, I would be a farmer's daughter, and a farmer's wife; and were I dependent upon my own exertions, to "bring up" or educate a family of children, I would sooner hire a farm, and with their assistance till it with my own hands, than struggle for subsistence by that life-destroying instrument, *the needle;* but only so, when used to such extent as is often the case, to *support* that life it too often *destroys.*

—*New England Farmer*
MAY 1857

CURE FOR RINGWORMS

Yellow Dock, root or leaves, steeped in vinegar, will cure the worst case of ringworm.

Whooping cough paroxysms are relieved by breathing the fumes of turpentine and carbolic acid.

THE WISDOM OF WIVES

A man's wife often knows more than he knows about a great many things, and while he need not lower himself in her estimation by admitting her mental superiority, it is sometimes well for him to silently recognize her superior intelligence and profit by it.

If he is a wise man he will not be too ready to come into accord with the opinions of his wife, but will affect a great deal of wisdom of his own, even though he knows that he has none.

It never increases a wife's respect for her husband to know that he is her inferior in anything; and it certainly does not increase her respect or her affection to have him intimate by word or look that she does not know anything at all.

The judgment of the average woman, regarding the disbursement of money, is often better than that of the average man. It is often better when it comes to spending money for domestic purposes.

It takes a shrewd shopkeeper or marketman to get ahead of the average woman, while a marketman who is yet new in the business finds it easy to work off stale wares on the average man, and the most conceited man might as well acknowledge frankly that his wife can attend to most of the affairs of her own household better than he can attend to them for her.

Women very often have the most acute perception regarding business affairs. There would probably be fewer failures in the business world if more men would "talk business" with their wives instead of taking it for granted that women "don't understand anything about business."

Many a successful business man owes his success to the keenness of judgment of a partner whose name does not appear in the firm name or the shop windows, and who is not supposed to have any connection with the business, and that partner is his wife, in whom he is wise enough to confide, and whose superior judgment, it is to be hoped, he properly appreciates.

A daily exchange of confidence and a mutual respect for each other's opinions will do much toward making the wheels of any domestic establishment run along smoothly.

—*The Household*
VOL. XXV, 1892

THE WIFE

Only let a woman be sure that she is precious to her husband—not useful, not valuable, not convenient simply, but lovely and

beloved; let her be the recipient of his polite and hearty attention; let her feel that her care and love are noticed, appreciated
and returned; let her opinion be asked, her approval sought, and
her judgment respected in matters of which she is cognizant; in
short let her only be loved, honored and cherished, in fulfillment of the marriage vow—and she will be to her husband, her
children and society, a wellspring of pleasure. She will bear pain,
and toil, and anxiety—for her husband's love is to her a tower
and fortress. Shielded and sheltered therein, adversity will have
lost its sting. She may suffer, but sympathy will dull the edge of
sorrow. A house with love in it—and by love I mean love expressed in words, and looks, and deeds (for I have not one spark
of faith in love that never crops out)—is to a house without love
as a person to a machine; one is life, the other is a mechanism.
The unloved woman may have bread just as light, a house just as
tidy as the other, but the latter has a spring of beauty about her,
a joyousness, an aggressive, penetrating, and pervading brightness, to which the former is a stranger. The deep happiness in
her heart shines out in her face. She gleams over it. It's fair and
graceful, and warm and welcoming with her presence; she is full
of devices and plots and sweet surprises for husband and family. She has never done with the romance and poetry of life. She
herself is a lyric poem, setting herself to all pure and gracious

*Charles Chapman, Custer Co., Nebraska. Solomon D.
Butcher Collection, Nebraska State Historical Society.*

melodies. Humble household ways and duties have for her a golden significance. The prize makes her calling high and the end sanctifies the means. "Love is Heaven, and Heaven is Love."
—*The Household*, VOL. I, 1868

The following paragraph is from an article entitled "Hints on How to Think," written in the early 1890s by the Reverend B. P. Raymond, President of Wesleyan University. It appeared with ninety-nine other essays in a volume dealing with the question of how to succeed. The passage reflects a prevailing attitude toward the land as well as larger cultural values, focusing clearly in its "romantic" analogy on the image of woman as another natural resource.

The North American Indian who lives in our great West does very little thinking; he does not summon himself to the task of asking and answering hard questions. He stands at the confluence of two mighty rivers, and only sees a promising pool for fish to supply his physical need, or a beautiful stream on which to dream while he floats his birch canoe. He sees upon the prairie only the buffalo herd, hears the thunder of its wild rush, but thinks only of buffalo skins to keep him warm when the winter moons return. He sees the mountains, but thinks only of the wild turkey or the fallow deer. He does not summon his thoughts to anything deeper or worthier than the supply of his physical necessities. The white man's mind acts upon this scene in quite a different way because he has trained himself to think. He sees the same streams and the same prairie and buffalo herd with its stalwart leader, but he thinks little or not at all of fish, or birch canoes, or buffalo meat, or skins; he sees the promise of a great city at that favored center. He sees the support of teeming millions in the vast prairies which lie fat and rich and wide about him. He sees the mountains, but no wild turkey; the fallow deer do not attract him, except it may be for a passing moment. He sees in the mountains the coal and copper, the iron, silver, and gold which make civilization possible and powerful. What is the difference between him and the North American Indian? Just this: the white man thinks, he applies his mind to the phenomena about him, asks a thousand questions, turns nature around and looks at her on every side, sees her in manifold relations, knows her, loves her, woos her, wins her, and what a bride she becomes to him! We may learn to think by thinking. Ask questions and then answer them, raise difficulties and then remove them.

—William C. King, *Portraits and Principles*
1894

MOTHER

There are three words that sweetly blend,
        That on the heart are graven;
A precious, soothing balm they lend—
        They're mother, home and heaven.

They twine a wreath of beauteous flowers,
        Which, placed on memory's urn,
Will e'en the longest, gloomiest hours
        To golden sunlight turn.

They form a chain whose every link
        Is free from base alloy;
A stream where whosoever drinks
        Will find refreshing joy.

They build an altar where each day
        Love's offering is renewed;
And peace illumes with genial ray
        Life's darkened solitude.

If from our side the first has fled,
        And home be but a name,
Let's strive the narrow path to tread,
        That we the last may gain.

                              —Mary J. Muckle
                         What Can a Woman Do
                                        1893

Photo on previous page:
Office of the Secretary of Agriculture.

LETTERS TO ALICE

Now that the orb of your life is rounding into full completeness, and to the holy name of wife will soon be added that of mother, I can only say with one of old, "Blessed art thou among women."

I know there are those who will talk to you in a different strain; those who "cannot see why these things must be," and who "marvel that women must be such sufferers," and so forth and so on *ad infinitum*. But never do you heed the croakers, Alice. Are they wiser than the God who made them?

Of course there are exceptional cases, instances where child-bearing is a curse rather than a blessing. There may be (mind you, I do not say there *are*) circumstances under which a woman is justified in using almost any means of escape from that which sickness or grinding poverty or I know not what else of evil, combine to render an intolerable burden. But notwithstanding all this, it still remains true that our loving Father who knows every need of woman's nature, every throb of her heart, every impulse of her soul, ordained that motherhood should be the crowning joy and glory of her life. Did He make a mistake? or have the times and the seasons changed, so that what was true of Rebekah and Rachel, is not true of Ann and Eliza?

They will talk to you of the suffering, the pang, the agony. It is all true, every word of it. We do go down into the Valley of the Shadow of Death for our children, Alice. But we come up from its depths again, bringing with us what repays us a hundred fold. Almost always. So few women, comparatively, die in childbirth, that we may regard life as the established fact, and its opposite as the rare exception that only serves to prove the rule. And it is anguish that one forgets so soon! Perhaps I ought rather to say, that its memory is lost, swallowed up in the joy. The inspired one who knew so well how to reach each chord in the human soul, drawing forth its subtlest music, says, "she remembereth no more the sorrow." What mother, especially what young mother, has not repeated these words over and over again, as she has lain upon her bed,—at rest after the conflict, at peace after the agony,—with the little form for which she has undergone so much clasped closely to her heart, and the small face nestling on her breast? Thank God that the remembrance of the sorrow is only as a dream, or as a "tale that is told," while the joy endureth forever!

MANAGEMENT OF STOVES

If the fire in a stove has plenty of fresh coals on top not yet burned through, it will need only a little shaking to start it up; but if the fire looks dying and the coals look white, don't shake it. When it has drawn till it is red again, if there is much ash and little fire, put coals on very carefully. A mere handful of fire can be coaxed back into life by adding another handful or so of new coals on the red spot, and giving plenty of draught, but don't shake a dying fire, or you lose it. This management is often necessary after a warm spell, when the stove has been kept dormant for days, though I hope you will not be so unfortunate as to have a fire to coax up on a cold winter morning. They should be arranged over night, so that all that is required is to open the draughts in order to have a cherry glow in a few minutes.

I hope you are cheerful and happy, Alice. So much rests upon it. It is almost fearful to think how much of the weal or woe of your child's whole life may depend upon your own frame of mind during these few months. The connection between the mother and the babe that she has as yet seen only in her dreams, is so close that if Physiology and Philosophy had taught us nothing, our own common sense might teach us this truth—a truth, alas! too often ignored or forgotten. You are truly your child's guardian now, as really responsible for the bias you give it, for the good or evil tendencies you engraft upon its yet unformed nature, as you will be by and by when it lies in your arms and your kisses fall upon its delicate, flower-like face. Perhaps you are even more so, for now it holds communion with you alone. No other influence comes between your soul and the slumbering spirit of your babe.

I do not flatter myself that I am telling you anything new, Alice. You have heard all this, I doubt not, time and again. But there are some truths that will bear to be dwelt upon, truths that need to be repeated over and over again to each generation. What you would have your child be, that you must be yourself. Do not fret; do not worry; do not be despondent. Do not seek the shadows, but, as far as may be, keep yourself in the clear sunshine of the soul. Do not indulge a passion or give way to an emotion that you will not be willing to see hereafter reflected in your child.

Do you say "This is an hard saying; who can bear it?" Perhaps it is, regarded in one light. But He that was born of woman, and who humbled himself to become Mary's loving and obedient son, looks tenderly and compassionately upon all mothers now; and for the sake of her at whose breast he was nourished, and whom he remembered in his dying agony upon the cross, he longs to sustain and to comfort them. Go to him, dear child, when the burden of your responsibility grows too heavy, and lay it at his feet. We try in our poor human weakness to carry so many loads that Christ is ready and willing to carry for us, if we will only let him.

But if you look at this matter merely as regards yourself, it is for your own good now and in the coming trial, that you should look on the bright side, and give way to no useless and idle forebodings. Therefore I say again keep out of the shadows and seek the sunshine; and finally, "Whatsoever things are true, whatsoever things are pure, whatsoever things are lovely, whatsoever things are of good report—if there be any virtue and if there be any

FOR CHILDREN TEETHING

Tie a quarter of a pound of wheat flour in a thick cloth and boil it in one quart of water for three hours; then remove the cloth and expose the flour to the air or heat until it is hard and dry; grate from it, when wanted, one tablespoonful, which put into half a pint of new milk, and stir over the fire until it comes to a boil, when add a pinch of salt and a tablespoonful of cold water and serve. This gruel is excellent for children afflicted with summer complaint.

Or brown a tablespoonful of flour in the oven or on top of the stove on a baking tin; feed a few pinches at a time to a child and it will often check a diarrhoea. The tincture of "kino"—of which from ten to thirty drops, mixed with a little sugar and water in a spoon, and given every two or three hours, is very efficacious and harmless—can be procured at almost any druggist's. Tablespoon doses of pure cider vinegar and a pinch of salt, has cured when all else failed.

praise, think on these things." Surround yourself as far as may be with beauty and with grace. Cultivate your flowers and take their loveliness to your inmost soul. Look not with eyes that see not upon the wonderful magnificence of the star-lit heavens, nor turn away from the daily miracles of sunrise and of sunset, heeding not their glory. There are hundreds about us who would go thousands of miles to see a veritable Titian or Leonardo da Vinci, who never open their eyes to behold the more glorious pictures that God hangs in his temple of the heavens.

Breathe the atmosphere of refinement and peace, and in this time of seclusion, when the world seems afar off, and the tumult of its strivings and its noisy ambitions fall deadened upon your ear, commune with your own heart and be still. It is a holy season, Alice, a time for thought and prayer. See that you use it well.

A WARM BATH WITH CUTICURA SOAP

You will take great delight in fashioning the little garments in which your baby's tender form will one day be wrapped. I know how you will brood over each one, how many hopes and fond thoughts and loving wishes will go into the making of the tiny robes, and what dreams and fancies you will weave in with the delicate embroideries. Ah! it will be better than the old days— not so very long past, either,—when you played with your dolls, and amused yourself with their toilets. I can see how you will busy yourself with thimble and needle in the seclusion of your own chamber, hiding your work at first, with a strange shyness, when you hear Philip's footfall upon the stair; but grown bolder at length, how you will timidly exhibit your pretty handiwork, and how he will wonder and admire, and laugh, perhaps, as he softly touches the daintily fashioned garment, and beholds its infinitesimal dimensions. I know just how you will arrange and re-arrange the drawer that you have appropriated to the little stranger, how you will fold and refold the soft, white dresses; how you will loop up the tiny sleeves with fresh blue and rose colored ribbons, and wonder which is the prettiest, a bow with floating ends or a simple shoulder knot. Well, well, my darling! be happy in dreaming of your new plaything. Let the small robings be soft and rare and dainty as your purse and your inclination will allow; but remember I pray you, that your own health is of more importance to your child than an exquisitely furnished wardrobe, and that delicate rufflings and richly wrought linen will be dearly purchased if at the expense of the strength and vigor that will be taxed during the coming year as it was never taxed before.

At last the long suspense, the weary waiting is over; and Philip's telegram tells me that you are the happy mother of a little son. Dear Alice, my heart is very full to-day. It seems so short a time since you were a baby yourself. Indeed, you were scarcely more than that when the love began that has "grown with our growth and strengthened with our strength," until now, when I am sitting here in the little library that has so often been brightened by your presence, writing to you of your child. Thank God for love and for friendship, and for all the ties that bind human hearts together! But thank him most especially in the midst of your newly born joy, for the mother-love that, Midas-like, changes whatever it touches to gold, and transforms pain and weariness, sleepless nights, anxious vigils, and it may be menial services, into something akin to worship.

Do you know that you will find a great deal of positive enjoyment in these hours of convalescence? The suspense is over; the trial hour is no longer to be dreaded; you are not strong enough to grapple with the cares of this "work-a-day" world; you can only lie at rest, putting by all your labors and anxieties until another day. It is a hard thing to say, but there are women to whom the few weeks—days, it may be—after confinement, are the only "breathing spells" they ever know; the only times when they do not feel the spur of necessity goading them onward. And even we who are more fortunate are apt to find ourselves entangled unawares in a net-work of petty cares, petty duties, social obligations, and I know not what besides. Perhaps we love our bondage and would not escape from it if we could. But it is good once in a while to be lifted up bodily, and placed upon clear ground once more, where we can look about us a little and try our wings.

Have you found a name for the baby? Of course it is the most wonderful child that ever was born; the prettiest, the brightest, and with *such* winning ways! You will hardly believe me when I tell you that thousands just as remarkable are born every day. Every child wears the aureole for a while at least, and we bow before it, worshipers at its saintly shrine. Each one, whether in royal palace or in peasant's cot, wears the monarch's crown upon its baby brow, and its small hand wields the sceptre over willing and admiring subjects. We are all kings and queens in the cradle, and each babe is a new marvel, a new miracle.

But to go back to the baby's name. Your grandfather, as well as *his* father, and your great, great, great grandfather, who came over in the Mayflower (or if not in that getting-to-be mythical

WOOD, (NEW) TO REMOVE TASTE FROM

A new keg, churn, bucket, or other wooden vessel will generally communicate a disagreeable odor to anything that is put into it. To prevent this inconvenience first scald the vessel with boiling water, letting the water remain in it till cold. Then dissolve some pearlash or soda in lukewarm water, adding a little bit of lime to it, and wash the inside of the vessel well with plain hot water, and rinse it with cold water before you use it.

vessel, in some other), rejoiced in the euphonious cognomen of Obadiah. I pray you, Alice, do not let the desire to hand down family names, lead you to bestow upon your boy an appellation that will be a torment to him all his days. Trained as you will train him, no regard for his ancestors, will be sufficient to deafen his ear to the uncouthness of such a name. Obadiah and Jedidiah, and the other *iahs,* have done yeoman's service. Let them rest now in the tomb of the Capulets. Neither need you in shunning Scylla fall into Charybdis. You need not call him Clarence Augustus, nor Roderick Angelo Fitzgerald; Napoleon Bonaparte, nor George Washington. But give your son a good, plain, honest name; one that will not be suggestive of dandyism and romance on the one hand, nor overshadow him with its own greatness on the other; a name that will fall smoothly from your lips now, and from the lips of a later love by and by; a name that is tender enough for a baby, and manly enough for a man. Call him John!

—*The Household*
VOL. I, 1868

Harper's Weekly, *Jan. 6, 1867. Courtesy: the Amherst College Library (Amherst, Massachusetts).*

THE OLD FASHIONED MOTHER

That old fashioned mother!—one in all the world, the law of whose life was love; one who was the divinity of our infancy, and the sacred presence in the shrine of our first early idolatry; one whose heart is far below the frosts that gather so thickly on her brow; one to whom we never grow old, but in the plumed troop, or in the gravest council, are children still; one who welcomes our coming, and never forgets us—never. And when, in some closet, some drawer, or some corner, she finds a garment or a toy that once was ours, how does she weep as she thinks we may be suffering or sad.

Does the battle of life drive the wanderer to the old homestead at last, her hand is upon his shoulder; her dim and fading eyes are kindled with something of the light of other days, as she gazes upon his worn and troubled face. "Be of stout heart, my son. No harm can reach you here." But sometimes that armchair is set back against the wall, the corner is vacant, or occupied by strangers, and they seek the dear old occupant in the graveyard. Grant you never have! Pray God you never may!

—*The Household*
VOL. III, 1870

TESTS OF CHARACTER

A great many admirable acts are overlooked by us, because they are so little and common. Take, for instance, the mother, who has had broken slumber, if any at all, with the nursing babe whose wants must not be disregarded; she would fain sleep awhile when the breakfast hour comes, but patiently and uncomplainingly she takes her timely seat at the table. Though exhausted and weary, serving all with a refreshing cup of tea or coffee before she sips it herself, and often the cup is handed back to her to be refilled before she had had time to taste her own.

Do you hear her complain—the weary mother—that her breakfast is cold before she has time to eat it? And this not for one, but every morning, perhaps, in the year. Do you call this a small thing? Try it and see. O, how does woman shame us by her forbearance and fortitude in what are called little things! Ah! it is these little things which are tests of character; it is by these little self-denials, borne with such self-forgotten gentleness, that the humblest home is made beautiful to the eyes of angels, though we

fail to see it, alas! until the chair is vacant and the hand which kept
in motion all this domestic machinery is powerless and cold!

—The Household
VOL. III, 1870

THE MOTHER'S ROOM

The core of the house, the dearest place, the one that we all love best,
Holding it close in our heart of hearts, for its comfort and its rest,
Is never the place where strangers come, nor yet where friends are met,
Is never the stately drawing room, where our treasured things are set.
Oh, dearer far as the time recedes in a dream of colors dim,
Breathing across our stormy moods like the echo of a hymn,
Forever our own, and only ours, and pure as a rose in bloom,
Is the centre and soul of the old home nest, the mother's darling room.

We flew to its arms when we rushed from school, with a thousand
*   things to tell;*
Our mother was always waiting there, had the day gone ill or well.
No other pillow was quite so cool, under an aching head,
As soft to our fevered childish cheek, as the pillow on mother's bed.
Sitting so safely at her feet, when the dewy dusk drew nigh,
We watched for the angels to light the lamps in the solemn evening sky.
Tiny hands folded, there we knelt, to lisp the nightly prayer,
Learning to cast on the Loving One early our load of care.
Whatever the world has brought us since, yet, pure as a rose in bloom,
Is the thought we keep of the core of the home, the mother's darling room.

We think of it oft in the glare and heat of our lifetime's later day,
Around our steps when the wild spray beats,
And the mirk is gathering gray.
As once to the altar's foot they ran whom the menacing foe pursued,
We turn to the still and sacred place where a foe may never intrude,
And there, in the hush of remembered hours,
Our failing souls grow strong,
And gird themselves anew for the fray, the battle of right and wrong.
Behind us ever the hallowed thought, as pure as a rose in bloom,
Of the happiest place in all the earth, the mother's darling room.

We've not forgotten the fragrant sheaves of the lilacs at the door,
Nor the ladder of sunbeams lying prone on the shining morning floor.
We've not forgotten the robin's tap at the ever friendly pane,

LINEN, CARE OF

When linen is well dried and laid by for use, nothing more is necessary than to secure it from damp and insects. The latter may be agreeably performed by a judicious mixture of aromatic shrubs and flowers, cut up and sewed up in silken bags, to be interspersed among the drawers and shelves. These ingredients may consist of lavender, thyme, roses, cedar shavings, powdered sassafras, cassia lignea, &c., into which a few drops of otto of roses, or other strong-scented perfume, may be thrown. In all cases, it will be found more consistent with economy to examine and repair all washable articles, more especially linen, that may stand in need of it, previous to sending them to the laundry. It will also be prudent to have every article carefully numbered, and so arranged, after washing, as to have their regular turn and term in domestic use.

Nor the lilt of the little brook outside, trolling its gay refrain.
How it haunts us yet, in the tender hour of the sunset's fading blush,
The vespers song, so silvery clear, of the hidden hermit thrush!
All sweetest of sound and scent is blent, when, pure as a rose in bloom,
We think of the spot loved best in life, the mother's darling room.

Holding us close to the best in life, keeping us back from sin,
Folding us yet to her faithful breast, oft as a prize we win,
The mother who left us here alone to battle with care and strife
Is the guardian angel who leads us on to the fruit of the tree of life.
Her smile from the heights we hope to gain is an ever-beckoning lure;
We catch her look when our pulses faint, nerving us to endure.
Others may dwell where once she dwelt, and the home be ours no more,
But the thought of her is a sacred spell, never its magic o'er.
We're truer and stronger and braver yet, that, pure as a rose in bloom,
Back of all struggle, a heart of peace, is the mother's darling room.

—The Art of Homemaking
1898

BLADDERS, PREPARED

Cut off the loose fat, wash in a weak solution of chloride of lime, and rinse in clear water. When drying, blow them tight and keep them expanded. Used to tie over jars, pots, etc., and to contain powdered pigments.

NOBODY KNOWS BUT MOTHER

Nobody knows of the work it makes
To keep the home together,
Nobody knows of the steps it takes,
Nobody knows—but mother.

Nobody listens to childish woes,
Which kisses only smother;
Nobody's pained by naughty blows,
Nobody—only mother.

Nobody knows of the lessons taught
Of loving one another;
Nobody knows of the patience sought,
Nobody—only mother.

Nobody knows of the anxious fears,
Lest darlings may not weather
The storm of life in after years,
Nobody knows—but mother.

Nobody kneels at the throne above
To thank the Heavenly Father
For that sweetest gift, a mother's love;
Nobody can—but mother.

—The Household
VOL. XXV, 1892

THE "OLD WOMAN"

It was thus, a few days since, we heard a stripling of sixteen designate the mother who bore him. By coarse husbands we have heard wives so called occasionally, though in the latter case the phrase is more often used endearingly. At all times, as commonly spoken, it jars upon the ears and shocks the sense. An "old woman" should be an object of reverence above and beyond almost all other phases of humanity. Her very age should be her surest passport to courteous consideration.

The aged mother of a grown-up family needs no other certificate of worth. She is a monument of excellence, approved and warranted. She has fought faithfully "the good fight," and come off conqueror. Upon her venerable face she bears the marks of the conflict in all its furrowed lines. The most grievous of the ills of life have been hers; trials untold, and unknown only to her God and herself, she has borne incessantly; and now, in her old age, her duty done, patiently awaiting her appointed time she stands more beautiful than ever in youth, more honorable and deserving than he who has slain his thousands, or stood triumphant upon the proudest field of victory.

Young man, speak kindly to your mother, and ever courteously, tenderly of her. But a little time and ye shall see her no more forever. Her eye is dim, her form is bent, and her shadow falls graveward. Others may love you when she has passed away—kind-hearted sisters, perhaps, or she whom of all the world you choose for a partner—she may love you warmly, passionately; children may love you fondly, but never again, never, while time is yours, shall the love of woman be to you as that of your old trembling mother has been.

—*The Household*
VOL. V, 1872

THE COMING GRANDMOTHERS

That means you and I, who are now in the prime of life, bearing the burden and heat of the day. The years roll on more and more swiftly—or seem to accelerate their passage—and the grey hairs come, one by one at first, and afterwards by scores.

GRANDMOTHER'S BEAUTY BATH

Ye olden dames bathed luxuriously. Here is one of their favorites:

Barley	2 pounds
Oatmeal	2 pounds
Fine bran	2 pounds
Rice	2 pounds
Bi-Carbonate of Soda	8 ounces
Borax	8 ounces
Dried lavender flowers	1 pound
Bay leaves	1 pound

Boil them for one hour in a sufficient quantity of rain water, and after straining carefully mix two quarts with the bath water.

The dread of growing old seems to me as unreasonable as the common fear of death. One does not like the prospect of becoming a burden to one's friends, but can not we prevent such a calamity by proper foresight and self discipline in these earlier years? Persons who honestly suppose that childhood is the "happiest stage of life," have little idea of the real value of life as a school, where most excellent lessons are to be had by all teachable souls. Such ones like to get *experience,* and it seems likely that coming years will not fail of yielding that, as past years have already done. When fresh lessons are set us in this great school of life, we often fail to see them in that light, and call them troubles and afflictions. I have great contempt for my own weakness in that respect. I should think I had lessons enough already, to begin to cooperate more cheerfully with the Great Teacher in the work of my own education; but I still shrink from my tasks, and forget how the great fact of Immortality throws all these light afflictions, which are but for a day, into insignificance.

How to get the *best* of these ever-present experiences, so that we may grow stronger and sweeter in spirit, as years go by—more cooperation with the Infinite Goodness, which underlies and works through all things for the ultimate good of the whole—that is the present and unceasing problem.

Just now, with most of us mothers, the way is marked out. Each day is full of duties crowding thick and fast upon each other. For many of us the way seems very straight and narrow. But by-and-by our babies will be busy out in the world. One by one they will fly away from the home nest, and *perhaps* there will then be some leisure—a little afternoon of life, when that work we do may be done from choice rather than from necessity. Then what?—Snuff-boxes and knitting work?—The former have pretty much gone out of use already, and when we have become grandmothers, will scarcely be known, great comforts as they were to the grandmothers a few generations ago. The knitting work of the dear grandmothers must not be scornfully mentioned, so greatly does it add to the comfort of thousands of families; and if machinery has not taken this work out of reasonable reach, by the time that my own grandchildren arrive on this planet, I, for one, shall cheerfully do my grandmotherly share of the family knitting. Just so of all the little helpful tasks that good grandmothers are wont to perform. There seems to me something almost angelic in the sweet patience and sympathetic assistance one sometimes finds

IN LAYING UP FURS

for summer, lay a tallow candle in or near them, and all danger of worms will be obviated.

in aged women. They seem to have ripened properly into human beings, and it delights me when such old women tell me, as some of them do, that their last days are their best days. It ought to be so. They may be mere children still, in scientific and literary attainments, and though this does not add to the charm of character, neither does it detract therefrom. It grows on me more and more forcibly, that St. Paul was right in his beautiful epistle in which we are taught: better than all knowledge, or doing of great deeds, are faith, hope, and charity—"And the greatest of these is charity."—A good loving heart greatly outweighs what we call knowledge. If to the loving womanly heart be added mental power and culture, then we have "A perfect woman nobly planned."

I fear this seems like preaching, and I must "draw to a close." This then, briefly, is the thought I wished to communicate: our seed time for our coming grandmotherhood—if we already have children—for our old age in any case—is not yet past. By regular and temperate habits, we may preserve or improve our health, so that we may be able to take care of ourselves, and perhaps help others in some way, when we are old.

—Faith Rochester
The American Agriculturist
VOL. XXXV, 1876

THE POWER OF MOTHER'S INFLUENCE

The sweetest, purest, strongest, most unselfish relationship in life is that of mother. God intended that this should be so. To this end is the little infant laid so helpless, the most helpless of all the animal creation, into the arms of a mother, who has gone down into the depths to receive it, and who should rise to the mount of self-purification and self-abnegation that she may promote its prosperity and happiness. ...

In whatever other relationship in life woman might or might not find a representative in man, in this he must utterly fail; he can never represent her motherhood. These maternal rights, duties, and obligations she delegates to none. In this, her crown of motherhood, woman stands peculiar, alone. The sweet joy, the strong tie, the unquenchable love, the untiring solicitude that swells with the first consciousness of a new life, and life of one's own life, and ends not in time nor eternity, is such that only experience can reveal, and even experience cannot understand. Awe, reverence, adoration, are emotions not too strong with

STARCHING

Fine things are best got up thus: Soak in cold water the night before; the next day wring them out, soap well, and pour boiling water over; rub out of that water, and soap a second time. Repeat the boiling water. When this has been done twice, rinse well in two or three waters, letting the last one have a little liquid blue in it. Let remain till your starch is made; get best starch, mix up well in a little cold water, then pour boiling water in, mixing all the time; put into a clean saucepan, and when starch is just on the boil, stir into it a small lump of sugar, or a very little bit of wax candle, with a little blue. When your starch has boiled for a minute, strain it through a piece of linen, and then starch your things (first wringing them out of the blue water). After they are starched let them dry; and two or three hours before ironing out, they must be well damped and rolled up tight in a clean cloth. Collars and lace should always be ironed out upon a piece of blanket or cloth, used only for that purpose. If linen be mildewed, wet it with soft water; rub with white soap; scrape some fine chalk to powder, and rub it well into the linen; lay it out on grass in the sunshine, watching to keep it damp with soft water, repeat the process the next day.

which to stand in the holy of holies of motherhood. This it is that makes the various Madonnas the most universally, reverently loved of all the works of art. It appeals to every thinking, feeling being.

> "*A mother is a mother still,*
> *The holiest thing on earth.*"

Through all the ages, the higher virtues have become more and more the vital moving forces in private and public affairs in proportion as the mother element has been respected and utilized. Our country to-day needs just this; it needs mothering; it needs to have the power of love for humanity transcend the love of wealth, or position. Mothers need the largest development, the utmost freedom and dignity, to enable them rightly to meet the demands of creating and educating the race.

Ben Jonson ascribed all his early impressions of religion to his mother's piety. She was a woman of distinguished understanding. Once when some one was asked whether Mrs. Jonson was not vain of her son, the reply was, "She has too much good sense to be vain, but she knows her son's value." How characteristic of

Harper's Weekly, June 17, 1871. Courtesy: Argosy Bookstore, N.Y.C.

motherhood! "She hid all these things in her heart." The world owes much to the early influences on the heart and life of the child. God pity the child who has an ungodly, worldly, frivolous mother! Mothers have special need of the power of the invisible, mighty love of the Divine to shed a softening charm. They need that protecting, all-embracing love that does not forsake its object because of weakness or sin. It is the mother who loves, and trusts, and hopes when all the world condemns. Mother's room, mother's heart, means home to the prodigal. When all other influences fail, this will often suggest the infinite love of God, and bring back the wanderer, worn by passion and the antagonisms of life, to the paths of purity and truth. Timothy was admonished that he should lead an exceptionally pure life because of the pious influence of his "grandmother Lois and his mother Eunice."

Hugh Miller derived from his mother his extraordinary genius for narrative. She possessed imaginative faculties, a creative power of fantasy that, with training and education, would have made her a power in the world of literature, either in poetry or romance. Untutored, these powers led her into the endless vagaries that were so powerful among the unlettered people of her day. Her son, surrounded with this weird atmosphere, early imbibed the uncanny notions, and they powerfully influenced him through life. He suffered paroxysms of terror in childhood. The influence of these early impressions, all his subsequent scientific education and research could not overcome. There is little doubt that eventually his early death was caused by this nervous strain. How important it is that mothers should be educated! Errors can be discovered only by intelligent thought. The mind must be trained to reason, to create ideals, to regulate imagination, to direct and modify emotion; all this can be accomplished only by education. What a shortsighted policy was that which established schools for boys before these opportunities were afforded girls!

Mothers should have strong bodies as well as carefully trained minds. To these should be added spiritual force and aspiration, for the influence pre-natal and post-natal is immeasurable, not less on mind and soul than on body. A mother whose waist is compressed, impeding the action of vital organs, cannot have a healthy child; neither can a mother whose mind has been compressed, circumscribed to a round of petty thoughts, be expected to influence her children to intellectual power. Like produces like.

EVERY KITCHEN NEEDS A BOX

containing balls of brown thread and twine, a large and small darning needle, rolls of waste paper and old linen and cotton, and a supply of common holders. There should also be another box, containing a hammer, carpet-tacks, and nails of all sizes, a carpet-claw, screws and a screw-driver, pincers, gimlets of several sizes, a bed-screw, a small saw, two chisels (one to use for button-holes in broadcloth), two awls and two files.

In a drawer or cupboard should be placed cotton tablecloths for kitchen use; nice crash towels for tumblers, marked T T; coarser towels for dishes marked T; six large roller-towels; a dozen hand-towels, marked H T; and a dozen hemmed dish-cloths with loops. Also two thick linen pudding or dumpling-cloths, a jelly-bag made of white flannel, to strain jelly, a starch-strainer, and a bag for boiling clothes.

In a closet should be kept, arranged in order, the following articles: the dust-pan, dust-brush, and dusting-cloths, old flannel and cotton for scouring and rubbing, large sponges for washing windows and looking-glasses, a long brush for cobwebs, and another for washing the outside of windows, whisk-brooms, common brooms, a coat-broom or brush, a whitewash-brush, a stove-brush, shoe-brushes and blacking, articles for cleaning tin and silver, leather for cleaning metals, bottles containing stain-mixtures and other articles used in cleansing.

All influence, good or bad, springs from the character and thought. This influence makes its way through an infinite variety of channels. The tone of the voice, the expression of the eye, the pressure of the hand, the unpremeditated act, all make indelible impression on the plastic heart of the youth. Each has its influence on the formation of character. "The world wants men," yes, and women, too. To obtain these, we must have the highest type of mothers. Happy the woman, who, like the mother of the Gracchi, can point to her children and exclaim with joy, "These are my jewels."

Frederick the Great, when he heard of the death of his mother and sister Wilhelmina, exclaimed, "This loss puts the crown on all my sorrows. My spirits have forsaken me. All gayety is buried with the loved ones to whom my heart is bound."

No position in life is superior to the influence of a mother's love. One of earth's noblemen said, "All that I am, all that I have been able to do, I owe to my mother."

—Mrs. Susan S. Fessenden
Portrait and Principles
1894

SOME MOTHER'S CHILD

At home or away, in the alley or street,
Wherever I chance in this wide world to meet
A girl that is thoughtless, or a boy that is wild,
My heart echoes softly, " 'Tis some mother's child."

And when I see those o'er whom long years have rolled,
Whose hearts have grown hardened, whose spirits are cold,
Be it woman all fallen, or man all defiled,
A voice whispers sadly, "Ah! some mother's child."

No matter how far from the right she hath strayed;
No matter what inroads dishonor hath made;
No matter what element cankered the pearl—
Though tarnished and sullied, she is some mother's girl.

No matter how wayward his footsteps have been;
No matter how deep he is sunken in sin;
No matter how low in his standard of joy—
Though guilty and loathsome, he is some mother's boy.

That head hath been pillowed on tenderest breast:
That form hath been wept o'er, those lips have been pressed;
That soul hath been prayed for in tones sweet and mild;
For her sake deal gently with some mother's child.

—Frances L. Keeler
The Household
VOL. III, 1870

WOMAN AS AN EDUCATOR

Whence flow the blessings that cluster around the family circle? Can they be traced to any other source than to that mother whose intelligence and purity have shed over it her mild and cheering influence?

The domestic circle, the cherished home of the affections, and the dwelling-place of every social virtue, was transplanted from Eden, and seems to be the only relic of paradise left to fallen

Sod House, Custer Co., 1888. Solomon D. Butcher Collection, Nebraska State Historical Society.

man. And who is the guardian angel charged by Heaven with its protection? We answer, thoughtful, patient and lovely woman. She

"Scatters around her, wherever she strays,
Roses of bliss on our thorn-covered ways;
Roses of Paradise sent from above
To be gathered and twined in a garland of love."

Who can estimate the influence of home upon the present and coming generations, for good or for evil.

Yet, woman is the central light and animating spirit of every true home. And here, she has the molding power in every family, and through the family she must educate the nation. In a literal sense, woman is the divinely commissioned teacher of our race. In this remark, we refer chiefly to maternal influence.

The mother *must* have the training of infancy and child-hood. And the power *she* has in molding the character and fixing the destiny of her child cannot be measured by human calcu-lations. This is the most susceptible period of earthly exist-ence, and the mother's smile and frown and tears and prayers have more educational influence than all the instruction of after years. ...

Let woman then accept the high position and important work assigned her. No sphere can be more exalted, no work more honorable. Let her be satisfied to be a *woman* and to act her part; proud to be called the educator of every generation, and earnest and faithful in the discharge of her important duties.

And if woman is to fulfill her holy mission she must be fit-ted for it by appropriate and extensive culture. The educator must be educated; in body, in mind, in heart. *Physical* development is of the first importance, as it lays the foundation for vigorous health and efficiency. The benefits thus derived, are not confined to the present, but extend to generations yet to come.

Social culture is indispensable for woman; for she is the soul, the ornament of the family and social circle.

It should be the aim and result of a liberal or limited course of study for young ladies, to secure that degree of refinement nec-essary to fit them to move with grace and dignity in good society; to preside over their own homes, entertain company, and every-where become the center and attraction of social life.

SMALL POX

To Prevent Pitting the Face—A great discovery is reported to have recently been made by a Surgeon of the English army in China, to prevent pitting or marking the face. The mode of treatment is as follows: When, in small pox, the preceding fever is at its height, and just before the eruption appears, the chest is thoroughly rubbed with Croton Oil and Tartaremetic Ointment. This causes the whole of the eruption to appear on that part of the body to the relief of the rest. It also secures a full and complete eruption, and thus prevents the disease from attacking the internal organs. This is said to be now the established mode of treatment in the English army in China, by general orders, and is regarded as perfectly effectual.

It is a well known fact, that disease is most likely to make its attack upon the weakest parts, and especially upon places in the system which have been recently weakened by previous disease; hence, if an eruption (disease) is caused by the application of croton oil mixed with a little of the Tartaremetic Ointment, there is every reason to believe that the eruption, in Small Pox, will locate upon that part instead of the face. The application should be made upon the breast, fore part of the thighs, &c., not to interfere with the posture upon the bed.

The highly disciplined mind must also be stored with the knowledge of science and art, and with general information upon all subjects that excite and interest mankind. The conversational powers should also be cultivated, and every other social habit that can add to woman's influence and usefulness.

Domestic training under the skillful eye of the mother, can alone fit the daughter for home duties.

Moral and *religious* culture furnishes the principal excellence of woman's noble character and crowns her queen of home and empress of the school-room, where her greatest power is felt and influence exerted.

Mothers, educate your daughters for *usefulness,* and not for the world of fashion and folly.

—*The Household*
VOL. I, 1868

ROCK ME TO SLEEP, MOTHER

Backward, turn backward, O, Time, in thy flight
Make me a child again, just for to-night!
Mother, come back from the echoless shore,
Take me again to your heart as of yore,
Kiss from my forehead the furrows of care,
Smooth the few silver threads out of my hair,
Over my slumber your loving watch keep—
Rock me to sleep, mother—rock me to sleep!

Backward, flow backward; O, tide of the years!
I am so weary of toil and of tears—
Toil without recompense—tears all in vain—
Take them, and give me my childhood again!
I have grown weary of dust and decay,
Weary of flinging my soul-wealth away—
Weary of sowing for others to reap;
Rock me to sleep, mother—rock me to sleep!

Tired of the hollow, the base, the untrue,
Mother, O mother, my heart calls for you!
Many a summer the grass has grown green,
Blossom'd and faded, our faces between;
Yet with strong yearnings and passionate pain,
Long I to-night for your presence again;
Come from the silence so long and so deep—
Rock me to sleep, mother—rock me to sleep!

IF BLACK DRESSES
have stains upon them, boil a
handful of fig leaves in a quart of
water, and reduce it to a pint, and a
sponge dipped in this liquid and
rubbed upon them, will entirely
remove stains from crape,
bombazines, &c.

Over my heart, in the days that are flown,
No love like mother-love ever has shone;
No other worship abides and endures
Faithful, unselfish, and patient, like yours;
None like a mother can charm away pain
From the sick soul and the world-weary brain;
Slumber's soft calms o'er my heavy lids creep—
Rock me to sleep, mother—rock me to sleep!

Come, let your brown hair, just lighted with gold
Fall on your shoulders again as of old;
Let it drop over my forehead to-night,
Shading my faint eyes away from the light,
For with its sunny-edged shadows once more
Happy will throng the sweet visions of yore.
Lovingly, softly, its bright visions sweep—
Rock me to sleep, mother—rock me to sleep!

Mother, dear mother! the years have been long
Since I have slept to your lullaby song;
Sing, then, and unto my soul it shall seem
Womanhood's years have been only a dream.
Clasped to your heart in your loving embrace,
With your light lashes just sweeping my face,
Never, hereafter, to wake or to weep—
Rock me to sleep, mother—rock me to sleep.

—Florence Percy
The Household
VOL. I, 1868

And, despite all the toil, hardship, pain, and danger involved in bearing and raising children, there was no tragedy so great as a woman who remained childless, failing to fulfill the "ultimate purpose" of her life.

THE SHADOW ON THE WALL

My home a stately dwelling is,
*   With lofty arching doors;*
There is carving on the ceilings high,
*   And velvet on the floors;*
A rich and costly building,
*   Where noiseless servants wait,*
And 'neath the escutcheon's gliding,
*   None enter but the great.*
But a happier home is near it,

A humble cottage small,
And I envy its sweet mistress
The shadows on her wall.

My pictures are the pride of Art,
And drawn by cunning hands;
But the painted figures never move,
Nor change, the painted hands;
Before the poorest widow
More gorgeous pageants glide,
Within the lowliest household,
More life-like groups abide;
And I turn from soulless symbols,
That crown my gloomy hall,
To watch the shifting shadows
Upon the cottage wall.

My stately husband never bends
To kiss me on the lips;
His heart is in his iron safe,
His thoughts are with his ships;
But when the twilight gathers
Adown the dusky street,
The little housewife listens
For sounds of coming feet;
And by the gleaming firelight
I see figure tall
Bend down to kiss a shadow,
A shadow on the wall.

My garden palings, broad and high,
Shut in its costly spoils,
And through the ordered paths all day
The silent gardener toils;
My neighbor's is a grass-plat,
With a hardy buttercup,
Where children's dimpled fingers
Pull dandelions up,
Where on a baby's silken head,
all day the sunbeams fall,
Till evening throws its shadows
Upon the cottage wall.

My petted lapdog, warm and soft,
Nestles upon my knee;
My birds have shut their diamond eyes
That love to look for me;

EAR WAX

Nothing is better than ear wax to prevent the painful effects resulting from a wound by a nail, skewer, &c. It should be put on as soon as possible. Those who are troubled with cracked lips have found this remedy successful when others have failed. It is one of those sorts of cures, which are very likely to be laughed at; but I know of its having produced very beneficial results.

63

The Empty Cradle. *Music Cover.*
Library of Congress.

HOW TO CRYSTALLIZE
GRASSES—

Take one and one-half pounds of
rock alum, pour on three pints of
boiling water; when quite cool put
into a wide-mouthed vessel. Hang
in the grasses, a few at a time. Do
not let them get too heavy, or the
stems will not support them. Again
heat the alum and add more
grasses. By adding a little coloring it
will give variety.

—Lottie May

Lonely I watch my neighbor,
*   And watching can but weep,*
To see her rock her darlings
*   Upon her breast asleep.*
Alas! my doves are gentle,
*   My dog comes at my call,*
But there is no childish shadow
*   Upon my chamber wall.*

My earthly lot is rich and high,
*   And hers is poor and low;*
Yet I would give my heritage
*   Her deeper joys to know;*
For husbands that are lovers
*   Are rare in all the lands,*
And hearts grow fit for heaven,
*   Molded by childish hands*
And while I go up lonely,
*   Before the Judge of all,*
A cherub troop will usher
*   The shadow on the wall.*

—Florence Percy
The Household
VOL. I, 1868

DAUGHTER

THE FARMER'S DAUGHTER

She may not in the mazy dance
    With jewell'd maidens vie;
She may not smile on courtly swain
    With loft bewitching eye;
She cannot boast a form and mien
    That lavish wealth has bought her;
But ah! she has much fairer charms,
    The farmer's peerless daughter!

The rose and lily on her cheek
    Together love to dwell;
Her laughing blue eyes wreathe around
    The heart a witching spell;
Her smile is bright as morning glow
    Upon the dewy plain;
And listening to her voice we dream
    That spring has come again.

The timid form is not more wild,
    Nor yet more gay and free,
The lily's cup is not more pure
    In all its purity;

Of all the wild flowers in the wood,
    Or by the crystal water,
There's none more pure or fair than she,
    The farmer's peerless daughter!

The haughty belle whom all adore
    On downy pillow lies,
While forth upon the dewy lawn
    The merry maiden hies;
And with the lark's uprising song,
    Her own clear voice is heard;
Ye may not tell which sweetest sings,
    The maiden or the bird.

Then tell me not of jewelled fair;
    The brightest jewel yet
Is the true heart where virtue dwells,
    And innocence is set!
The glow of health upon her cheek,
    The grace no rule hath taught her,
The fairest wreath that beauty twines
    Is for the farmer's daughter.
        —The New England Farmer
        OCTOBER 1853

Photo on previous page: Watson Ranch School, 1904.
Solomon D. Butcher Collection, Nebraska State Historical Society.

What Shall the Farmers' Daughters Do?

MR. EDITOR:—Your columns seem to be open to the remarks of your many readers, and not a few of them take advantage of the opportunity thus offered, of making known their various opinions upon agricultural, as well as some other subjects, and of learning those of others upon the same.

The farmers have written upon the advantages and disadvantages of large farms and small farms, of good farms and poor farms, the best manner of raising neat stock, horses, sheep, hogs and poultry; and the ways in which a man commencing the world without a dollar, can in a few years acquire a good farm well stocked, a good home, with all the comforts and many of the luxuries of life, have been ingeniously set forth, much to the encouragement, probably, of many who were on the point of "giving up the farm," and betaking themselves to some more genteel or lucrative business.

Pleasures and enjoyments for leisure hours, books, papers, lyceum lectures, and debating clubs, for the long winter evenings, and the most approved methods of intellectual culture, have been recommended; and "farmers' sons" have discussed the subject whether they had better remain at home on the farm, or seek a situation in the city, where they can enjoy privileges not found in rural districts. And even farmers' wives have made some useful suggestions in your valuable paper.

But it occurs to me that households are rare in which the farmer, his wife and sons, comprise the whole family. It is true that compared with the sons, the daughters are considered by the lords of the soil as quite insignificant beings. Now, Mr. Editor, *I* (being one of the latter class) do not expect to convince you or your readers that I am of equal importance in the world as my brothers; or that my claims to consideration and interest should be mentioned the same day as theirs. But having been a reader of the *Farmer* sometime, I have often hoped and vainly looked for some article indicating the best course for the class of which I am a representative to pursue.

There is a large family of us, some already are come to years of maturity; we have many wants to supply, and the respected head of our family has so many calls for his surplus funds that there is next to nothing left for the girls. Now shall we stay at home and be content with the limited means and advantages afforded us, or shall we leave the homes of our childhood,

NIGHT DRESS

The flannel, cotton, linen, or silk, worn next the skin through the day, should always be replaced, on retiring, by a suitable night-dress. This should be of the same material with that which is taken off. If we wear flannel through the day, we need it quite as much at night.

FOR THE TOILET TABLE

A nice hair pin receiver may be made from a round collar or cuff box. The cover is not used. Cover the bottom and sides neatly with some merino or anything convenient, the color of the worsted to be used, scarlet being the most serviceable. Crochet in split zephyr, a strip to cover the sides and sew it on. Fill the box with black curled hair, such as upholsterers use. Crochet a circular piece for the top in the open-stitch, finished with shells, tacking it on the covered edge of the box just inside the shells. It is not a thing of beauty but is so convenient and easily made that it becomes quite necessary.

—Mrs. Olive Green.

tear ourselves away from brothers and sisters, and from parents, when we most need their council? Shall we stick to the farmhouse kitchen, and assist in lightening the task of our mother, or shall we leave her to toil alone, while we seek from home some of the few employments which are open to females?

Now, sir, if you or some of your able correspondents will advise us; and also among the few kinds of employment, which is to be recommended, or least objectionable, you will greatly oblige.

—A Farmer's Daughter
The New England Farmer
MAY 1857

THE IDEAL FARM GIRL

I do not know of any subject pleasanter to write about than the girls. They are the light and life of things. What a dreary world it would be any way you could fix it without the girls to enliven and adorn it. But I am asked to write of the farm girl—the ideal farm girl—who is not found on every farm, nor in every community. More farm girls of a high type would make more farmers of a similar sort.

The farmer's daughter who is cheerful and content with farm life, and is not seeking for avenues of escape from the (so-called) drudgery of house and home work, and country living, but is doing the best she knows where she was born, need not be a dull, spiritless girl by any means. Some of the most intelligent and brightest women I ever knew have been farmers' wives and daughters. They could write well, teach Sabbath school classes, and entertain their friends in true hospitality and geniality. All the farm girl needs is grace and grit to keep her on a par with those who are looked upon as being more favored than she, in that they have rich papas and servants to do the work, and plenty of time to do as they please—which means to grow indolent and lazy.

The farm girl is all right until she gets herself worked into the notion that she is capable of something higher than helping her folks at home—that there is a "career" for her that will lead on to wealth and distinction, and she must leave the paternal roof and go in pursuit of the good things she feels sure are laid up for her somewhere. When she feels herself pretty well assured that she is of better stuff than her mother, and that she will marry no "hayseed" for a husband and settle down for life to domestic drudgery as she did, there is trouble brewing for her that will sooner or later overwhelm her. "Pride goeth before destruction."

Rewards come to those who have earned them, and the farmer's daughter has as good an opportunity to win them as any other; but she must not be working for glory and self-elevation, but simply to do her duty, and make the most of her talents—it may be only one—that the Creator in his wisdom has endowed her with. If her parents can not afford to give her a classical education, and send her away to some advanced school or college to be polished and perfected, she can get on right well without it; for self-made women, like self-made men, are the ones the people lean on—the ones who can remove mountains of difficulties that are in the way of success.

The farm girl who has been used to making things hum at home, who has milked the cows, helped in the garden, cleaned house and baked bread and cookies can outstrip the city girl with do-nothing propensities when she gets into the class room with her. Country air and exercise have given her health, and health counts largely in mental pursuits. And this same healthy body will help her at home to store up knowledge from books and observation that will be of great service to her. She should have a home paper, a magazine or two, and thus will she be able to keep in touch with the affairs of the day. Books are cheap and plenty, and when one can read and write there is no height in knowledge they may not attain by their own push and perseverance .

An unabridged dictionary is an education of itself if well used. The ideal girl does not read simply to get through the book and have done with it, as she would wash and scrub, but reads for a purpose. Is there a word that she does not understand she will not pass it idly by, but consult her dictionary and get the true meaning in the sense the author intended. When she first adopts this plan—and it should be early in life—she will find herself ransacking the dictionary a good part of her reading hours, but it will pay; the day will soon come when she will only have to resort to this authority occasionally for a full understanding of the text before her.

First and foremost the farm girl needs to lay aside unholy ambition. It is worse than useless to spend time in repining because she is not a man, and can not stalk abroad and accomplish wonders and be somebody of consequence as he can. Very few men get to be anything particular, and such as do oftener than otherwise attribute their good fortune to having had an humble-minded, good mother.

FEATHER BEDS

These ought to be cleaned every spring. There are several ways of doing this, but the following is recommended, as it cleans both tick and feathers: Contrive, if possible, some sort of a platform that you can set up in the yard, on which to lay your beds for cleaning or airing. Failing this, use a back porch. Wash the platform clean, and lay on it the feather bed, and let it remain there during the night in the dew. In the morning, before the dew is off, take a pail of clean, cold, soft water, and, with a new whisk broom, wet and rub the upper side of the bed for some time. Let it lie in the sun until it is dry, which will not be for several hours. Turn it over and treat the other side in the same way, and continue the process until the white stripes in the ticking look as clean as new. This treatment of the feathers makes them "lively."

God made women to be mothers, we can not blot that out, and can hardly plan for ourselves better than he planned for us. Think of a young girl educated only in music and dancing and such lore as the average school affords, and what sort of a home is she likely to preside over?

She may look for money and try marrying to place herself beyond the need of work; but let me whisper, dear girls, there are very few men in this country who can afford to support a wife in idleness—very, very few. A well-known writer has said, "that five out of ten of those who marry to be supported are thrown back upon their own resources within a few years, with the added weight of one, two or five babies to be maintained, and perhaps the husband as well." Marrying for money is the poorest sort of a poor business. Riches take wings and fly, and it is far better to fortify yourself while very young with the practical knowledge of the duties of home-making that sooner or later will be likely to fall to your lot; for if you have no call to use this knowledge it is far easier to abandon it than to pick it up when necessity forces it upon you. The good housekeeper has something in her possession that will always command a good living. There is demand for good housekeepers that exceeds the supply.

The ideal farm girl will not forget to study housekeeping in all its departments. She will make a special study of economy in all things. Waste has wrecked many a household; it has kept many a family desperately poor and dependent that had the wherewithal to lay by something for a rainy day had genuine thrift been practiced. She will not want everything her neighbor has, but will consider carefully the cost and whether she can afford to indulge in the needless luxuries that are abounding and tempting the weak of to-day. She will not fritter away time in vanity that might, if well used, make her an ornament for any position in life. There is no happier fireside on earth than the farmer's. Many who have gone from the old farm and its healthful recreations and delightful evenings at home, look back longingly and lovingly to the happy days and peaceful content of the old home where father and mother and brothers and sisters dwelt.

In view of the fact that woman was made to be a helpmate for man, and guardian spirit for the little ones of the family, are we not disorganizers of society and enemies of the home life when we abandon love and marriage and their attendant anxieties and cares to take up the world's work, and make for our-

STANDARD TOILET POWDER

A good standard toilet powder for safe everyday use, or for occasions when such is required, is composed as follows:

Talcum	10 drams
Wheat starch	1 dram
Orris root (pulverized)	1 dram
Oil rose geranium	2 drops
Oil of Bergamot	1 drop

selves a name and fame that are not accorded to the wives and mothers in the quiet country homes where good men and women are raised?

We have a notable instance of this in the late lamented Frances E. Willard, who forsook the plighted love of her girlhood for a public life and labor in a needed reform, and died broken-hearted in the prime of life, in the midst of her distinguished career—with the work she set out to do unaccomplished. We can not find long life and peace and happiness if we rebel against an institution that God has ordained.

My ideal farm girl will try right at home to make it happier and better, and lighten the work of her mother. In so doing she will fortify herself to preside with wisdom and discretion over her own household should she be permitted to have one. She will extend a helping hand beyond her own borders when possible, and make the neighborhood better for her having lived in it.

If there is a broader field needs her, she will be sought for it. She need not go out of her way in pursuit of honors, they will find her. Thus will she be helping to elevate the farmer's home and business—a most noble work to be engaged in.

—Mary Sidney
The Farm Journal
MARCH 1903

THE RED ANT

Where they are troublesome, it is said that sage leaves, fresh picked, will keep them away, if scattered in places you wish to protect. Green hickory bark will scatter ants.

Childhood's Happy Days. *Lithograph. Library of Congress.*

A MOTHER'S DUTY TO HER GIRLS

MEDICINAL FOOD

Spinach has a direct effect upon complaints of the kidneys; the common dandelion, used as greens, is excellent for the same trouble; asparagus purifies the blood; celery acts admirably upon the nervous system, and is a cure for rheumatism and neuralgia; tomatoes act upon the liver; beets and turnips are excellent appetizers; lettuce and cucumbers are cooling in their effects upon the system; beans are a very nutritious and strengthening vegetable; while onions, garlic, leeks, chives and shalots, all of which are similar, possess medical virtues of a marked character, stimulating the circulatory system, and the consequent increase of the saliva and the gastric juice promoting digestion. Red onions are an excellent diuretic, and the white ones are recommended raw as a remedy for insomnia. They are tonic, nutritious. A soup made from onions is regarded by the French as an excellent restorative in debility of the digestive organs. We might go through the entire list and find each vegetable possessing its especial mission of cure, and it will be plain to every housekeeper that a vegetable diet should be partly adopted, and will prove of great advantage to the health of the family.

Modern education, so far as girls are concerned, busies itself with teaching them a little—a very little—of everything under the sun, except that which it most behooves them to know. In spite of the utter denial of nature in much of the modern philosophy—in spite of the efforts of the strong-minded to eliminate the womanhood from our women, every true woman will continue to find her fullest development and her serenest happiness as wife and mother.

And yet, who does not know that, with all her learnings, no hint concerning the things which shall constitute the chief interest in her probable future is ever given her, either at home or in school? In fact, the subject is as sedulously avoided as if it were prohibited by the laws of God and man.

The difficulty lies mainly in a false notion of what purity is. The old-fashioned idea, that women should be guarded from all knowledge of evil, is hardly practicable in these days of newspapers, French novels, and free-and-easy manners. A knowledge of the utter corruption of human nature must in some degree reach the most sheltered women of the present day, and it lies with every mother to accept the responsibility of seeing that it comes in the right way. If the alternative were between the knowing and not knowing of certain things on the part of young girls, a mother might feel a natural pang at the thought of disturbing the vestal purity of the girlish imagination; but it is usually a very different alternative from this. The choice lies too often between knowing the right things and knowing the wrong—between looking at the most solemn realities of life in an earnest and reverent spirit, or in making them the subject of mysterious and giggling confidences and *double entente*, though mothers may fondly dream otherwise.

It is quite time that we—women and mothers—should face this question square, and that we should come to a true idea of what constitutes purity. Purity means spotlessness, not mere ignorance. It is a mental poise—that attitude toward evil which can only be taken and maintained where a knowledge of evil exists. It is not what one knows that constitutes impurity, but what one loves.

A mind waking up to the life around it feels naturally a profound interest and curiosity in regard to all unexplained phenomena which are rare enough to attract attention. This curiosity is not ignoble; it is as healthy and normal as physical hunger. It is one of nature's demands, which has a perfectly natural means of supply. A wise mother will watch the development of this wonder, and, as the time seems ripe for it, will gently appease it, not by silly fables, but by facts. No mother has a right to permit her daughter to grow up ignorant of the laws which she must obey if she would be healthy, and strong, and useful. Still less has a mother a right to permit her daughter to marry without the fullest notion of the responsibilities she is about to assume.

It is an immense advantage to a woman, in every way, to have made her children her companions. The habit of talking with them and explaining difficulties of various kinds will open the way for such teaching as this, and if, in addition, she has informed herself in scientific matters, so that she can lead the way from physiological botany to human physiology, she will find the familiarity with scientific terms and the habit of dealing with the subject impersonally a great aid.

If the task be too difficult, there is still another resource. For the younger daughters, there are admirable books, containing all necessary information and without a suggestion of indelicacy, which may be substituted for personal counsel. For those who have left the family circle and upon whom the sweet dream of maternity is dawning, I know no better book than "The Mother and her Offspring," published by Harper and Brothers.

When a natural and healthful curiosity is met by a frank and simple statement of facts, the greatest danger is avoided. All temptation to discussion of these matters among girls is removed. Knowledge, instead of weakening and corrupting the character, really strengthens and purifies it, if it be the right kind of knowledge, rightly given. There must be a pure and a right way of looking into whatever God has ordained. Let us seek until we find it, and then gently guide our daughters till they find it too.

—S. B. H.
Scribners
VOL. XXI, NO. 5
MARCH 1881

STUDYING FRENCH TO MARRY A FARMER

It is a matter of deep regret, to all thoughtful persons, and one of ominous significance, that so many girls of the present generation are brought up without any positive purpose, or any end in view at all adequate to satisfy the demands of their nature and probable condition in life. Much as has been said about the dignity of labor as the basis of our republican independence and prosperity, it cannot be denied that the great mass of the young women, born and reared in families not actually oppressed by want, do hold all manner of manual toil in positive contempt, and scarcely apply themselves to toil of any kind, even intellectual. They have but one purpose in the future, and that is to marry. The manner of their bringing-up, being left almost entirely to fond mothers; these mothers have for them also but one object, to have them marry *well*, which means, being interpreted, so they will not have to work. They are taught everything which is supposed to make them pretty, or add to their natural fascination, with no regard to what will make them useful. They know how to make calls, embroider slippers and pincushions, be frightened elegantly at mice and spiders, play croquet and the piano, to have a smattering of French, and be pert and superficial in all things of the least possible consequence. The girl, brought up in this way, whose only design is to marry, and for whom the only design is to marry *well*, not having definite ideas of marrying "well," and true to the instincts of her nature, loves "John the mechanic," or John the farmer, or some other John, who is a laborer, or something less,

Ashfield (Mass.)
Historical Society.

and in spite of opposition and advice marries him. Soon after the honeymoon has gone into its last quarter, and she finds that John's shirts want washing, and pants want patching, and stockings want darning, and collars want ironing; that there are meals to get, and beds to make, and rooms to sweep, and furniture to dust, and an immense amount of work to do, she finds herself able to make about the same use of what she has learned, as the young minister does of his college mathematics when he comes to prepare sermons, or the entry clerk of his Greek and Latin, in making out invoices. What does she know about all these things? It frets her, it vexes her, it makes her cross, it puts John out of sorts, and sets the whole system of things by the ears, and that chiefly because she has been brought up to know all about something which will never do her any particular good, and nothing about that which will. The result is she will soon break down in spirits, and then in health, and become the partner of an ill-conditioned and unhappy home, which state of things might with a little previous discretion on the part of her parents, been for the most part avoided. I would not be understood as saying a word against the French and frolic, calls and croquet, pianos and pincushions, but that they are secondary to the weightier matters of the household, and that whoever, in the education of their girls, puts these lesser accomplishments before the greater, puts the cart before the horse, the beautiful before the useful, the dessert before the dinner, and is adding a sweet element of confusion to some unhappy home.

—Hard Knox
The Household
VOL. 1, 1868

Poor Nelly—A Life Sketch

Seventeen years ago the summer visitors in the little village of Mantelwood were generally asked, first, whether they had seen the big spring, and secondly, what did they think of the little beauty of the village, Nelly Haynes?

These were the two boasts of the little town. The spring was a fountain of great strength and clearness, and the little girl was the daughter of the carpenter, a child of such remarkable beauty that the whole village was proud of it.

Her mother felt that some lofty fortune was in store for her child. She worked hard to buy the young girl finery, while her

PREMIUM BREAD

The Rhode Island Society for the promotion of Industry gave the first premium on domestic bread to Mrs. Hiram Hill, of Providence. The following is Mrs. Hill's recipe for making the bread exhibited by her: For two loaves of the ordinary size, take two potatoes, pare them, slice very thin, and boil quick until quite soft; then mash it to a fine pulp, and add, little by little, two quarts of boiling water, stirring until a starch is formed; let this cool, and then add one-third of a cup of yeast. This forms the "sponge," which should remain in a moderately warm place for ten or twelve hours, or over night, until it becomes very light and frothy; even if a little sour, it is of no consequence. When the "sponge" is ready, add flour, and work it in until you have formed a stiff, firm mass. The longer and more firmly this is kneaded, the better the bread. Let the kneaded mass remain say from half to three-quarters of an hour to rise, then divide into pans, where it should remain, say fifteen minutes; care being taken that it does not rise too much and crack: then put the loaves into a quick oven, and bake, say three-quarters of an hour. If the oven is not hot enough, the bread will rise and crack; if too hot, the surface will harden too rapidly, and confine the loaf.

BRANCHES

of the elder-bush hung in the dining room of a house, will clear the room of flies. There is an odor which the insect detests.

CALF'S EARS STUFFED, AND FRIED

Parboil eight well scalded and soaked white calves ears, cook in a stew pan with white stock, made with a glass of vinegar, one ounce of flour and water to cover the ears; add salt, an onion, with four cloves, some pepper corns, and a half pound of chopped beef suet. Cover and cook slowly till the ears are done, about one hour; drain, pare, remove the centre with a small, round tin tube; let cool, fill the inside nicely with a cooked force meat, roll in bread crumbs, immerse in beaten eggs, roll in crumbs again, and fry in deep, hot fat. Drain, dish on a folded napkin, garnish with parsley and lemon, and serve with tomato sauce.

brothers and sisters wore coarse clothes. As she grew older, Nelly was perpetually seen upon the street, sitting on boxes at the shop doors, while a group of admiring men and boys surrounded her, delighted with her saucy replies to their teasing jokes.

"What was the harm?" her mother said. "Everybody was proud of Nelly; everybody loved her."

The constant praise unfitted Nelly for work in the house. Her homely sisters cooked, sewed and lived indoors, but she could not tolerate such hard labor, and her foolish parents felt that the beautiful girl was surely fitted for a higher fate than to be a kitchen drudge.

School tired her, too. She played truant often, but her teachers could not find it in their hearts to be stern with the gay, pretty creature.

As Nelly grew towards womanhood, the county rang with praises of her beauty. She was eagerly sought for at picnics, suppers, dances.

"Why not let the child have her fun?" her proud mother said. "She will be young but once."

Her sisters, quiet, modest girls, married tradesmen, and went to homes of their own. Nelly scorned such a humble fate. Such beauty as hers, she felt, needed magnificent gowns and jewelry to adorn it.

Before she was sixteen, all of the county had heard not only of her beauty, but her bold habits of life. Much, however, was forgiven her because of her ignorance and innocence. But time came when those excuses availed no longer.

Nelly disappeared. There were startled, shocked whispers and then—silence. Her name was never heard in the town, nor even in her father's house.

A year passed. In one of the large Western cities a wretched woman, outcast and starving, was placed in a van to be taken to the city hospital. She was dying when they took her out, having swallowed poison. But in the room where they hastily laid her, she found strength to cry for her mother and to tell her name. The matron of the hospital asked her if she had no message for her friends.

"I have no friends," she said. "I—missed my chance in the world, somehow."

When they brought her home dead, the villagers stood around the coffin, looking with pity at the lovely face which they knew so well.

"Poor Nelly!" they said. "It was her beauty that was to blame for all."

Was her beauty alone to blame?

Nelly's story is true. But in every town and village there are young girls, as yet ignorant and innocent, going down the path which led her to ruin.

—*The Household*
VOL. XXV, 1892

THE HORSE-SHOE'S GREETING
TO THE FOUR-LEAVED CLOVER

Ho, little country cousin,
  What brings you to the city?
We've sad hearts by the dozen;
  To join them were a pity.
I wonder you can sever
  From home and friends, though humble,
Trefoil and cinquefoil clever,
  The honey-bee and bumble.

You've come to spend the season
  At Mrs. Grundy's asking?
Ah! then I know the reason;
  In fashion's smile you're basking.
You've come awhile to "queen it";
  I shall be superseded;
I know you did not mean it,
  So no excuse is needed.

Poor child! your prospect's dreary;
  Indeed, my heart aches for you;
Of fashion soon you'll weary;
  I've been through it before you.
They'll stiffen you and bend you
  In every shape they fancy;
Gentility they'll lend you
  By direful necromancy.

They'll paint you, carve you, mould you,
  They'll work you up in crewel;
In silver or in gold you
  Will make a charming jewel.
They'll hang you o'er the lintel
  As lonely as an isthmus;

FOR THE CURE OF CANCER

Put water with the ashes of red oak bark, and boil it down to the consistence of molasses, and cover the cancer with a coat of it. In about an hour afterward cover it with a plaster of tar, which must be removed after a few days, and if any protuberance remain in the wound, apply more potash and the plaster again, until it shall wholly disappear.

You'll pose upon the mantel;
    You'll mope on cards for Christmas.

On reticules you'll dangle;
    On soup-tureens you'll swelter;
In maiden's hair you'll tangle
    And strive to hide for shelter;
You'll stare from each shop window
    On throngs of lovely ladies,
Till, jealous as a Hindoo,
    You'll wish you were in Hades.

You'll go to balls and operas;
    You'll whirl in giddy dances,
And sit up stiff and proper as
    The dames in old romances.
You'll perch on ladies' fingers,
    And flash among their laces
Till scarce a vestige lingers
    Of all your rural graces.

And tired of city pleasure,
    For green fields you'll be sighing,
Where life affords some leisure
    'Twixt natal day and dying;
Where hearts wear all the graces,
    And winds go straying over
The old familiar faces
    And sweet young heads of clover.

"East, West—home's best," though trysting
    Be kept in lowliest cottage,
And love makes royal feasting
    Of e'en a mess of pottage.
Ah me! I've long been pining
    To see the dear old smithy
With ruddy forge-fire shining,
    Remembered still, though mythy.

And now, I feel with rapture,
    From home no more I'm banished;
I scarce regret your capture—
    Your rural pleasure vanished.
For, with your happy coming
    I make my happier parting.

A CERTAIN CURE FOR CANCER

Take an egg, pour out the white, then stir into the yolk fine salt until it is quite thick; then put it on the cancer as a plaster; continue it until it is cured.

Thanks, thanks, sweet friend, this gloaming
    Shall see my hasty starting.

Good-bye, sweet friend, and bless you;
    Ere home my way I'm wending
Let me once more caress you;
    The darkest night has ending.
Just think, when things look stormy,
    Poor little four-leaved clover,
"The horse-shoe reigned before me;
    My reign will soon be over."

—C. M. St. Denys
The Continent
1882

State Historical Society of Iowa.

WORKERS

I believe that there is no class of women so really well off as those in their own homes and competent to minister to the wants of their families. ...

And the daughter, too, if needed there, can find her truest place, at least a large share of the time, in her father's household, not fearing manual labor shared with her mother, and making herself companion, teacher, and mutual assistant in all things. There may be rough work to be done, and the hours seem crowded with cares; yet her place is really an enviable one. In these times, when so many worthy women and accomplished young ladies are thrown upon themselves for support, when the cities are full of women, as well as men, seeking labor, yet finding little or none, it seems to me that work is one of the greatest blessings that women can ask for; and to those in their own homes, where it comes unsought for and ever ready, it should be welcomed rather than repelled. As I have already said, there may be too much required of one pair of hands, but even that is preferable to seeking yet finding nothing to do.

There *are* women, and young girls, who must find employment in the great outside world, and to some this seems better than the quiet yet toilsome duties of home. But fortunate, I think, are those (certainly in these times) where the family hearthstone welcomes them, the family board opens for them, and the family labors are shared by them. If the family purse is not deep, there is home comfort; if the toils are arduous for some of the weary ones, there is at least home shelter and home rest for them.

Just as I am penning this, there comes an article in our daily paper concerning the shop girls in New York city. After mentioning that the girls are required to stand constantly from seven in the morning till seven at night, with only an hour at noon for dinner and rest, and that this is producing incurable diseases, the writer says: "The girls do a fearful amount of work for wages ranging from $3 to $7 per week; and, severe as it is, were they all to quit to-morrow there would be ten thousand not only willing but anxious to take their places."

"What kind of a life is it that compels a girl to work twelve hours per day for say $8 per week? She pays $6 per week for board, for which she gets a little hall bed-room, without fire, and the vilest table imaginable. Her washing she does partly herself, but that which she has to hire done costs her at least $1 per week. This leaves her a dollar for clothes, medicine, and what luxuries she has. And, miserable as this life is, there are twenty thousand girls in this city to-day who would cry for joy to get it. The number who live in garrets, on such food as they can get for nothing, is almost appalling."

Let women and girls in their comfortable homes look on such pictures as these, as well as of the thousands of women trying to pick up bread from the needle's point, and then ask themselves if their lot is so very hard after all. To a young girl in the country, the sum which some of these girls get in the cities might seem large; but what is it when their actual living, and poor at that, is taken out? And then think of the thousands who can get positively nothing to do! ...

In writing of these things we are not taking the ground that all womankind are to be house and home helpers, because we know this cannot be, and also know that the world outside has work for many to do. But for the majority of women home is their true kingdom, and the never-ceasing routine of domestic cares and labors their proper sphere of action. For those who do nothing, and would

> *"Be carried to the skies*
> *On flowery beds of ease,"*

we are not writing; but for the many who have heart and hands full—so full as oft to grow dispirited in their tasks—we would give a more cheering view of their lot. Labor of some kind is a part of the discipline of life, and also one of its grandest behests.
—*The Household*
FEBRUARY 1883

Maxims for Farmers' Girls

The art of being loved should be the first thought of a girl approaching womanhood; for with that will come all the arts of housewifery. No young woman need to expect to win and keep the love of a man worth loving, without exercising this art. The secret of this art is all embodied in the "small, sweet courtesies of life."

The art of preserving includes more than pickles and peaches. A husband's love must be preserved as well as won.

BUTTER, TO PRESERVE FRESH

Melt it in a well-glazed earthen pan set in a water-bath at a heat not exceeding 180°Fahr., and keep it heated, skimming it from time to time, until it becomes quite transparent; then pour off the clean portion into another vessel, and cool it as quickly as possible, by placing the vessel in very cold water or ice. This is the method employed by the Tartars who supply the Constantinople market. In this state it may be preserved perfectly fresh for six or nine months, if kept in a close vessel and a cool place.

Rancid butter may be restored by melting it in a water-bath with some fresh burnt and coarsely powdered animal charcoal (which has been thoroughly freed from dust by sifting) and straining it through clean flannel. A better and less troublesome method is to well wash the butter, first with good new milk, and next with cold spring water. Butyric acid, on the presence of which rancidity depends, is freely soluble in fresh milk.

FOR SPRING, SUMMER, AND FALL,

husk beds ought to be in use in every family, and would be if better known. There is no better time for procuring husks than when the corn is being harvested, and the husks will be much nicer and cleaner when corn is cut and shocked, and not become so dry and weather-beaten. A good husk bed will last from twenty to thirty years. Every farmer's daughter can supply herself with such beds against time of need at a trifling expense.

No one who has not tried them knows the value of husk beds, which is such that some persons think that straw and mattresses would be entirely done away with if husk beds were once tried; that they are not only more pliable than mattresses, but are more durable, and the first cost is but little. To have husks nice they may be split after the manner of splitting straw for braiding. The finer they are the softer will be the bed, although they will not be likely to last as long as when they are put in whole. Three barrels full, well stowed in, will fill a good-sized tick, that is, after they have been split. The bed will always be light, the husks do not become matted down like feathers, and they are certainly more healthy to sleep on.

To preserve beauty, you must preserve health. That is preserved by moderate labor, cheerfully performed; by generous diet, quiet sleep, and proper dress.

Health is woman's richest jewel. Its casket is the heart. Its location is within a chest that should never be rudely exposed to injury. Keep that well covered, though all the limbs should be exposed. You need never fear cold if properly clothed. See that sitting-room and sleeping-rooms are well ventilated. Do not neglect exercise nor recreation.

"Laugh and grow fat." It is an old proverb, and a true one. Boisterousness is not mirth. The meaning of the maxim is, Always be cheerful, and thankful for health, and more health will follow.

Hugging the stove will never gain health. That comes from air and exercise. A flower fades in a hot-air room. Beauty does the same. Health, contentment, happiness, and matrimony should dwell together. When you are reasonably sure that they will in your case, you may contract marriage. Love may bring care; the want of it may bring sorrow. No one has a right to ask to be exempt from a share of the cares of life; but, before you make this contract to leave your mother, be sure that you have learned every household duty that she can teach. One of the most important things for you to learn about household duties is, not to depend upon borrowing. There is nothing that will render you unwelcome to a new neighborhood quicker than this. However kindly disposed and pleasant your neighbors may be, they will soon grow cold if they find that you are an habitual borrower—sending for a little tea or sugar to-day, a little soap or salt to-morrow, and bread or butter next day. In sickness, you may send to a neighbor for medicine and assistance, and they will be freely given. In health, avoid borrowing as you would a pestilence.

Indolence is the parent of languor. That, as a general thing, is true, although there are cases where languor comes of ill health or fatigue. But, unhappily, listlessness is a state that city ladies, and sometimes farmers' girls, fall into. To prevent this, exercise freely in the open air. Do not be afraid of walking. It is one of the most healthy kinds of exercise that girls can take. Wear strong shoes, and take long walks.

You will never die on horseback. This is an old and very true proverb. We can not give better advice to farmers' girls than this: learn how to ride well, and ride much. Walking, sometimes, is fatiguing, while a canter, upon an easy-going horse, invigorates body and mind. Many a poor, diseased liver has been restored to health on horseback. Roses will bloom upon pale cheeks, rushing through the air before sunrise.

A New Hampshire farmer was congratulated upon the healthy appearance of his girls, and asked to explain the cause. He said, "It is because their diet has always been wholesome, plain, and simple, yet abundant. They drink water or milk, never having used tea or coffee. They have exercised every day in the open air, assisting me in tending my fruit trees, and in such other occupations as are appropriate for women; and their dress has never been such as to hinder free respiration of our pure mountain air, which is a better panacea than druggists' remedies."

—*Facts for Farmers*
VOL. II, 1866

The Apple Bee. Harper's Weekly, *Nov. 26, 1859. Library of Congress.*

FARMERS' GIRLS

Up in the early morning, just at the peep of day,
Straining the milk in the dairy, turning the cows away,
Sweeping the floor in the kitchen, making the beds up stairs,
Washing the breakfast dishes, dusting the parlor chairs.

Brushing the crumbs from the pantry, hunting the eggs at the barn,
Cleaning the turnips for dinner, spinning the stocking yarn,
Spreading the whitening linen down on the bushes below,
Ransacking every meadow where the red strawberries grow;

Starting the "fixens" for Sunday, churning the snowy cream,
Rinsing the pails and strainer down in the running stream,
Feeding the geese and turkies, making the pumkin pies,
Jogging the little one's cradle, driving away the flies;

Grace in every motion, music in every tone,
Beauty of form and feature thousands might covet to own,
Cheeks that rival spring roses, teeth the whitest of pearls,
One of these country maids is worth a score of your city girls.

—Hellen M. Ladd
The New England Farmer
JUNE 1854

RHEUMATISM

To a hand full of blue flag root add a pint of good spirits; let it stand a week. Dose, a spoon full three times a day, and increase by degrees to three tablespoons full a day. An Indian remedy. Or, apply a poultice of hot potatoes; renew as often as it becomes hard or cool. It is said to be a very excellent remedy.

WHICH, MISS OR MRS.?

Sooner or later, most women have to decide the question, whether they shall accept the title of Mrs., or retain that of Miss to the end of the chapter, and there is no question, perhaps, concerning the present life, on which depends so much of weal or woe. It is conceded by all, that married life is more complete and has possibilities of much happiness than falls to the lot of unmarried people, and it is equally evident that it has greater responsibilities, and has also a possibility of much suffering, disappointment and misery, and therefore one should not enter upon married life without serious thought, and earnest prayer to Him who seeth all things from beginning to end.

The late Dr. Dixi Crosby once gave this advice to a patient of his: "Never take a pig for the sake of his sty." To be sure, there are instances where women have married for a home, knowing well they didn't give that love they were capable of giving, and yet they have found much contentment, and even happiness. However, great respect for the husband elect, and congeniality of taste to a tolerable degree, are necessary for such a result. Even then it is a hazardous undertaking, and it is a sin and a shame to urge any to take such a step against their inclinations, as is sometimes done, for the probabilities are, it will bring only sorrow and life-long regret. As a rule, never give the "casket without the gem," the hand without the heart. One cannot expect to find smooth sailing on "matrimonial seas," unless, at least, she embarks with a good supply of true love.

Wait for the genuine article, girls. You will know it when it comes, and with that founded on respect, any good, sensible, unselfish girl need not be afraid to change Miss for Mrs., when she is asked to do so. Neither need she be afraid to be an old maid. The time is past when maiden ladies are objects of derision, except now and then perhaps, to some simpering, sentimental school girl, and it is possible this same spinster she makes fun of, might have been in the place of this school girl's mother. Certainly, there are such cases.

If you choose a life of single blessedness, you will be in good company, for many of the most gifted and lovable women of our day, belong to this class, and are examples of executive ability as well as of great grace of manner, and sweetness of character. It must be confessed though, that such a life has a tendency to develop certain traits of disposition which are always disagreeable, and hence should be carefully guarded against. One is selfishness. To be self-centered in all one's endeavors and affections, is evil, and only evil, although it may be the most natural thing in the world for one to become so, who has no one in particular depending upon her for help or happiness. It behooves an old maid then to compel herself to get interested in some individual, or some cause, which will call out effort for the comfort and well-being of others. Let her give of her substance as she is able, even making self-sacrifice sometimes, and always give largely of that "love that thinketh no evil, that suffereth long and is kind."

It is quite natural too that a woman who has the "bread and butter" and raiment problems to solve, and thus may have much to do with men in a business capacity, it is quite natural, I say, for such a woman to become brusque, loud and overbearing. With a little watchful care, this and other disagreeable ways may be avoided.

MORNING AND EVENING MILK

There is usually a small difference, in the amount of solids in the milk yielded in the morning as compared with that in the evening. The difference may amount to about one-half per cent, and is mostly represented by butter fats. Any thing which tends to annoy cows, as hot weather in the summer, or cold weather at nights (especially in winter), has a corresponding effect in lessening the yield of solids apart from the total quantity of the milk. Thus, in the summer the cows are most comfortable during the night, and the milk is therefore usually richest in the morning; but the reverse may be the case under a different set of circumstances. Even watering the cows with ice-cold water in winter will frequently cause a decrease in the milk.

Choose some occupation which you have a predilection for, then work with a will, but in sweet, modest, womanly ways, and you will find a place among the best ladies of the land.

—L. O. U.
The Household
VOL. XV, 1882

How to Get a Husband

From an excellent communication published in a contemporary, we copy the following, "expressly for the girls."

"Being old, and therefore allowed license for teasing the girls on matrimonial subjects, I consult them about their future prospects often, and find that the opinion obtains with them that the young men were never so slow in proposing as in these days, which, we must admit, gives them a good, not to say all-powerful reason for not taking a husband. Now, young ladies, the whole secret with nine-tenths of you, of not being able to get off your parents' hands, is simply that you don't know how to work. You can't make a pair of breeches. You can't tell, for the life of you, the difference between bran and shorts, or which cow gives the buttermilk. The young men generally have no fortune, and to marry with them now, rest assured, relates more to making a living with the assistance of a loving industrious helpmate, then indulging in opera music, moonshine and poetry. Do you know what they say of one of your butterfly young ladies who has held them in the parlor by the hour listening to 'elegant nothings?' Nineteen times out of twenty, it is this: 'Well, she's all right for an evening's entertainment, but she will not make a good wife.'

"There is no possible objection to the accomplishments of music, painting, and the like, as such, but the idea is to be able to set these prior amusements aside for the period when the stern duties of married life call for your practical knowledge. Show the young men that you can do your part of double business; that you can cook a meal's victuals on a pinch; that you can sweep up, and dust, and darn old stockings, and save a penny towards an accumulated pound; that you will not be a dead expense to him through life. Believe me, young friends, as many true, heroic, womanly hearts beat over household duties as flutter beneath the light of a parlor chandelier. Your kiss is just as sweet, your smiles just as bright, your heart as happy and tender, after a day's exertion in a sphere worthy of true womanhood, as in places

of dissipation, frippery and silly amusement. Have an ambition to do your part in life; cultivate industrial habits, and let the parlor accomplishments go with the higher accomplishments I have roughly enumerated. It is astonishing how soon a domestic young lady is found out and appreciated. It is because she is such a rare exception to the general rule."

—*The Household*
VOL. III, 1870

To Whom It May Concern

"You would rather lay your daughter in the grave than to see her standing at the marriage altar." You see I quote your very words; but begging your pardon, my dear old friend,—I do not believe them. Doubtless you thought you were speaking the truth; yet in reality you were dealing in the hyperbole of our childish day, when we "hoped to die," if things were not thus and so. You know in your heart of hearts—and I know it as well—that though your tears might flow as you placed the orange blossoms in her hair, they would be wrung from you by no such anguish as would be yours if you were about to consign her to the darkness and silence of the tomb. So do not say this again, dear Rachel; and above all things, do not say it to your child, thus forcing her to feel, if she believes your words, that marriage, God-ordained and heaven-appointed, is something worse than death.

But the truth is, she will not believe them. She will think that her mother is a croaker; and, by and by, when some brainless, or heartless gallant comes along and whispers soft nothings in her ear, and you feel compelled to say to her—"My daughter, do not give yourself to that man; he is selfish, unprincipled; you can not trust him"—how much will your caution influence her heart or life? She may yield to you; but it will be under protest. She will feel that you object to marriage in the abstract; to the love rather than to the particular lover.

"But there are so many unhappy marriages."

True; and there are so many happy ones. Why not let one statement balance the other?

"But," you say again, "do you really believe that your fact would balance mine?"

Most assuredly I do, and overbalance it. So do you. You do *not* believe, my friend, that take our country through—or our own town, if you prefer it—the unhappy marriages are in the

TO COOL THE BLOOD

Take eight ounces of sarsaparilla, three ounces of root licorice, six ounces of wild cherry bark, one-half ounce of mandrake, one ounce of gentian, one-half teaspoonful each of cinnamon and red pepper. Boil in three gallons of rain water till reduced to one-half. Sweeten a very little. This is a fine drink for cooling the blood: Abstain from sweets while using it.   —M.H.N.

A ROYAL DISH—MUSH AND HOW TO MAKE IT

It would be hard to find a cook too modest to claim a knowledge of mushmaking, says *Woman's Home Companion;* yet how many, even among experienced housekeepers, make good mush? Boiling water, cornmeal and salt—what simpler than to put together and cook them?

Yet mush of indifferent meal properly made may be better than that made of the best meal wrongly handled. The water must be freshly boiled and salted, and all the meal as it goes in must encounter the same boiling temperature, to burst the starch cells, as direct heat "pops" corn. Therefore, making mush takes time, for the meal must be added so slowly as not to stop the boiling, as well as to avoid lumps.

A thick iron pot, porcelain lined, is the best thing to cook it in, and a wooden spoon or paddle should be used for the stirring. Sprinkle the meal in slowly with the left hand while stirring with the right.

The proportions of the ingredients will vary with the quality of the meal or its character (whether crushed or cut), but an average rule would be four quarts of water, two and a half pints of meal and two scant tablespoonfuls of salt. When all the meal has been smoothly stirred in, cover the pot closely and stand it where it will give an occasional bubble for three or four hours, or half the day.

Do not disturb the surface, as stirring permits the "extractives" or flavors to escape. Mush made of good meal by the above method, and served with rich cream, is a royal dish.

majority. You do not believe that God's plan of human life is a failure. You do not believe that He implants in two hearts the impulse that leads them to single each other out of all the world, to unite their love, their fortunes and their destiny; and that at the same time He makes these two hearts so subtly antagonistic, so ruled by opposing passions and desires so far asunder in thought and feeling that the bond that binds them together is a life-long torture. You do not believe that this is true in the majority of cases.

Unhappy marriages there are; and far too many of them. Marriages that should never have been thought of; hearts whose sole watchword is endurance. We would not ignore this fact, or shut our eyes to the lesson that it teaches; while at the same time we must affirm that by far the greater proportion of husbands and wives are happy in their homes and happy in each other. God and Nature do not make such awful blunders as must be predicated of them if this is not true. The homes that are scattered all over New England, whether stately mansions enriched by all the appliances of wealth and taste, or humble cottages where the busy mother prepares with her own hand the evening meal for sire and son—these multitudinous homes in town and country, in villages or hamlet, on the farm or in lonely mountain places, are not—as some would have us believe—hells. Doubtless many of them have their skeletons, big or little, as the case may be. But every heart, whether in or out of wedlock, has its graves, where lie buried hopes and dreams and aspirations without number. Every heart has its own skeleton—locked up in some secret closet, mayhap, overlaid with dust and cobwebs—but still there, ready to frighten its owner when in some unguarded hour the door flies open. But it is not fair to presume that these graves, these skeletons, are any more frequent in married than in single life.

Neither are any of these homes actual heavens. But I believe that most of them are as near heaven as anything we poor mortals can find on earth. The stars have shone upon no perfect Edens since the angel with the flaming sword barred Adam out of Paradise. Therefore it is well that the young should not expect too much. Marriage, like life, is a means, not an end.

"But you have had so many cares."

Yes—and your daughter, if she marries, will have them too. But will she not have them if she does not marry? From the age of twenty to thirty, doubtless the married woman has, as a rule, more cares than she who is unmarried. But homes break up; fathers and mothers die; brothers and sisters form newer and stronger ties; the old home circle is scattered far and wide. After middle life the scales hang evenly again, or the weight preponderates upon the other side.

Yet has this much to do with the question? Are the two words care and sorrow synonymous? By no means. And care, rightly understood, when it does not roll upon one like an avalanche, crushing and destroying, means growth. How many a limp, flaccid nature, seemingly inert, passive, inane—how many a light and frivolous one, wholly absorbed in ease and pleasure, has rounded into a noble and beautiful womanhood when the necessity of caring for others has drawn it out of its own self-seeking? The more there is to draw any human being, whether man or woman, out of self, out of a perpetual regard for his or her own comfort or convenience, out of the round of wholly selfish pursuits or pleasures; the more he or she is the central sun of other systems, giving out light and warmth and life to other planets, the nobler and the happier will that human being be.

Did it ever occur to you, dear Rachel, that we make a mistake when we inquire too deeply into the sources of our happiness?

Happiness is a delicate flower, and it will not bear much handling. We may count the pistils and stamens, note the beauty of the corolla and the form of the calyx, and inhale the fragrance floating from its tiny censer. But if, in our eager pursuit of knowledge, in our devotion to science, we carry our examination a little too far, the flower will lie torn and fading in our clasp, a crushed, unsightly thing. It is best to take "the good the gods provide" without inquiring too closely into its source and origin.

Introspection is morbid, unhealthy. The soundest body is least conscious of its own organs. It is hardly aware that it has lungs, or a heart, or a liver. Carlyle tells us that he did not discover that he had a stomach until he was over twenty, and that he has not been unconscious of the fact for an hour since!—which may perhaps account for his misanthropic cynicism. The healthiest soul is the one that is so in harmony with God that it does not need to be perpetually studying itself, searching for points of accord and discord. And the healthiest heart is the one that is openly and frankly a loving heart, not stopping to ask why it loves, or to wonder if it gives more than it receives, or to question if the objects of its love are fully worthy. It simply loves—and so it "touches God."

—Julia C. R. Dorr
The Household
VOL. V, 1872

THE EARLY WOOED AND WON

A young and modest bride art thou
        In all thy early bloom;
And now art gone from friends away
        To grace another's home;
We know full well thy few brief days
        Of triumphs now are done;
Yet happiness shall now repay
        The early wooed and won.

Thine is a young and guileless heart,
        Confiding, pure and warm;
Unsullied by a breath of shame,
        Or passion's fiery storm;
In Hope deferr'd thou hast not passed,
        Until Hope's race has run;
But chains of purest love now bind
        The early wooed and won.

Thy smiles of bliss have ceased to grace
        The halls of joy and mirth;
For thou now find'st thy dwelling-place
        By thy fond husband's hearth;
Thy hours of duty, joy and love
        In brightness have begun;
And may all happiness be thine,
        Thou early wooed and won.

—Finley Johnson
Peterson's Magazine
OCTOBER 1857

USE A CLOTH

to wash potatoes. It is no trouble to keep one for this purpose, and it will save hands and time. Some prefer a brush. Tie a strip of muslin on the end of a round stick, and use to grease bread and cake-pans, gem-irons, etc. Have two large pockets in your kitchen apron, and in one of them always keep a holder. A piece of clam or oyster shell is much better than a knife to scrape a kettle, should you be so unfortunate as to burn any thing on it. If you use a copper tea-kettle, keep an old dish with sour milk and a cloth in it, wash the kettle with this every morning, afterward washing off with clear water, and it will always look bright and new. Cut a very ripe tomato and rub over a kitchen table to remove grease. The juice will also remove stains from and whiten the hands.

EPITAPH ON THE UNMATED

No chosen spot of ground she called her own.
In pilgrim guise o'er earth she wandered on;
Yet always in her path some flowers were strown.
No dear ones were her own peculiar care,
So was her bounty free as heaven's air;
For every claim she had enough to spare.
And, loving more her heart to give than lend,
Though oft deceived in many a trusted friend.
She hoped, believed, and trusted to the end.
She had her joys;—'twas joy to her to love,
To labor in the world with God above,

And tender hearts that ever near did move.
She had her griefs;—but they left peace behind,
And healing came on every stormy wind,
And still with silver every cloud was lined.
And every loss sublimed some low desire,
And every sorrow taught her to aspire,
Till waiting angels bade her "Go up higher."

—Mrs. M. L. Rayne
What Can a Woman Do
1893

The joys of equality were experienced only in childhood, for all too soon choices must be made in destinies fulfilled. Note the options projected for those "girls wild as a feather."

From the Collection of Historic Northampton, Northampton, Massachusetts.

91

BOYS AND GIRLS TOGETHER

Raking in the meadows,
Riding on the hay,
Racing down hill shadows,
Pulling posies gay;
Hunting for the hen's nest,
Hunting for the cow;
On the fence at see-saw,
Jumping from the mow;
Gaming out at moonlight,
Playing hide and seek,
Fishing in the mill-pond,
Sailing vessels fleet;
Loitering by the wayside
On the road to school,
Butterflies a chasing,
Wading in the pool.

Hurray! life never comes but once!
So never mind the weather;
We are young and happy now,
Boys and girls together.

Swinging in the wildwood,
Playing bat and ball,
Kindling ruddy bonfires,
Climbing nut trees tall;
Sitting on the house roof,
Singing on the style,
Making dolls of pumpkins,
Marching Indian file;
Blowing airy bubbles,
Reading funny books;
After fruit and berries,
Wading in the brooks;
Playing games of marbles,
Hiding up the lane,
Jack-o'lanterns making,
Raising "merry Cain."

Boys can be mischievous,
Girls wild as a feather;
But there is nothing half so gay
As boys and girls together.

HOW TO MAKE
SWEEPING CAPS

Any girl who values a clean head with bright hair, will cover it up while sweeping; coquettish little sweeping caps may be made by cutting a piece of bright pink, blue or gray cambric in a circular shape, and making a shirr within two inches of the edge (which should be hemmed) and running in an elastic or a piece of narrow tape, with which it can be drawn up to fit the head.

—Mrs. Hoy

Harry'll grow a sailor,
  Hennie'll buy and sell,
Mark'll be an artist,
  Mamie'll be a belle,
Willie'll go a soldier,
  Frankie'll stay at home,
Sadie'll marry Herbert,
  Jack'll marry Rome;
Ed and Pete'll "farm it,"
  John'll be a fool,
A vulture of a lawyer,
  And Jane'll keep a school;
Nellie'll reign in Paris,
  Bobbie'll break his heart,
Hermie'll be a minister—

And we'll always live apart;
  But we'll look back to golden days,
Through memory's "specs of leather,"
  When we were jolly boys and girls—
Boys and girls together.

—*The Household*
VOL. I, 1868

DON'TS

Don't begin a journey until the breakfast has been eaten.

Don't forget that a new born infant's eyes may be injured by rubbing them with its fingers before the nurse has washed the child. Have on hand an obstetrical bandage, which consists of cheesecloth, the two edges of which are rolled in and then doubled over a second time. Carefully wipe the baby's eyes, and wrap this bandage around the head and eyes and pin it.

—Geo. E. Abbott, M.D.

HOMEMAKER

To a Little Housewife

O little Housewife! clean and spruce,
*   Thy use one heart divines;*
A rosy apple full of juice,
*   And polished—till it shines!*
A tidy, tripping, tender thing,
*   A foe to lazy litters,*
A household angel, tidying
*   Till all around thee glitters.*

To see thee in thy loveliness,
*   So prudent and so chaste,*
No speck upon the cotton dress,
*   Girdled around thy waist;*
Thy ankle peeping white as snow,
*   Thy tuck'd-up kirtle under;*
What shining dishes. row on row,
*   Behind thee stare and wonder.*

While round thy door the millions call,
*   While the great markets fill,*
Though public sorrow strikes us all,
*   Singing, thou workest still;*

Yea, all thy care and all thy lot
*   Is ever sweet and willing,*
To keep one little household spot
*   As clean as a new shilling!*

The crimson kitchen firelight dips
*   Thy cheeks until they glow;*
The white flour makes thy finger tips
*   Like rose buds dropped in snow,*
When all thy little gentle heart
*   Flutters in exultation*
To compass, in an apple tart,
*   Thy noblest aspiration!*

O Housewife! may thy modest worth
*   Keep ever free from wrong;*
Blest be the house and bright the hearth
*   Thou blesseth all day long!*
And nightly may thy sleep be sound,
*   While o'er thee, softly, stilly,*
The curtains close, like leaves around
*   The hushed heart of the lily!*
*   —The Household*
*   VOL. III, 1870*

Photo on previous page:
McCormick Collection, State Historical Society of Wisconsin
(WHi (X3) 14321).

A really good housekeeper is almost always unhappy. While she does so much for the comfort of others, she nearly ruins her own health and life. It is because she cannot be easy and comfortable when there is the least disorder or dirt to be seen. A fine musician is always pained and made miserable at a slight discord that is not noticed by less trained ears, and a fine housekeeper is just as unhappy as she can be at a little dust or disorder which the ordinary mortal does not see.

—*The Household*
JANUARY 1884

THE BUSY HOUSEWIFE

The farmer came in from the field one day;
His languid step and his weary way,
His bended brow, his sinewy hand,
All showed his work for the good of the land;
    For he sows,
    And he hoes,
    And he mows,
  All for the good of the land.

By the kitchen fire stood his patient wife,
Light of his home and joy of his life,
With face all aglow and busy hand,
Preparing the meal for her husband's band;
    For she must boil,
    And she must broil,
    And she must toil,
  All for the good of the home.

The bright sun shines when the farmer goes out,
The birds sing sweet songs, lambs frisk about;
The brook babbles softly in the glen,
While he works so bravely for the good of men;
    For he sows,
    And he mows,
    And he hoes,
  All for the good of the land.

How briskly the wife steps about within,
The dishes to wash, the milk to skim;
The fire goes out, flies buzz about—

SIMPLE DISINFECTANT

The following is a refreshing disinfectant for a sick room, or any room that has an unpleasant aroma pervading it: Put some fresh ground coffee in a saucer, and in the centre place a small piece of camphor gum, which light with a match. As the gum burns, allow sufficient coffee to consume with it. The perfume is very pleasant and healthful, being far superior to pastiles, and very much cheaper.

97

FOR THOSE WHO WISH
TO MAKE DOWN QUILTS

or cushions and have not the
poultry from which to pluck the
down, let them try the down from
the milkweed pod which grows in
nearly every state in the Union
without cultivation or other care.
Make a bag the size of a common
quilt and in the early autumn
(about the last week in August in
Kansas) take a grain sack and go
"down" gathering, along the river
bank, in the hedge rows, on the
edges of the meadows, you will
find them everywhere. Gather the
pods before they are ripe enough
to open, and put them in a dry
place for a few days until they
begin to shrink, then by opening
the pods the seeds can all be
removed as quickly and easily as
one can pass them through her
hands, and the down dropped into
your quilt and treated exactly as
you would feather down. They are
so light and soft they make a
splendid substitute for the goose
and duck down, and have the
advantage of being free for all.

For the dear ones at home her heart is kept stout;
 There are pies to make,
 There is bread to bake,
 And steps to take,
All for the sake of home.

When the day is o'er, and the evening is come,
The creatures are fed, the milking done,
He takes his rest 'neath the old shade tree,
From the labor of the land his thoughts are free:
 Though he sows,
 And he hoes,
 And he mows,
 He rests from the work of the land.

But this faithful wife, from sun to sun,
Takes her burden up that's never done;
There is no rest, there is no play,
For the good of the house she must work away:
 For to mend the frock,
 And to knit the sock,
 And the cradle to rock,
All for the good of the home.

When autumn is here, with its chilling blast,
The farmer gathers his crop at last;
His barns are full, his fields are bare,
For the good of the land he ne'er hath care;
 While it blows,
 And it snows,
 Till winter goes,
 He rests from the work of the land.

But the willing wife, till life's closing day,
Is the children's guide, the husband's stay;
From day to day she has done her best,
Until death alone can give her rest,
 For after the test,
 Comes the rest,
 With the blest,
In the farmer's heavenly home.

—Henry Davenport Northrop
Crown Jewels
1887

W hile some writers simply idealized domestic life in terms of glow ing health and joyful occupation, others found it necessary to imbue domesticity with a higher sense of meaning and accomplishment.

HOUSEKEEPING AND HOMEKEEPING

I know there are those whose superior wisdom can influence the minds of their laboring sisters better than I can, still when I think of this subject, I feel as though I must add my mite, poor though it be. We are too apt to consider the necessary work that the household requires, nothing but drudgery. Do we, who have the superintendence of the housework, and participate therein, strive to make it what it ought to be? It is the work of our homes, the most blessed work that woman can do; for from our homes the influence goes out all over the land to make the rising generations better or worse.

It is not only housekeeping, but something more, it is homekeeping. It is not merely the mechanical performance of a round of duties each day, but it is an art that brings into use all our latent ingenuity, and requires a keen sense of the beautiful, with firmness and perseverance, to overcome all the petty trials and difficulties that are forever crowding around the path of a housekeeper.

Homekeeping is an art that needs just as finished an education, and as thorough a practice, to become an adept, as what are termed the "fine arts," but why fine arts? I know not, for if homekeeping is not one of the fine arts, what is? To be sure there is the coarser work the same as there is in everything. The painter must know how to properly clean his brushes, and palette, he must mix his paints, and oils, and if the picture does not suit, perhaps the canvas will have to be cleaned so as to commence again; but the toil is forgotten, for he works for an object, for a crowning beauty.

And should we not toil as unceasingly through all these little duties, doing faithfully, still not dwelling too much on the trivial, but through all keeping and recognizing a higher beauty that shall bless us while we labor, and make life's picture perfect in its completeness? We cannot, like the artist, efface our work, for we are building for eternity; let us then give the seemingly uncomely labors more abundant comeliness.

Order and harmony should be every housewife's motto; as the old saying, "a place for everything and everything in its place."

I do not say the bread should never be burned, or the room never littered; for all these things will sometimes happen to the best of housekeepers. But I do say there should be neatness and order, not meaning that every chair should be set back as though it were glued there, and the whole house wear a look of primness and coldness that repels one, and dampens the spirits of every one that comes in, but that all things should be refined and perfectly natural, from the kitchen to the parlor, and all blend and harmonize in true beauty without confusion or disorder. Every housekeeper can and should be just as much a lady as though she never entered the kitchen and partook of the labors there.

Housekeeping does not exclude those other employments that have of themselves so large a share in our world. Music, drawing and painting, and also literary pursuits, they all have their place in the model housekeeper's domain, and help to make life and home beautiful.

The housekeepers and homekeepers of our land have a large field of labor. Oh! that they realized more fully the great and noble work, which if entered into in spirit and in truth would be theirs. Housekeeping has a direct influence on the inmates of the household, and remember that the influence of our homes, and the teachings and practice of the home life, act directly upon the nation, so if we would have our nation pure, upright, and truly great, we must begin at our homes, and make them pure, honest and wholesome.

—A. M. R.
The Household
VOL. XIV, 1881

FURNITURE CREAM

Shred finely two ounces of beeswax and half an ounce of white wax into half a pint of turpentine; set in a warm place until dissolved, then pour over the mixture the following, boiled together until melted: Half a pint of water, an ounce of castile soap and a piece of resin the size of a small nutmeg. Mix thoroughly and keep in a wide-necked stone bottle for use. This cleans well and leaves a good polish, and may be made at a fourth of the price it is sold at.

THE HOUSEKEEPER'S SOLILOQUY

Well, at last my house is all cleaned;
From garret to cellar I've been,
Not a cobweb I'm sure's to be seen,
Or grease spot how ever so thin—
I've whitewashed, and papered, and scrubbed,
And dusted, and polished all through,
Till I'm sure that I ought to be dubbed
Royal mistress of household ado.

Now if I could only sit down,
And composedly fold up my hands,
And say that my work was all done,

And duty had no more demands,
If when clean, it would only stay clean,
   How pleasant and nice it would be,
To feel that no dirt could be seen,
   And nothing expected of me.

But no, that is never the case:
   I must daily look over each room,
Little fingers and foot prints erase,
   And be busy with duster, and broom.
My watch must be careful and close,
   My hand must be willing and true,
For if I should sleep at my post,
   The enemy's work you would view.

And 'tis thus with some Christians I've thought,
   Who confess all their folly and sin,
And cleanse their heart out as they ought,
   From impurities gathered within,
And then feel safe and secure,
   And neglecting the duster and broom,
Their lives become vile and impure,
   Long before the next cleaning day comes.

Yes, the Christian's life's something like mine—
   If the heart is kept loving and pure,
And governed by precepts divine,
   That can patiently work and endure
The dust which self-righteousness leaves—
   The cobwebs of envy and pride—
The dark stains which selfishness gives,
   Must be constantly banished aside.

If I strive with a daily survey
   To keep my house comely and neat,
I must watch o'er myself as I may,
   That my life may be full and complete;
For a house is not home if the heart
   Lies unswept of its passions and sin,
And Patience can best do her part,
   If Love is the matron within.

—Kate Woodland
The Household
1877

DIPHTHERIA

A gargle of sulphur and water has been used with much success in cases of diphtheria. Let the patient swallow a little of the mixture. Or, when you discover that your throat is a little sore, bind a strip of flannel around the throat, wet in camphor, and gargle salt and vinegar occasionally.

THINGS FOR A YOUNG HOUSEKEEPER
TO REMEMBER

When you especially realize your tired feet, and aching back, and coarse, red hands, try also to appreciate the greatness in littleness, the nobleness underlying the pettiness of your office. If you belong to the noble army of martyrs who are daily sacrificing themselves upon the domestic altar,—conscious that they are capable of higher service,—let these words of Ruskin's encourage you.

"Every action, however mean or inconsiderable, is capable of a peculiar dignity in the manner of it, and a still higher dignity in the motive of it. For there is no action so light but it may be done to a great purpose, and ennobled therefore."

—Lydia Shillaber
Mrs. Shillaber's Cookbook
1887

From the Collection of Historic Northampton, Northampton, Massachusetts.

B ut all attempts to attach a higher meaning or purpose to the rural woman's life had to be measured against the day-to-day demands made on her.

How to Keep House

MONDAY.—This day has been considered the universal washday in America, thereby making Monday the most dreaded day of the week. Now, by changing washing from Monday to Tuesday, you have Monday to make all of your preparations in, and thus avoid both annoyance and anxiety. You can utilize Monday by doing odd jobs, such as washing windows, brightening the silver, cleaning stair-rods, etc., etc. A host of them will come crowding into the housekeeper's mind, and she will find that the day is not long enough to get them all done, and some must take their turn on the next Monday. There is that closet you have so long been anxious should be cleaned; that jar of preserves to be attended to, or they will spoil; and various incidental matters of this kind in addition to the "odd jobs." Monday will be a busy and much valued day. It is a good time to select for all these extras, just after the rest of Sunday, and before the regular rush of the week's housework begins.

But you must save time from this work that your servant may, towards evening, help you to prepare the clothes for the next day's wash. Direct her to divide them into three parcels, the fine, the more common, but not much soiled, and the really dirty. While this is being done you can put down on your list the number of articles of each kind. It is well to do this, even with honest servants, for, if anything is missing, the owner is sure to insist that it was lost in the wash, and the list will at once show whether the charge is correct. Have ready three tubs of cold, soft water, and put in the clothes, having first rubbed soap over the parts most soiled, and leave them to soak all night.

TUESDAY.—After breakfast, place your wash-boiler on the stove, place in your washing fluid and several pieces of hard soap cut up in shavings, together with the required amount of soft water. Put in the fine clothes, and boil them twenty minutes. Take out with as little water as possible, and without wringing, put into clear, cold water. If there are any soiled spots remaining on the clothes, they should be rubbed out before wringing from this water into the bluing water. The tub of bluing water is set near

CLOTHES, TO BRUSH—

CLOTHES, TO BRUSH—

Have a wooden horse to put the clothes on, and a small cane to beat the dust out of them; also a board or table long enough for them to be put their whole length when brushing them. Have two brushes, one a hard bristle, the other soft; use the hardest for the great coats, and for the others when spotted with dirt. Fine cloth coats should never be brushed with too hard a brush, as they will take off the nap, and make them look bare in a little time. Be careful in the choice of the cane, do not have it too large, and be particular not to hit too hard. Be careful also not to hit the buttons, for it will scratch, if not break them; therefore a small handwhip is the best to beat with. If a coat be wet and spotted with dirt, let it be quite dry before brushing; then rub out the spots with the hands, taking care not to rumple it in so doing. If it want beating, do as before directed, then put the coat at its full length on a board; let the collar be towards the left hand, and the brush in the right. Brush the back of the collar first, between the two shoulders next, and then the sleeves, etc. observing to brush the cloth the same way that the nap goes, which is towards the skirt of the coat. When both sides are properly done, fold them together, then brush the inside, and last of all the collar.

the other, so that the articles shall fall into it from the wringer. Put your second division of clothes into the boiler, in the same water from which the fine things were taken, and repeat the same process; but, if you have a third boiler full, it will be better to prepare fresh water. Take the clothes out of the blue water, and rinse in cold soft water, wring out, and hang out to dry. With this plan of washing, and fair weather, the clothes will all be hung out by noon, unless the wash is very large, and the servant will have the afternoon for cleaning up the kitchen and wash-room, putting away the tubs, boiler, etc., and making herself tidy. In the evening, the fine clothes and most of the starched things are to be sprinkled and folded, ready for ironing; and the bread is to be "set," for the next day's baking.

WEDNESDAY.—The baking this morning need not be as large as that done on Saturday, and it should be done as early as the morning work will allow, so that the servant may not be hurried in beginning the ironing, and do her work badly. She can easily do the ordinary fine ironing of a family and her other work in this part of the day. But, if there is much ruffling on ladies' dresses, and fine work on children's clothes, it will require a whole day's hard work to do it, and, in such a case, the mistress should hire some one to assist, or do all the ordinary housework herself. In the evening, the plainer and coarser clothes are to be sprinkled, and folded for ironing.

THURSDAY.—In the morning the ironing is to be finished. Where it is stipulated in the bargain that the servant should have half a day every week, this is the best afternoon to give her. It is the leisure interval between ironing and sweeping; and, as it is the day usually given by housekeepers, it enables the girl to meet her friends when she goes out.

FRIDAY.—Besides the every day sweeping, dusting, and putting to rights, it is necessary to devote one day in the week to this special duty, and Friday suits best for the purpose. The sitting-room, dining-room, halls, and stairways must be swept often, but once a week will be found generally sufficient for the rest of the house. To do this thoroughly and well will require the whole of a day in addition to the ordinary work. In the evening the bread must be set to rise for the next day's baking.

SATURDAY.—This is the busiest day of the week. There is the regular morning work; then the baking; then the scrubbing and scouring. And the latter part of the day should be occupied in preparing everything for the next day, so that Sunday shall be a day of rest for all as far as practicable. The whole breakfast can be so arranged as to occupy but a very few minutes in cooking, and, in winter, nearly everything for dinner can be prepared; and, in summer, most things will keep well on ice, or in a cool cellar. The Sunday dessert can always be made on Saturday. But do not let the Saturday's work run into the evening.

SUNDAY.—Do not work at all on this day, except what is actually necessary for comfort. If you see a dusty corner, or a dim window pane, let it alone until the next day. Some putting of things to rights there must be, some making of beds and cooking. But there is no need of getting up especially elaborate dinners on this day, and, if Saturday afternoon has been employed as it should have been, your cooking will not occupy very much time. There are people who will stuff a turkey and roast it, and cook three or four vegetables, and stew cranberry sauce for dinner, and yet will not make up a pan of biscuit for supper, because "it is wicked to work in flour Sundays!" This is only one of a dozen senseless ideas of the same kind. The idea is not that any particular kind of work is in itself sinful on this day, but that it is the day set apart for Christian worship, and you and your family desire to attend church; and to have the servant attend also, and, if there were no higher principles involved, all creatures need a rest one day in seven.

—*How to Keep House*
1882

TO CLEAN STOVE-PIPE

A piece of zinc put on the live coals in the stove will clean out the stove-pipe.

GRANDMOTHER BROWN

Oh, those were busy days! Besides the everyday routine of cooking, cleaning, washing, ironing, and baby tending, there were many things to be done that nowadays women might consider extras. I never did any gardening—that was thought to be men's work in our house—and I never milked any cows or made the cheese. But I looked after the chickens and eggs and butter. We stocked up with big Shanghais, but we couldn't afford to live on chickens that first year. I would never sell all our cream, but always saved enough to make good butter. I never made soft, runny butter; you could always cut a slice off *my* butter. Only the other day, Lizzie said to me: "I can just see how you used to work your butter, Mother. I can see you shaping the roll, tossing it over and over and rolling it, and tapping it at the ends, making it so pretty!"

I often did the washing with and without help. There was no running water in the house in those days. Still, we women had it pretty convenient with a well on the porch and a good cistern. In summer we washed under the cherry trees.

There was always enough cooking to be done, and at threshing time we had to lay in unusual quantities of food to feed the extra hands. The men of the countryside helped each other in their harvesting, and the neighbor women took turns helping each other feed the men. Often, at those times, Dan'l would let Charlie come in the house to help me. Until Lizzie was twelve years old, Charlie was my chief assistant in ironing and making pies. He would take the moulding board down cellar where it was cool and where flies didn't bother him, and would roll out as fine a batch of pies as threshers ever ate.

One of my best helpers in time of stress was my neighbor, Mrs. McChord. She was the loveliest woman. There never was such a neighbor. She used to help me pick hog guts all day long. The men would bring in the whole entrails of a hog they had butchered and lay them on the table before us. There is a leaf of solid lard above the kidneys, you know, which is considered the best. All along the entrails is fat which we would pick off. This gut fat is just as clean as any of the animal, but I had a notion that it didn't go in with the other lard and always put it by itself.

And the sewing we had to do! I think I had more faculty for that sort of thing than most women have, but, goodness knows, it was hard enough for the most skillful of us. Probably it was I who made the first knit underwear for babies. At least I used to feel very proud of the beautiful gauze-like shirts I'd make for my babies out of the tops of my old white cotton stockings, and I never knew any other woman who thought of doing it.

I even made the men's clothes at times. Dan'l came home from Fort Madison, one day, bringing cloth for a suit. "Why, Dan'l, I never cut out a man's coat," I told him. "Well, if you can cut a coat for the boys, why not for me?" he asked. Emma Farnsworth was to come and help me; her mother had been a tailoress. She was amazed. "You don't mean to tell me you cut out this coat!" she exclaimed. "Are all these chalk marks yours? Why,

CHEESE PUDDING

In a cup of new milk dissolve a piece of butter the size of a walnut and pour over a tablespoonful of bread-crumbs; let it soak, then add two eggs well beaten, and one-half of a pound of finely-grated cheese. Pour the mixture into a well-buttered mold and bake in a quick oven. Serve as hot as possible.

—E.J.A.

he'd have sold a cow before he would have done that himself." I
suppose I *was* a big simpleton to do such work. Oh, no. I guess it
was right. It didn't hurt me, and it saved money. We got ahead.

—Harriet C. Brown
Grandmother Brown's Hundred Years
1929

An Industrious Woman

A Michigan woman made 191 pies, 140 cakes, 84 loaves of bread,
729 biscuit, 156 fried cakes, and 1,026 cookies in her statistical
year, which closed September 1st. This, in addition to caring for
her children and doing her regular housework. This list may aid
those men who sometimes wonder whatever a woman does with
her time.

—*Success with the Garden and Farm*
DECEMBER 1897

The Story of a Busy Life Briefly Told

Two things I have been taught in my long farm life: one is, that
work never kills, and the other is, that we must calculate work
beforehand in order to save steps and do a great amount of work.
I am fifty-eight years old. Have been on a farm all my life until a
year ago, when we built a new house on one end of our farm
which opens on a public road and is retired from farm labor.
My father was a farmer and a minister of the old school, who
believed in no salary, but believed in working for a living. I
learned to milk when seven years old, and always did my share
while at home. I was sent to school, but at fourteen commenced
to teach a district school on a third grade license. I soon received
a second and then the first grade. I boarded around. I was
married at nineteen, and then my farm life began in earnest.
We always kept a dairy, from twelve to fourteen head. When
we were married we did not own a foot of land. My husband
and I bought thirty acres the day after we were married, join-
ing the old homestead of his people with whom we lived. They
owned fifty acres, but there was a mortgage of three hundred
and fifty dollars on that. We took care of them until they died,
paid the mortgage, bought enough more to make us two hundred acres. We had a sugar orchard and made from three to five
hundred pounds of sugar and a great deal of sirup every year.
We kept sheep and always worked up the wool, spun, wove, and

made full cloth for men's wear and for flannel sheets. We knit our own socks and stockings. I would always rise in the morning at four or half past, winter and summer, and have built my own fires, milked from four to eight cows, prepared the breakfast and had it at six. Until about ten years ago we made butter, and since then have sent it to a factory. I always did my own churning, and many are the books of poems, histories, stories, and newspapers I have read through while churning. I am the mother of eight children, five of whom are living. The others died when small. The oldest living is thirty-six and the youngest is twelve. Three of them have graduated from high school and been a number of terms at an academy. One has been for five years at Cornell University. I have always done my own washing and weaving of carpets, as I have a large house and it is furnished with rag carpets. I make my own garden and have helped rake hay and husk corn. One fall, alone, I husked between five and six hundred bushels. I had one daughter and she was at home at that time; so I did no housework while husking, although I attended to the milk and butter, milked, and got breakfast. One summer I piled up one hundred cords of wood and did my own housework. You will say there was no call for this. We were married the first year of the Civil War. In '63 my husband was drafted, paid his three hundred dollars, and stayed at home. That had to be met in hard times for the farmer. Not many modern wives would think they could pull flax, cut corn, dig potatoes, and do all things on a farm that we used to do. All this time I had a hired girl only a year and a half. We made our own table linen and toweling, spinning and weaving it, and our flannel dresses. I have been with the sick a great deal, and always went to church and Sunday school, and attended societies which belonged to the church. To-day I can walk a mile or more as quickly as any one. At the present time I have two old people to care for; one of them is eighty-six and the other is eighty-three. There are five in our family, and I am doing all the work myself, and am going to take the teacher to board next year. So you see, work does not kill and there must have been some calculation to save steps. My husband says, "You helped earn and saved more than I did." The boys many times say, "If it had not been for your pushing and helping us to school, we never could have done so well." All this time I have kept up with the general reading of the day.

I never counted my steps but once and that was when I spun a skein of woolen yarn. I went a little over a mile.

—Cornell Reading Course for Farmers' Wives
The American Kitchen Magazine
VOL. XIV, OCTOBER 1900–MARCH 1901

. . .

To be a home-maker is not an easy task. It requires much patience, bravery, foresight, and endurance. It calls for some knowledge, thought, and skill. It demands great hopefulness, tenderness, and, above all, unselfishness; but, though it is so difficult, it is none the less a grand privilege—a privilege which none dare think slightingly of; for is not the position of home-maker one which, nobly performed, will bring to every good woman the promise spoken of in the Bible, that "her children will arise and call her blessed?"

—Mrs. John A. Logan
The Home Manual
1889

To Tell a Good Housekeeper

How can I tell her?
By her cellar,
Cleanly shelves and whitened walls,
I can guess her
By her dresser;
By the back staircase and hall;
And with pleasure
Take her measure
By the way she keeps her brooms;
Or in peeping
At the "keeping"
Of her back and unseen rooms;
By her kitchen's air of neatness,
And its general completeness,
Where in cleanliness and sweetness
The rose of order blooms.

—*The Household*
VOL XXV, 1892

WOMEN'S UNDER-GARMENTS

I still receive repeated inquiries in regard to women's sensible underclothes. It does not seem to me necessary to send anywhere for patterns. The idea is very plain. Make a long-sleeved, high-necked, easy-fitting waist, with buttons around the bottom. Gore this over the hips, and put on two or three rows of buttons if you like, one row for the drawers and one for skirt; another row, the middle one, for "dress drawers," if you use them. The remainder of the combination garment (a combination of waist and drawers, which together make a complete and comfortable undersuit), consists of drawers which may be cut like any garment of the kind, of cotton for summer use, open in the usual way, and so high in the back as to admit of leaning far over without bursting the buttons from the back of the waist; or they may be made for winter long and close at the ankle, left open at the bottom for a few inches to admit of their lapping smoothly under the stockings. There is room for individual taste and preference in several respects, as whether the waist and drawers shall be permanently united or buttoned together (I prefer the latter for my children and myself), whether the waist shall be made close-fitting or more like a sack, and whether the drawers shall be closed or not.

The seemingly endless tasks and crises of keeping house were often viewed by the men as a great burden on their lives—a disruption of routine and household tranquility, and an unwarranted demand on their attention. Ideally it should all have been done without their notice. The perfect homemaker worked silently and invisibly.

THREE ROYAL RULES FOR THE QUEEN OF THE HOUSEHOLD

First. Be systematic! "An hour lost in the morning may be chased all day"; and a duty omitted till a more convenient season may put the whole domestic machinery out of gear.

Second. Be punctual! and require others to be so. Do not have it understood that you furnish "meals at all hours." The table should be the *rendezvous* from which neither business nor pleasure should keep any member of the household. The mealtimes will be the most cheerful seasons of the day to the whole family, with the right sort of a meal and the right sort of a family.

Third. Be serene! A prompt and systematic housekeeper may be a great tyrant. If the greatest good of the greatest number requires a change of routine, do not be upset by it. The greatest good is a happy home, which is an impossibility without a happy mistress. Even the unexpected arrival of company to dinner, on the busiest of days, should be met with equanimity. Cordial hospitality is good sauce, even though there be a scant supply of pudding.

—Lydia Shillaber
Mrs. Shillaber's Cookbook
1887

TO BRIGHTEN GILT FRAMES

Take sufficient flour of sulphur to give a golden tinge to about one and one-half pints of water, and in this boil four or five bruised onions, or garlic, which will answer the same purpose. Strain off the liquid, and with it, when cold, wash with a soft brush any gilding which requires restoring, and when dry, it will come out as bright as new work.

A SONG OF CLEANING HOUSE

Sing a song of cleaning house!
Pocket full of nails!
Four-and-twenty dustpans,
Scrubbing brooms, and pails!
When the door is opened,
Wife begins to sing—
"Just help me move this bureau here,
And hang this picture, won't you, dear?
And tack that carpet by the door,
And stretch this one a little more,

And drive this nail, and screw this screw;
And here's a job I have for you:
This closet door will never catch,
I think you'll have to fix the latch;
And oh, while you're about it, John,
I wish you'd put the cornice on,
And hang this curtain; when you're done
I'll hand you up the other one!
This box has got to have a hinge
Before I can put on the fringe;
And won't you mend that broken chair?
I 'd like a hook put up right there;
The bureau drawer must have a knob,
And here's another little job—
I really hate to ask you, dear—
But could you fix a bracket here?"
> *And on it goes, when these are through,*
> *With this and that and those to do—*
> *Ad infinitum and more too,*
> *All in merry jingle.*
> *And isn't it enough to make*
> *A man wish he was single? (Almost.)*
> —*The American Kitchen Magazine*
> VOL. XIV, OCTOBER 1900–MARCH 1901

As important as the efficient management of the household was the responsibility to "keep up appearances," both in public and within the family circle. Respect and respectability were woman's work.

ALICIA'S IDEA

That is to say, That "in addition to keeping the house clean and neat, the housekeeper should pay careful attention to her person and her dress." It is not an intemperate demand of the husband that the person of the wife should be generally in an acceptable condition. The paramount intention of the marital relation is an increase of happiness. At the bottom of this intention, as sort of a first principle of action, as the starting point of expectation, is that subtle, elementary principle, we call LOVE. Now everybody knows what the basis of Love between the sexes is. That which attracts, captivates, enthralls. It is not a hard matter for woman to *gain* love; it *is* a much harder matter to keep it. If the wife would expect to be always loved, she must manage to be

111

generally *lovable*. If she puts the neatest foot, the cleanest dress, and the richest embroidery forward, as a maid, let her not be disappointed if she is expected to put the same forward as a wife. If she is loved for the neatness and delicacy of her surroundings first, let her expect to be so always, that she be not disappointed.

—*The Household*
VOL. I, 1868

ADVICE FOR HELEN

MY DEAR NIECE:—I am glad you are housekeeping, at last, for I am sure all married people, and, perhaps, unmarried ones, are happier in homes of their own.

You ask for advice, so I will begin, and, besides, Helen, I feel somewhat troubled over one remark you made. You said John came in to dinner one day, and you had been so busy sewing that you had entirely neglected the dinner, so he had to wait while you prepared it. To be sure, he told you it was no matter, and praised you for being so quick. That may do very well now, it shows your husband to be good natured, and I suppose you haven't "got settled" yet. But, my dear, I want to impress upon

*Solomon D. Butcher
Collection, Nebraska State
Historical Society.*

you, the necessity of punctuality. The lack of it will cause loss of time, and, consequently, loss of money, and, alas! loss of temper, both to you and your husband. Begin right. Form the habit of punctuality now, for, by and by, when your household may be increased, it will be more difficult to do the right thing at the right time.

And don't allow yourself to make work. For instance, if you have crumbs or shreds on the table, don't brush them on the floor, thereby necessitating the use of a broom. Or, if cutting paper, don't allow the bits to scatter over the carpet, but keep them on the table. Then when you come in from your morning walk—and, by the way, I want to say, don't let anything but sickness or storm prevent that walk. You say you think more of John's comfort than of your own, and I don't doubt it, but remember it is decidedly for John's comfort that his little wife keep well, and how can one be well without some exercise in the pure, open air—but when you come in, don't throw your cloak on one chair, and your hat and gloves on another, or on the table. If you do, very likely you will soon see Mrs. C. coming, and they will be carried from a sitting room to a parlor chair. Then Mrs. C. will want to look at your new chromo, and they will be hastily transferred to the bed room, and so on. Better put them in their places, at first.

Well, my dear, I have much more to say, but have already written a longer letter than I intended, so I'll only give you one of my recipes for a quick breakfast. Have your frying pan well heated, spread with pork fat, or butter, then lay on slices of cold potato left from yesterday's dinner, sprinkle with salt, and fry till nicely browned, turn to cook on both sides. If eaten when hot, they make a nice dish. Bits of meat are no objection.

Now I must stop writing to get dinner for Uncle Reuben, for you know, "Practice what you preach," is one of the maxims of

—Aunt Emma
The Household
VOL. XIII, 1880

NEVER ON ANY ACCOUNT
use coal-oil to make the fire burn more quickly. In making the fire, as soft wood burns more quickly than hard, it is better to have some with which to start it, filling up with hard wood. If the wood is good and properly placed you will have a bright clear flame, yielding a great amount of heat which should be utilized for cooking purposes, by so arranging the draught that none of it is wasted. This can only be done by one who so perfectly understands each part of it as to economize in the use of fuel. The fire needs constant attention, as it is poor economy to let the fire go partially out, as in adding fresh fuel the heat is wasted until the stove and oven are again heated to the right temperature for cooking.

How reassuring it must have been for the young farmer to expect that he could, if he were careful, choose a housekeeper for desired traits and characteristics, in much the same way he chose his livestock.

S o compelling was the image of rural life and homemaking that many women leapt
at the chance to experience them. No matter that most American girls, indulged
in their upbringing with great freedom, were not usually trained for the responsibilities they were expected to assume. Carefree, optimistic girls brought to the country
unprepared were often devastated by the shock of its demands.

THE ANCIENT AND MODERN IN HOUSEKEEPING

The conveniences for housekeeping at the command of young
married couples were never so complete as now ... the services
of a servant may be entirely dispensed with, so complete are the
labor-saving devices, provided the feminine head of the household is endowed with knowledge of the culinary art. It may be
safely asserted that under such conditions the cost of ailments
to a couple need not exceed one dollar a day. A first breakfast of
coffee and rolls, a luncheon equivalent to a second breakfast,
and a dinner to which a more generous impulse may be given,
with clever management, need not exceed in cost the sum named.
But it all depends upon the woman. Fortunately, physiognomists
have established certain rules whereby such a one may be se-
lected. They have clearly indicated the physical characteristics
which accompany the feminine love of good living, and the possession of natural aptitude in the preparation of culinary dain-
ties. A woman of this sort, it is affirmed by them, will have a
broad face, sparkling eyes, short nose, round chin, and moist
lips; will be rather comely than beautiful and very plump, even
to a suggestion of *embonpoint*. A woman of this description,
however, is predisposed by temperament to a certain indolence
not conducive to neatness. That one, on the contrary, to whom
nature has denied skill either in the preparation or enjoyment
of gastronomic delights, is described by the physiognomists as
possessing a long face and nose and large eyes. She has black and
straight hair, and is invariably thin and angular. On the other
hand, what she may lack in culinary ability is compensated for
by a nervous and intense love of order. As a happy medium is
rarely attainable, those young men of moderate resources who
are lovers of good living under economical conditions, and contemplate matrimony, need not be at a loss in selection.

—*Good Housekeeping*
1895

We are going to live on a farm! Going to take lots of comfort, lots of health, and enjoy to the utmost, all the good things of earth which it is our privilege to possess; and as it is my belief, country homes have been despised, farms considered the abiding place of unhappy spirits only, I am anxious to tell you of our farm home that is to be. The house—I believe that's the first object of attention to ladies, and for them I am writing—is a small affair, a little brown story and a half building, containing five rooms and a tiny L. Facing the street are two rooms with front entry and staircase between. At the back is a long sunny room which occupies the remainder of the ground floor; opening from this is the L which contains an ample closet, milk room, and a tiny place which I mean to wash in. Two quite roomy, and at the present time quite spidery chambers complete the humble dwelling.

Then there is a barn, and nice new wood house, and a cute little hen house. I shall raise chickens; I have only five biddies and a pert rooster to commence with, but they will answer till I am able to buy more. We have a cow, a gentle mild eyed creature whose confidence is mine already and whose capacity for chewing potatoes and turnips is wonderful. The "cow subject," was at first a difficult one to settle, as times were so hard and money so very scarce; but a real determination, and a careful economy of the little we do have, finally furnished the means, and when I survey our prize I feel that we are amply paid for the little self denials we were forced to practice.

To be sure, I was obliged to stay at home when cousin Emma had her wooden wedding, and Tommy has found it convenient to remain indoors on frosty days because his overcoat was worn thin and shabby, and he had no warm gloves, but we've got the cow! Tom says, "the cow is like the old woman's andirons, for now we must have a pig." Of course we must, and shall, although the getting may be a long way ahead.

Some one, whose ideas are placed on large roomy dwellings may think the little five room house almost too small for comfort. But it is large enough for two, and, let me whisper it, quite ample enough for my modest supply of furniture. The sunny room will be my kitchen, I have no carpet as yet, only a big bag full of carpet rags which owing to my propensity to "make over" old clothes does not gain so very fast. But with lots of good comfortable rugs the floor will do nicely.

CEMENT CRACKS IN FLOOR

Cracks in floors may be neatly but permanently filled by thoroughly soaking newspapers in paste made of half a pound of flour, three quarts of water and half a pound of alum mixed and boiled. The mixture will be about as thick as putty, and may be forced into the crevice with a case knife. It will harden like papier-mache.

I have a fine supply of house plants for the two south windows, a sewing machine for the east, and two respectable rocking chairs for the west window. The sunniest front room will be a sitting room, the other my "spare bedroom." I have no parlor furniture as yet, so the time more fortunate ladies spend in caring for parlor "pretties" I shall devote to my flower garden and chickens.

Tom has excellent taste for gardening and I have stored in my cellar a fair supply of dahlias and gladiolus, and in my kitchen a goodly array of soap boxes in which my flower seeds have been sown. Already, mignonette, asters, petunias, candytuft, and nasturtium are an inch high and a careful examination of other boxes leads me to expect pinks, phlox, balsams and zinnias in a few days. Verbena seed never seems to come up, so I have trimmed off all the slips from the four thrifty plants and have them rooting for my garden.

I wish some one who has experience would give me a few ideas about raising herbs. I'd like a little herb bed, it is so handy to have your own pure herbs in time of sickness. Will the same soil and care flowers receive be right for them; and when are they ready for cutting and drying? It seems strange that farmers as a general thing pay so little attention to such things. A neighbor to whom I applied for advice about my herbs declared he had no time or money to expend for such foolishness, and advised me to use my warm corner for beans, or something which would bring in money and require less care. To my certain knowledge they expended two dollars for cough syrups and other uses during the past winter, and were obliged to ride three miles to an apothecary's at that. Now I'd rather raise my own sage, boneset, saffron and summer savory, if some one will tell me how. The chamber over my spare room I shall use for store room, and in it hang the herbs if they succeed well, and on the floor spread the butternuts if the big tree bears.

We don't expect to farm for profit as the world understands the term. With our hearty appetites we shall probably eat all the fruit and vegetables. Tibbie will want all the pumpkins, grass and hay, the pig and biddies will dispose of corn and oats. But we shall have a comfortable home, plenty to eat, and to enjoy to the full that free happy life which is given all God's creatures to enjoy who strive for it in the right way. And can we not live nearer Him when everything which surrounds us, every little flower,

---

ADULTERATION OF FOOD

The subject of food adulteration is one of momentous importance to every household. The manufacture of spurious articles, and the adulteration of the genuine, has become so common that there is scarcely anything that is safe from this fraudulent practice. This evil has become so universal that it extends to drugs and medicine supplies, as well as food, and is employed in the manufacture of wines, lager, rum, brandies, and other alcoholic liquors to a fearful extent. Physicians assert that many valuable lives are sacrificed from the failure of adulterated medicines to secure the expected result. Nearly all of our groceries and spices are capable of adulteration. Much of the tea, in order to give it color and weight, is poisoned with prussic acid, mineral green, arsenite of copper, verdigris, clay, etc. The coffee that is bought in packages is rarely pure, but consists of various compounds mixed with a small proportion of coffee, such as peas, chicory, stale bread, etc.

the dear birds and the thousand objects which throng our farm homes are evidences of his handiwork and constant reminders of the Father who so lovingly provides for all his children?

Of course farm houses in summer cannot help being a trifle flyey when barn and pig-pen are near and the milk is kept in the house. But a few yards of mosquito netting helps wonderfully and if now and then a few flies are seen buzzing in some newly painted room, try to think that country flies are much more bearable than city bed bugs and cockroaches.

—Eva A. B.
The Household

E conomy and efficiency were the particular provinces of the woman. It was a large part of her household responsibility to save and patch and make do. This required her to be both innovator and master mechanic, which often simply increased her opportunities for failure.

VOL. XI, 1878

THE NOTE BOOK OF A HOUSEKEEPER NUMBER EIGHTEEN

What a knack some women have for saving! Now there is Mrs. Raymond, the greatest hand to plan and get along with small means. She will make a good, serviceable garment out of what some women would put in the carpet rags or the rag bag. Nearly all of her little girls' sacques for neighborhood and school wear are made of her husband's cast off clothing. One of them is now wearing a sacque (formerly a pair of pantaloons,) of some light colored, heavy material. Trimmed with black velvet it makes a very neat little sacque. When first made up one would never have suspected its history. It has been outgrown by one of the girls as "best sacque," and is now serving a younger one for every-day wear. Also, there is now in the family a beaver cloak or ulster, a good, serviceable garment for general wear, which—the other side out—formerly did good service as an overcoat.

In some households garments are seldom brushed; left hanging (often right side out,) in dusty rooms; never cared for or kept in repair as they should be, and when some larger rent occurs, are thrown aside to be replaced by others soon in like manner to be ruined. This is very wrong. It is as much the wife's

FOR GENERAL USE

copper and brass cooking utensils are not the best, because of the great care necessary to keep them clean and free from poisonous deposits, a work that *can never be trusted to servants.* Care should be used in cooking in tin vessels, as they are liable to be affected by acids, oils and salt, but not to the same extent as copper. For all ordinary cooking purposes, if tin vessels are kept clean and free from rust, no injury will result. A little whiting or dry flour may be used to polish tin with. If a kettle is to be used for cooking fish, heat it first over the fire; if an odor arise, it needs cleaning as above, before using. If the same gridiron has to be used for broiling steak, that has been used for fish, in addition to cleaning it as above, heat it over the fire, rub well with brown paper, then with an onion. In washing tin-ware use soft water and soap, and wash well, rinse with hot water, wipe well, and put on the hearth or stove to dry perfectly; once a week wash tin-ware in water in which a little sal-soda has been dissolved.

province to save as it is the husband's to earn. It is poor encouragement, indeed, for the head of the household to provide for his family's comfort and see everything go directly to waste and ruin. Surely whoever be care-taker and housekeeper has a duty here, in every department of her important office.

"In my travels" I recently saw a coat deemed past usefulness. It was a long dress coat of fine, good material, the wrong side bright and fresh, looking like new. Having a right to advise, I suggested that it would make over nicely into a sacque for the little girl; but as the idea of bothering with old clothes did not seem to meet with favor, it is still only an old cast off coat. Economy is a matter of deep importance to this family, and there are so many ways in which such a garment might be used to advantage. It would make a neat housejacket for the housekeeper herself, or a good, warm basque to wear with that black skirt of hers, trimmed to match, they would look exceedingly well together; trimmed with bias folds of black silk like one that Mrs. Raymond made of an old black broadcloth coat, it would look well with almost any skirt, and last a long time. Or it would make a neat dress coat for the little boy; or a vest for the good old farmer at the head of the household—a good, presentable vest to wear about home on Sundays, to wear when he goes to town to trade, or on any common "dress up" occasion when he wishes something a little better than for "every day," yet does not like to wear his best; then there would be enough left to make caps for each of the two boys. Oh, be sure we would find some use for it.

Mrs. Raymond and I being on very intimate terms, make free to speak our minds to each other; no fear of being misunderstood. Only the other day I said to her, "Marcia, if you had what some women waste, it would clothe your family comfortably." So it would, and elegantly, too.

To be sure her husband's clothes are not patched "patch upon patch"; that were economy of one sort, it is true, but we doubt if it be always the best economy. After being worn and repaired as much as seems advisable, they are ripped, sponged (or sometimes washed), and pressed, and, if necessary or admissible, they are turned the other side out, and made to last in other garments for months and sometimes years.

One use to which she puts old pantaloons (full cloth, etc.,) is to make leggings for girl's out-door wear in winter; just the thing for girls who go to school, and an article of clothing, by the way, that all women, especially in the country, should possess. Mrs.

Raymond makes them to button closely the entire length outside and fasten down firmly around the foot by means of a leather strap and a button or a buckle, thus effectually precluding the snow about the top of the shoe and the ankle. The leggings should be long and may be supported by attaching them to a strap buttoned to the waist on which are the buttons for supporting the skirts.

I know a lady who once turned a faded overcoat of her husband's, making it up again very nicely, the only expense being for such little items as thread, twist, braid, etc. It was a double breasted coat, and the way she managed the button holes was to carefully pick out the stitches and re-work. The coat appeared new when done and did excellent service. However, in "cheap times" this might not be wise economy; but in those days clothing was high, and as economy was essential, in fact the only other alternatives being rusty coat or none at all, it seemed splendid management.

In cutting out men's garments of heavy material there are often pieces left not large enough to be of much use for patches. These do nicely to make caps for the boys. There is a neat style of cap in eight pieces; six pieces in the body of the cap and two side pieces to turn down over the ears at will, the side pieces being joined in a seam at the back, and sewed in with the cap at the bottom, two buttons and an elastic loop connecting the ends in front. If of heavy material, the side pieces need no lining, but may be simply finished around the upper edge, and around the points, with a binding.

I recently made one of ladies' cloth for a little boy. The cap proper was lined and slightly wadded; the side pieces were of muskrat fur (the light colored part of the fur,) which was lined with the ladies' cloth, so that when they are turned over the ears the cap is all alike.

The cap keeps its shape better if of thick material; then side pieces of the cloth without lining are sufficient. They may be made to be really elegant, if one has the proper materials; but, after all, their greatest worth is in their comfort, and that may be secured with but small expense.

—Gladdys Wayne
The Household, VOL. XIV, 1881

WE WOMEN: A GENERAL INFORMATION CLUB

Our moderator was in the chair. We all brought our own work, sewing, knitting, tatting, crocheting, darning, and dear old Auntie Slater brought a very substantial job of patching.

THE ELDER LEAF BANDAGE

Gather elder leaves, together with the flower if possible; steep a handful of them in one or two quarts of boiling water. If, on awakening with heavy eyes, or suffering with a headachy feeling, or troubled with a sense of ennui, lie down for an hour, first laying the steeped leaves, after they are cool, across the forehead and eyes, binding them in place with a soft cloth. The effect is wonderfully sedative, as well as clarifying to the mind.

CHICKENS

should never be cooked the day they are killed; the flesh is then stringy and slippery. They should be drawn as soon as killed and the inside wiped out with a cloth, not washed. A little piece of charcoal laid inside will aid in preserving, but is unnecessary if they can be hung in a cool, airy place. If the feet, after being skinned, are cooked with the rest of the chicken, they will add richness, as they contain gluten, but they may be removed before sending to the table.

Auntie Slater was the first one called on, and she said with humble apology, that by the permission of the ladies she would continue on in the same " jovial subject." She said her old man found a shirt and two pairs of denim overalls in Westerfield's barn, when he was there threshing rye. The painter, a man from York state, had left them when he started for home. Dan Westerfield said they were of no use, but if they were cleaned they would make good carpet rags for filling. Now it happened that a brother of Mr. Slater's was a painter himself and knew how to clean up such clothes and make them as good as ever, and this was how the painter's cast-off clothing was cleansed: About five cents' worth of baking soda was put into the water, enough to cover the garments, and they were scalded in that until the paint dissolved, when they were washed in suds the usual way. No vestige of paint or soil remained, and the clothing was as clean as though no paint had ever touched it. This item of practical knowledge is worth remembering.

Aunt Sally inquired if any person present had any question to ask. Nancy McCarthy held up her hand, and the question was one that has perplexed many and many a housewife—how to make nice pie crust. Of course there are ways of making it crisp and flaky, but when one is hurried there is no time to roll out and spread on lard, and roll up and roll out and spread again, and roll up and out so many times on a marble slab, and with ice cold fingers. Yes, there was a way, simple, easy, sure, and one that never failed, and was always nice and good, and never missed once. Use the same measures of water and lard. Knead so that it will barely hold together. This is the best and most uniform way of making pie crust known. It never fails of being just right. The vote of thanks was unanimous.

"Any more questions?" said Aunt Sally. Another hand went up.

Mrs. Emmett had learned how to sharpen a butcher knife and bread knife, "all her own self." She had seen a great deal of trouble in trying to worry along with dull knives, and finally she had purchased one of the steel sharpeners that butchers use, and then she had asked the jolly butcher, a good fellow, as broad almost as he was long, how to use it successfully, and presto! she knew and could tell others. This raised a shout of hilarious merriment and one little creature, Cad Remington, said "Hoop-e-la!" with all the abandon of a rude boy.

"Why, the dawn of the millenium draws nigh," she said, "when a woman can put an edge on the bread knife herself!"

And this was the way: Hold the steel with the handle from you, and then strike down from the end towards you first on one side and then on the other with the blade of the bread knife, the point of the knife going toward the handle of the steel. Any woman can sharpen the knives then herself, and put an end to drubbing them on the stovepipe or the top of a crock, or grating them roughly over a sandstone. It is too bad! Women do the most of the cutting up of meats with a dull knife, round-edged, barely fit to be used, nothing more. Bread, that would otherwise be nice and good and aesthetic enough to make people partake, whether they were hungry or not, is often haggled into thick, uneven blocks or slices with knives that are dull or over thick and not fit for any known use. And then the demand came up from patient, long-suffering women asking where steels could be purchased, how much they cost, and all about them. We were all very glad for this item of news.

Somehow the talk turned upon washing dishes, and one woman, one of the best housekeepers in the neighborhood, said she was almost afraid to give the women the benefit of her ideas on this all important subject, for fear of being laughed at. No woman likes to be the butt of jokes and merriment, but perhaps some one could face the censure and ridicule and do, not "like other folks do," but the better way.

TO PRESERVE LAMP CHIMNEYS FROM BREAKING

Place a cloth in the bottom of a large pan, fill the pan with cold water, and place new chimney in it; cover the pan, and let its contents boil one hour: take from fire, and let chimney remain in the water until it is cold.

Bureau of Agricultural Economics, National Archives.

121

She said washing dishes three times a day took so much time that she established a plan of her own: Washed the dishes well in warm water in which was a little rub of hard soap, and then rinsed them thoroughly in plenty of hot water, and turned them on their edges in a large wooden bowl, in the bottom of which was a folded towel to absorb the water that drained from the dishes. Generally the dishes were left in the bowl in the pantry until needed for the next meal. Sometimes, if she had leisure, she set the table as soon as the dishes had dried, spread a square of netting over, closed the dining room door, and so much was ready toward the next meal. One duty follows another, so that the busy housemother is obliged to save time and steps as much as possible. Some of the wise women shook their heads, and looked "smart," as much as to say, "It might do for some folks, but not for me."

Well, one thing is certain, and "we women" ought to know it by this time, brains are required in all kinds of work, especially housework. We see the lack of brains every day. We must think. We must contrive and plan and put this and that together, and note results. We often think of what an old Irish woman said to us once in the depot at Albany. It was in the night; our train did not leave for a long while, and to put in the time as pleasantly as possible, we took a cup of coffee at the restaurant, a little while before our train was due. The poor old weary woman asked us in a hesitating whisper if the coffee were good. We told her it was. Then she took a cup steaming hot, and while sipping it, said: "Yes, it's good; I like coffee that has some sense to it."

Agnes Leonard was the next one called. She had baked bread the day before, after the recipe given to THE HOUSEHOLD some time ago by Persis, only instead of using her kind of dry yeast, she took a cent's worth of baker's yeast. This is her recipe: Take one cent's worth of yeast and thicken it into a batter about four o'clock. Stand it in a warm place, but do not cover it closely. By bed-time it will have risen to the top. Then mix up the bread with about twice the amount of tepid water that there is of yeast, add a pinch of salt and a spoonful of lard, knead well, and stand the bowl in a moderately warm place till morning. Have the pans greased ready and the loaves can be moulded before breakfast, and the baking done almost with the morning's chores. It is a wonderful saving of labor to bake bread after this plan, and the best of it is that the bread is of the finest kind, sweet, moist, delicious and bready. It will not be that kind that will crowd the top of the oven and spill

CEMENT FOR KNIFE HANDLES

Set handle on end, and partly fill cavity with powdered resin, chopped hair or tow, chalk, whiting, or quicklime; heat the spike of the knife and force it into its place. Equal parts of sulphur, resin, and brick-dust also make an excellent cement.

TO RENDER LEATHER BOOTS WATERPROOF

Melt over a slow fire, one quart of boiled linseed oil; one pound of mutton suet; three-quarters of a pound of yellow beeswax; and half a pound of common resin; or smaller quantities in these proportions. With this mixture saturate the leather of new boots and shoes, having previously made them rather warm.

over the sides of the pan, not great, ungainly, unshapely loaves, but very good ones, with a delicious, nutty flavor.

Mrs. Weatherbee was called next. She said she knew nothing; had nothing to tell.

Aunt Betsey Slater told her it would be of use to some of "us poor bald creeters" if she would tell how she kept her hair in such good condition; tell us what she put on it to make it grow and be so glossy and soft. And the smiling answer was: "Nothing ever goes on my hair; no oils, washes, pomatums, no mixture of cantharides and alcohol; nothing but clipping the ends every new moon and brushing it frequently and gently." "In the new of the moon," made some of the girls pucker their mouths and look wise, and we asked Mrs. Weatherbee why the new of the moon in preference to any other stage, and the answer was that if she set a time and lived up to it, it became a habit and she would not neglect it. For this reason only, she set the first Tuesday after every new moon to trim the ends of her hair.

The conversation turned upon shoes, by some means, and the moderator forgot her dignity, and we all talked together. The minister's wife told us something new. She says her new shoes, made to order in one of our large cities, feel just as comfortable on her feet as though they were old ones that she had worn a year. Her village shoemaker takes her measure just right, sends it to the firm with whom he deals, and her shoes are made to fit splendidly, and are soft and easy and comfortable from the first time she puts them on. She has one enlarged joint and this is taken into kindly consideration. She used to have a very troublesome corn on the side of her foot, which was skillfully removed by a physician who had mastered the art, and then she began wearing those rarely made shoes, and ever since she has enjoyed freedom from pain, and her feet have been a blessed comfort to her. The name of the city manufacturer was jotted down by half the women and girls present.

Then the subject of lace, ruches, *crepe de lisse*, linen collars, and all manner of neck wear came up for discussion, and in the end common cotton lace was at a discount. Let whatever you wear be honest and in good taste. For common wear at home, lawn frills, and linen collars, and ties of mull or lawn are pretty, easily done up and none of them signify sham. *Crepe de lisse* is always in good taste, though expensive and easily broken and soiled. Linen collars are honest, and ties tell what they are, and why they are worn, and what they mean. Real lace will last, with care, for

TO PREVENT HAIR FROM TURNING GRAY

The hair should be well brushed every day, and be wet at the roots with strong sage tea. One ounce of borax to every quart of the tea. Wet the scalp, and then brush for fully ten minutes. This will make harsh, rough hair, smooth and glossy.

123

many, many years. For Sundays and great church occasions, even a farmer's wife could afford this out of her "butter-and-egg fund."

A lady visited us once who had been lecturing in Boston. While she was here she did a nice washing of herself. She did not boil the clothes, just rubbed soap on them, laid them in a tub, poured warm water over and let them lie half an hour or while she read aloud to us one of Mrs. Browning's finest poems. We remember how she turned over the peck measure and sat down beside us where we were stringing beans out on the stoop. We liked her way of washing very much. The clothes were put through two suds and two rinses and came out nicer than ours which were boiled ten minutes.

But we were talking about good lace. While she stood clear-starching her best things, she laughed and said: "This choice bit of lace, just enough to go 'round my neck, I bought in New York. The first evening I lectured in Boston, some ladies to whom I had been introduced, in passing out behind me remarked in a scathing whisper: "Oh, her lace is cotton!" And that was why I bought this lovely piece, at a price that seemed to me extravagant. I could not bear the thought of giving offence."

We thought of this incident lately, when a beautiful woman who was an agent for something of general benefit to her sex, called here, was pleased, conversed awhile, and finally asked the privilege of staying all night. It was not our pleasure, and we told her so, kindly and frankly. She insisted; we saw no reason why, when every moment was precious to us, that we should be obliged to entertain a stranger, and we shook our head positively, probably thinking of the "cotton lace" incident.

She looked at us from head to foot in a puzzled way. We knew she was not accustomed to hear a "nay," but always had her own sweet will.

"I'm astonished," she said; "I should think you would be glad to have me stay with you all night, or for a whole week, even; I should think you would welcome me—a woman from Boston—one who could tell you more new things than you could learn in a year in this out-of-the-way quiet place."

Mrs. Benedict, when called on, said the last thing she had learned was how to manage in taking bad or bitter medicines. Make your own wafers by mixing up a thin flour paste, heat two flat-irons until they are "neither too hot nor too cold," then grease them a little, and drop a bit of the paste on the face of one turned

EQUAL PARTS

of ground mustard and flour made into a paste with warm water, and spread between two pieces of muslin, form the indispensable mustard plaster.

A GINGER POULTICE—This is made like a mustard poultice, using ground ginger instead of mustard. A little vinegar is sometimes added to each of these poultices.

A STRAMONIUM POULTICE—Stir one tablespoon of Indian meal into a gill of boiling water and add one tablespoonful of bruised stramonium seeds.

WORMWOOD AND ARNICA are sometimes applied in poultices. Steep the herbs in half a pint of cold water and when all their virtue is extracted stir in a little bran or rye meal to thicken the liquid; the herbs must not be removed from the liquid.

This is a useful application for sprains and bruises.

LINSEED POULTICE—Take four ounces of powdered linseed and gradually sprinkle it into a half pint of hot water.

up between your knees, then place the other iron on it, let it remain an instant, and your wafer is made. It may take a little effort to get things to work well, but one will hit it after awhile. When you go to take the medicine, wet the wafer first, to soften it, lay the powder on one side and turn the other side over it like a turn-over pie. This is an excellent way of getting bitter medicines down without the taste remaining in the mouth.

Aunt Sally gave her own contribution, a recipe for making nice cabbage slaw for dinner. Take an ordinary sized head of cabbage, trim of the coarse, outer leaves and cut the head into shreds. Then make a dressing by beating up an egg, stir enough flour in to make a smooth batter, pour half a cup of thick, sour cream in, and one cup of good cider vinegar; stir these ingredients together, and pour them into a spider where there is about two tablespoonfuls of good meat frying, let it boil up and when slightly cool pour over the cabbage, or stir the cabbage in the spider.

The academy bell rang just here for the meeting of the festival committee, and some of the ladies had to leave. As it was nearly evening we all concluded to go home.

We meet next time at Kitty Sanderson's, out at Poplar Grove, on the hill.

Aunt Sally will be away then, on a visit to her sister's, and she hailed out, as she rode home on her pacing pony, that we must not "cut up" in her absence, but be good girls.

—Rosella Rice
The Household
MARCH 1883

Virtue, morality, healthy ambition, manners, character, and ideals were the products of home influence, and the home was the province of the homemaker. She took possession of the house and filled it with extensions of herself until house and woman became an amalgam—a mystical presence. Her mission was not merely to furnish, decorate, and maintain the home, but above all to provide the spiritual force that held it together.

Home! What a hallowed name; how full of enchantment and how dear to every heart. How it touches every fiber of the soul, and strikes every chord of the human heart with its angelic fingers. Nothing but death can break its spell. What tender associations are linked with home! what pleasing images and deep emotions it awakens! It calls up the fondest memories of life, and opens in our nature the purest, deepest, richest gush of consecrated thought and feeling. "Home, home, there is no place like home."

Home is the greatest school of life. Few can receive the honors of a college education, but all are graduates of the home. The learning of the university may fade, its knowledge may moulder in the halls of memory, but the simple lessons of home, impressed upon the heart of childhood, defy the rust of years, and outlive the vivid pictures of after life.

Those who are best acquainted with the world, and who have read most extensively, know that the most telling influence upon life comes out of and radiates from the home. It is the home which often, in boyhood, has formed beforehand our most famous scholars, our most celebrated heroes, and our most devoted missionaries. Even when men have grown up reckless and reprobate, and have broken all restraints, human and divine, the last anchor that held them and the last cable they were able to snap, was the memory that bound them to a virtuous home.

—Margaret E. Sangster
The Art of Homemaking
1898

HEALTHY HOMES—CLEANLINESS

Now, boys and girls (and I ask the girls particularly to pay attention to this—old girls, if there are any such, as well as young girls), I am going to talk to you of healthy homes and cleanliness. To begin with, then, what think you is the best method to raise a man above the life of an animal? Why, replies Mr. Smiles, to whom I am mainly indebted for what follows, to provide him with a healthy home. The home, is, after all, the best school for the world. There—children grow up into men and women; imbibe their best and their worst morality, and have their morals and intelligence, in a great measure, well or ill-trained. Men can only be really and truly humanized and civilized through the institution of the home. In the good home are domestic purity and moral life, and in the bad one, individual defilement and moral death. Character and disposition are the result of home training; and if through bad physical and moral conditions, these are deteriorated and destroyed, the intellectual culture acquired in the school may prove an instrumentality for evil rather than for good.

IF YOU WOULD AVOID WASTE IN YOUR FAMILY,

attend to the following rules, and do not despise them because they appear so unimportant: "Many a little makes a mickle."

Look frequently to the pails, to see that nothing is thrown to the pigs which should have been in the grease-pot.

Look to the grease-pot, and see that nothing is there which might have served to nourish your own family, or a poorer one.

See that the beef and pork are always *under* brine; and that the brine is sweet and clean.

Count towels, sheets, spoons, &c. occasionally; that those who use them may not become careless.

See that the vegetables are neither sprouting nor decaying: if they are so, remove them to a drier place, and spread them.

Examine preserves, to see that they are not contracting mould; and your pickles, to see that they are not growing soft and tasteless.

But the home should not be considered as a place for eating and sleeping merely; but as one where self-respect may be preserved, and comforts secured, and domestic pleasures enjoyed.

Three fourths of the petty vices which degrade society, and swell into crimes which disgrace it, would shrink before the influence of self-respect. To be a place of happiness, exercising beneficial influences upon its members, and especially upon the members growing up within it, the home must be pervaded by the spirit of comfort, cleanliness, affection, and intelligence. And in order to secure this, the presence of a well-ordered, industrious, and educated woman is indispensable. And here I wish to speak particularly to girls. Many of you will soon be women, and ultimately wives and mothers, and you ought to know how important it is to have clean, healthy, comfortable homes. Besides, so much depends upon the woman that we might almost pronounce the happiness or unhappiness of the home to be woman's work. No nation can advance except through the improvement of the nation's homes; and they can be improved through the instrumentality of women alone. Women must *know* how to make homes comfortable; and before they can know, they must be taught.

Women, therefore, must have sufficient training to fit them for their duties in real life. Their education must be conducted throughout with a view to their future position as wives, mothers, and housewives.

Too frequently, young men attach little or no importance to the intelligence or industrial skill of young women; and they only discover their value when they find their homes stupid or cheerless. Boys and men alike are caught by the glance of a bright eye, by a pair of cherry cheeks, by a handsome figure; and when they "fall in love," as the phrase goes, they never bethink them whether the "loved one" can mend a shirt or cook a pudding. And yet, and bear the fact in mind, Jenny, the most sentimental of husbands must come down from his "ecstatics" as soon as the knot is tied; and then he soon enough finds out that the clever hands of a woman are worth far more than her bright glances; and if the shirt and pudding qualifications be absent, then woe to the unhappy man, and woe also to the unhappy woman! If the substantial element of physical comfort be absent from the home, it soon becomes hateful; the wife, notwithstanding all her good looks, is neglected; and the liquor saloon separates those whom the law and the church have joined together.

TO BEAUTIFY THE HAIR

The hair may be made more beautiful and darkened by taking four ounces of bay rum, two ounces of olive oil and one drachm of the oil of almonds. Mix, shake well and apply.

127

Men are really desperately ignorant respecting the home department. If they thought for a moment of its importance, they would not be so ready to rush into premature housekeeping.

A healthy home, presided over by a thrifty, cleanly woman, may be the abode of comfort, of virtue, and of happiness. It may be the scene of every ennobling relation in family life. It may be endeared to a man by many delightful memories—by the affectionate voices of his wife, his children, and his neighbors. Such a home will be regarded, not as a mere nest of common instinct, but as a training ground for young immortals, a sanctuary for the heart, a refuge from storms, a sweet resting-place after labor, a consolation in sorrow, a pride in success, and a joy at all times.

—John Fraser
Youth's Golden Cycle
1885

THE HOUSEHOLD—HOUSES AND HOMES

Setting aside, once for all, sentimental theorizing, though never the sentiment, which is a very different thing from its maudlin and gushing sister, apt as people are to confound the two, it must be made plain that for each one of us in any life that seeks to do worthy work, a home is the chief essential. Circumstances may limit us to simply a room or two, but no matter how narrow the quarters, a woman can fill them with the spirit of home—a place where thought is free and work untrammeled and love the keynote of the life lived within it.

If there were no other distinction, setting women apart and above men, this one most noble and precious gift of homemaking would be sufficient to mark the more spiritual quality of the one sex above the other. Only the finest and rarest men can infuse their personal qualities into the very walls of such spot as they make home, and even then they admit that a woman must fill out and complete the whole work.

But this is something quite apart from the home on which masculine writers have spent millions of weak and nauseating words; the home where the woman greets her lord always with that inevitable smile—the perennial grin of a deprecating slave, and is in an also perennial hurry to provide hot slippers and a general poultice of little attentions and self-obliterations. Such duties, welcomed with delight where love rules, are as well, perhaps better, performed by any servant, where it does not, yet are often preached as the chief part of that whole duty of women expounded with glibness by most men, and with double glibness by the most selfish or least likely candidate for warming anybody's slippers with his own hands.

"He for God only; she for God in him," is the word of a master poet, and with Miss Cobbe I am heartily glad that a master poet put into terse and quickly-refutable form the statement which has been the text at many a school commencement, and wherever most men have addressed women or girls just entering womanhood upon that inexhaustible subject of their duties— not to themselves or to the world, but to man, taken as representative and sum of all that a woman can ever know or desire.

It is no part of my purpose to underrate the life of men and women together. When a union of the two *is* a union—a blending of many forces in one, and a joint progress toward the same end—the noblest and most perfect life this world can hold is then and there made possible. But we do not need statistics to prove to us that in this nineteenth century many women do and must remain unmarried. Even though in actual fact the numbers in both sexes are nearly equal, there are many localities— England for one, New England for another—for both of which the same statement may be made. Emigration, war and many other causes have emptied the country of its able-bodied men, and left women to live their own lives as they can. The possibility of marriage is for all women—the probability limited—but, married or unmarried, the same traits that would make the double life harmonious, will be equally powerful in the single. There is work of one sort or another for every human being not set apart by disease or mental incapacity, and no life need be lonely or cheerless unless, indeed, the power to make a home has been left out.

For there are a few women—and it is a pitiful fate—who seem as helpless in this respect as men, and whose lives are spent in a disorder and barrenness which need not exist had there been any training in the principles which underlie all home-making, and are as distinct factors in the problem of life as the laws that govern a mathematical formula. No matter how shielded the life, how comfortable or luxurious, the personal virtues of love and truth and justice and unselfishness, which is at its highest a union of all, must be the foundation, or we have not lived at all. To any true home these virtues must be brought, else neither in daily routine nor in the conflict of duties owing to one and another in

WATERPROOF FOR TWEEDS

Take two pounds four ounces of alum and dissolve it in ten gallons of water. In like manner dissolve the same quantity of sugar of lead in a similar quantity of water, and mix the two together. They form a precipitate of the sulphate of lead. The clear liquor is now withdrawn, and the cloth immersed for one hour in the solution, when it is taken out, dried in the shade, washed in clean water and dried again. This preparation enables the cloth to repel water like the feathers of a duck's back, and yet allows the perspiration to pass freely through it.

the family, or in social life, on small or large scale, as the case may be, can there be the faithful performance of each in turn. To all home-making this is the key-note, and for all harmony one's own life must first be in tune, responding then, as all lives can, surely as vibration answers to vibration, in swelling chorus or in mighty orchestra.

—Helen Campbell
from *Todd's Country Homes* by Sereno E. Todd
1870

TO CLEAN BLACK KID GLOVES

A good way to clean black kid gloves is to take a teaspoonful of salad oil, drop a few drops of ink into it, and rub it over the gloves with the tip of a feather, then let them dry in the sun.

—Tanner

OUR SITTING ROOM

Our sitting room has a bright rag carpet and rug and an oil cloth mat for the coal stove. The walls are covered with a pretty gilt and satin paper. It is furnished with sofa, cushioned chairs, and cane seated rockers. But it's not this I want to tell you about, but the knick-knacks, all made at home, the home with mother before I came to the new one.

In a corner by a north window is the tiniest of cottages, with veranda, graveled walks, lake, rocks and grove, made as follows: "He" fitted a board into a corner, wide enough for the purpose, fastened with brackets to the wall. The cottage is made of pasteboard covered with moss, at the right is a slight rise of ground, with evergreen twigs for trees, fastened with glue—no roots. A foot path, graveled, leads into this grove, starting from the front door, while another leads to the shore of a lake, a piece of mirror, with a few bushes and one gigantic (?) rock peeping

J. W. Speese Family, Westerville, Nebraska, 1888. Solomon D. Butcher Collection, Nebraska State Historical Society.

130

in. In the chimney of the cottage, who knows of the end of a cigar, put there while the building was in progress? Of course, I did not smoke the cigar. The board is entirely covered with moss.

Then there is a bracket covered with moss, with a bird's nest on the shelf, while fastened a little above, the mother bird is perched with wings spread, looking into the nest. In fact, she never looks any where else, for her body is made of—not pea straw, nor is her tail made of hay, but of things equivalent—arsenic, I believe, and cotton batting.

I have white curtains at the windows, made of bleached cheese sacking, inexpensive, but good enough for me. Across the top where they are gathered, is a band of autumn leaves, pressed, and pasted in place. On the curtains are large ferns, gracefully curved, and also pasted. They have been much admired.

I will not speak of kitchen and pantry, for it is four o'clock, time to start supper. Shall I tell you what we are to have? Hulled corn and milk, principally, bread and pie, conditionally, with a cup of tea for my "gude mon," so tired and hungry.

—Eva A.
The Household
c. 1870

At the heart of the home was the kitchen, the work center and the emotional and psychological core of the house. It was a place for comfort, sustenance, community, and consolation, and it was where you could always find Mother. The kitchen was the rural woman's undisputed base—her anchor and her power, and as such, lent itself to endless sentimental and nostalgic excess. It was also the focus for all the skills and knowledge she had to master and use, and the setting for the larger part of her burdens.

MY MOTHER'S OLD KITCHEN

How sweet to my sight was my mother's old kitchen
As prompted by hunger I entered therein;
The kettles and sauce-pans, they look so bewitching
And a halo of glory surrounding the tin.
The bag of old Java—the coffee-mill by it,
The tea-urn and caddy, on the shelf just above;
The jar of nice pickles and all the good victuals,
And the juicy mince pies which so dearly I love.
The tender crust pies; the spicy mince pies,
The sweet juicy pies, which so dearly I love.

My mother's old kitchen, was always the haven,
　　Where in childish distress, I put in for relief;
And the tablets of mem'ry will ever be 'graven,
　　With the pastry collations that smothered my grief.
How eager I'd tease, while my mother was making,
　　For a squirrel-shaped pattie, or sometimes a dove,
And with lips that were wat'ring, I'd watch while 'twas baking,
　　The juicy mince pie which so dearly I love.
　　　　The tender crust pie; the spicy mince pie,
　　　　The sweet, juicy pie, which so dearly I love.

With my alphabet plate and the pattie upon it,
　　I 'd haste to the door-step, that fronts on the street;
Nor sweet cake, nor pudding could win my heart from it,
　　Though luscious with spices and everything sweet.
And though since my childhood, I've been a wild rover,
　　O'er life's stormy billows, I return like the dove,
To rest in the old kitchen, till the turmoil is over,
　　And partake yet again of the pies that I love.
　　　　The tender crust pies; the spicy mince pies,
　　　　The sweet, juicy pies, I so dearly still love.

—C. L. Whitman
The Household
VOL. I, 1868

Our habits of luxury in town life and our relegation of kitchen work to the hired maid, have robbed us of much of the pleasure we used to have in simpler days. But I am sure there are still sunny kitchens in which the cat purrs by the fire, while the brisk mistress steps to and fro, doing her baking and ironing her sweet smelling linen, fragrant with the purest air and the blessing of the light. There the boy studies his Latin grammar and adds up his sums, and the girl tells how she went to the head in spelling, and how the teacher asked her to be class monitor for the day. The dear grandfather pottering about the garden and the barn comes to the kitchen to rest, and to smoke his meditative pipe. The sweet old grandmother sits in the pleasant window with the long gray sock she is knitting, and the baby plays on the floor, or sleeps in the cradle which stands in the darkest corner. Here, in the best of cooking-schools, the daughter learns housewifely management, here the bone and sinew of the land are nourished, here our patriotic American citizens are bred up to stand sturdily for God and their country.

The kitchen is the heart of the home, and the mother is queen of the kitchen.

—from *The Household Guide*
by Mrs. J. L. Nichols and Ann Holnerson, 1893

OUR KITCHEN

"Co-operative Kitchens!" Heaven forbid! Heaven probably will not interfere: but surely woman will. If there never was a house large enough for two families, there never will be a kitchen large enough for a dozen. It is not strange that some of our women want to get rid of their kitchens, such looking and smelling dens as they are, and will always remain.

Cowper sang "The Sofa," and glorified the teacup. I proclaim the kitchen, with a hearty desire to rescue it from its abused condition. It is nonsense for men to bemoan their grandmothers, because they spun and wove, while we do neither. If they worked perpetually, you may be sure it was because they had to, not because they wanted to do so. They would have been just as glad to have availed themselves of steam looms and sewing machines as a refuge from endless drudgery as their granddaughters, if they had only had them.

Yet it would be vastly better for our generation if we consulted those dear old ladies oftener than we do; better if we imitated them more closely, not in their piety only, which on the whole was too self-abnegating, for it did injustice to some of the best powers God had given them and increased the depravity of man in making a bigger tyrant of him. But there is no danger of our imitating them too nearly in their personal interest in their kitchens. It is for the woman of the nineteenth century to hold in her development the equal balance of physical and mental culture. She cannot do this and neglect her kitchen. No matter how far at times she may rise above it, it will always do her good to come back to it: and, if it is the kitchen it ought to be, she will ever feel delight in returning to its homely brightness and savory smells.

I am sorry for that woman who does not treasure in her heart somewhere the memory of a beloved kitchen. Perhaps it was grandmother's kitchen, or mother's. May be it was in the country. You can hardly be happier again than when you played on its floor a little child. I love such a kitchen; not the discarded one of a fine villa, but the honored kitchen of a thrifty farm house. It faces the east, and takes the sun's first "good morning." Thus its busiest hours are full of brightness, and its restful

FINE BLACKING FOR SHOES

Take four ounces of ivory black, three ounces of the coarsest sugar, a tablespoonful of sweet oil, and a pint of small beer; mix them gradually cold.

afternoons full of serene light and peaceful shadows. Its wide door opens on a grassy yard where "the old oaken bucket hangs in the well." What a yard it is! Its clover grass is a paradise for bleaching; its irregular paths ran through the dandelions down to the garden, whose luscious vegetables offer a daily market for the ready hand, and out to the orchard where the ruddy apples hang.

There is an old lilac bush by one window, a sweet briar by the other, while morning-glory bells cluster about both. Beside one is a stand full of plants, which in the winter flourish in the morning sun. On its ledge there is a work basket—a marvelous basket—into whose depths I sometimes dive, through piles of stockings, through bundles and bags, through scissors and thimbles and pins, down to a needle-book (certain to be at the bottom, if only through my impetuous poking) in whose pocket I am sure to find a whole literature of domestic recipes, heart poems, and editorials on the state of the nation.

Beside the basket is a little old chair, with a warm cushion. This is the mother's chair and this is the mother's corner, not to be invaded. Then the old kitchen has a deep fire-place, a vast brick oven, and a modern stove. It has a great pantry, whose wide shelves are filled with glittering milk pans, all set for cream; and a store-room, in which you may find everything for cheer, from the barrels of flour and sugar, the rows of sweetmeats, dear to every housewife's heart, to bunches of dried catnip hung up for the cat, and pennyroyal enough for every stomach-aching baby in town. The old kitchen floor is painted a clear gray, brightened by gay home-made mats. It has a deep throated clock, that rules its days; a book-rack filled with books and newspapers, and colored prints on its walls. It has an arm chair, a sewing chair and a chintz covered lounge. There is nothing in it too fine for its place. It is only a kitchen, after all, yet a joy to behold and to enjoy.

There is a parlor in this house, proud in a bright grandmother-made carpet, of the most intense stripes; in haircloth furniture, as shining as a beetle's back; in a profuse pile of old daguerreotypes and a new photograph book. On its walls old gentlemen sit in venerable frames, with high collars, stiff enough to break their necks; and old ladies sit in others, in mutton leg sleeves and bristling caps, who look down with a mild severity on the chignons of their descendants. When the minister comes, or the children from town, this parlor is opened and furnished.

But, somehow, sooner or later all the company gravitate back into the old kitchen; for the glow, the cheer, the love are there.

Do you realize how much every life takes on of the hues of its surroundings? And what a minister of good as well as a minister of beauty you may be when you make your kitchen as perfect as a kitchen as you have already made your parlor as a parlor? It cannot be measured, the wretched health, the morbidness, the misery, the vice even, which have had their birth in the dark, unventilated dens which are called kitchens, in which so many women drag on their weary lives.

And when the girl of our time grows up to regard the kitchen of her home as something more than a hole to be shunned, in which Bridget was born to drudge; when she brings into it, instead, her calico apron and smiling face; when she devotes to its service a portion of the cultivated powers now wasted in idleness, if not in sin, we shall see the beginning of that royal race of women for whom we longingly wait and in whose advent we so devoutly believe.

—Mary Clemmer Ames
The Household
VOL. III, 1870

SUNSHINE IN THE KITCHEN

A greater part of us American women are our own house maids; although we do the honors of the table, and entertain our callers, yet we are supposed to perform, in some mysterious way, the duties and tasks of the kitchen. Though the ruffles of our aprons are ironed faultlessly, and the flavor of the puddings is delicious, it didn't happen by chance. In short, the kitchen is the room where much of our lives are spent; the key to the beauty of our homes.

Time and money are often lavished to adorn the parlor with "charming little notions"; the chambers are types of neatness and seem inviting—this is all right—but way down in the kitchen, the walls are dingy, the paper soiled, the chairs and table old and gloomy. We are prone to feel in our hearts what our eyes behold—our lips to utter what is in the heart.

Can it be well for us to have our kitchens dreary? O! rather let the sunshine in. It will take a little money perhaps, but only a few dollars. Have the kitchen painted and white-washed; get some bright, cheery wall paper; take down those dark paper curtains and put up some white ones—an old sheet will do— bring out a

DON'TS

Don't forget that discharges from the bowels and bladder of a typhoid fever patient must, from the first, be carefully disinfected. Bi-chloride of mercury solution, 1 in 500, and sulphate of iron are good disinfectants.

—*The Nurse*

Don't forget that it is dangerous to health or even life to ride in an open carriage or to sit at the open window of a car or room after exercising.

—*The Analyst*

Do not forget that dusting-powders, especially diamond and gold dust, cut the hair, and cause it to become brittle, dull and lifeless, close the ducts and check the growth. Hair-pins cut the hair and injure the scalp. Women should wear the hair as loose as possible, especially at night. Before retiring it should be let down, combed, and tied with a loose ribbon, or placed in a loose net or cap of light material.

—*Medical Bulletin*

rose bush or a twining vine from the "other room"—you can spare it, there are others left—place it in the window, it will grow and blossom just as well and it will be a joy to you. No wonder the work seems tiresome when there is nothing beautiful around.

Paper on the shelves of the pantry make it look neat and tidy; newspapers will do. (I don't mean THE HOUSEHOLDS, but dailies and such like). Cut them a little wider than the shelves and point the edges, arrange the dishes neatly upon them and you will see the good effect.

When there is "sunshine in the kitchen" the men folks are apt to be good natured and once in a while will take notice of the scraper at the door—(sometimes I have wondered if they knew that article was invented for their own especial use). Labor is honorable and the command obligatory, "Whatsoever thy hand findeth to do, do it with thy might," but don't shut the sunshine out of your kitchen and out of your hearts.

—Jennie
The Household
VOL. I, 1868

A Good Recipe

Here is a recipe which I once read, and always remembered it because of its goodness. I send it that others may try it.

> *Take a gill of forbearance.*
> *A pinch of submission.*
> *Twelve ounces of patience.*
> *A handful of grace.*
> *Mix well with the milk of the best human kindness.*
> *And serve with a radiant smile on your face.*

Please try it when you feel all out of patience and everything seems to go all wrong, and see if it doesn't help you.

—Mrs. R. A. B.
The Household
VOL. XXV, 1892

Give us a home nest bright,
Give us the faces dear,
And where is the world's delight
Like to our fireside cheer?

Plaudits for those who seek
Laurel and lasting fame,
But leave us the lips that speak
Our humble, household name.

—*The Farm Journal*
SEPTEMBER 1902

PART TWO
BURDENS, COSTS, RESPONSES

"Until Death Alone Can Give Her Rest"

AUGUST.

Lithograph on previous page:
Gleason's Pictorial, *Aug. 19, 1854.*
Courtesy: Argosy Bookstore, N.Y.C.

THE FARMER'S WIFE

"Born an' scrubbed, suffered and died."
That's all you need to say, elder.
Never mind sayin' "made a bride,"
Nor when her hair got gray.
Jes' say, "born 'n worked t' death";
That fits it—save y'r breath.

Hamlin Garland's bleak impression of Middle West prairie woman leaves little room for whatever joys there may have been, but there is no arguing that the amount of work rural woman had to do was all but overwhelming. While not all farmers' wives of the period were burdened, ill used, unhappy, tired, and sick—often to the point of decline or insanity—the fact remains that many of them did pass their lives in this soul-destroying context.

At the middle of the nineteenth century (and still, in many respects, at its close), rural life was narrow and hard. Even in the settled and civilized East life was demanding and unsure, but beyond the mountains to the Mississippi, the Northwest Territory, and the Great Plains it was, at every stage, a tenuous venture. No matter what satisfactions it offered, daily life there was a wearing, monotonous, isolated existence. Wherever she lived, the role of rural woman was sharply defined and her horizons limited. What she had to do more than filled her days and took all her strength.

Some women of the time appeared to glory in their work—they had the "gift." Many did not, and these women slowly went under or wore out, paying the price of continuous attrition. It was not simply that they worked so hard in such a narrow sphere (rural men certainly shared an equal burden) but rather that they had no choice. What the rural woman did went without saying, and she spent her life trying to live up to virtually impossible expectations. A man could farm here or there, or not at all. Within certain limits, he was able to choose, but his wife's options were inevitably narrowed to keeping house. He was the initiator, the leader, the force that could effect change. He was the self-sufficient, independent spirit, but it was the woman who had to support him and the family, on a day-to-day basis, wherever and under whatever conditions prevailed.

Most of the work that rural woman did was sheer drudgery—endless, repetitive work, doing and redoing, making and remaking, running as fast as she could in order to stay in the same place, but always striving to make that place perfection. The term drudgery is used again and again in the popular literature as a descriptive term—kitchen drudge, household drudge—with little or no opprobrium attached.

Woman's work never attained a recognition or dignity of its own. Serious articles on farming or rural life rarely mentioned the woman's contribution for its own sake or in its own terms but only as it related to man's work and well-being. And the costs to her, in exhaustion, "fretfulness," and incapacity, were less a concern for her own well-being than for the smooth and serene functioning of the family. She was, and had to be, the spiritual center of the home, an innate, rocklike presence. If she crumbled, so did the family.

Often, too, the scope of her work extended into that of her husband's. Besides the house, she had charge of the farm garden, the maintenance of livestock and poultry, and whatever outside work related to "civilizing" the farm. At special times of the year, if she did not work the fields herself, she provided room and board for the extra help that did. Yet her husband rarely found himself drawn into the active management of home or children.

What developed in popular literature to justify and secure her position of self-lessness and sacrifice was an all-encompassing, sentimental idealization coupled with a persistent coercive prodding to do even better. Farm life was, after all, a good life, secure, protected, removed from the world's corruptions. Woman's status was blessed, and the giving of herself was a fulfillment of the highest ideal.

By the second half of the century, however, "the sweet bird content to sing in its small cage" began to notice the bars of the cage. After all, Susan B. Anthony was out there with sixteen sober Rochester housewives committing a federal offense by trying to vote in the 1872 presidential election.

But most rural women either failed to see the bars or were too cowed by habit or social custom to object. Better the security of the cage. It was true perhaps that the weekly newspaper, the increasing variety of store-bought commodities, the new indoor pump or parlor stove, and the occasional time to look up or sit down had begun to stir some murmurings, or to create an awareness of how badly the homemaker was used, but the alternatives were always presented in lurid shades of danger and depredation. Besides, the overwhelming demands of just keeping the household running on course took precedence over expanding perceptions. Those who allowed dissatisfaction to enter their lives were offered only one "respectable" solution, which was to make of their drudgery a legitimate and respected profession. They could attain self-esteem by becoming better at the jobs they had to do. While this attempt at improving their lot helped, it still did not deal with the crux of the problem—the freedom to choose their own vocations and direct their own lives.

As for the issue of alternatives or rights, it was the brave rural woman indeed who could stand up against public opinion or popular authorities such as O. S. Fowler, who wrote that the woman's movement "is conducted chiefly by dissatisfied wives or else unmarried croakers." Choice, independent action, and success were masculine concepts and their prerequisites—aggressiveness, strength, boldness, logic, efficiency—were seen as exclusively male characteristics. A woman "succeeded" only insofar as she was able to manifest these masculine traits. Except in the domestic sphere or in other limited fields of endeavor, she ventured forth at great hazard to her "natural" being, and except in rare circumstances of unique talent or incredible perseverance, pursuits outside these limited fields were closed to her. The growing awareness expressed in the agitation for rights and opportunities was opposed by a determined effort (mounted by both women and men) to maintain the traditional order. Not only must women be made to accept the rational purpose of their lives, they had to see that purpose as a blessing bestowed, rather than a burden imposed.

This section attempts to juxtapose some perceptions of burden and cost with the domestic myth and to present some of the responses these perceptions called forth. Along with these responses came the inevitable backlash that all too frequently succeeded in smothering attempts at change. The viewpoints and arguments presented here represent a wide range of popular view and opinion. They are contentious, contradictory, passionate, tentative, ambivalent, and often agonized. Since, for the most part, the rural woman lived out her life in this teeter-totter of confusion and conflict, I have tried to present them in this way.

OVERWORK & ISOLATION

WHAT IS THE GAIN?

There are many overworked, nervous mothers striving hard to do their duty as wife, mother and housekeeper.

Self-sacrifice comes natural to women. Much of it is born in them, and what is not is ground into them from their childhood by education. For the sake of her home duties a girl gives up amusements and privileges which her brother would never be expected to forego for the like reason.

As she grows older, this spirit grows, encouraged by all tradition and outside influence. Often its power masters her altogether, and her life becomes one long devotion to endless labor and acceptance of unpleasant things, that the pleasant part of living may be kept sacred for the rest of the family.

The purely useless side of this entire self-abnegation must sometimes strike the beholder. Such effacing of individuality is not uncommon. And it gives as little real benefit to the family as it does to the individual.

Putting aside the moral effect on the younger members of a family, brought up to regard their mother as a machine run for the family service, does the woman who so gives herself for the well-being of her family really accomplish all she desires?

If she works without pause or slackening, day in and day out, does she always feel satisfied, with the admiring onlookers, that it is the noblest way to so spend her health and energies?

If she renounces all recreation and higher life for herself, and gives up all communion of mind and spirit with her husband and children, is the reward adequate that is paid to them in a better kept house, a more beautifully supplied larder or handsomer clothes?

If over-fatigue causes her to become petulant or complaining, is not the atmosphere of home more greatly injured than the added cleaning and cooking can repair?

If she is too worn out to give sympathy and help to the children's joys and sorrows, what do the finer clothes and furniture obtained avail?

And if, as sometimes happens, outraged nature gives way, and others must step into the breach, do their own work and the played-out woman's as well, and take care of her into the bargain, what has she gained by her extreme efforts that she has not lost by the break-down?

Photo on previous page:
Independence on the Plains—
Gathering Chips. *Kansas State Historical Society.*

144

A life laid down in a worthy cause is not lost, but gained; but is this cause worthy?

—*The Household*
VOL. XXV, 1892

THE HOUSEKEEPER'S TRAGEDY

One day, as I wandered, I heard a complaining,
*   And saw a poor woman, the picture of gloom;*
She glared at the mud on her door step ('twas raining),
*   And this was her wail as she wielded her broom:*

"Oh! life is a toil, and love is a trouble,
*   And beauty will fade, and riches will flee,*
And pleasures they dwindle, and prices they double,
*   And nothing is what I could wish it to be.*

"There's too much of worriment goes to a bonnet;
*   There's too much of ironing goes to a shirt;*
There's nothing that pays for the time you waste on it;
*   There's nothing that lasts us but trouble and dirt.*

"In March it is mud; it's slush in December;
*   The midsummer breezes are loaded with dust;*
In fall the leaves litter; in muggy September
*   The wall paper rots and the candlesticks rust.*

"There are worms in the cherries and slugs in the roses,
*   And ants in the sugar and mice in the pies*
And rubbish of spiders no mortal supposes,
*   And ravaging roaches, and damaging flies.*

"It's sweeping at six, and it's dusting at seven;
*   It's victuals at eight, and it's dusting at nine;*
It's potting and panning from ten to eleven;
*   We scarce break our fast ere we plan how to dine.*

"With grease and with grime, from corner to centre,
*   Forever at war, and forever alert,*
No rest for a day, lest the enemy enter—
*   I spend my whole life in a struggle with dirt.*

"Last night, in my dream, I was stationed forever,
*   On a little bare isle in the midst of the sea;*

POKE-ROOT,

boiled in water and mixed with a good quantity of molasses, set about the kitchen, the pantry, &c. in large deep plates, will kill cockroaches in great numbers, and finally rid the house of them. The Indians say that poke-root boiled into a soft poultice is the cure for the bite of a snake. I have heard of a fine horse saved by it.

PRACTICAL METHODS
AND RECEIPTS FOR THE
CARE OF KITCHEN
UTENSILS

1. Attention to details is very
necessary.
2. Sand or bath brick is excellent in
cleaning wooden articles, floors,
tables, and the like.
3. If you use limestone water, an
oyster shell in the tea kettle will
receive the lime deposit.
4. Boil in the coffee pot, occasionally, soap, water and washing soda.
It should always be bright to insure
good coffee.
5. If skillets are very greasy, a little
sal soda in the water will neutralize
the grease, and so make them
much easier to wash.
6. Pans made of sheet-iron are
better to bake bread and cake in
than those made of tin.
7. Bottles and cruets are cleaned
nicely with sand and soap suds.
8. Iron pots, stoneware jars and
crocks should have cold water and
a little soda placed in them on the
stove and allowed to boil, before
using them.

My one chance of life was a ceaseless endeavor
To sweep off the waves ere they swept off poor me.

"Alas! 'twas a dream—again I behold it!
I yield; I am helpless my fate to avert."
She rolled down her sleeves; her apron she folded:
Then lay down and died, and was buried in dirt.
—*The Household*
VOL. III, 1870

DESPONDING MOTHERS

"I have done nothing to-day but keep things straight in the house," you say wearily at the close of it. Do you call that nothing? Nothing that your children are healthy and happy, and secured from evil influence? Nothing that neatness, and thrift, and whole-some food follow the touch of your fingertips? Nothing that beauty in place of ugliness meets the eye of the cheerful little ones, in the plants at your window, in the picture on the wall? Nothing that home to them means home, and will always do so to the end of life, what vicissitudes soever that may involve? Oh, careworn mother, is all this nothing? Is it nothing that over against your sometime mistakes and sometime discouragements shall be writ-ten, "She hath done what she could"?
—*The Household*
JANUARY 1884

SOMETHING TO DO

A good man has said: "The three grand essentials to happiness are, something to do, something to love, and something to hope for."

Something to do! Did that good man ever hear of any one who had a surplus of that first "essential"? Did he ever think of the manifold operations of washing, ironing, cleaning, baking, mending, and making that steal away the time and strength of so large a portion of feminine humanity? Did he ever calculate the number of journeys from cellar to attic that the supervision of one's household requires? Did he ever count the ingredients that one day furnishes for that "essential to happiness"?—attending to marketing, "fixing off" for school, sewing up the rips in papa's gloves, brushing his broadcloth, meekly receiving sundry in-junctions as to the mending of "that other coat" and the pur-chase of a necktie, with the exclamation, "Really, these old slippers are getting the worse for wear." Then, preparing for and entertaining company, house-cleaning, moving, etc., *ad infinitum;* bringing about day by day and month by month, the inevitable condition of hands full, head full, heart full, which is wearing so many lives away.

"But then, you have a sewing machine, and the best help to be obtained."

"Yes, the sewing machine is a blessing, but it will not cut nor baste, nor darn, nor sew up gloves, nor put on buttons and hooks and eyes. And it is often out of order, besides. Help! But Betsey was sick, and Kate wasn't honest, and Mary got married, and then we had a foreign ignoramus who didn't know a tureen from a washtub, followed by a long vacancy on the culinary throne, and now in the reign of Bridget the Sixth, don't we almost wish for another interregnum?"

Something to do! My dear sir: probably you have enjoyed that comfortable state of just enough to do, which does not preclude your settling down for a nap, after dinner, or taking a little walk, when you want fresh air. Perhaps you never were obliged to defer for days and weeks an answer to a letter of friendship or business. Perhaps you were never called from the depths of Emerson's essays to make a johnnycake for dinner. Perhaps Longfellow and Tennyson were not sealed books to you, until a midnight watch beside a sick friend unclosed them for an hour. Perhaps you can read the "latest intelligence concerning the Impeachment Trial" within a week from the time it is printed, or can have, any day, an undisturbed afternoon to devote to John Stuart Mill and political economy. In no other way can we understand that assertion about "something to do" without any qualifying clause, or account for your existence in this busy world, without being sometimes a little tired of it.

Who will propose to the weary ones a remedy?

—*The Household*
VOL. XIV, 1881

DISH-WATER AND DISH-WASHING

These are the most discouraging elements of house-work! I say this awful truth because I have proved it, you have proved it, your neighbors have proved it and the stranger within your gates has sighed because of the disheartening truth. Don't anybody attempt to contradict me; don't even shake your head. I tell you I know it, and it

9. Never allow the handles of knives to be placed in hot water.

10. A discolored brass kettle can be cleaned nicely by scouring it with a little vinegar and salt, and washing it well afterwards with hot water and soap.

11. Scrape the dough from your rolling pin and wipe with a dry towel, rather than wash it.

12. Don't put your tinware or iron vessels away damp, always dry them first. And scald out your woodenware often.

13. Steel or silver may tarnish in woolen cloths. A chamois skin or tissue paper is very much better.

14. Don't use a brass kettle for cooking until it is thoroughly cleaned with salt and vinegar.

15. Don't allow coffee or tea to stand in tin.

16. Don't allow knives with wooden, horn or bone handles to lie in hot water; wash the blades in as hot water as you please, but keep it off the handles as much as possible.

17. Don't heat new iron vessels too quickly. Heat them gradually, and they are not so liable to crack.

makes me cross to have anybody give the remotest intimation that my word or knowledge admits of a doubt.

The sweeping and the dusting is discouraging enough, but there is this consolation. It isn't the same dirt which you swept before.

Washing is bad enough, but the dreadful monotony can be broken by high winds, broken lines, snow squalls and scrubbing. Ironing is hard enough, but the clothes are sometimes too dry, sometimes too wet, irons hot or irons cold.

Cooking is awfully tame, but it isn't the same flour, the same sugar, the same eggs, the same soda, the same salt, and so on to the end of the endless variety of ingredients needed. There is, too, a sort of wicked solace in the thought that, while you labor to use all these articles, it creates a necessity for labor to supply the new demands. Every loaf of bread and cake, every pie, every pudding, every soup, every boil, every fry isn't the same dead awful same.

But those dreadful dishes! you carry them to the table and put them grimly in the same set places at morn; you take them off after breakfast and set them down, poor, white, inanimate unthinking, clayey clods, by the side of the dish-pan. You rinse them in water that looks just like the liquid in which you rinsed them last.

You put them one after another into the same dish-pan, you scald the same knuckles day after day, you tip them in the same dripping-pan, you wipe them with a dish-towel that looks just like the other five, you set the mute things in the same places on the pantry shelves, you wash the same villainous-looking griddles, spiders, kettles and pans, you scrape and pumice the miserable "catch on places," you wash the dish-cloths in the same way that your mother, grandmother, and great-great-great-grandmother did, hang them on the same old nails or bushes your childhood knew, wash the dish-pan inside and out in the same old wearing way, and are done in time to turn around to put them in the same old speechless places on the dinner table.

You are fortunately, or unfortunately, given strength enough to play your part in the same miserable drama again, rinsing, washing, scalding, scouring, and are in time to take the miserable hackneyed porcelain back for tea, and then there they will sit on the kitchen table by the side of the almost immortal dish-pan, staring at you unblinkingly with the same white, unthinking, soulless eyes.

You rinse, scald, wash and scour again, and put the dead pictures of discouragement upon the same shelves and the next

---

A WARMING-PAN

full of coals, or a shovel of coals, held over varnished furniture, will take out white spots. Care should be taken not to hold the coals near enough to scorch; and the place should be rubbed with flannel while warm.

---

morning there they sit, winking, winking, stupidly and harm-
lessly, staring, staring, mutely and appealingly, the same white
plates, cups, saucers and bowls, and away you go, ferrying them
over to the breakfast table; and so on and on to the end of the
century, if you are unkindly spared so long.

Hence, I repeat: Dish-water and dish-washing are the most
discouraging elements of housework.

There's the occasional recreation of breaking a plate, a valuable tureen, or glass, but there comes another to its funeral; it
finds its place on the same pantry shelves and tables, and is prepared to stare as relentlessly as its predecessor.

There is no change, no respite. Your folks will never learn to
eat from unwashed plates, and so the stolid ferrying, the grave
placing, the wearying rinsing, the unending washing, the aggra-
vating scalding, the voiceless wiping, the unblinking gazing, the
inanimate grouping, the changeless bush and the ever youthful
pan will live on and on from decade to century (and no machine
will ever come to a successful rescue,) and dish-water and dish-
washing must continue to discourage, dishearten, weary and ag-
gravate girls and women who cannot learn to be content with
monotony and labor which is dead compulsion—no more.

—C. Dora Nickerson
The Household
N. D.

LABOR-SAVING MACHINERY IN THE KITCHEN

While the various operations of the farm are being carried on by
the help of valuable labor-saving machinery, are not far too many
farmers a little negligent in regard to the conveniences provided
for performing the never-ending work of the kitchen and dairy-
room? Is the same willingness generally manifested for buying
new machines for the house, when the old ones become worn out
or get out of fashion, as when the mowing machine or cultivator
needs repairs or replacing by new or better styles? Are not the labors of the wife and of the house servants too often looked upon
as unproductive and of minor importance, compared with the
out-door work of the men folks?

Clean clothes to wear, clean, soft and well-aired beds to sleep
in, good, wholesome, nicely cooked meals, three times a day, and
tidy and attractive rooms to live in, do not, perhaps, at first
thought, seem to be as productive of wealth as the sale of the

TO KILL EARWIGS, OR
OTHER INSECTS, WHICH
MAY ACCIDENTALLY HAVE
CREPT INTO THE EAR

Let the person under this
distressing circumstance lay his
head upon a table, the side upwards
that is afflicted; at the same time, let
some friend carefully drop into the
ear a little sweet oil or oil of
almonds. A drop or two will be
sufficient, which will instantly
destroy the insect and remove the
pain, however violent.

149

matured crops from the farm, but for what do we sell our farm products except for the purposes of securing just these very home comforts we have named? Without these, what would our lives be worth? And with them, do we men folks on the farm realize how much they have cost, of hard labor and constant care, on the part of wives and daughters?

We have visited a good many farmers' kitchens, and have noticed a wide difference in the convenience provided for carrying on the everlasting routine of house-work. We have one large farm-house in mind, where the wife is mother of a numerous family of boys and girls who have been reared to manhood and womanhood, where all the water used in the house is brought in pails from a spring some twenty rods distant, and all the way up hill, at that. This mother, who is still living, though bent almost double by the weight of years, may be seen, almost any day, with pail in hand, going to or from the spring, over the well-worn path, which was first

Photograph by permission of Minnesota Historical Society.

marked by the tread of ancestors, nearly a century ago. The labor of two men for two weeks would be sufficient to secure permanent water from a cistern within ten feet of the kitchen sink.

Washing day is one of the hardest days on the farm, when the men-folks fail to furnish a full supply of water and dry wood at a convenient distance from the centre of operations. With good, dry wood, piled under cover, plenty of water, a good cook stove with ample boiler, or a large, clean, set kettle that is not used for boiling swill, the washing of a medium-sized family may be done with comparative ease and dispatch, even without any of the patent washing or wringing machines, so freely offered for sale in our village stores, or exhibited at the agricultural fairs from one end of our country to the other.

—*The Household*
VOL. XIII, 1880

DEAR HOUSEHOLD—Will you admit one from the far West to your circle? I want to tell you about our home, nestled among the mountains on the Pacific Coast. We live on a ranch in a small valley, half-way up the western slope of the Sierra Nevada Mountains, a kind of temperate zone between the snow-capped mountains and the torrid valley of the Sacramento, a very pleasant place to live, with magnificent scenery about us everywhere.

We have a fine view of Mt. Shasta, eighty miles to the north of us, which an Eastern person would take to be only some ten or fifteen miles away, owing to the clear atmosphere of this coast.

Our principal crops here are fruit, hay, beans and potatoes. Of fruit we have apples, peaches, pears, plums, prunes, nectarines, apricots, quinces, figs, cherries, grapes and berries of all kinds on our ranch; also almonds, walnuts and chestnuts.

I am a farmer's wife and enjoy it. I would not exchange the freedom and quiet of farm life for all the city luxuries. While I am writing, the thermometer is nearing 100° Fahrenheit, while I can look out of my window and see perpetual snow only thirty miles away. The heat here is not nearly so oppressive as in the Eastern States.

My heart aches for those overworked mothers, for I used to be one of them; but twenty-five years' experience in housekeeping has taught me that we do a great deal of unnecessary work.

Let me tell them something that will, perhaps, make their cross seem lighter. I have raised a family of four children to be grown-up men and women, and I have but one hand—my left

TO REMOVE FRECKLES

The following lotion is highly recommended: One ounce of lemon juice, a quarter of a drachm of powdered borax and half a drachm of sugar; mix in a bottle, and allow them to stand a few days, when the liquor should be rubbed occasionally on the hands and face. Another application is: Friar's balsam, one part; rose water, twenty parts.

hand being amputated at the wrist before I was married—and I have never had hired help in the house except in sickness.

Now, dear sisters, if you are blessed with health and all your limbs and faculties, just try to look on the sunny side of life and make the best of your situation. When you feel despondent, visit some one less favored with conveniences and help than yourself, after which your own cares will seem lighter; or do as I do—take up THE HOUSEHOLD and read and rest; act upon the good advice given in its pages. I shake hands with you all across the continent, and bid you good afternoon.

—Mrs. Wm. Weigart
The Household
OCTOBER 1891

A bird of a somewhat different feather from the one described on page 139, the following perception of "The Farmer's Wife" is somewhat at odds with the idealized view. Even here, however, her understanding of the oppressive load she had to carry yields in the end to the ultimate rationale. Both poems, it is worth nothing, were written by men.

THE FARMER'S WIFE

Up with the bird in the early morning—
  The dewdrop glows like a precious gem;
Beautiful tints in the skies are dawning,
  But she's never a moment to look at them.
The men are wanting their breakfast early;
  She must not linger, she must not wait;
For words that are sharp and looks that are surly
  Are what men give them when meals are late.

Oh, glorious colors the clouds are turning,
  If she would but look over hills and trees;
But here are the dishes and here is the churning—
  Those things must always yield to these.
The world is filled with the wine of beauty,
  If she could pause and drink it in;
But pleasure, she says, must wait for duty—
  Neglected work is committed sin.

The day grows hot and the hands grow weary;
  Oh, for an hour to cool her head
Out with the birds in the winds so cheery!
  But she must get dinner and bake the bread.

The busy men in the hay-field working,
　　If they saw her sitting with idle hand,
Would think her lazy, and call it shirking,
　　And she could never make them understand.

They do not know that the heart within her
　　Hungers for beauty and things sublime;
They only know that they want their dinner—
　　Plenty of it—and just "on time."
And after the sweeping and churning and baking
　　And dinner dishes are all put by,
She sits and sews, though her head is aching,
　　Till time for supper and "chores" draw nigh.

Her boys at school must look like others,
　　She says, as she patches their frocks and hose;
For the world is quick to censure mothers
　　For the least neglect of children's clothes.
Her husband comes from field of labor;
　　He gives no praise to his weary wife;
She's done no more than has her neighbor;
　　'Tis the lot of all in country life.

But after the strife and weary tussle
　　With life is done, and she lies at rest,
The nation's brain and heart and muscle—
　　Her sons and daughters—shall call her blest.
And I think the sweetest joys of Heaven,
　　The rarest bliss of eternal life,
And the fairest crown of all will be given
　　Unto the way-worn farmer's wife.

　　　　　　　　　　—California Farmer
　　　　　　　　　　　　The Household
　　　　　　　　　　　　　c. 1878

E. B., the Missouri farm wife we met earlier, unburdens herself to her *Household* sisters in a not unfamiliar litany of woe, but here, obviously, was a cry of pain that came too close for comfort. The letters following E. B.'s show how such complaints (and their implications) were deflected, rationalized, or even turned back onto the complainer. Nevertheless, as Olive Oldstyle puts it in the last letter, it's all right to complain. It frees the mind, and afterwards the "general harmony" is none the worse.

OVERWORKED FARMERS' WIVES

May I take refuge here a little while? I would like to be "speaker of the house" for a few moments, in behalf of about twenty-five thousand farmers' wives, who have for the past three months been going through very nearly what I am about to relate. Truth compels me to confess that I am in no very gracious mood this afternoon, for I have just come in to rest from a three hours' conflict with an obstinate churn, and it is the same thing five days out of every week.

Now, butter-makers come to the front, for all housekeepers in the country will admit that this is a subject of great importance to every farmer's wife, who has to do the churning in connection with all the other laborious work, found I verily believe, only within the precincts of a farm-house kitchen. Oh, but I am tired ! Do let me draw one good long breath, and lean back in the cushioned chair, so as to be comfortable, before I begin to talk again. For weeks and weeks, I might say months, we have had workmen to cook for. First, the plow boys, then the harvesters and the wheat stackers, and the end is not yet, for hay harvest is at its height and next week the threshers are coming. The threshers are coming! Those four words may appear very insignificant to the uninitiated, but to those who have "been there" they contain a world of meaning. I do not wonder that the medical statistics show that there are more farmers' wives in the lunatic asylum than any other class. Poor things, I don't doubt it. I have been going all spring and summer like a well-regulated clock, am set running every morning at half-past four o'clock, and run all day, often until half-past eleven P.M. I am beginning to think with that sensible writer and woman philosopher, George Eliot, that "leisure is gone, gone where the spinning wheels and the slow wagon, and the peddlers who brought bargains to our doors on sunny afternoons, have gone," and leisure at present is nothing but a "will o' the wisp" to allure poor overworked farmers' wives on to greater efforts. Then the cradle at our house is still on duty. It is occupied at present by baby number twelve, and the fragment of time between half past eleven and half past four is spent in "wooing nature's sweet restorer," and endeavoring to persuade the fretful baby to do likewise. My weary limbs are scarcely stretched for repose, before red dawn peeps into my chamber window, and the birds, in the whispering leaves over the roof, apprise me by their sweetest notes that another day of toil awaits me. I arise, the harness is hastily adjusted and once more I step upon the tread-mill.

TO CLEAN TEETH

Take of good soft water, one quart; juice of lemon, two ounces; burnt alum, six grains; common salt, six grains. Mix. Boil them a minute in a cup, then strain and bottle for use; rub the teeth with a small bit of sponge tied to a stick, once a week.

In addition to all this toil and trouble we have had Mrs. Elite and her sister Miss Stylish, their nephew Bon Ton, and his cousins to make a protracted visit of several weeks, and not a shade of a darky could I get! We did have some kind of excuse for help for a few days, but for the life of me I could not tell whether it was "help" or not. But my friends have all gone now. The back of the last polonaise and dress coat has vanished in the distance. The wheat harvesters and the hay stackers have gone to work and make work for some other household, and weary and foot-sore I feel like rushing off up stairs, and locking myself up in the chamber we call peace; but instead of that, I am pouring my sorrows into the ear of a sympathizing (?) public, or, perchance, into the hospitable waste basket. But truly I can exclaim with the queen of Sheba, "the half has not been told." I trust no one will consider me inhospitable, as it would be unjust, for I know I am hospitable and so are my neighbors, but our friends are unfortunate in their selection of a time for visiting.

During the growing season farmers are very busy. Necessity compels them to hire several extra hands, and the burden and heat of the day fall with full force upon the already overworked farmer's wife. Many, many times during the summer have I prepared breakfast for Ned, the boys and the hands between five and six o'clock, and they would be off. Later, between eight and nine our guests would sit down to their breakfast, and then at twelve o'clock, as we have to be prompt with our meals, the table would again be spread for between fifteen and twenty-two persons. Is it any wonder that I have become slightly demoralized, and have come to condole with every woman who reads THE HOUSEHOLD, and can take in the situation?

In the August number, "grandma" asks if this life is worth the living. Well, judging from my present gloomy standpoint, I should say it is not.

But there is an after thought which brings peace like a balm to my spirit. If we ever each day do the very best we can, God will at last crown our efforts with abundant success; and in that sweet hereafter we, if faithful, can look back upon our toils and labors as but stepping stones to that gracious rest which is prepared for those who have done the best they could.

—E. B.
The Household
VOLS. XI and XII; 1878, 1879

PRACTICAL RULES FOR
KEEPING POULTRY

1. A little glycerine applied occasionally to combs and wattles will prevent injury by frosting.
2. A great source of contagion is the drinking troughs. Remember this if roup should make its appearance in your poultry house.
3. In place of "tonic," drop a nail into the drinking trough and allow it to remain there. It will supply all the "tincture of iron" required.
4. If you feed whole corn, place it in the oven and parch it occasionally and feed smoking hot. The fowls appreciate it in the cold, frosty weather.
5. A little linseed or oil meal given once a week in the soft feed will promote laying. This will not come under the heading of "dosing the fowls with medicine."
6. Do not throw your table scraps into the swill barrel. Give them to the chickens.
7. One of the most important points in the keeping of ducks is to give them clean, dry quarters at night. They are very prone to leg weakness in cold, damp quarters.

E. B.

Well, I wonder if there is really such a woman as E. B., with such an overburdened life to lead? I have lived all my life away in the depth of the country, as a city sister calls it, right with and among farmers' wives, and to save my life, I cannot understand how E. B. has managed to live. I am the daughter of a farmer, the granddaughter of a farmer, and the wife of a farming physician, but I do not begin to see into the perfect tangle of work into which E. B. has got. Why, I remember well how dreadful seemed the task of cooking one meal daily, and how we thought that by dividing the cooking between mother, aunt and myself, we might get along. This was just after freedom, and of course we have been improving since then, and now I can get along nicely with a small girl as help. Things down south are quite different to the way you do. I remember once a Marylander boarded with us, and we were doing our own cooking and housework, and once I complained, when he made the remark, "Why, you ladies down here don't know what work is." So you see E. B. may imagine a great deal that is not real. I am in a thickly settled neighborhood of farmers' wives, and I cannot point to a single instance where they lead such a work life as E. B. Of course farmers in the backwoods do labor hard, but then there is a vast difference in surrounding which makes their work light, too. For instance, in the matter of washing; their children in summer wear almost nothing, and in winter wear very dark, thick clothing which they seldom change more than once weekly. So you see their week's washing would not equal more than two day's washing for a more favored family.

And their houses are small, making their housework necessarily light. I don't think E. B. belongs to this class, so her multiplicity of duties are still a puzzle.

—Clyde Wayne
The Household
MARCH 1883

FARMERS' WIVES

In a recent number of your most readable paper, I see an article written by E. B., headed "Overworked Farmers' Wives." Said article excites in my mind both sympathy and curiosity. Sympathy on account of the laborious life the writer seems to lead, curiosity as to how she manages her household affairs.

Near the outset of her article, she incidentally refers to a three hours' conflict with an obstinate churn.

Dear woman, allow me to say that such a conflict should never occur. Throw away that churn and get a better one, or get a thermometer, and by its use get the cream at the right temperature before commencing the conflict, and thereby save four-fifths of your time and labor. I am intimately acquainted with a farmer's wife who has, on an average, churned twice a week for twenty years past, and I am pretty certain that in all that time the conflict has rarely exceeded half an hour.

I am also somewhat curious to know what E. B. finds to occupy her time from half past four o'clock in the morning till half past eleven at night. Circumstances in a farmer's family may occasionally be such as to render necessary this early rising, and this extending of work into the night, but how it comes to be an every-day occurrence, I cannot see. Please allow me again to refer to a farmer's wife that I well know, who is almost invariably in bed at or before nine o'clock in the evening, and just as rarely out until after five o'clock in the morning, and who very frequently finds time for an after dinner nap.

E. B. says the cradle is still in requisition in her house, and is now occupied by number twelve. Where, let me ask, are all those twelve children? If any of them are gone to their eternal rest, they no longer add to the toils of the mother. If they have gone out into the world, we presume they have homes and cares of their own. If they are still at home, they most certainly will share the labors of the household, and take some of the burden from the shoulders of the overworked mother. How is it?

E. B. alludes to another matter, in which she strikes a sympathetic chord in the heart of every farmer's wife, and in the heart of the farmer as well, and that is in regard to the visits of friends at inopportune and unseasonable times. That which otherwise would have been a pleasant and acceptable visit is often only a burden and a vexation because of being improperly timed. I have known of people receiving downright shabby treatment, in consequence of making their visit to a farmer's home when all the male members of the household were toiling in the harvest field, and the female members more than usually busy on account of hired help being added to the family at this busy season of the year. In cases of this kind, the possession of a little common sense, and the exercise of a little forethought on the part of the visitors

8. Feed your fowls just what they will eat up clean. Fat hens or pullets are poor layers, and the latter is just what you don't want just now, with eggs at 28 and 32 cents per dozen.

9. Fowls over three years old are not, as a rule, good for breeders. The males are unable to properly fertilize eggs for hatching, while the stock is usually weak. Four years is generally considered a "ripe old age" for a fowl.

10. Each hen, if properly kept, will lay from 200 to 250 eggs a year.

11. Liver and intestines are an excellent food to make hens lay.

12. Keep an abundant supply of lime where the hens can easily get at it, if you desire your hens to lay well.

13. Always clean the nest well and put in fresh straw before the hen begins to sit.

14. It is best in breeding to cross or mix the breeds more or less every year. It improves the flesh and general health of the fowls.

15. Pullets are better layers than old hens. Keep your stock young by disposing annually of the old broods.

16. Keep at least one rooster for every eight hens if you desire vigorous young chickens.

17. It is a good plan to change roosters every year.

18. Roosters are best at two years of age.

would be well in place. I do not think that farmers as a general thing can be charged with a lack of hospitality, or, if so, it is in consequence of that hospitality being abused. I know I give voice to the sentiments of many when I say to our friends, come in leafy June, come when the apples are ripe, come when we can take you out and show you the beautiful autumnal tints, come when we have the long winter evenings, for reading, for conversation, or for games, as the taste may be, but don't come in seed time—don't come in harvest. But this is a digression.

The reading of the letter of E. B. gives rise to serious thought on one matter and that is this: Where are the thousands of our young farmers to get wives? If the statements of E. B. are read and believed by the marriageable girls of the land, they will be slow to place themselves in a position where there is a prospect of having to bend their backs to such a burden. Dear girls, let me whisper in your ear that E. B. has overdrawn the matter, and painted a darker picture than the facts in the average case could warrant. When she wrote that article, she must have had a fit of the blues, or her bread would not rise, or the cow had kicked over the milk pail.

Next time she writes, let us hope she will give us the bright side of her life, for a bright side there certainly is. That a farmer's wife has much to do, there is no denying, but twenty-five years experience on a farm leads me to the conclusion that if they work eighteen out of the twenty-four hours, it is a self-imposed task, and not necessarily connected with the business.

—Pat
The Household
JANUARY 1883

TO MAKE THE TEETH WHITE

A mixture of honey with the purest charcoal will prove an admirable cleanser.

FROM ANOTHER FARMER'S WIFE

In the October number of THE HOUSEHOLD, E. B. relates the experience of an over-worked farmer's wife. It was read to the members of our family circle, and this is what "our farmer" said about it: "Surely that woman's husband is one of the most thoughtless and selfish of beings. There is actually no need of any farmer's wife being such a slave as E. B. describes. Whenever a farm is large enough to demand hired help for the farmer, the farm is large enough to demand and provide good help for the farmer's wife, unless it happens that there are girls in the family who have been taught to assist the mother, while there are no boys large enough to help the father. If the farmer lives in a community where no white girls will work out and where no darkeys are to be had, then the best thing that he can do is to let her keep the handiest boy they have in the house to assist her with the heavy work. I have never known of it hurting a boy a particle to have a practical knowledge of housework.

"But surely, in a family where baby number twelve is in the crib, there are girls large enough to assist in the housework if no other help is to be had. If the boys have to help their father with his work, it is only just that the girls should help their mother. At no other time and place will they acquire practical knowledge of the details of household economy and management so easily, as in their mother's home. And in this country, where there is so little hereditary wealth, it is essential that every girl should thoroughly understand domestic affairs.

"One evil effect of a mother being such a drudge, is that when her sons go into homes of their own, some of them without doubt will expect their wives to 'do as mother did,' and the girls, well, what will they not be tempted to do to escape a life of such drudgery as their mothers had.

"People who delight in drawing unfair comparisons always select overworked women, and say something like this: 'Yes, farmer's wife is only another name for slave. They work the hardest, and have the least time and money to use for rest and recreation. They have no time and money for travel, or books, or any other kind of pleasure. They have nothing but one eternal round of work, work, and save, save, until the grave gives them rest, or they become disabled.'

"I have spent my whole life upon a farm and have seen much of farm life in many states, but I have never yet seen any need of making such a drudge of woman upon the farm as E. B. portrays. That many do so, does not justify the practice. In every instance that has come under my notice, it has been the result of selfishness or thoughtlessness, and in a few instances, of gross brutality. But these characteristics of human nature are not indigenous to the farm. No humane man allows his farm animals to be overworked, much less ought he to allow his wife, the mother of little children, to undertake such an unjust portion of labor.

"The talk about the overtasked farmer's wife being a martyr, and getting her reward only in the future, will not benefit her family and the world half so much as it would for her to demand simple justice at the hands of her family, and teach them that the

CHAMBER, MANTEL, AND TOILET COVERS

White Marseilles, thin *pique* or Allendale quilting, edged with white ball, or twisted fringe, makes nice covers for toilet stands, or chamber mantels, especially where cottage furniture is used. If the furniture is very handsome black walnut, or rosewood, elegant mantel covers may be made by tacking patent maroon velvet on a thin board, and edging it with bullion fringe.

wife and mother has rights which it is their duty to recognize and respect, and that one of those rights is the opportunity to obtain rest and recreation."

—*The Household*
MARCH 1883

DEAR SISTERS:—How the Band has grown! I wonder if our editor is not proud of his great family. What industrious house-keepers they are, and how well united! Not a word of slander—not a bit of envy or jealousy in any of these monthly "sociables," but all are friendly, and seem desirous of imparting something for the general good of the sisterhood. Occasionally one comes in and makes a speech spiced with a little indignation, but after "freeing her mind," she is all right, and loving and lovable again, and the general harmony is not disturbed. ...

—Olive Oldstyle

Girls and Ox Team on the Road. Frank Leslie's Illustrated Newspaper, *April 30, 1859.*

The next three excerpts concern the dilemma of women who lacked the aptitude for housekeeping. Since homemaking was considered part of woman's nature, not merely something that she did, women such as these became vulnerable to oppressive censure. Hence the tentative stances and almost desperate entreaties. Note especially the letter from a Southern woman with its unstated conclusion: Women are the new slaves.

People generally think that all women, young and old, whatever their taste, in whatever direction their talent lies, ought to do housework. If a young man has a taste for any particular vocation, he is expected to follow it, and he is awarded great commendation for proficiency in that vocation, no matter how little he may know of anything else. If he takes naturally to journalism, it is not considered his duty to work with hoe and spade all his life. But custom and prejudices have marked out one vocation for women and that is housework, and unless she excels in this she receives wholesale denunciation.

Men are apt to sneer at a woman who is inefficient in household duties, but did man ever think that if his own sex were to follow any one special business there might be some who would prove incompetent? For instance, should Agriculture be laid down as the only God-allotted sphere of man, should we not be likely to see as great a number of slack farmers as we do now of housekeepers? We expect man to attain an excellence in one direction only, namely, one for which he has a particular taste. Is it not insulting, then, to require that all women who, from time immemorial, have had almost no advantages of education compared with men, and many of them who already excel in some departments of learning, should attain the very maximum of excellence in housewifery for which some have no taste?

Of course we do not deny that it is better to be a good housekeeper than a poor one, but truly no one ought to expect all women to like housekeeping equally well. It will be a great lesson when people learn that women have as noble aspirations as ever beat within the breast of any man. Every far-sighted person can see that there is as much difficulty in the tastes of women as in those of men, and he who knows it not, understands not human nature aright.

—*The Household*
VOL. V, 1872

HOW TO MAKE A BIRD

Take a good-sized cork for the body of the bird, cut two wooden toothpicks of equal lengths for the legs; a third one cut shorter and stuck into one end slanting will serve for the neck. Make the head of a piece of beeswax or bread rolled into a ball, and take the sharp end of a toothpick for the beak, using bright glass beads for eyes. Take a long feather for the tail and two shorter ones for the wings. Cut a large cork in half and fasten the legs in the rounded side, making a stand for this comical bird, which may be varied in many ways by the addition of feathers.

COFFEE-BAG RUG

Cut the coffee-bag—if not procurable, any coarse sacking may be substituted—into the size and shape desired; then cut pieces of wool into strips half an inch wide, and, with a coarse needle, darn them in and out lengthwise through the material, not drawing them flat to the foundation, but leaving loops nearly an inch in height between each stitch. Taste in arranging the colors is of course needed. After the darning is finished, the whole surface is evenly clipped. A very pretty style is to make a black border, and fill in the centre with grey, dotted at intervals with circles of blue or scarlet. Or the centre may be darned haphazard with a variety of bright colors. Other combinations will suggest themselves.

A VOICE FROM KENTUCKY

For many, many years Kentucky enjoyed a widespread admiration for her prosperous, beautiful homes, and her open-hearted, generous people. Even when her southern sisters were bleeding under the scourge of warfare, a happy destiny seemed to weave a protecting mantle about her, and when the dark cloud cleared away her soil showed only an occasional foot-print, here and there, of the iron-hoofed war horse.

But not only in devastated towns and ruined homesteads are we to look for the real and more lasting effects of a great national struggle, and like all the states that, actively or passively, participated in perpetuating that dark blot which lay for long years on our country, Kentucky has realized a great internal change, felt far more within the homes and hearts of her people than appears outwardly. It is in the rural districts, in the beautiful country homes that this radical difference is most perceptible, and where may be most plainly read the plaintive legend, "Times are changed."

And is it necessary to say that it is the housewives, the women of the south upon whom these changes have fallen with effects the most real and palpable. Born, irresponsibly, under a system that wove invisible chains of inactivity and dependence around the hands that held the key of real shackles enslaving others, the war found and left the southern woman wholly unfitted to cope with the practical, actual duties of the household, and characterized by a guiltless ignorance of all such matters, wholly incomprehensible to her northern sisters, trained from childhood in the bracing atmosphere of wholesome activity.

And with the abrupt termination of that system, there fell, with no previous preparation, upon weak shoulders and delicate hands a burden of domestic care augmented a hundred fold by long years of indulgence in superficial luxuries now grown to necessities. The household machinery that had run so smoothly for generations back ceased suddenly, to be replaced by hands sadly inadequate to the task both in strength and skill.

But, if the heroism of southern men has gained a place in immortal song and story, not less may be said for the southern woman of the womanly bravery with which she has met and borne her heavy portion.

Not sitting down with folded hands to mourn the past or grieve for lost comforts, she has with patient disregard of physical disability, and of all fastidious instincts instilled by time and custom, nobly put her shoulder to the household wheel, meeting every dictate of necessity with a calm and womanly will. Throughout this southern country of ours it is but a common sight to meet women who had reached gray hairs never having made a cup of coffee, broiled a steak or kneaded a loaf of bread; women who all their life having sat or presided at tables laden with every delicacy, yet who with her own hands could not have concocted a single dish. Can you wonder, then, that when with the same hospitable, generous customs still existing, with the same demands that characterized the old regime still to be met, the weight of household care should indeed have fallen heavily amid conditions that had altered all things else, leaving now those to execute who were accustomed merely to order and be obeyed.

Never shall I forget the first time in all my life that I stood in my kitchen without a servant, large or small, about "the place," helpless in the truest sense of the word.

We were eight in family, myself and husband, a grown son and daughter, and four boys all large enough to render general assistance; so you would have thought the situation not a very dreadful one, nor do I think we should have been so much dismayed when the last domestic heartlessly quitted the premises, had not the unexpected intelligence arrived simultaneously that two gentlemen would drive a distance of thirty miles to take supper and spend the night with us. This complicated matters considerably, for our visitors would arrive with ravenous appetites after such a ride on an intensely cold day, and a suitable meal must be provided, and their comfort be considered generally.

Jennie, my daughter, looked at me, and I looked at Jennie, while my husband and oldest son looked compassionately at us both, visions of kitchen duties and perplexities rising before me. We were miles from a bakery, a confectioner, or a market house, and not a friendly or a mercenary hand nearer to lend the sorely needed aid. There was evidently nothing to be done but to go bravely to the seat of war and begin operations.

"O, we will have no difficulty," I said reassuringly, "Jennie and I would be helpless simpletons indeed could we not get a simple meal for only ourselves and two visitors."

My husband looked infinitely relieved, but when I have detailed results, dear readers, results which to my mortification, I assure you to be perfectly true, you will not wonder that even while speaking, there was a vague sense of misgiving deep in my heart.

HOUSEKEEPER'S ALPHABET

APPLES—Keep in dry place, as cool as possible without freezing.
BROOMS—Hang in the cellar-way to keep soft and pliant.
CRANBERRIES—Keep under water, in cellar; change water monthly.
DISH of hot water set in oven prevents cakes, etc. from scorching.
ECONOMIZE time, health, and means, and you will never beg.
FLOUR—Keep cool, dry, and securely covered.
GLASS—Clean with a quart of water mixed with table-spoon of ammonia.
HERBS—Gather when beginning to blossom; keep in paper sacks.
INK STAINS—Wet with spirits turpentine; after three hours, rub well.
JARS—To prevent, coax "husband" to buy "Buckeye Cookery."
KEEP an account of all supplies, with cost and date when purchased.
LOVE lightens labor.
MONEY—Count carefully when you receive change.

Crowding the stove with fuel with more regard to the temperature without than the rules of baking, we were already on the scene of action.

"What shall we have, mother?" asked Jennie.

"Only the simplest tea, my dear," I answered promptly; "tea and coffee, biscuit, nice corn batter bread and broiled ham; the gentlemen can surely make out with that."

Easy enough it was to enumerate the few and unpretentious dishes, but now came the tug of war.

"Let us make the corn bread first," suggested Jennie. "I have an idea it takes longer to bake than biscuit."

So together we began with careful measurements and anxious solicitude the preparation of that bread dear to the Kentucky heart, and although by no means quite certain of success, we soon placed it proudly in the oven.

"Now the tea and coffee," suggested my aide-de-camp again, and readily assenting, we turned our attention to these beverages.

"How much tea, mother?" asked Jennie.

"We only need two cups," I answered, meditatively, "but it must be good and strong; about half a teacup of tea, I should say, and a pint of water."

In they went, and the coffee being next most cautiously measured by thoughtful guessing as to quantity, the two were soon boiling away and exhaling unmistakable fragrance. The ham was sliced thin and placed in a skillet on the rear of the stove with an indefinite idea of being in readiness, and we turned to the formidable biscuit, naturally the chief dependence of the supper table. I will say just here that in a southern household the wheat bread principally relied on and most generally used is the kind known as beaten biscuit, the *modus operandi* of which I am now competent to impart to any one desirous of learning. It is certainly a very delightful bread and most simple in construction, but, as I have found by personal experience, dependent for excellence upon a certain sleight of hand or skill by no means possessed by Jennie or myself at the time to which I refer. Briskly we set to work administering a very full measure of salt, a very scant allowance of lard, wholly disproportionate quantities of flour and water, and then began the process of beating as we had seen old Aunt Dinah do many a day.

I beat, and Jennie beat, and all the four boys took their turn at beating, and still the obstinate dough would not assume the whiteness and lightness we deemed necessary. The evening was growing on apace, the guests had arrived and were waiting patiently and hungrily for supper, my husband and Guy looked in occasionally with that wistful look that often follows in the course of several hours, a lunch dinner, and I could only encourage them by the promise that "it would not be long now.

And finally the biscuit were ready for the oven, though I saw Jennie had rolled them far too thin, and left them forlorn looking in general; but there was no time to remedy palpable errors now, so we opened the door silently. O, horrors! In our busy preoccupation we had entirely forgotten the corn bread in the red-hot stove, and now only a black scorched form met our dismayed eyes.

"O dear, dear!" cried Jennie, "they will have to do as best they can with biscuit."

I tried to meet the accident as philosophically as possible, but my courage was fast failing. Completely choked with the superfluity of fuel, the stove by this time began giving all manner of trouble, and naturally, the more we poked and stirred, the worse it grew. It seemed as though those biscuit would never bake, but were slowly drying up, evidently becoming each moment less palatable and tempting both in appearance and probable taste.

A hard white crust at last warranted us, however, in removing them, and with discouraged mien I began placing them as neatly as I could on the plates, while Jennie brought a dish for the ham.

"O, mother, it is just as hard and dry as the chips under the stove!" she cried, "do look at it please!"

And of what avail was my perplexed, hopeless gaze. I had simply been ignorant that a little lard and the brief action of fire were necessary to make meat what it should be, but there was nothing now to be done but to grace my table with this additional, scarce edible dish.

"Pour out the tea, Jennie," I said in a tone of distress, but as the peculiar looking beverage flowed from the teapot, I could but gaze wonderingly at it; both in color and odor it was scarcely recognizable, a fact not to be wondered at if my measurements are remembered. I said nothing but turned to the coffee; surely the fates were in arms against me! The coffee had slowly boiled away till scarce two cups were to be drained from the slightly scorched grounds.

NUTMEGS—Prick with a pin, and if good, oil will run out.

ORANGE and lemon peel—Dry, pound, and keep in corked bottles.

PARSNIPS—Keep in ground until spring.

QUICKSILVER and white of an egg destroys bedbugs.

RICE—Select large, with a clear, fresh look; old rice may have insects.

SUGAR—For general family use, the granulated is best.

TEA—Equal parts of Japan and green are as good as English breakfast.

USE a cement made of ashes, salt, and water for cracks in stove.

VARIETY is the best culinary spice.

WATCH your back yard for dirt and bones.

XANTIPPE was a scold. Don t imitate her.

YOUTH is best preserved by a cheerful temper.

ZINC-LINED sinks are better than wooden ones.

& regulate the clock by your husband's watch, and in all apportionments of time remember the Giver.

"Just pour in hot water, mother," said Jennie in low tones of desperation, "and I won't take any, and I'll tell the boys to eat very sparingly to-night."

And this was the supper to which at a late hour we and our hungry friends sat down. Burnt corn bread, flinty, miserably baked biscuit, ham like chips, tea of a strength that would have been dangerous could it have been swallowed, and coffee deficient in quantity and quality.

Can you imagine my feelings as I sat in my chair endeavoring to appear the agreeable hostess, dispensing reputed hospitality? We rose from the table as hungry as we sat down, and I am persuaded our guests made an early move for bed to seek forgetfulness in sleep, while the household exchanged a weary goodnight as we gloomily thought of the morrow.

—L. L. R
The Household
VOL. XV, 1882

TO BLEACH STRAW HATS, ETC.

Straw hats and bonnets are bleached by putting them, previously washed in pure water, in a box with burning sulphur; the fumes which arise unite with the water on the bonnets, and the sulphurous acid thus formed, bleaches them.

Happy is the woman born with that mysterious gift called "Faculty." Her life is serene with the calmness of conscious power. The innate depravity and malice of all household goods and implements never dares show itself to her. Every atom of her domestic machinery knows its appropriate niche, and it is simply impossible that it should ever be elsewhere. Her rooms are beautiful in the perfect order and spotlessness of every article therein; and her table is a marvel of snowy damask, glittering china and silver, and incomparable viands.

All this is the work of her own hands for the superlative housekeeper is apt to dispense with the blundering aid of Bridget and Katy. More wonderful still, she is never hurried—always has plenty of time for reading, writing, or the demands of society. Marvelous are her doings in the eyes of the unfortunate whom fate has placed in the position of housewife, but whom nature intended for something entirely different. "She is no housekeeper," is the half pitying, half scornful remark of her friends, and she is herself conscious of the humiliating fact; a fact the more painful to her, because she often has an intense admiration for a clean, well arranged, well ordered home, and a shuddering antipathy for its opposite.

But how is she to do the creative work of evolving order out of chaos, when the very pans and kettles know she is incapable of ruling them? The manner in which her culinary arrangements display total depravity, would almost make one believe in the existence of malicious kitchen brownies inviting them to their wicked behavior. Neither prayers, entreaties, nor added yeast can induce her bread to rise at the proper time; and when it is sadly put away, unbaked, because of its heaviness, then in the night when nobody expects or wants it to rise, it overflows the tins, spreads itself over the table, and is happy if it can drip on the floor. It would never dare play such a practical joke on the housekeeper with "faculty."

Every movable article in the house is constantly getting in the way when not wanted, and persistently hiding for the purpose of occasioning a search. This unsuccessful housekeeper works hard, because her work is always at a disadvantage and is harassed constantly with the thought of tasks still undone. Servants without a skillful guiding hand only add to the general confusion. Is this woman's life a total failure because she is an incompetent housekeeper? Do we not all know women who are ministering angels to the sick, or whose cheerful temper, brilliant conversation, or generous sympathy, make their presence eagerly welcomed anywhere, but whose peculiar housekeeping excites the smiles of their friends and the sneers of their enemies?

What can be done for these unfortunates? Shall they give up a work for which they are not fitted, and apply themselves to that which they can do well? In many cases this is impossible. Or, can they, having no liking for the work, take up the burden of housekeeping, and by diligent study of THE HOUSEHOLD and patient daily effort finally attain the highest success? We will wait for a reply.

—Grace R. Bartholomew
The Household
VOL. XI, 1878

DRAUGHTS FOR THE FEET

Take a large leaf from the horseradish plant, and cut out the hard fibres that run through the leaf; place it on a hot shovel for a moment to soften it, fold it, and fasten it closely in the hollow of the foot by a close bandage.

Burdock leaves, cabbage leaves, and mullein leaves are used in the same manner, to alleviate pain and promote perspiration.

Garlics are also made for draughts by pounding them, placing them on a hot tin plate for a moment to sweat them, and binding them closely to the hollow of the foot by a cloth bandage.

Draughts of onions, for infants, are made by roasting onions in hot ashes, and, when they are quite soft, peeling off the outside, mashing them, and applying them on a cloth as usual.

The value of a wife's duties in relation to her husband's work was a subject of misunderstanding and contention. Her attempts to communicate some sense of what she was required to do and its effects on the quality of her life were rarely credited and often the subject of derision.

Man's Way and Woman's Way

After harvest, as usual, the voice of the steam-thresher was heard in the land, and one afternoon, after the great, odd, awkward thing had, with a hiss and a screech, invaded our domain, and settled itself to its task of devouring the wheatstacks behind the orchard, I was rolled out in my chair to watch the operation—the first time for many years such a thing has been possible to me. It was a sight worth seeing, and I felt well repaid for my trouble.

Men think it pays to have plenty of help on such occasions. It does pay. But when it comes to woman's work, they look at the matter in a totally different light.

This is not because farmers, or other men, wish their wives and daughters to work themselves sick. They have no idea they are making drudges of their dear ones, and taking all pleasure out of their lives. On the contrary, the good men usually have the idea that they are the most indulgent of husbands and fathers. If you were to penetrate to the inmost thoughts of their hearts, you would probably find that in their eyes "the women folks" have, on the whole, a very easy time of it. They have only to "get the meals on," and "do a few chores round," and have plenty of time to play, or "fix themselves up," which "fixing up" is made to include the family sewing, and all tidying of the house of course.

Men have no conception of what is preliminary to "getting the meals on," and making the house pleasant and cool and restful for tired and hungry fieldworkers. They do not sympathize with the house-worker's fatigue, because they do not understand its cause. If compelled to notice it, they say, "Well, let things go." The weary woman wonders and asks what she shall let go.

"Oh, something. There's no need of getting so tired. I don't see what there is to be tired about."

The next remark may very likely be that there will be extra hands to dinner, wanted at twelve sharp, which fact makes necessary new and laborious arrangements.

It seems a little strange that the average man should be so impressed with the idea that household work is of little consequence, when as soon as the exhausted workers are forced to let things go, he is the first to feel the discomfort and inconvenience that arises. The house is in confusion; meals are irregular; the men wander about seeking rest and finding none, until health comes back to the stricken household, and the old order of things begins again—no lesson learned.

Men are apt to think housework wholly consists in getting meals, and getting meals consists in putting a few things on the table. No wonder they do not see the necessity for getting tired

NIGHTMARE

This is a complaint which comes when the sleep is disturbed. It is the dreaming of something horrible and the person feels that it is something from which he cannot escape but is the victim. He attempts to scream for help but usually his effort is in vain. Nervous and overworked people are especially subject to it. It is due to poor circulation. It is not only unpleasant but dangerous. The best remedy is to bathe each morning in cold water on arising, eat plain foods, little or no meat, tea or coffee, and breathe deeply for fifteen minutes each night before retiring.

—B. S. Y.

over that, especially as they measure the labor by their own strength, not taking into consideration the weaker muscles and nerves of women and girls.

They do not stop to think how their own toil is sweetened to them by the fact that it is out of doors. The broad, sweet face of nature is ever before them, and, although they may not realize how its soothing, calming influence helps them, the influence is at work, the help is afforded, nevertheless. The sun may be hot, but there is a fresh breeze blowing. Even if sultry, the heat is very different from the stove heat in the vitiated air of the house. When the farmer follows his plow, his eyes rest on long reaches of meadow or wood or upland; when he whets his scythe, or rides on his mower, his nostrils catch the breath of clover blooms, wafted by the same refreshing breeze that cools his heated forehead. The blue sky is above him, fields and woods before him, sweet, pure, fragrant air about him, and all that gentle, indefinable influence of the free, open country at work upon him, affecting him, whether he knows it or not.

The women, who, by the greater sensitiveness and impressibility of their nature, need even more than he this soothing, calming influence, are shut within the four walls of the usual farm-house kitchen, sweltering in the close, stove heat, necessary to baking and broiling, breathing in the hot air, perfumed only by cooking meat and vegetables, giving many a longing glance through the window or open door, but knowing that liberty to bathe in the delights lying just outside is not for them.

A few years ago I saw in one of our popular magazines an article deploring the tendency of young people to leave the country to seek employment in cities, drawing a dark picture of the life and final fate of many a young girl who, attracted by the glitter and dash of town life, foolishly leaves her country home and friends in the hope of a brilliant future elsewhere. This was illustrated by a picture entitled, "The home she might have had," a tree-shadowed, quaint old farm-house. In a hammock slung between the trees before the house reclines a young woman in flowing robes, her baby in her arms, the image of happy leisure.

This is a very pretty idea; but how about its truth? How many farmers' wives have time to lie in hammocks with their babies, even on Sunday—that day of rest to all except women? Even on Sunday the meals must be prepared, the house put in order, and the children kept tidy.

EGG PAPER

Soft, tough paper cut to fit jars, and dipped in a saucer of white of egg, put over steamed jars of fruit or preserves, will keep them better than all the late inventions. When the jars and fruit are scalded hot as possible, it will keep them nicely. For jellies and all kinds of pickles, it makes a cheap, convenient cover. The paper must turn over the rim of the jar.

169

If help enough were provided for the house so that the work might pass off naturally, steadily, smoothly, without hurry, as man's work does, women could spend more time out of doors, and would become, in consequence, healthier and happier, and so more agreeable and lovable. They would learn to love the farm-life, and be in no haste to leave it. For there is no life on earth so sweet and independent, so filled with pure interests and pleasures, as the country life, if made for both men and women what it ought to be, and what it might be.

—Helen Herbert
The Household
SEPTEMBER 1884

How Much Is a Wife Worth?

No man will deny that a good wife is a treasure. Her care and labor certainly secure him many comforts; but how much would he consider them worth in dollars and cents? It is a great comfort to a man to have his three meals properly cooked and prepared at hours that suit his convenience. He can swallow a dinner in twenty or thirty minutes that it has taken most of the wife's forenoon to prepare. He thinks it a good dinner; but how high an estimate, think you, would he put upon the labor of preparing it if required to state the worth in money?

American Progress.
Chrome Lithograph, 1872.
Library of Congress.

With what astonishment and disgust would he look upon his table if set with dishes that had not been washed since last used; but how high a money value would he be willing to put upon the one unromantic item of washing dishes, which, nevertheless, takes so large a share of woman's time?

With what satisfaction he puts on the clean, smoothly ironed shirt and his nicely darned socks! They do not look much like the ones he pulls off to throw into the wash. Some one has had to rub pretty smartly to get the dirt all out; some one strained over the hot flat-irons to make the shirt so glossy; some one spent an hour, perhaps while he slept, to darn those unsightly holes in the heels of those stockings. And if a farmer it was his wife, most probably that did it all; and not this week only, but every week as sure as the weeks come round. Now he does appreciate cleanliness, notwithstanding his protestations against washing days and house-cleaning; does he own that it is worth anything in money if done by his wife?

Then comes the care of the milk and butter. Every day it must be attended to at the proper time, the cream churned, the butter made and carefully worked and salted. He is proud that his wife makes good butter, and quite happy to have customers tell him, 'You have the best butter of any one around here.' But then, are not the cows his? Does he not furnish the food? Does he not milk and take care of them? Is her part really worth anything in dollars and cents?

Then, again, her energies are taxed early and late in the care of her children. She is, of course, an interested party here; but then she don't pretend to own but half a share. Is it really worth nothing to soothe, amuse, correct, teach and watch over his half of the little folks as her own? This is real brain-work. Where is the man who will say that this care of their children does not require all a woman's wit and wisdom? But if asked to put a pecuniary value upon this part of a wife's and mother's care and labor, to how high a figure think you it would amount?

A farmer's wife, who really does her own work, or faithfully oversees its being done, which is by far the most trying part, has no easy task; but we would ask for her only what is justly due her. If there is any standard by which her services can be rightly estimated, we would like to know it. We wish to know whether there be any surplus in her favor—whether when she asks for a few dollars for some purpose not strictly necessary (a pocket book for

AN OX'S GALL WILL SET ANY COLOR

silk, cotton, or woollen. I have seen the colors of calico, which faded at one washing, fixed by it. Where one lives near a slaughterhouse, it is worth while to buy cheap, fading goods, and set them in this way. The gall can be bought for a few cents. Get out all the liquid, and cork it up in a large phial. One large spoonful of this in a gallon of warm water is sufficient. This is likewise excellent for taking out spots from bombazine, bombazet, &c. After being washed in this, they look about as well as when new. It must be thoroughly stirred into the water, and not put upon the cloth. It is used without soap. After being washed in this, cloth which you want to *clean* should be washed in warm suds, without using soap.

instance), she ought to feel that she is asking for her husband's hard-earned means, or whether she has a right to feel that it is her due? How much must a wife credit to her husband's generosity? How much use with a clear conscience as her own faithfully earned portion of their joint labors?

Young men will do wisely to give this matter a serious thought, lest they make the mistake of taking a wife's labor and attentions as a matter of course, as a right, instead of feeling that, with his name, he gave his wife an equal right to his cares and labors, joys and sorrows, and also an equal right to a proper use of the money which she has done her part to earn or accumulate. A wife, a farmer's wife particularly, has too much toil and perpetual watchfulness to make her life desirable, if, with it all, she is to be considered a beggar, a recipient of charity instead of a joint partner with her husband in all that he has.

—Mrs. H. W. Beecher

The Perplexed Housekeeper's Soliloquy

I wish I had a dozen pairs
Of hands, this very minute;
I'd soon put all these things to rights—
The very deuce is in it!

Here's a big washing to be done,
One pair of hands to do it,
Sheets, shirts, and stockings, coats and pants,
How will I e'er get through it?

Dinner to get for six or more,
No loaf left o'er from Sunday;
And baby cross as he can live,
He's always so on Monday.

And there's the cream, 'tis getting sour,
And must forthwith be churning,
And here's Bob wants a button on—
Which way shall I be turning?

'Tis time the meat was in the pot,
The bread was worked for baking,
The clothes were taken from the boil—
Oh dear! the baby's waking!

Hush, baby dear! there, hush-sh-sh!
I wish he'd sleep a little,
'Till I could run and get some wood,
To hurry up the kettle.

Oh dear! oh dear! if P—comes home,
And finds things in this pother,
He'll just begin and tell me all
About his tidy mother!

How nice her kitchen used to be,
Her dinner always ready,
Exactly when the noon bell rang—
Hush, hush, dear little Freddy.

And then will come some hasty word,
Right out before I'm thinking,—
They say that hasty words from wives,
Set sober men to drinking.

Now isn't that a great idea,
That men should take to sinning,
Because a weary, half-sick wife,
Can't always smile so winning?

When I was young I used to earn
My living without trouble,
Had clothes and pocket money, too,
And hours of leisure double.

I never dreamed of such a fate,
When I a-lass! was courted—
Wife, mother, nurse, seamstress, cook, housekeeper,
chambermaid, laundress, dairy woman, and scrub
generally, doing the work of six,
For the sake of being supported!

—*F. D. Gage*
The Household
1868

Most often it was the women themselves who made sure that "accepted standards" were maintained and hardships accepted with cheer and optimism.

WAS SHE TO BLAME?

"I do declare," exclaimed Mrs. John Smith, "if that Mrs. Marshall isn't the most shiftless woman I ever knew! She's the poorest housekeeper in the village."

"Yes!" chimes in Mrs. Jones, "she is the miserablest wife ever a man had. Who wonders her husband has no energy?"

"Not I!" responds Mrs. Smith, "he never has a dinner fit to be eaten, nor a room fit to sit down in when his work is done. His clothes are never mended until it is too late to make them look nice, and the children are always in a squall when he comes home. Poor man! I pity him from the bottom of my heart."

Whether the little sigh that followed this tirade, did come from the bottom of her heart we leave the reader to judge. It was a well-known fact, that before the aforesaid Mr. Marshall met pretty Lizzie Lewis, he had been a welcome guest at the house of Mrs. Smith's father, and it had been currently reported in the village, that John Smith had been accepted, in very chagrin, when the more favored lover proved inconstant.

These things were well known in the sewing circle, where all this gossip was going on, but no one ventured on opposing remarks, for Mrs. Smith was the wife of one of the few men of comparative wealth that the little village possessed. "Comparative," for men are deemed immensely rich in a small town or village, whose property would not amount to a year's comfortable income in a city.

Mrs. Foster at whose house the sewing circle was holding its session, was a new comer in the village. She was a lady of high culture and sympathising heart. Being herself a housekeeper of undoubted excellence, she could afford to defend one whose character in this respect was assailed.

"Come! come! ladies," said she with a thoughtful smile, "you are cutting up that poor woman's reputation faster than you do the pieces for that quilt. Isn't it almost time to be sewing them all together again? It may be pleasanter work, besides being more serviceable."

Some received the gentle rebuke kindly, as it was intended; a few, among whom were included Mrs. Smith, seemed inclined to resent and debate the matter.

"Well, for my part," said Mrs. Smith tartly, "I think if a woman neglects her husband and children in that way, she must expect to be talked about."

A VARNISH TO PREVENT THE RAYS OF THE SUN FROM PASSING THROUGH WINDOW OR OTHER GLASS

Pound gum tragacanth into powder, and put it to dissolve for twenty-four hours in whites of eggs, well beaten. Lay a coat of this on your glass with a soft brush, and let it dry.

"Are you sure she does neglect her husband and children?" asked Mrs. Foster quietly.

"Sure!" was the indignant reply, "Are not the children always ragged and dirty? And don't he always have to wait for his dinner, and hold a squalling baby while she hurries it up?"

"As for the children," said Mrs. Foster, now really roused for the defense, "I happen to know, that the little crowd are all carefully bathed every morning, at all seasons, and in hot weather every night before retiring. It is not their mother's fault that they dig in the dirt all day, while she is busy with other work, and their rosy cheeks and bright eyes would indicate that they are far better off, than those who are *kept clean* by being deprived of air and exercise. With regard to the husband, I would simply ask, if it is such a hardship for him to amuse his own baby a half-hour's time while his overtasked wife hurries up the family dinner? Had we not better give a little pity to her, who is obliged to take care of it all day in the midst of so much work, and all night, when she so much needs rest."

"I declare I never thought of that," murmured several ladies with pitying looks.

"She might, at least, wash her own dress once in a while," spitefully replied Mrs. Smith.

"It would be very easy for you, Mrs. Smith," responded the defender of the absent, "to order your servant to wash a calico dress, that is, if you ever condescended to wear one. It is not quite so easy for a poor woman who has but the one cheap print, to keep it always clean and whole, in the midst of so much dirty work, and with that little crowd of children claiming every moment's time."

"I declare, Mrs. Foster, you are quite a Woman's Right's woman!" said Mrs. Jones, anxious to turn the conversation, and hide Mrs. Smith's too apparent discomfiture.

"Any kind of rights, you please, Mrs. Jones," said Mrs. Foster, smilingly, "so they be really *rights,* and not usurpations. I will not even restrict you to *human* rights, as some have done, for even the birds of heaven, and the beasts of earth, have their rights also, as sacred in the eye of their Maker as are our own. The woman who gives her whole time to her family, and even overtasks her slender stock of physical strength for them, while her brain is constantly occupied with a routine of petty economies, and her temper grows irritable through want of sleep and the constant strain upon her nervous system, is often condemned by us as a poor housekeeper, because she cannot work the miracle of accomplishing certain desirable results with insufficient means. Meanwhile, other women, with ample means, few or no children, and every kind of convenient arrangement in their houses, perhaps well-trained servants, or womanly daughters to assist, are complimented as capable housekeepers because neatness and order reign in their households.

"Meanwhile the careless or indolent husband, who spends money enough for tobacco in a few weeks to buy his wife a decent dress, or in a few months a sewing machine, a wringer or some other assistant in her labor; and who wastes time enough in lounging round smoking the vile weed, to lend her a helping hand occasionally when some heavy work is to be done, is really pitied as a martyr, because he has to wait half an hour for his dinner, or tend the worrysome child whose nerves have been tuned to agony by that very tobacco smoke."

"Dear me! Mrs. Foster," laughed some of the ladies, "what a public lecturer you would make!"

"I should pity your husband," said another, "if he were a user of tobacco."

"Or if he ever offended you in any way," sneered a simpering old maid, who believed that the least difference in opinion was a proof of matrimonial infelicity.

—Mrs. Julia A. Carney
The Household
VOL. III, 1870

A DAINTY ADDITION TO ANY ROOM

is one of the now popular rose-jars. A delightful potpourri can be made by the following tested recipe:

1/2 peck of rose leaves
1/2 pound of common salt
1/2 pound of common brown
    sugar
1 oz. of storax
1 oz. of benzoin
1 oz. of ground orris root
1 oz. of ground cinnamon
1 oz. of ground mace
1 oz. of ground cloves

All the above are to be pounded and mixed.

Add all sorts of sweet flowers and the leaves of orange and lemon verbena, but no leaves that are not in themselves aromatic. Put the ingredients in a rose-jar and stir frequently with a *wooden* spoon.

OVERLOOKED

"Ha, ha, ha!" Aunt Patty laughed a loud, good-natured laugh that was just like her cheerful, energetic self, and looking up I saw her coming toward me, her broad face brimfull of merriment, while she held out an empty cup in one reddened hand.

"Ha, ha, ha! If that don't beat me! You see, I took a cup from the shelf just now to get some short'nin' for my cake;—a little short'nin' makes this kind o' cake better, you know. Wall, when I got into the buttry, I found out I'd forgot my knife; so I went back after that, and then I couldn't find my cup nowhere. I looked all round in the buttry, then I come back and hunted my table over, but to find it I couldn't; so I went to the cupboard after another, and here I'd had the cup right in my hand all the time! Ha, ha, ha!"

I laughed with her a little, and then she walked off, saying to herself, "I'm growin' forgitful, awful forgitful."

Aunt Patty is not so unlike the rest of the world after all, I thought to myself: and this little incident over which she is so merry is just what we are all doing, I fear.

The world is teeming with dissatisfied spirits; we find them everywhere, flitting hither and thither, much like aunt Patty, looking for cups of happiness, seeking for something that shall bring peace and delight. Oh, these searchings would not be always so sadly disappointing if we did not keep overlooking our blessings so, reaching beyond the treasures that lie at our feet while we are vaguely longing for others which are greater. Restless mortals, pursuing uncertain phantoms of earthly joy, how often do we hold in our hands the very things we covet, the very joys and blessings that our souls are craving. Heart-sore and foot-sore we go through the world, rushing eagerly on after some far-off vision of excellence, and how seldom do we look into the present for the realization of these blissful dreams! Always thirsting, we still pass unheeded the myriad fountains that are gushing up in our pathway; always hungering we still look beyond the rich repasts which are spread before us every day.

Ah, why is it that we spend our strength for that which profiteth not? Why are we never satisfied? Why, save that the scales of unbelief and ingratitude are clinging to our eyes, making us so blind that we cannot see the blessings that are within our reach; so blind and so ignorant that we do not see we already have in our hands just what we need to fill up the measure of our bliss, do not know that in the common things which we thrust aside are the elements of just that meat which our souls are craving.

Thus it is that we keep straining our darkened eyes to catch glimpses of brighter days, days that we fancy belong to the dim, golden sometime, and never, never see them; that we keep turning away from the daily bread which is given us, and are always, always famishing.

Blinded and deluded, must we go on in this frantic, thankless search? Must we keep plodding along this dreary thoroughfare all our days? Nay, verily, so long as the voice of Him whose earthly mission was to open the eyes of the blind is calling to us, "Behold, I show unto you a more excellent way." We have only to lift up our aching eyes that the films may be wiped away from them; have only to inquire "Whither," with willing and obedient minds, that we may find that glorious highway.

Then, with purified visions, shall we see clearly to gather up the sweet and beautiful treasures that are thickly scattered all along our pathways. Every life is full of these precious fragments, needing but the touch of a thankful, reverent heart to form them into a glorious pattern; and there is no heritage so overshadowed by tempest clouds, so embittered by disappointments, or so narrow in its round of stale, commonplace experience, that it may not yield abundant cheer and satisfaction.

The duties which seem to us very irksome, the demands which are stern, even our heavy burdens and allotments, these are our disguised blessings, our fountains of joy that shall fill our lives with richness and verdure.

Yes, our very trials and griefs are blessed in their ministry, drawing us nearer God; and all the little cares that fill up our days, making a great whole, which seems grievous and often grows very tiresome, these are not the meaningless trifles which we sometimes think they are, not empty cups yielding no satisfaction, but filled with a sweetness which is ready to make our lives fragrant.

When we learn that true excellence lies not beyond the circle of our common spheres, that true nobility and pure happiness seek the level of our humblest walks; when we learn to look below the level of our superficial lives into the sparkling undercurrent that imparts to them a glad vitality, then shall we see how all the hours are crowned with glory, how excellent and beauteous are even our plainest, most thankless duties.

Putting forth obedient hands unto the cares and claims of the present, however lowly they may seem to us, taking them up reverently and holding them in the light of our Father's love, they will surely yield us all the sweetness which our hungry souls are craving; they shall be our passports to higher homes and everlasting joys.

—A. W. Q.
The Household
VOL. III, 1870

DEAR HOUSEHOLD:—There is a little article, in the September number, entitled "The Bright Side," in which is quoted a thought from Miss Mulock, that gentle and sweetest of writers, that brings forcibly to my mind a noble, womanly woman.

Cultured, refined and of great intellectuality; strong, yet mild; patient, yet full of fire; brave, cheerful, steadfast through

TO CLEAN TURKEY CARPETS

To revive the color of a Turkey carpet, beat it well with a stick till the dust is all out, then with a lemon or sorrel juice take out the spots of ink, if the carpet be stained with any; wash it in cold water, and afterward shake out all the water from the threads of the carpet; when it is thoroughly dry rub it all over with the crumb of a hot wheat loaf, and if the weather is very fine, hang it out in the open air a night or two.

every trial; left to bear the heavy burden of direful poverty alone, her spirits never failed to meet every trying ordeal with cheerful bravery.

Often I have seen her walking the small piazza of her home, softly singing, when I knew her heart was well nigh breaking, with its load of unshared sorrow.

"Dear friend," I said to her one day, "how can you sing?"

"I must sing," she answered, "or the tears would drown out my life; besides, my little ones are so much happier when mother smiles and sings. I would not darken their lives even in the smallest degree. Little by little, as I sing, peace, rest and contentment, something akin to happiness, creeps slowly and softly into my heart. The burden of life seems less hard to bear.

"I have always found that it helps one so much through the roughest and dreariest day to sing bright and cheerful songs."

"But do you not find it very hard?"

"Yes, at first; but now it has become a habit.

Photograph by permission of Minnesota Historical Society.

"I often sing unconsciously, and thus save my face from many a sorrowful shade that would cast a cloud of gloom over my household. I heard my little child saying, one day, to her brother, 'Neddie, don't cry; that will only add to your pain. Sing, like mamma does, and then the pain will sail away into the air with the song. Perhaps it will go straight to God, and He will make it well.' How little I suspected that I was teaching my children to bear the ills of life bravely, piously and cheerfully."

If all of us HOUSEHOLD sisters would imitate this noble woman, it would lighten a little the burden of our daily duties, and smooth away the dozen daily annoyances that bring a frown to our foreheads and drawn, hard lines around our mouths.

—Myra Joe Rhesa
The Household
VOL. XXV, 1892

To the rural woman's burden of overwork must be added the special circumstances of isolation and loneliness, which she endured with the knowledge that there was little chance of escape or amelioration. Often removed geographically to remote and sparsely settled areas, tied to a house where the casual and varied contacts so often a natural part of her husband's daily rounds were limited or nonexistent, she lived in a world that was often a small and joyless box. Whatever friends, social life, contacts, or escapes were possible to her she intensely valued.

Moving on was the great American game. While the demands implied by this decision were shared by husband and wife, the choice and commitment to move often were not. Opportunity and adventure for the man could mean disorientation and dread for the woman. For someone whose existence was largely defined by the sense of community she had made, the leaving of friends, company, culture, cherished items, and associations meant demolishing the armature of life.

The need for contact and shared experience found an outlet frequently in the outpouring of letters to the widely circulated magazines. How women valued and jealously guarded their sense of sisterhood can be seen in the three letters addressed to a request by one husband for representation in "their" magazine. The fact that the editor of *Household* was a man, however, seemed never to be a question at issue.

GRANDMOTHER BROWN

And so it was that the Brown family came to Iowa.

"How did it seem to you when you got over your excitement about the gold and looked around you?" I asked Grandmother Brown.

"Oh, my heart sank. 'Don't let's unpack our goods,' I said to Dan'l. 'It looks so wild here. Let's go home.' But we had bought the farm and there we were.

"We lived there fourteen years, and I was never reconciled to it. I had never lived in the country before. The drudgery was unending. The isolation was worse. In time, we knew a few families with whom we had friendly relations, but they were very few. At first we had the Oliver Browns across the way. They were always great readers, were educated and sent their children away to school. But they were frontiersmen by nature, always moving West, and a couple of years after we came to Iowa they sold their farm and moved on.

"We had a good farm of rich black soil. But it is people that really make a country, not soil. Those who had settled in that neighborhood were of American stock, but it was poor in quality. I like to be with people who know something, who want something. One of our neighbors let three years go by before she came to see us. 'I woulda come before,' she said, 'but I heard you had Brussels carpet on the floor!' Why, she should have come to see what it was like. She was mistaken about the carpet, anyway.

"Soon after we came to our farm there was a Fourth of July celebration not far from us in a grove on Lost Creek. I packed a picnic luncheon and took my children over. Long tables were set for dinner. There was plenty to eat of a kind—but the people had no more manners than so many pigs. They stared not only at us, but particularly at the jelly cake I had set on the table. Without apology, they grabbed at my cake and gobbled it down.

"The nearest town to us was Augusta," continued Grandmother Brown. "It was about two miles away on Skunk River, a narrow winding little stream not entirely without beauty. Augusta once showed some signs of life, though not a very cultivated life. It had two mills and two blacksmith shops, and several stores. But now it's a strip of desolation, all grown up with weeds. You can't find it on the map."

"As you became prosperous, weren't you more reconciled to be on your Iowa farm?" I asked Grandmother Brown.

"No," she answered. "I took satisfaction in the improvements we had made, but it seemed to me that our life grew more burdensome each year. The family was larger. It seemed to take more strength to keep things going, and I had lost some of my courage

181

when our little Lottie died. And I couldn't see much opportunity in that part of the country for my children.

—Harriet C. Brown
Grandmother Brown's Hundred Years
1929

DEAR HOUSEHOLD:—I would like to tell the sister who wants to know how to have griddle cakes light when they come on the table, to put in one egg, or as many more as she can afford, and I stir the batter a little stiffer than my mother taught me. Mine are always good and light.

I wonder if those sisters who live in Montana and Oregon, have neighbors, or if they live almost alone, and if they are not homesick, and if there are others in Dakota, and if they like. The women that I know about, though I have not seen them, do not like, and cry half of the time. I think it is a desolate place. The wind blows so most of the time one don't dare go out. We have had a number of fine days lately, but all that were here last year say the wind blows harder in winter than in summer, and it is so cold you don't want to stay out long.

Most of the crops around this way were a failure, it was so very dry, with such hot winds, and an early frost finished the vines. Some wheat fields yielded four bushels to the acre and some twenty-one bushels, but the most ten or twelve. The largest yield will be boomed through the country as the "average yield."

If people knew just what they were coming to, there would be no such rush here as there has been. The water is bad and hard to get. Our well is forty-two feet deep, and the water tastes badly and makes us sick so we cannot drink it, but get what we use in the house, a mile away. Many have to go two miles. When there is a well with good water there are enough to patronize it. The "beautiful streams of clear water for man and beast" are scarce and muddy to a New Englander. The lakes are full of grass. My husband went fishing twice, but the fish were "out" and I was very much disappointed.

But my husband has suddenly warned me to "hurry up" and go out riding, and as it is the first time for six weeks, perhaps I had better go.

—Mrs. Ben
The Household
c. 1870

There are few social events in the life of these prairie farmers to enliven the monotony of the long winter evenings; no singing-schools, spelling-schools, debating clubs, or church gatherings. Neighborly calls are infrequent, because of the long distances which separate the farmhouses, and because, too, of the lack of homogeneity of the people. They have no common past to talk about. They were strangers to one another when they arrived in this new land, and their work and ways have not thrown them much together. Often the strangeness is intensified by differences of national origin. There are Swedes, Norwegians, Germans, French Canadians, and perhaps even such peculiar people as Finns and Icelanders, among the settlers, and the Americans come from many different States. It is hard to establish any social bond in such a mixed population, yet one and all need social intercourse, as the thing most essential to pleasant living, after food, fuel, shelter, and clothing. An alarming amount of insanity occurs in the new prairie States among farmers and their wives.

—E. V. Smalley
Atlantic Monthly
SEPTEMBER 1893

DEAR HOUSEHOLD:—As I sit by my window this evening, I would like to bring some of you that have always lived in the city, away out here in south-western Minnesota, and see what a fearful yet grand thing a prairie fire is, where the flames shoot away as if trying to reach the clouds, then a fierce gust of wind takes the cinders, and in an instant it is beyond you, yet it has been thorough as it passed. You have only to prepare by burning around your dwellings some still evening, and you are safe. Do you say, "I would be afraid to live there?" The healthfulness of the climate would make up for the disadvantages. I have lived near a town of six hundred inhabitants for four years and have never known of a death from any fever in that time, in or about the place.

I wonder if any of the sisters have tried making a comforter without batting. The warmest one I have I made by first laying the lining on the floor, then spread smoothly all the old patched flannels, knit or cloth, and some old print, everything in fact that was too good for the rag-bag and too poor for the carpet; I then laid the cover on, tacked it to frames, and tied.

Here is a pie that differs from any I have noticed, and is as good as fresh apple: One cup of fine bread crumbs, one cup of

TO REFASTEN THE LOOSE HANDLES OF KNIVES AND FORKS

Make a cement of common brick dust and rosin, melted together. Seal engravers understand this recipe.

sugar, two cups of water, one third teaspoonful of tartaric acid, and spice to taste.

—Minnie
The Household
1883

TO GET RID OF A BAD SMELL IN A ROOM

Place a vessel full of lighted charcoal in the middle of the room, and throw on it two or three handfuls of juniper berries, shut the windows, the chimney, and the door close; twenty-four hours afterwards, the room may be opened, when it will be found that the sickly, unwholesome smell will be entirely gone. The smoke of the juniper berry possesses this advantage, that should anything be left in the room, such as tapestry, &c., none of it will be spoiled.

DEAR HOUSEHOLD:—I have long watched an opportunity to slip quietly into your circle of kindly faces, and have listened to your instructive converse for three years. I am a simple western housewife, living in the wilds of far away Missouri, and I look eagerly each month for your coming. In all the books and periodicals with which my sickroom is supplied (for I am a weary invalid), there is none so welcomed, so prized as THE HOUSEHOLD. So many bright familiar faces, so many kindly voices are there, that I long to have you break the monotony of my life by speaking to me, and helping me to bear the trial and privation of pain and poverty. For, dear sisters, I possess no golden "sesame" to open the door to ease and comfort; only what the hand of love can do to brighten my life, is cheerfully done. And I long to hear from you, one and all. Many thanks for the sweet breaths of sunshine your monthly visits bring to my clouded life. Am I welcome?

—Waif
The Household
VOLS. XI, XII; 1878, 1879

In nearly every other occupation than farming, the hardest worker finds a daily relief from his toil, and from the suggestion of toil, in a home that is entirely apart from his industry. However arduous and anxious and long continued the work, there comes a time when the workman goes into a new sphere, where the atmosphere is entirely changed. His home is a place of rest and pleasure, or at least a place of change. The pen and the hammer are left in the counting-room and in the shop, and however far the home may fall below his desires and ambition, it is at least free from the cares of the day's occupation. The American farmer has no such relief. His house is a part of his farm; his fireside is shared by an uncongenial hired man, his family circle includes too often a vulgar and uninteresting servant, and from one year to another, his living room being the kitchen and work room of the busy farmhouse, he rarely knows what it is to divest himself of the surroundings of his labor and business, and to give himself over to the needed domestic enjoyment and recreation. It is this feature of his life more than any other, which seems objectionable. If it is objectionable for him, it is infinitely more so for his wife and daughters who, lacking the frequent visit to the town or occasional chat with strangers, and the invigorating effect of open-air work, yield all the more completely to depressing cares. They become more and more deficient in the lightness and cheerfulness and mental gayety to which in any other occupation the chief toiler of the family would look for recreation at his own fire-side.

It is easy to say that the farmer's lot must be made more cheerful, attractive, and refined, and less arduous, but it is by no means easy to see how the improvement is to be brought about. The cardinal defect is the loneliness and dullness of the isolated farm-house. Intelligent and educated young women, brought up among the pleasantest surroundings, marry young farmers and undertake their new life with the determination that, in their case at least, the more obvious social requirements shall be met. During the earlier years after marriage they adhere to their resolution,

Women's Bureau, National Archives.

and are regular in attendance at the church and public lecture, and they keep up, so far as possible, social intercourse with their neighbors. But as time goes on, as the family increases, as toil begins to tell on health and strength and energy, they drop out, little by little, from the habit of going abroad, until often for weeks together they never exchange a look or thought with any human being outside of their own households. Aside from the overworked members of their own families, their companionship is confined to hired men who smell of the stable, and to hired girls with whom they are yoked in the daily round of household duties.

—*Atlantic Magazine*
MAY 1877

DEAR HOUSEHOLD:—I want to enter your charmed circle this quiet evening, to talk with the "Jeans" of our Band a little while. The Jean of the December number, whose letter I have just been reading, is but one of a large sisterhood who are "going to sleep over their books," "embroidering till their eyes ache," and growing "sick and tired of their own music," and, generally, of themselves too. This disease, for disease it is—a real moral stagnation—can never "be cured by being endured," as the old saying runs. It must be fought against till driven out of the field, and the fighting will overcome the "all work and no play" which make the Jeans such dull girls. There are many things to quarrel with in the lives which such girls lead, and there are also, many pleasant ways in which the war may be carried on.

Among young people in quiet country homes there is a strong tendency to morbid fancies. A settling down to the idea that they are "buried alive," and that there is no use in trying to do anything, a feeling which does not often attack the busy mother or aunty in the family. The village library—if there be one—has generally few books which can do more than increase the dullness, while a lack of even that source of entertainment is felt as another cause for complaint, few towns having the "book club" which is working wonders in its way. It may be enjoyed to a small extent, a beginning made, by three or four readers putting together what money they can spare, and subscribing for even two of the best magazines. It is surprising how many pennies and nickels can be laid aside during the year towards increasing the book fund for the next season. A club which can enjoy the visits of Harper's, the Century and Atlantic, with the Bazar to assist the

lovers of fancy work as well as the makers of their own dresses, has something to help itself out of a fatal dullness. Then a "Mutual Improvement" society can be formed in any place; no matter if it commences with but two or three members, it can, and will grow if rightly managed, for I never heard of the town even in the back woods where there was but one young person.

Let us look at the Jean who has aroused the sympathy of many a reader of her little letter. She has books, she has music, she has long winter evenings! How many girls who have neither of these might envy you these same long winter evenings in which you "hate" your music and "go to sleep" over your books. If your music is so bad, make it better. Read better, stronger, more helpful books. Perhaps the social qualities of some of those neighbors might develop wonderfully under a little cultivation, and the feeling that we are of some use in the world, some help to any of our fellow beings, is a powerful antidote to dullness. You would not stand alone long in your endeavor to elevate yourself and others. There is a latent longing in every one of us for something better, which needs but a touch sometimes to fire it into a living power, and outward appearances are very deceitful. The greatest men of our age have been the dullest youths, the same may perhaps apply to women, in a measure, and while we may not attain greatness, still it is always better to aim higher than we can expect to attain, leaving some steps to climb rather than to sit down resignedly half way up the hill. There may be nothing half so fine as we imagine at the top, but we want to find it out for ourselves, and can too, with little assistance aside from a strong determination to succeed.

Jean, fill up those long winter evenings with study and recreation. The "Mutual Improvement Society" will reduce the number, one each week, the preparation for it, another. Give one evening to the elder children in the neighborhood. In two hours of the early evening you may gain pleasure and they instruction which will last a lifetime. Not an evening school is intended by this, but reading aloud some good books, talks about the best writers, little sketches of history, a fine poem perhaps for a change, it will lead the young minds into broader channels of thought, and help them to know what to do with the long winter evenings when they come to them. Send for the new systems by which you can master some one of the languages which you may not understand, by yourself. Send for music that you will not grow tired of. Read English history and Scott's novels together.

TO KEEP PLANTS WITHOUT A FIRE AT NIGHT

Have made of wood or zinc a tray about four inches deep, with a handle on either end, water-tight— paint it outside and in, put in each corner a post as high as the tallest of your plants, and it is ready for use. Arrange your flower-pots in it, and fill between them with sawdust; this absorbs the moisture falling from the plants when you water them, and retains the warmth acquired during the day, keeping the temperature of the roots even. When you retire at night, spread over the posts a blanket or shawl, and there is no danger of freezing. The tray may be placed on a stand or table and easily moved about.

Read Dickens, and Thackeray, and Shakespeare, George Eliot, and Miss Mulock. Why, there are hosts of things to do; so many, that we shall not be surprised if next December you ask, "How can I do all I wish in so little time?" instead of the pathetic question, "What shall I do with the long winter evenings?"

—Emily Hayes
The Household
FEBRUARY 1883

WHERE ARE THEY?

THE HOUSEHOLD seems like a monthly meeting and greeting of some scattered family. We feel like shaking hands as each familiar name appears. But, sometimes, when families meet after long separation; dear familiar faces are missed from the social circle;—loved voices are no more heard; and to the question, "where are they?" the answer comes, "gone to the land from which no traveler returns. So in THE HOUSEHOLD we miss some names which had grown familiar, and look in vain for a cheerful greeting, or listen for a strain of sadness, and watch in vain for some token that they still live and will return some day. But we look, and listen, and watch in vain: and to our anxious question, what has become of our old friends? where are they? Echo answers, "where are they?" and we are no wiser than before.

There was one who touched the key note of our sympathy; who gave one sad wail of anguish, one piteous cry for help, and then became silent as the grave.

Was "Marah" the child of some busy imagination? Did some one write that appeal in behalf of the many hungry, aching hearts who sigh for sympathy; or was there a real woman who wrote and signed her name Marah, because she had drank deeply of the bitter waters? How we longed to go to her, and clasp her in our arms, and tell her of one Friend who is true, tender, loving, faithful. One who pities her and counts all her tears,—whose great heart is sympathizing in all her loneliness. He knows and understands it all; for "He came unto his own, and his own received him not!" Ah Marah! you received coldness in return for your love and faithfulness, and you are grieved, and your heart is hungry, O! so hungry! Cold hearted people may boast of their strong minds, and smile disdainfully at what they term your childish grief; but we know, and the dear Lord knows that a true and loving wife longs for kind words, loving smiles, and expressions of tenderness, such as first won her heart from him to whom she has given all. But the loving, pure and faithful Jesus received more than mere coldness. "He was wounded in the house of his friends." He was reviled, spit upon, and slain by those he come to save. He was a man of sorrows, and has measured every depth of suffering and knows how to pity, and is able to deliver.

Is Marah still alive? Has the cloud passed by and left only sunshine and brightness? If so, she ought to tell us, so that we may not waste sympathy; for there are other aching hearts who need all we have. Is she still grieving because bright hopes have faded, and the rosy hues which made her sky so beautiful on her wedding day have vanished and left only a murky sky and twilight gloom? Cheer up Marah! I believe there is light in the future for you if you will trust in Him who was wounded for our transgression, and by whose stripes we are healed. Carry your sorrows all to Him and He will deliver thee and give thee, not only the sunshine of His love, but also that for which you sigh, the love and companionship of your husband. I have known husbands as cold and indifferent as yours, who had no desire to hear their wives read or sing, and who thought all petting childish and silly;—and some of those same husbands have learned to appreciate a kind word, and even relish a little petting themselves. And when their wives try to make home comfortable and bright for them, they see it and express their gratitude. Courage Marah! your bright days are coming. I see them in the future; be patient, be kind and faithful still, and bide your time; and when it comes, thank God with your whole heart, and with your husband travel on to that better land where sorrow and disappointment never will come.

—Olive Oldstyle
The Household
c. 1875

MR. CROWELL:—I want to enter my decided protest against granting that "husband of a subscriber" his request, "That a page be devoted for the special purpose of hearing from husbands." Who wants to hear from them, I'd like to know. Don't we hear enough from them at home, without having them enter our HOUSEHOLD, to criticize, mock, and rail at our domestic experiences, our cooking recipes, and our confidential letters? There are few enough papers that are wholly devoted to women, and THE HOUSEHOLD is our own, our very own, where no irritable

TO TAKE SPOTS FROM WASH GOODS

Rub them with the yolk of egg before washing.

TO PREPARE RENNET

Take the stomach of the calf, empty it, and stew it plentifully with salt; let it lay for a day or two, then stretch it out on two sticks, and dry it in the sun; a piece of dried rennet, the size of your hand, is sufficient for a quart of water; a tablespoon full of the water will curd a quart of milk.

husband should be allowed to come and disturb our peace with his grumblings. A whole page, indeed! Perish the thought! "We husbands have to pay for the subscriptions of our wives to the paper," and "in view of the fact, surely we can meekly ask for just one page." Humph! there it is again, a whole dollar and ten cents a year for his wife a paper! How magnanimous some men do feel toward their wives, who wash, iron, make, mend and cook for their board and clothes, if once in a while they give them half a dollar, or money to subscribe for THE HOUSEHOLD! They feel then, that the paper partly belongs to them. When the justice is conceded to a wife to have a purse of her own, with even half the money in it, for service rendered, that her servant girl has, she will not be compelled to ask for every dollar she may wish for a magazine or paper. Where is the man who thinks it even necessary to inform his wife when he subscribes for his political paper? And what oceans of papers there are for him to take, and read, and write for, if he wants to, that are entirely devoted to men's business, without even one little column given to the interests of women. Yet this man has the audacity to wish to have a hand in

Custer County, 1887. Solomon D. Butcher Collection, Nebraska State Historical Society.

our housekeeper's paper, because forsooth, it was out of his purse it was paid for! Because the "wives rush in their letters without even consulting their husbands whether they like it or not." Preposterous (?). Away with him! Make an example of him for his impudence! Women "may not be convinced by an argument unless it be in the shape of a new dress or hat," but they are altogether capable of looking after their paper, without any aid, suggestions, or advice whatever, from any discontented, interfering husbands. Very tenderly,

—Lenore
The Household
FEBRUARY 1883

What are you going to do with the man who has dared to sue for a page in behalf of himself and the other ten thousand martyrs who "pay for THE HOUSEHOLD for their wives." Let's make him some tar cookies, fill his hands with sugar plums, petition congress to send him to India as minister of the women folks' affairs, anywhere but within the circle where he hopes to reign supreme. What does he know about how mother or any one else cooks, all he has to do, is to eat the things, isn't that enough?

Oh, I believe these men think they are losing their thrones reared in the midst of their homes. They think their wives are learning too many new-fangled notions from THE HOUSE-HOLD, and, Mr. Crowell, they will be pushing you out of your editorial chair, saying they will teach you how to manage a woman's paper. Let us hold the fort while we have it.

—"Young" Mrs. Carrie R. Alsobrook
The Household
MAY 1883

I also felt like exclaiming three cheers for Lenore, when I read her letter in the February number, that the men had no right to a page in our paper. A page! I say not even one letter, for when they are allowed that as L. Farnham was in the same number, they come grumbling because their wives happened to make failures with their pies. I wonder if failures were not sometimes made before THE HOUSEHOLD was ever thought of. And I feel now, as I often do, like saying, "Oh, the ingratitude of this world!" Instead of appreciating and thanking us for our economical recipes, practical hints, etc., he goes so far as to say he would like us to help

A CHEAP FUEL

One bushel of small coal or sawdust, or both mixed together, two bushels of sand, one bushel and a half of clay. Let these be mixed together with common water, like ordinary mortar; the more they are stirred and mixed together the better; then make them into balls, or, with a small mold, in the shape of bricks; pile them in a dry place, and use when hard and sufficiently dry. A fire cannot be lighted with them, but when the fire is lighted, put two or three on behind with some coals in front, and the fire will be found to last longer than if made up in the ordinary way.

furnish the material for the work we suggest. Did you ever see so much audacity? No, we would politely remind you, worthy gentlemen, that these pages are our very own, and while we have the rein in our own hands, we intend to hold it firmly, and I honestly think that ere the pile of brick-bats has been exhausted, all those who have attempted to intrude, will feel like doing as the craw fish did, "back right square out," and leave us alone in our glory.

—South Carolina
The Household
JUNE 1883

ILLNESS &
DECLINE

FARMERS' WIVES

Happiness and health are handmaids. Whatever tends to promote one promotes the other. The art of love is the art of good housewifery. Tidiness wins, negligence loses husbands. Home is made happy by woman's constant care. Smiles and neatness are sauce for homely meals. An orderly house with poverty, is better than confusion with wealth. A fretful woman is every man's horror. A woe-begone look has given many a heart-ache. A happy house always wears a cheerful look. To take a social meal in such a house needs no second invitation. A husband is blind to a wife's faults who always strives to please. Do not give vinegar to your husband's friends. Honey is sweet, and its taste lies long upon the tongue. Policy sometimes requires sacrifice. A friend may seem an ill-bird to-day, who, in after-years, will think it no hardship to lend you his wings. With those, you or your children may soar out of despondency.

—Solon Robinson
Facts for Farmers
VOL. II, 1886

SHORTNESS OF BREATH

Take a quarter of an ounce of elecampane root, half an ounce of powder of licorice, as much flour of brimstone, and powder of anise seed, and two ounces of sugar candy, powdered. Make all into pills, with a sufficient quantity of tar. Take four large pills when going to rest. This is an incomparable medicine for an asthma. Or, take half a pint of the juice of stinging nettles; boil, and skim it, and mix it up with as much clarified honey. Take a spoon full morning and evening.

"None of the many mysteries displayed by the study of life has been to mankind more unintelligible than that of disease, and nothing is more striking about this than the terribly disproportionate amount of suffering which falls to the lot of women. All my life I have been engaged in the study of their special ailments, and no conclusion is more firmly rooted in my mind than a devout thankfulness that I belong to the other sex."

—Sir Lawson Tait FRCS *in* a lecture—1890

WOMAN AND HER DISEASES

An imaginative poet avers that woman is the link connecting Heaven and earth. True it is, we see in her the embodiment of purity and heavenly graces, the most perfect combination of modesty, devotion, patience, affection, gratitude and loveliness, and the perfection of physical beauty. We watch with deep interest the steady and gradual development from girlhood to womanhood, when the whole person improves in grace and elegance, the voice becomes more sonorous and melodious, and the angles and curvatures of her contour become more rounded and amplified, preparatory for her high and holy mission.

Photo on previous page:
Solomon D. Butcher Collection,
Nebraska State Historical
Society.

The uterus, or womb, and ovaries, with which her whole system is in intimate sympathy, render her doubly susceptible to injurious influences and a resulting series of diseases from which the other sex is entirely exempt. By their sympathetic connections they wield a modifying influence over all the other functions of the system. Physically and mentally, woman is man modified, perfected,—the last and crowning handiwork of God. When, therefore, this structure so wonderfully endowed, so exquisitely wrought, and performing the most delicate and sacred functions which God has ever entrusted to a created being, is disturbed by disease, when the nicely-adjusted balance of her complex nature deviates from its true and intended poise, the most efficient aid should be extended in order that the normal equilibrium may be regained, her health restored, and her divine mission, on which human welfare so largely depends, be fulfilled.

Treating the Wrong Disease. Our improved and perfected system of diagnosing, or determining, the *exact* nature and extent of chronic affections, which, in most cases, we are able to do at a distance, and without a personal examination of the patient, as will be more particularly explained in the appendix, or latter part of this little book, has enabled us to avoid the blunders so often committed by the general practitioner, who not infrequently treats those afflicted with chronic ailments peculiar to women, for long weeks, and perhaps months, without ever discovering their real and true disease, or condition. Thus, invalid women are often uselessly subjected to treatment of dyspepsia, heart disease, liver or kidney affections, sick headaches, and various aches and pains, as if they were *primary* diseases, when in reality, they are only so many local manifestations, or *symptoms,* of some over-looked derangement, or disease, of the womb. For, as we have already intimated, every organ of the system is in *intimate* sympathy with the uterus, or womb. Any disease, either functional or organic, of this organ, is at once manifest through several, if not all, the sympathizing organs of the system. When we receive a sharp blow upon the elbow, the pain is felt most keenly in our little finger. Just so in diseases of the womb; often the most distress is felt in organs or parts of the system quite distant from the real seat of disease. On this account, thoughtless, easy-going and ignorant physicians are misled, and very commonly mistake the invalid's disease for some affection of the stomach, heart, liver, kidneys, or

other organ, when really it is located in the uterus. Cure the disease of the womb, and all these disagreeable manifestations, or symptoms, vanish. Their cause being removed, the various dependent derangements, and disagreeable nervous sensations and sufferings rapidly give way, and vigorous health is firmly re-established.

—E. B. Foote, M.D.
Health and Disease
1895

If special danger threatens, as fire or foes, the male naturally stands at bay, while the mother snatches her infant and flees for safety. That is, man naturally fights, while woman runs.

Often in the extra nervous women of these days of female nervousness, this cautiousness becomes overstrained, morbid, and virtually insane, so that many females are in a state of perpetual fear and terror. The rustling of a leaf alarms, and the jolting of the carriage or shying of a horse frightens them; thus rendering themselves and all around them miserable. If their "darlings" fall sick they "call the doctor"; do this and that in a half frenzy of fear; and thus often kill their children by the very means taken to save them. This is "too much of a good thing." Such should offset this tendency by their sense; and remember that they are always more "scared than hurt."

—O. S. Fowler
Sexual Science
1875

NOVEL READING

Novel reading redoubles this nervous drain begun by excessive study. What is or can be as superlatively silly or ruinous to the nerves as that silly girl, snivelling and laughing by turns over a "love story"? Of course it awakens her Amativeness. In this consists its chief charm. Was there ever a novel without its hero? It would be Hamlet played without Hamlet. Yet how could depicting a beau so heroic, lovable, and dead in love, fail to awaken this tender passion in enchanted readers? To *titillate Amativeness,* mainly, are novels written and read. For this they become "vade mecums," and are carried to table, ride, picnic, walk, everywhere. It is doubtful whether fiction writers are public benefactors, or their publishers philanthropists. The amount of nervous excitement, and consequent prostration, exhaustion, and disorder they cause is fearful. Girls already have ten times too much excitability for their strength. Yet every page of every novel redoubles both their nervousness and weakness. Only Amazons could endure it. Mark this reason. Amativeness, that is, love, and the nervous system, are in the most perfect mutual sympathy. Love-stories, therefore, in common with all other forms of amatory excitement, thrill. In this consists their chief fascination. Yet all amatory action with one's self induces sexual ailments. It should always be with the *opposite* sex only; yet novel-reading girls exhaust the female magnetism without obtaining any compensating male magnetism, which of necessity deranges their entire sexual system. The whole world is challenged to invalidate either this premise or inference. Self-abuse is worse, because more animal; but those who really must have amatory excitement will find it "better to marry," and expend on real lovers those sexual feelings now worse than wasted on this its "solitary" form. Those perfectly happy in their affections never read novels, because *real* love is so much more fascinating than that described.

—O. S. Fowler
Sexual Science
1875

DRINK FOR JAUNDICE

Tie up soot and saffron, equal parts, in a cloth to the size of half of a hen's egg, let it lie in a glass of water over night; in the morning put the yolk of an egg, beaten, into this water, and drink it. Do this 3 mornings, skipping 3, until 9 doses have been taken.

On Female Health in America

During my extensive tours in all portions of the Free States, I was brought into most intimate communion, not only with my widely-diffused circle of relatives, but with very many of my former pupils who had become wives and mothers. From such, I learned the secret domestic history both of those I visited and of many of their intimate friends. And oh! what heartaches were the result of these years of quiet observation of the experience of my sex in domestic life. How many young hearts have revealed the fact, that what they had been trained to imagine the highest earthly felicity, was but the beginning of care, disappointment, and sorrow, and often led to the extremity of mental and physical suffering. Why was it that I was so often told that "young girls little imagined what was before them when they entered married life"? Why did I so often find those united to the most congenial and most devoted husbands expressing the hope that their daughters would never marry? For years these were my quiet, painful conjectures.

CAUTIONS IN VISITING SICK ROOMS

Never venture into a sick room in a violent perspiration (if circumstances require a continuance there for any time), for the moment the body becomes cold, it is in a state likely to absorb the infection, and receive the disease. Nor visit a sick person (especially if the complaint be of a contagious nature) with an empty stomach; as this disposes the system more readily to receive the infection. In attending a sick person, stand where the air passes from the door or window to the bed of the diseased, not betwixt the diseased person and any fire that is in the room, as the heat of the fire will draw the infectious vapor in that direction, and much danger would arise from breathing in it.

But the more I traveled, and the more I resided in health establishments, the more the conviction was pressed on my attention that there was a terrible decay of female health all over the land, and that this evil was bringing with it an incredible extent of individual, domestic, and social suffering, that was increasing in a most alarming ratio. At last, certain developments led me to take decided measures to obtain some reliable statistics on the subject. During my travels the last year I have sought all practicable methods of obtaining information, and finally adopted this course with most of the married ladies whom I met, either on my journeys or at the various health establishments at which I stopped.

I requested each lady first to write the *initials* of *ten* of the married ladies with whom she was best acquainted in her place of residence. Then she was requested to write at each name, her impressions as to the health of each lady. In this way, during the past year, I obtained statistics from about two hundred different places in almost all the Free States.

Before giving any of these, I will state some facts to show how far they are reliable: In the first place, the *standard of health* among American women is so low that few have a correct idea of *what a healthy woman is.* I have again and again been told by ladies that they were "perfectly healthy," who yet, on close inquiry, would allow that they were subject to frequent attacks of neuralgia, or to periodic nervous headaches, or to local ailments, to which they had become so accustomed, that they were counted as "nothing at all." A woman who has tolerable health finds herself so much above the great mass of her friends in this respect, that she feels herself a prodigy of good health.

In the next place, I have found that women who enjoy universal health are seldom well informed as to the infirmities of their friends. Repeatedly I have taken accounts from such persons, that seemed singularly favorable, when, on more particular inquiry, it was found that the greater part, who were set down as perfectly healthy women, were habitual sufferers from serious ailments. The delicate and infirm go for sympathy, not to the well and buoyant, but to those who have suffered like themselves. ...

It must be remembered, that in regard to those marked as "sickly," "delicate," or "feeble," there can be no mistake, the knowledge being in all cases *positive,* while those marked as "well" may have ailments that are not known. For multitudes of American women, with their strict notions of propriety, and their patient and energetic spirit, often are performing every duty entirely silent as to any suffering or infirmities they may be enduring. ...

—Catherine Beecher
Letters to the People on Health and Happiness
1855

The rural woman was required by her vocation to be healthy, strong, and contented. The well-being of her family and the nation demanded it. Yet, in an inordinate number of cases she was not. Subject to what appeared to be continuous and baffling disorders, suffering from a wide range of chronic illnesses, incapacities, exhaustion, anxiety, and nervous disorders, she was often a frail and failing presence whose physical capacities were not up to the demands of her calling.

While this prevalence of sickness and decline was a cause of great concern, it was generally accepted as the inevitable result of her imperfection and "peculiar" anatomy. Woman was a natural invalid and the causes put forward, the cures proposed, and the speculations concerning this "fact" were all influenced by a vast body of misinformation, prejudice, and myth. Women were seen as victims of themselves—not wronged by men, but rather by God, who had made them women.

The work that they did and the conditions under which they did it, while seen as factors in that sickness and decline, were rarely fully credited.

The Bright Beyond.
Song Cover, 1884. Library of Congress.

199

"Mother Wasn't Very Strong"

No, she was not strong. She had never been very strong. Farmer Grey knew, when he married her. Eight children called her mother. She made all of their clothes and did her own housework, and yet, "mother was not very strong."

Farmer Grey said it often and always regretfully.

Perhaps he was unselfish enough to wish that she were stronger for her own sake, but I fear not. He was a very robust, active man, and exceedingly anxious to "get along" in the world. Therefore, I fear that his regret for mother's feebleness was simply a regret that she could not do more to help him in his schemes for "getting along."

She herself regretted that she was not stronger.

"Father works so hard," she would say, "I feel that I am not so much help to him as I might be if I were a real strong woman."

What more would she have done? What more could she have done? And, what more should she have done?

She kept the house in order. She did a loving, God-fearing mother's duty by her children. She was up early and to bed late. She was busy every hour of the day. She milked and made butter, worked in her garden, cooked for "hands," raised and sold chickens, but never had a dollar of her own.

She could and did, "when father was rushed," go out into the fields and drop corn for half a day, and then come into her hot stuffy little kitchen and get dinner for fourteen people, and yet— "mother was not strong."

She often wondered if she would ever be strong. She would sit on the kitchen door-step some nights long after the others were in bed, dreading the coming of the morrow and hoping it wouldn't be so very hot. She was afraid she might "give out." She would lean her aching head against the unpainted doorframe, cross her tired hands listlessly in her lap, close her eyes and "wonder" about many things.

Some of her neighbors, with families only half as large as her own, kept a strong hired girl in the kitchen the year round.

She often wondered vaguely how it would seem to have a girl in her kitchen; she wondered how it would seem for her to be away from home over night.

The fondest hope of her life for ten years had been that she might visit her mother, who lived two hundred miles away. She said she wouldn't be afraid to go "such a long ways" alone, and

SORE NIPPLES

Put twenty grains of sugar of lead into a vial with one gill of rose-water; shake it up thoroughly; wet a piece of soft linen with this preparation, and put it on; renew this as often as the linen becomes dry. Before nursing, wash this off with something soothing; rose-water is very good; but the best thing is quince-seed warmed in a little cold tea until the liquid becomes quite glutinous. This application is alike healing and pleasant. ...

"father" had often said she should go if "such and such a thing turned out well."

These things often "turned out well," but mother never made that visit.

"One thing and another," she said, kept her at home; and one day a messenger came, bringing the news of her mother's death. She would have liked to have gone, even then, to see once more that beloved face, even though it was cold in death.

But father said that, "seeing as she could do no good there was no use wearing herself out making the trip," so she stayed at home, grateful to father for his thoughtfulness in not wanting her to "wear herself out."

But she was so utterly worn out one day, so worn out in body and mind and soul, that when she clasped her tired hands over her breast in sleep they were never unclasped again in this world. There was no response of "Yes, I'm coming," when father called her in the gray dawn of a November day.

The Father who had truly loved her, and who had helped her bear her heavy burdens through all these twenty years, had called her in the night, and I think she was glad to say, "Yes, Father, I'm coming."

—J. L. H.
The Household
VOL. XXV, 1892

TIRED OUT

I heard a sad story yesterday of one woman's hard experience for a year in consequence of overwork in years preceding. She seemed to bear the strain of nerve and muscle pretty well, toiling on without complaint, until a more critical time of life came—a few years before her fiftieth birthday—when nature would endure no more. She who had spent herself unsparingly for others, was now almost as helpless as a baby. Only great patience and toleration of all her whims saved her from insanity. She had most unreasonable and uncontrollable crying spells, and a strong dislike for some of her former good friends. Her physician counseled the family to bear with her as with a sick child, and by their tender care and patience she at last came through her troubles, to be again the companion and friend of her husband and children, but never again the drudge which they had thoughtlessly allowed her to be before her long illness.

RHEUMATISM

To a hand full of blue flag root add a pint of good spirits; let it stand a week. Dose, a spoon full three times a day, and increase by degrees to three tablespoons full a day. An Indian remedy. Or, apply a poultice of hot potatoes; renew as often as it becomes hard or cool. It is said to be a very excellent remedy.

DESTROYING RATS

Corks, cut as thin as sixpences, roasted or stewed in grease, and placed in their tracks; or dried sponge in small pieces, fried or dipped in honey, with a little oil of rhodium; or bird-lime, laid in their haunts, will stick to their fur and cause their departure.

If a live rat be caught, and well rubbed or brushed over with tar and train-oil, and afterwards put to escape in the holes of others, they will disappear.

Poisoning is a very dangerous and objectionable mode.

Every day, now, I am longing for tidings from a friend very near and dear to me, though more than a thousand miles away. She too is "tired out," and has been flat on her back for long weary weeks, unable to bear even the sound of her baby's sweet prattle for more than a few minutes at a time, sucking her food through a tube because she cannot sit up to eat. Nobody knows what made her sick. When at last her wearied nerves and muscles gave way, she was unable to leave her bed; when the doctor came, he said she looked as though she had been sick six months. She answered that she had "been *tired* for six months." He said it was a case of simple exhaustion, and that perfect rest and careful nourishment were all her case required in the way of cure. But it is slow work, this rebuilding a constitution so long over-taxed and gradually undermined. I have often whipped myself up when nature begged for rest, by thoughts of this woman's example. I supposed I did not work so hard as she, and what she could endure why could not I? This was foolish reasoning, since no two human beings are made exactly alike, and each must work according to individual capacity. And now I see that even she who worked on so patiently and self-sacrificing, and so seemed to bring a reproach upon us weaker sisters, could not endure all things. Her case must serve as a "warning" instead of the "shining light" it once seemed.

I know another woman whose heart is sometimes very heavy and sometimes rather bitter during the weary months that precede confinement. To me alone has she poured out her full heart. Alas! alas! how little help can any of us give another. Yet sympathy is genuine help after all. This woman's mother-heart is sometimes almost broken. She is almost constantly tired out and discouraged. No other ambition has been so strong as the desire to be a good mother to her children, but now she finds herself so cross and irritable that she can scarcely bear the sound of her children's voices. Night and day she has their constant presence, never one moment free from care. She has also many financial worries—little matters of business to attend to for her husband, and many a makeshift to eke out the family support. She has read, and knows well, the common theory of a mother's responsibility for the health and disposition of her children, yet her nerves and muscles are constantly over-taxed with care and work beyond her present power. She longs constantly for rest, but when she can lie down occasionally for a nap, she thinks of her children's neglected education and other matters, and she cries herself into a headache instead of sleeping.

—Faith Rochester
American Agriculturist
VOL. XXXV, 1876

FARMERS' WIVES

Do we really wish to see ourselves as others see us? There is a chance, then, for any of us who are farmers' wives to see a portrait of ourselves painted pretty vigorously—whether quite truthfully or not each farmer's wife should judge for herself. I refer to a chapter in Mrs. Woolson's "Woman in American Society," entitled "Farmers' Wives." I will quote from the work, with some italicizing as I copy Mrs. Woolson's words. It should be remembered that Mrs. Woolson is a New England woman.

"Her constant labors are carried on within four bare and narrow walls, without change of scene or hope of variety. It is not strange that her strength becomes impaired, and that she often finds herself at middle age afflicted with disease. And the physical weakness which must inevitably result from such a life is greatly increased by an astonishing ignorance of the manifold causes that tend to produce it. This is especially the case in towns lying remote from the great centers of intelligence. Practices and food that cities have learned to discard as most pernicious are still clung to in our farmers' homes without any suspicion of their injurious effects. *Visitors avoid, if they can, their diet of fried pork, their feather beds, their cotton coverlets, and their ill-aired rooms, and gladly escape out of doors for exhilarating rambles through field and forest; but these are supposed to be mere whims of their guests, indulged in without reason.*

"This peculiar animal food (pork), which intelligent people have learned to abjure, is usually cooked in the very manner which renders it most indigestible—by soaking in boiling fat, in other words, by frying. The wholesome bread raised by pure yeast, once the pride of our farm-houses, has given place to abominable compounds whose chemical ingredients are ruinous to both teeth and stomach. Everywhere around these houses sweeps a current of pure air; but it is as carefully excluded from the rooms as if it were a poison. Fortunately, however, it possesses the witch's privilege, and enters unbidden through cracks and key-holes. Walking is nowhere held in such ill repute as in these same towns, where there is so much beauty in earth and sky to tempt one abroad. It is an offence in the eyes of all for a woman to be seen sauntering along the roads, and gadding about is held to be one of the heinous sins. A horse and wagon must be brought to the door if the distance to be traversed is but half a mile, so that daily exercise in the open air is indulged in only by school children and those who work in the fields. These influences of *excessive toil, lack of diversion, unhealthy food, and ill-aired rooms, submitted to partly from necessity and partly from ignorance as to their results, can not but seriously impair the health of all who experience them.*"

Well! Does the coat fit? Here is another—try this. I find it in the private letter of a gentleman whose position and years and culture and habits of observation give weight to his words. He says: "Do you know the absolute cheerlessness, loneliness, wretchedness, almost hopelessness of a large share of farmers' wives? Work and bear children—that is the whole story."

But this is too bad! The farmers' wives whom these pictures fairly portray are not readers of these columns—at least, not many of them. And besides, if we are farmers' wives how can we help that? We wouldn't like to divorce ourselves from our husbands, nor to divorce them from their farms. I don't wonder at all that observers have begun to say such things about the lot of the average farmer's wife, but they may be too sweeping in their statements and too limited in the application. A good many wives and mothers in other fields of labor—mechanics and tradesmen's wives—might be described in almost the same way, though to be sure these generally live in villages or cities. It will do us no harm to consider the criticisms upon our shortcomings, and to go to work at once to improve our condition.

They complain of our ignorance. Well, knowledge is worth something; but I have good authority for saying that charity or love is far better. Patience and faith on our part are worth more to our children than any scientific information we could give them. But let us give these dear children, and give our husbands and maid-servants and man-servants and ourselves every chance we can to get health and knowledge and happiness.

I would like to go on now and speak of the advantages of the farmer's wife over her town sisters, for I would not like to have any discontented woman strengthened in unwise dissatisfaction by what is here written. Let every farmer's wife think over these advantages for herself. She will find them many if she looks deeply.

Each situation in life has disadvantages as compared with others, and each has its compensations. The fact is, we are all getting stirred up and unsettled, and any person who thinks his or her present lot too hard had better look well before leaping into what seems a better situation, or it may be just "out of the frying-pan into the fire."

—Faith Rochester
American Agriculturist
VOL. XXXII, 1873

OUR GRANDMOTHERS

It is simply impossible for any woman to do the whole work for her household and make her life what woman's life ought to be. This is a rule that admits of no exception and no modification. The machinery of the family is so complicated and so exacting, that one woman cannot have the sole charge of it without neglecting other and equally important matters. The duties which a woman owes to society, and to the moral and spiritual part of her household are just as imperative as those which she owes to its physical comfort. And if she alone ministers to the latter the former must be neglected, and the latter will hardly be thoroughly accomplished.

I know all about our noble grandmothers. I have heard of them before. I think we could run a race with them any day. But if we cannot, whose fault is it? If the women of to-day are puny, fragile, degenerate, are they not the grandchildren of their grandmothers—bearing such constitutions as their grandmothers could transmit? It was the duty of those venerable ladies not only to be strong themselves, but to see to it that their children were strong.

A sturdy race should leave a sturdy race. It was far more their duty to give to their children vigorous minds, stalwart bodies, healthy nerves, and firm principles than it was to spin, weave and make butter and cheese all day. We should have got along just as well with less linen laid up in lavender; and if our grandmothers could have waited, we would have woven them more cloth in one day than their hand looms would turn out in a life time.

But there is no royal road to a healthy manhood and womanhood. Nothing less costly than human life goes into the construction of human life. We should have more reason to be grateful to our ancestors if they would have given up superfluous industries, called off the energies from its perishable objects, and let more of their soul and strength flow leisurely in to build up the soul and strength of the generations that were to come after them.

CARPETING, CHEAP

Sew together strips of the cheapest cotton cloth, of the size of the room, and tack the edges to the floor. Then paper the cloth as you would the sides of a room, with any sort of room paper. After being well dried, give it two coats of varnish, and your carpet is finished. It can be washed like carpets without injury, retaining its gloss, and, on chambers or sleeping-rooms, where it will not meet rough usage, will last for two years, as good as new.

Nobody is to blame for being born weak. If this generation of women is feeble compared with its hardy and laborious grandmothers, it is simply because the grandmothers put so much of their vitality, their physical nerve and moral fibre into their work, that they had not the sufficient quantity left wherewithal to endow their children; and so they wrought us evil.

—The Household
VOL. III, 1870

BLEEDING AT THE LUNGS

Eat freely of raw table salt, or take a teaspoonful three or four times a day of equal parts of powdered loaf sugar and resin.

Exposure to intense cold and sudden changes in temperature will produce lockjaw more quickly than a wound.

To prevent wounds from mortifying, sprinkle sugar on them. The Turks wash fresh wounds with wine, and sprinkle sugar on them. Obstinate ulcers may be cured with sugar dissolved in a strong decoction of walnut leaves.

BUSY LIVES

"I don't say as I think John's second wife lazy," said old Mrs. Perrin, one day, to a friend of mine, "but she isn't a bit like poor Selina. She lets things go, and don't seem to have no ambition; while Selina—well, I tell you, she was a master worker. The year before she died she not only did all the work of the house, but she saw to the milk of twelve cows, tended the bees, and sold cheese, butter, eggs, soft soap, and dried corn and apples. She took the prize at the country fair for her quilts, and she preserved one hundred jars of fruits, and put up two hundred cans of tomatoes to sell to the town store. And she had to see to her three children, too, and John had four hired men all summer for her to feed and wash for."

"Ah," said Mrs. B., "I don't wonder she died! If I had have been in her place I'd have died, too, and been very glad to go."

Mrs. Perrin looked over her spectacles at Mrs. B. with a wondering look.

"La!" she said, "women was made to work. You don't believe in these women who lie 'round, do you?"

"No," said Mrs. B., "and I don't believe in women who make slaves and household drudges of themselves, either; particularly, when it isn't necessary. John Perrin was able to hire help, and Selina ought to have had it. I remember well how tired her white face looked in the coffin, and how glad I was to see her hands at rest for once."

Men are none too thoughtful, take them as a class. They grow used to seeing their wives and sisters work, and think nothing of it. They allow them to do many things for which they are unfitted. I recollect reading in THE HOUSEHOLD about a year ago of some sister who had to pull all the wood for her fire out from under the snow, and chop it, too. Now I think it the business of the husband to see that his wife is provided with fuel ready to her hand. No wonder men have two or three wives during a life time, when women work at chopping and hauling.

Selina Perrin never took a breathing space. It was work, work, from dawn to nine o'clock at night, and she grew at last into the belief that hours spent in bed were wasted. It was no wonder that the delicate machinery of body and mind wore out at last.

A couple of weeks ago I read in the New York Tribune of a woman who bore and brought to manhood and womanhood fourteen children. She never had hired help for more than a week at a time: she made all the clothing for both husband and sons, as well as that for herself and daughters, spinning and weaving the material. At ninety-eight she is hale and hearty. But not one woman in five hundred could have done so much. There is a limit to the capacity of human nature. There is an old saying that "it is better to wear out than to rust out," and it is often quoted to me by a little woman to whom I preach frequently on the text, "Don't do so much." She has six little children and keeps only one servant, consequently she has a great deal of work on her hands. She is forever sweeping, dusting and cleaning, and is almost worn out at thirty. Her husband will certainly have to look for a second wife before many years are past if she continues to overwork herself as she is now doing. Her face wears a strained, anxious look all the time, she is nervous and fretful because she is exhausted. The children say, "How mamma scolds," and her husband is irritated by the constant fretting going on about him. If he speaks to her about it she cries as if her heart would break and wishes she was dead. Yet she cannot make up her mind to let things go; to be indifferent as to dust on the parlor mantel and the prints of tiny fingers on the window panes. She knows she is wearing out, but she is determined not to rust. Even at night she cannot rest. The children must be put to bed at seven o'clock. That takes an hour always; for the baby is a little night-owl, and crows and kicks long after the eyes of his little brothers and sisters are closed. Then he wakes her up half a dozen times during the night to nurse. She has no system about his nursing, though he might earlier have been taught to sleep through the night without food. From eight to nine o'clock she busies herself in picking up and putting away in the nursery, dining-room and parlor, and then the stocking basket with its "holey" contents comes out to keep her employed until ten, when she retires, almost too tired to fall asleep.

Is she doing right thus to wear out body and brain so rapidly? Wouldn't it be better far to preserve her health and strength that she may live to bring up her little children? How hard it would be for her to reflect on her death bed that because of her folly in wearing herself out she must leave her darlings to be reared by stranger hands, or at the best relatives who cannot feel toward them the tenderness of the mother, and will not be lenient to their faults and weaknesses. A clean, well-ordered house is delightful, certainly, no one can dispute its charm; but its cleanliness and orderliness should not be accomplished at the expense of the exhaustion of the wife and mother.

—Florence B. Hallowell
The Household
VOL. XV, 1882

The physical health and capacity of a woman were often viewed by society as a material advantage for someone else rather than a matter of her own well-being and happiness.

"A Valuable Wife for Somebody"

"A young lady recently sheared twenty sheep, and cooked dinner besides, all in one day! A valuable wife for somebody!"

Yes, "a valuable wife," that is all! Nobody says, "She can make her own living," or "she can take care of herself." Nobody advises her to "stick to her shearing" and lay up something for a rainy day, but every one holds up both hands for exclamation points, and cries, "What a valuable wife for somebody!" just as if a woman was "somebody's wife," or nothing.

Wouldn't it be possible for Miss Tennessee to follow shearing, year after year, and be quite as respectable as those who marry Smith or Jones, "because it is so hard for a woman to get along alone?"

"Twenty sheep and dinner beside!" says widower Podge to himself. "Maria never could do that. It took her about all the time to get the meals, and see to the children. Such a woman could help a man. Why, she'd save hirin' one hand, and board and wages together; that is considerable in a year."

So he puts on his best suit and drives over, not to say as an honest man would, "Miss Tennessee, I have heard that you are a splendid worker and that you can shear twenty sheep in a day, and get dinner too; so I came over to tell you that I'd like to marry you, for I have a large farm, but it is not all paid for yet, and lots of cows and hogs and sheep, besides five children, and I want a woman who can work hard to help me get along in the world." Ah, no, he knows better than to begin that way; so he puts on his very sweetest smile, and wonders if her "father could be induced to sell that roan horse," and he calls several times before he finds Mr. T. at home, and every time he talks about—well, everything but work, and that he never hints at, except to feel so sorry that "Mrs. Meek has to work so much beyond her strength," and to fear that "Fanny Gregg is sewing herself into a consumption," and he is so good that tired Miss Tennessee thinks it would be so nice to have a husband who would know when a woman had done enough; so she "falls in love" with the wooer and marries him, and he takes her home, and is much disappointed to find that she does not cook or wash dishes a bit faster than other folks. And she does not wash, and bake, and mop, and iron, while he is doing the morning chores, but takes two days for it, just as Maria did, and he begins to believe that he has been cheated!

Then he thinks that he will hurry her up a little, so he gathers up all the sacks on the place and wants them washed and patched, and then he says, "Can't you milk that heifer? She is so afraid of men," and when she hints that she would like to have a new carpet he thinks that "so smart a woman can make her own carpet," and, woman like, this "valuable wife" tries to do all that is expected of her, and in a few years she is all broken down; "not what I expected her to be at all," says the astonished husband.

Mrs. Podge herself looks back regretfully to her sheep shearing days. "I used to do some great day's work then," she says; "but it was not drag, drag, all the time, for if I was very tired, I rested next day and got over it, but since I've been married I haven't had a minute's rest. If I do leave the work and the children, I have them on my mind all the same. And I used to lay up a little money, too, but I have not saved a cent since I got married. I boarded Hopkins a good while, but that went on a horse Podge bought of him, and although it was called my horse, it was traded with others for a threshing machine, and that was traded for something else; and so it goes, whatever I earn.

"Oh yes, Podge takes care of me when I'm sick, and gives me victuals, and pays my doctor's bills, but he has not the least idea that I have a *right* to it all, and growls that women don't care how much they are sick, for it all comes out of men's pockets.

"Well, if I hadn't married I might have had enough money to take care of myself, when I'm sick, without asking for it, and I

UNIVERSAL LINIMENT

One pint of alcohol and as much camphor gum as can be dissolved in it, half an ounce of the oil of cedar, one-half ounce of the oil of sassafras, aqua ammonia half an ounce, and the same amount of the tincture of morphine. Shake well together and apply by the fire; the liniment must not be heated, or come in contact with the fire, but the rubbing to be done by the warmth of the fire.

should not have worked half so hard for it, either. If I had my married life to live over I would have more help, because help costs no more than doctors do. I believe Podge thought I was made of cast iron and never would wear out. I only wish that I had known enough to take care of myself before it was too late."

There is any number of "valuable wives" for any number of husbands, but how many can keep "a valuable wife" after they get her?
—*The Household*
VOL. V, 1872

O f all the "inherent" and disturbing weaknesses of women, perhaps the most pervasive and irksome was the so-called female tendency toward fretfulness and "fidgeting." Regardless of the reason, the solution was simple: Don't do it. Don't grieve—be cheerful and count your blessings.

THE GOOD WIFE

Those who have heard the lecture of the Rev. Dr. Willitts, on the "Model Wife," will recognize the following amusing verses, which were written for Dr. W. by a friend:—

> *It is just as you say, Neighbor Green,*
> *A treasure indeed is my wife;*
> *Such another for bustle and work,*
> *I have never found in my life.*
> *But then she keeps every one else*
> *As busy as birds on the wing;*

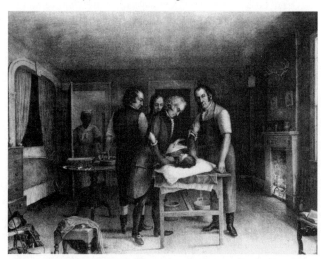

First Ovariotomy.
Lithograph, 1878.
Library of Congress.

There is never a moment for rest,
    She is such a fidgety thing.

She makes the best bread in the town;
    Her pies are a perfect delight;
Her coffee a rich golden brown;
    Her crullers and puddings just right.
But then, while I eat them, she tells
    Of the care and worry they bring;
Of the martyr-like toil she endures;
    Oh, she's such a fidgety thing!

My house is as neat as a pin;
    You should see how the door-handles shine;
And all of the soft-cushioned chairs,
    And nicely swept carpets are mine.
But then she so frets at the dust,
    At a fly, at a straw, or a string,
That I stay out of doors all I can,
    She is such a fidgety thing!

She doctors the neighbors? O, yes;
    If a child has the measles or croup,
She is there with her saffrons and squills,
    Her dainty made gruels and soup.
But then she insists on her right
    To physic my blood in the spring;
And she takes the whole charge of my bile;
    Oh, she is such a fidgety thing!

She knits all my stockings herself;
    My shirts are bleached white as the snow;
My old clothes look better than new,
    Yet daily more threadbare they grow.
But then if a morsel of lint
    Or dust to my trowsers should cling,
I'm sure of one sermon at least,
    She is such a fidgety thing.

You have heard of a spirit so meek,
    So meek that it never opposes,
It's own it dare never to speak—
    Alas! I am meeker than Moses!
But then I am not reconciled
    The subordinate music to sing;

The American Wringer Co.'s
HORSE-SHOE BRAND
ROYAL
WRINGER
WARRANTED 5 YEARS

211

I submit to get rid of a row,
She is such a fidgety thing.

It's just as you say Neighbor Green,
A treasure to me has been given,
But sometimes I fain would be glad
To lay up my treasure in heaven!
But then every life has its cross,
Most pleasures on earth have their sting;
She's a treasure, I know, Neighbor Green,
But she's such a fidgety thing.
—The New Practical Housekeeping
1890

FRETTING

Perhaps there is no failing so common among American women, and, at the same time, so detrimental to the comfort of the household as fretfulness. So universal is it that the housemother who can go through the ordinary routine of the day without unjust, and unwise fault-finding and censure of some, or all of the members of her family, is a very rare exception. It does not require any great occasion of profound annoyance and disturbance; the most trifling circumstance is usually sufficient; a child leaves the door open, the men are ten minutes late to their dinner, a pocket handkerchief is blown off the clothes line, the teacher is sick and there is no school; any little thing however unimportant, will ruffle the temper and give that fretful whine to the voice which effectually banishes peace and equanimity from the house.

It reminds me of nothing so much as the electrical sparks which prick your fingers when you smooth pussy's fur the wrong way. And trifles alone seem to have this irritating power. Let great troubles fall upon the household, and the peevish fretful woman becomes a very Spartan and works heroically through difficulties the most obdurate, and circumstances the most annoying, without a word of complaint. This faculty of fretting is seldom or never exercised except on members of one's own family. The woman who has kept her children in a chronic state of hatefulness all day, who has driven her husband from the house in a towering state of disgust, and cultivated the spirit of contrariness in her servants, till they are prepared to call sweet, sour, and black, white; will be as gentle as a summer morning should a neighbor call, or a peddler rap at the door, or a tramp ask for his dinner.

212

It is one of the mysteries of this mysterious disease that precisely the persons she loves best, who have the strongest claim upon her forbearance, and on whom her happiness so entirely depends; just these and no others does she make to suffer. If she has occasion to send an errand by her neighbor's husband and he forgets it she smilingly assures him it is no matter, if her visitors' children leave the doors open in fly-time, or track in the mud, she bears it patiently; but her own husband whom she loves utterly, and her precious children for whom she would make any sacrifice and bear any suffering, she will wound with a sharp word or an ill-timed or undeserved reproof when it would seem to be so much easier to spare them; the effect on the husband is of course different, as temperament and disposition differ. Many men bear it patiently, some don't notice it at all; others consider it a feminine vagary, infinitely beneath their consideration, and some are so outrageously ugly, that their wives dare not fret at them, but in that case the servants and children get a double share.

But the meanest of all is to fret at the children. The husband can go off on business, or he can at least have the satisfaction of answering back; the servants can find another place, and be fretted at by another woman, but the children have no business; they must not answer back; and they can't move on. They can only bear. The delicate and sensitive live in a state of chronic irritation, the timid and secretive learn to lie; the sturdy and bold grow belligerent and ugly. Their childhood is despoiled of its beauty and happiness and one way, or another, they suffer for it all their lives.

Fretfulness seldom shows itself, at least to any extent, until maturity. Marriage seems especially to develop it; old maids, notwithstanding public opinion, seldom fret. The childless woman is quite as likely to be fretful as the mother of a household, and sometimes an irritable and exacting woman will become gentle and patient after the birth of a baby.

There are four causes which operate powerfully to produce and increase this evil; probably there are many more, but, as far as my observation goes, these are the most potent. The first is overwork. I am well aware there are fretful women who do not work, but the great mass of American housewives in moderate circumstances, work from twelve to sixteen hours every day; enough to exhaust the nerves and temper of the strongest of us. Day in and day out, year after year, the work goes on; do the housework,

THE MOTHER'S MEDICINE CHEST

In travelling or for use at home, it is very desirable to have at hand a few remedies valuable in accidents or sudden sickness.

A small box will hold the following articles:

Absorbent cotton
Sticking plaster—rubber plaster is best, because it requires neither heat nor moisture for its application.
Bandages of muslin or flannel
Thread and needles
Pins
Vaseline
1. Aromatic spirits of ammonia
2. Tincture of Assafœtida
3. Oil of cloves
4. Hoffman's Anodyne
5. Syrup of Ipecac
6. Laudanum
7. Magnesia
8. Mustard
9. Paregoric
10. Spiced syrup of rhubarb
11. Turpentine
To these may be added, if there is room, camphor-water, essence of ginger, lime-water, and sweet spirits of nitre.

213

BURYING ALIVE

To know when death has really occurred and so prevent burying alive, hold a candle to any portion of the body, a blister will soon rise; if on puncture it gives out a fluid substance, death has not taken place; if it emits air only, it is perfectly certain that life has become entirely extinct, for which we offer but one reason among others, in case of actual death the blood is congealed in a sense, there is no moisture, simply a little air, this being rarefied under the flame, raises up the skin; if there is life, the flame causes an inflammation and nature, in her alarm, sends increased material there for repair, a kind of glairy fluid, and this being sent there in excess, causes the skin to rise; inability to feel the pulse or heart beat; cold skin, no dew on a bit of glass, none of these are conclusive, as there has been life, when none of these were observed.

Another sure sign of death—stick a needle an inch or so into the supposed corpse. In the living tissues the needle will soon become tarnished and oxidised, whilst in the actually dead it will retain its polish.

---

bear and tend the children, make and mend, and have the knitting always handy to fill in the spare moments.

Another cause is indoor confinement. It is not alone that we breathe the vitiated air, deficient in oxygen, till the nerves are starved, and so irritable as to cause constant suffering, but we lack the companionship of nature, the touch of her gentle hand, the repose of her strong, calm heart. How many of us have gone from the care, and labor, and noise, and turmoil of our busy homes to sit in the peaceful presence of an aged mother; and though few words were spoken, we have gone away strong and rested. Nature is our mother; she never grows old, she is always vigorous, gentle, powerful. Brooding under her mighty wing, nestling on her ample breast, we cannot fail to gather strength and peace.

Another cause is loss of individuality. When a woman marries, in one sense she ceases to exist. She is absorbed into her husband. His life goes on much the same as before; marriage is to him an incident; an important one, doubtless, but still an incident. But it has changed the whole tenor of her existence. Whatever her natural bent or preference may be, now she must keep his house; and she has not an occupation, a duty, or a thought, but revolves around him. Not an hour of the day can she be herself, she is only his wife. Doubtless there are many (and for them let us thank God,) whose personality is too strong for absorption. They are the salt of womankind; strong, calm, self-poised. The fountains of their peace strike deep into the eternal soul; they quench their thirst at no man's pitcher.

There is yet another cause, but I hesitate to mention it; women are not loved enough. In marriage she gives more than man, she risks more, and all women feel that they have a right to the full measure of the price for which they give so much. When their daily life grows barren, and the husband treats them like any member of the family, and with far less courtesy than he does the servants, what wonder that they feel the injustice of it, and nothing is more natural than for a discontented and unhappy woman to fret.

—N.
The Household
VOL. XI, 1878

DON'T FRET

Don't fret, don't! You cannot afford to, any more than a farmer can afford to sow his garden with noxious weeds. Look in your mirror the next time you are fretting, worrying, brooding over something gone entirely wrong, that should have gone entirely right. Do you recognize yourself? Lines between eyes that look gloomily into yours, eyes out of which the glad sparkle is departed, lips compressed into a hard, unloving, unlovely look, and a dark shadow resting upon the whole countenance. Can you afford to see that face often? Can you afford to let your friends see it?

I think it was Thackeray who wrote of a man that was homelier than he had any business to be; surely that description may well apply to many of the feminine gender. Cannot you think dear reader, of many old ladies whose faces mirror their character? One lovely placid face seems before me now, kindness and love beaming from every feature; mild benevolent eyes, tender mouth, lips just ready to part into a smile half sad, yet wholly sweet. Wasn't she beautiful, and wasn't every hair of her grand old head loved and honored by every one? "She was a handsome girl," I have heard some of the old people say, "and a handsomer couple never walked into the old D——meeting house" than she and her stalwart young husband, as they passed up its aisles, a groom and bride. Trouble came to her as it comes to all, her first born died, and the mother-heart within her breast was about broken by the blow, while the much loved husband went many years before her to a heavenly home.

In contrast with her peaceful face, I see another, peevish, fretful, unlovely, a burden to herself and those around her; "she is a great trial," they said of her, and when they laid the poor head down to its quiet rest under the daisies, hardly a tear fell upon the unconscious, tranquil clay, yet there were those left that called her by the name of mother. Ah! sisters, don't fret. You can't afford it. Don't grieve, dear hearts, into spiritual darkness. Do you lose property? Rejoice that life, health, and friends are spared. Does a friend prove false? A greater heart than thine was grieved by cruel desertion, denial, and betrayal. Does the dreaded dark-winged angel of Death, bear from your agonizing grasp your choicest flower? Dear heart, remember that love can never lose its own; your loved ones are no less yours after they have passed the grim portals we call "death" but which to them is but the threshold over which they step into a glorious higher life. To most of us it is "the little foxes" that spoil the fair adornment of our lives, the little crosses, little cares, little troubles, while for some crushing sorrow we gather up all our energies, all our Christian faith, and meet it bravely.

The best antidote for any trouble that seems poisoning our daily lives is a good dose of "count over your mercies." If one dose does not cure repeat it every day, in no homeopathic quantity. Be happy and you'll be good. Be good and you'll be pretty. If you are plain looking now, look better. If you are beautiful now, keep beautiful. And finally in order to be so:

> "*Do noble deeds, nor dream them all day long,*
> *And so make life, death, and that vast forever,*
> *One grand sweet song.*"

—Alma

There were deeper psychic disorders and depressions, not unrelated to fretfulness but usually the result of more specific traumas or activities that were woman's special province; these disorders too were perceived to grow from her special nature.

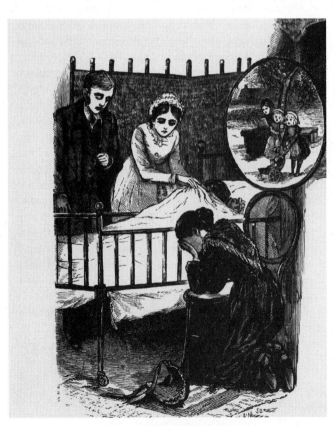

The Changing Year.
Cassell, Petter, Galpin & Co.,
N.Y.C., 1883.

216

GRANDMOTHER BROWN

"Isolated as you were, dear Grandmother Brown, you must have had many anxious hours when sickness came," I said.

"Yes," she answered. "The country doctor of those days wasn't much help. I learned to rely on myself. When my little Lottie was dying I just did everything the doctor said. But after she was gone, I said to myself: 'Never again! When the next trouble comes, it will be between me and my God. I won't have any doctor.' I recalled the old saying: 'I was sick and wished to get better, took physic and died.'

"I had a pretty hard test. Three of my children, Charlie, Lizzie, and Gus, came down at the same time with scarlet fever. All but Will were ill, and I was expecting another baby. Nevertheless, I nursed them through without the help of doctor or nurse, as I later did my brother's son, after we moved to Fort Madison [Iowa]. I didn't call the doctor until the baby was almost there. 'I can't have that baby now,' I thought desperately, 'while these children are so sick.' I had my bed set up in the sitting room, where I could direct an old woman of the neighborhood in nursing the sick children, while I lay in the next room with the new baby. I gave them no medicine and no food except the juice of grapes and of canned peaches. When they began to get better, I gave them a little egg soup—that is, egg beaten up with salt and hot water. I kept them cool and clean. One good thing about the old house was that you could let the windows down from the top. I had a clothes horse hung up with wet sheets to cool the room. I kept a bottle of slippery-elm water sitting in the well curb all the time and gave them some of it frequently to soothe and heal their parched mucous membranes. I never gave them water that had stood in the house, but took it always fresh from the well. 'You make such hard work of nursing,' Dan'l used to say; but it is care with the little hard details that makes the difference between good and poor nursing. Dan'l was not to be depended on in illness, because he could not keep awake. If anyone was sick, it was Will who helped me through the nursing.

"When Charlie began to dry up, after scarlet fever, he was yellow all over. Old Doc Farnsworth came over for potatoes one night. 'Now you can go in and see the boy, if you want to,' Dan'l said. But Farnsworth wouldn't look at him. He was mad because I had ignored him throughout the illness.

"More and more I came to rely on my own judgment in illness. When there was a smallpox scare, we called on Dr.

COUGH SYRUP

Take half a pound of dry hoarhound herbs, one pod of red pepper, four tablespoonfuls of ginger, boil all in three quarts of water, then strain, and add one teaspoonful of good, fresh tar and a pound of sugar. Boil slowly and stir often, until it is reduced to one quart of syrup. When cool, bottle for use. Take one or two teaspoonfuls four or six times a day.

217

THE FLAVOR

of cod-liver oil may be changed to the delightful one of fresh oyster, if the patient will drink a large glass of water poured from a vessel in which nails have been allowed to rust.

Farnsworth to vaccinate us all. Three more babies came to us for him to usher into the world. But the rest of the time I ministered to the family myself. That is, with the help of good Dr. Gunn. Dr. Gunn was the author of a big book entitled *The House Physician,* which told how to care for the sick and make them remedies from the herbs that grew all around us. Whatever the ailment, from hiccoughs to tapeworms, I consulted Dr. Gunn.

"I think I have an instinct for nursing. When my youngest sister was a new baby, only a day old, she had a spasm. I was just fourteen years old and had never seen anyone have a convulsion. My mother was in bed, of course, and there was no one about just then except Sister Libbie and a servant girl. I called them to bring a pail of water, and I dashed it on the baby's head. Soon she relaxed and was all right. 'Child, whatever put that into your mind?' said Ma. I don't know; I just instinctively seemed to know what to do when people were sick.

"Whenever one of my children was ailing, the first thing I tried to do was to clean him thoroughly, inside and out, to open skin and bowels, and then put him to bed. The warm bath would bring out any latent trouble. Of course we had no stationary bathtubs in those days. But I had a large wooden tub. I put a board across it and made my child sit on it, gave him a washcloth, and took another with which I washed his back and feet. Then he'd climb into bed and usually sleep off his disorder.

"Once Dan'l and a girl named 'Liza, who was working for us, were taken sick the same day. 'Liza wanted the doctor. He came and looked at them both. 'They're in for about three weeks' sick spell,' he said. I didn't give Dan'l the doctor's medicine. Instead, I put him through one of my scrubbings and gave him some grated rhubarb. When the doctor came next day Dan'l was out chopping wood, but 'Liza was in bed. Sick for three weeks and more—sure enough!

"Surgery has made great strides during my lifetime. It's wonderful. Just see what the surgeons have done for Gus— given him a new opening to his stomach. But they don't know much more about drugs than they ever did. Except that they've learned to use them less. That's good.

"I've done a little surgery myself in a modest way. Once my baby Herbie touched his hand to a hot stove lid that I'd taken off the stove and put on the floor. He burned himself cruelly, and I was afraid that his fingers would be drawn up when they healed. I made a splint out of a thin board and bound the fingers to it."

"That wasn't the only time Mother saved my fingers," commented Herbert. "I cut off three of them one time when I was cutting sheaf oats for my pony in a cutting box. I rushed into the house with the ends of my fingers hanging by shreds. Mother washed them, fitted them together carefully, and bound them up so that they grew into perfectly good fingers again. Another time she saved my foot. I was running barefoot down the street in front of the Court House. They were repairing the roof, and the sidewalk was covered with old shingles. I ran a rusty spike straight through my foot. Mother pulled out the spike and syringed the wound with hot salt water and hot soda water until she washed away every bit of the rust. Saved me probably from lockjaw."

"There was one time," reflected Grandmother Brown, "when I was forced into performing a really important surgical operation. While we were living on the farm a woman came to live temporarily with our neighbors, the McChords, while her husband was in the war. She was about to have a baby. Dr. Farnsworth was away. No midwife could be found. All the help the poor woman had was what three of us neighbor women could give her. She had had children before and said that none had ever been born to her without the help of a knife. She begged us to help her. Oh, it was terrible. I could see that the body of the child was unable to break through into the world. She suffered horribly. None of the other women would do anything. 'It can't be born without a knife. It can't be born without a knife,' the poor thing kept saying. I was afraid to use a knife for fear of sticking it into the baby's head. Finally I just plucked up my courage and tore the membrane with my finger nail. The baby was released and the mother relieved. That night Dr. Farnsworth stopped to see me. He had been to see the mother after being told, on reaching home, that she had sent for him earlier in the day. 'I came to congratulate you,' he said to me, 'for having had the moral courage to *do* something. That woman couldn't have lasted much longer. She would have gone into spasms and died.' The baby lived to be an old woman, and died here in Fort Madison only recently."

—Harriet C. Brown
Grandmother Brown's Hundred Years
1929

"Protect us, O God, from diphtheria!" These ringing words uttered by my father at morning prayers were my first introduction

---

CAUDLE FOR INVALIDS

A highly nourishing caudle for invalids is made with two moderate spoonfuls of manioca stirred into a quart of cold water, with a little butter, a blade or two of mace, and some grated lemon peel. Boil a quarter of an hour or twenty minutes, stirring constantly that it may be quite smooth. Sweeten with refined honey, or sugar if preferred. Add spice to taste, and one glass of brandy or white wine. Should the mixture become too thick, stir in a little boiling water while the mixture is yet warm.

---

to the tragedy of diseases. The atmosphere in our home that morning was tense. Father and mother ate no breakfast, and we children, not knowing why, left the large platter of fried mush, which usually quickly disappeared, practically untouched. Soon father left home dressed in his Sunday clothes. Mother, pale and silent, continued to walk the floor, wringing her hands and going to the window now and then to look down the road. I followed and looked up and down the road too, but saw nothing. Some hours later a long line of teams came slowly down that road. Driving the lead team, a strange one, was my father, and beside him sat a man I did not know. In the bed of the farm wagon were three oblong boxes. Following were spring wagons, farm wagons, and a large number of men on horseback. Questions directed to my mother brought no answer. Father returned home after many hours and cryptically announced as he came in the door: "Five more." Mother sank into a chair and covered her face with her apron.

As days wore on I learned that the wagon had borne the coffins containing the bodies of three of my playmates. Five more followed in quick succession. Eight of the nine children in that one family died of diphtheria in ten days. There remained only a baby of nine months. The mother took to carrying this child constantly even while she did the farm housework. Clutched to her mother's breast, this child seemed inordinately wide-eyed as though affected by the silent grief which surrounded her. I used to steal away without knowing why and visit this home. There was something fascinatingly tragic about it. Watching that mother, I was learning then, though I did not know it, that it is not the dying but the living who suffer.

—Arthur E. Hertzler
The Horse and Buggy Doctor
1938

MY BABY DEAR IS DEAD

The trees their green are waving,
The sky is blue you say;
My eyes are dull with weeping,
And a cloud is on the day.
I hear among the branches
That sway above my head,
A requiem sad and lonely,
My baby dear is dead.

I want to hold him gently,
*   And kiss him and caress,*
And watch the laughing features
*   Of beaming loveliness.*
O, yes, I want my darling,
*   My arms are wide outspread,*
He runs no more to fill them,
*   My baby dear is dead.*

His life was a June morning,
*   So radiant, fair and sweet,*
The sunshine came in gladness
*   With the patter of his feet.*
We thought of flowers and angels
*   When we saw his merry face,*
And caught in all his movements
*   A gleam of heavenly grace.*

We trembled as we held him,
*   And heard his baby voice,*
For we felt 'twas heavenly music
*   That made our hearts rejoice;*
And jealously we clasped him
*   Lest the angel hand should come*
And woo from out our household,
*   Our precious little one.*

While I miss his face of beauty,
*   And his presence rare and sweet,*
And yearn to hear the patter
*   Of his tripping little feet,*
I smile, for now a glory
*   About my soul is shed,*
The angels have my darling,
*   My baby is not dead.*

—E. O. P.
The Household
VOL. XIV, 1881

It Is Better So

When the baby died, we said,
With a sudden, secret dread,
"Death, be merciful, and pass—
Leave the other"; but, alas!

While we watched he waited there—
One foot on the golden stair,
One hand beckoning at the gate—
Till the home was desolate.

Friends say, "It is better so,
Clothed in innocence to go";
Say, to ease the parting pain,
That "your loss is but their gain."

Ah, the parents think of this!
But remember more the kiss
From the little rose-red lips;
And the print of finger-tips.

Left upon a broken toy,
Will remind them how the boy
And his sister charmed the days
With their pretty, winsome ways.

Only time can give relief
To the weary, lonesome grief—
God's sweet minister of pain
Then shall sing of loss and gain.

—Nora Perry
The Household
VOL. XXV, 1892

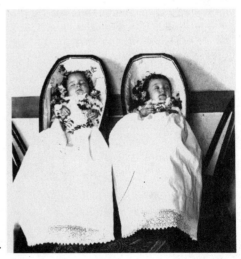

State Historical Society of Wisonsin (WHi (V2) 724).

AGED ONE HOUR

A tiny bark from a hidden shore—
No chart, no helm, no sail, no oar—
Drifting out on the unknown main,
Only to sink from sight again.

A little life, so pure, so brief;
One moan, and then a sweet relief;
A shadow thrown on some hearth-stone;
A whispered prayer, "Thy will be done."

—*The Household*
JANUARY 1892

A SUBSTITUTE FOR MILK OR CREAM

Beat up the whole of a fresh egg in a basin, and then pour boiling tea over it gradually, to prevent its curdling; it is difficult from the taste to distinguish it from rich cream.

GRANDMOTHER BROWN

"When Frank was four years old little Carrie was born. 'Brown, come here,' Dr. Farnsworth called to Dan'l. 'She's a little Venus. I've brought a good many babies into the world, but never one of prettier shape.' It seemed for a while almost as if our lost Lottie had come back. Yes, she was a little beauty, but she was never well. The nurse bathed her till she was chilled. It was the Fourth o' July, but it was a cold day. And then the baby nursed my hot milk. It seemed to poison her. I weaned her,— tried cow's milk, goat's milk,—but nothing helped. Twice a doctor came all the way from Burlington to see her and advise me. But she never thrived. I tried in every way I could to tempt her appetite. I made her the dain-tiest food I could devise; made it taste nice, look pretty. Trimmed her tray and dishes with flowers. 'Baby want some more?' I would coax, but she would always shake her head. She understood ev-erything I said to her. She loved me. But she never talked or walked. She was just too weak. I carried her about on a pillow. As I went about my work I used to think my heart would break as I looked at her lying there, so frail and beautiful, and I so power-less to help her. To have lost one lovely little girl so suddenly and then to watch this one die so slowly—oh, it was more agony than I deserved! She breathed her last one morning at daybreak, when ev-eryone else in the quiet house was sleeping except us two. And when she died, I knew that in seven months I should bear another child."

—Harriet C. Brown
Grandmother Brown's Hundred Years
1929

223

HOUSE-KEPT WOMEN

In the State Reports concerning the condition of Insane Asylums, it is mentioned as one of the chief causes of the excess of female over male lunatics, that women live in-doors too much, and breathe too little out-door air.

—*American Agriculturist*
VOL. XXXV, 1876

The records show that, of the whole number of females admitted to the Connecticut Hospital for the Insane from the beginning, which is 558, 215 are housewives, and of course for the most part the wives of farmers. When one considers the method of life of this class of persons, it does not seem so surprising. Take for illustration a young farmer's wife. She may not be very strong physically at the outset; but be that as it may, she enters into all the plans of her husband with alacrity, she assumes the entire control of the house and does her own work; this is well enough at the outset; but soon she enters upon the maternal state, and a young and increasing family becomes a part of her care, and draws upon her in a two-fold way; she bears not only the physical strain of child-bearing, but also continues to perform her own household duties. Her husband's business still increases, adding more yet to her already multiplied duties; but still she presses on, and so continues, till her pale, anxious face and weary step tell of a constitution broken at once mentally

PREPARING THE DEAD FOR BURIAL

The first duty is to close the eyes, pressing the lids gently down and holding them a moment until they will stay closed. The old way was to lay a coin on each eye, but this is rarely necessary. If the jaw inclines to drop it may be held in place until set by a handkerchief tied over the head, and the limbs should be straightened. The body may then be washed and a clean nightdress put on, or a sheet folded around it and be stretched on a hard bed, or on boards laid on slats.

The body is dressed just before putting in the coffin, usually in the person's own clothes, shrouds being now rarely used,

Woman's Ward, Convalsecent Hospital. Frank Leslie's Illustrated Newspaper, *May 5, 1877. Courtesy: Argosy Bookstore, N.Y.C.*

and physically. This is no imaginary picture, but one enacted continually among our farming people to-day. The average farmer's wife is one of the most patient and overworked women of the time. One has only to attend one of our village churches on some Sunday in the summer to obtain a critical view of our overtaxed farmers and their wives; a glance over such an assembly reveals a set of faces whose very lineaments are drawn and wrinkled from overwork; they tell of lives of constant, unremitted toil, the signs of which even a Sabbath day's rest cannot at all efface.

—*The American Farmer*
1884

The Household—Farmers' Wives

Over the broad sweep of country stretching from the Atlantic to the Pacific, wherever the plowshare has turned the virgin mould, and manly industry has plowed and planted, dug and reaped, are dotted isolated dwellings; in each, when the day is done, sits the house-mother beside the house-band, with their sons and daughters. Wherever the implements of the farmer are found, there, too, are found household utensils. The food which the labor of one produces, the labor of the other prepares; and much more than that. The farmer works from sun till sun; the farmer's wife frequently till far into the night. Who can compute her dreary and incessant toil, under all sorts of deprivations? It is a toil so excessive as to shrivel the charms of womanhood, exhaust the nervous system, bow and stiffen the frame, weaken the springs of life and leave its harsh traces upon every faculty and organ. Yet she is the wife of him whose calling is first, most necessary, and so most honorable, of all avocations.

But the farmer's wife—can we not coin a term and call her farmeress?—is so often a pathetic figure in a beautiful setting! Around are hill and dale, meadow and stream, lovely under any light, at every hour, with nature's own tints and forms—she, too, should be in harmony with these. But, after her first youth is over, does her form, face and expression indicate a real correspondence between nature and her soul? This cannot be. Her days are spent in that work which, however faithfully done, seems to leave no positive effects. The only apparent result is a sense of comfort which is appreciable only by its loss.

Is the case over-stated? One significant fact alone replies. The statistics of the chief lunatic asylums of this country show that

though we have seen a nicely-ironed and snowy sheet draped across the chest, and to the feet, which looked very well. One or two articles of underwear are all that are needed and the dress or coat is usually cut down the back as it may be made to fit more smoothly thus. The hair should be neatly arranged as worn when living. Flowers are now more used to place around the room than in the coffin, though a small bunch may be laid in the hand, and colored flowers are as much used as white. If a person has been tenderly cared for while living, all that is needed is a decent and orderly burial. A splendid funeral will never atone for past neglect. Too many persons "save all their flowers to give to the dead" instead of giving the kind attention and sympathy their hearts hungered for while living.

While the conditions in country neighborhoods are different, and neighbors and friends come in their own carriages, still happily the old custom of having a great dinner of "funeral baked meats" to which even near neighbors came, is now becoming obsolete. The grief-stricken family do not feel like preparing a feast and would appreciate more a quiet friendly call to cheer their loneliness when the funeral is over.

—Ruth Brown

from farmers' wives are found the largest percentage of those whose light of reason has been quenched in terrible and hopeless darkness. Constant fatigue, monotony, want of society, with its social stimulus and interchange of thought, the hopelessness of any change of routine, prove too much to endure, and the poor, tired brain reels with thoughts of a cheerless past and hopeless future. The horses and oxen plowing in their master's field have before them the panorama of nature; they breathe the free winds of heaven; but her outlook is narrowed to the four walls of her house, which in time becomes a prison of torture.

A leading agricultural paper of this country, situated centrally, and having opportunity of speaking for all sections, published these editorial remarks only two months ago:

> The fact is, and has been for a long time, that the farmer's wife is expected to do the work of three or four women, with very imperfect facilities often for doing the work of one. She must be cook and provide three hearty meals each day. She is laundry maid, dairy maid, kitchen girl, mother, wife, nurse, seamstress; she raises pigs, calves, and poultry, and in a pinch helps in the field. Her husband in his work will have mowers, reapers, all the modern machinery—what has she? Just her two hands, and in nine cases out of ten her kitchen is ill-arranged, and she must draw water, bring in wood and do everything at a disadvantage. Who ever knew a farmer's wife to sit down in the middle of the day and rest an hour? Yet every hired man claims this as his right.

Nor is this class a restricted one. None is so widespread, and none, hitherto, have had so little consideration. It forms a sisterhood which, until the time of Granges, had no affiliation, stimulus or incentive. Sunday was literally a day of rest. The unwonted quiet, a kind of solemn hush, which rested like a spell over the face of nature, the long ride to the "meeting-house," the psalm-singing by the rustic choir, the prayer ranging to the "uttermost parts of the earth," the setting of the congregation into their places, the sermon, roaming over some subject foreign to the thought, all soothed the weary nerves and oiled the wheels of life. Blessings on that rest for the farmeress! We see her now, leaning back in the stiff pew, nodding to the rhythm of the preacher's voice as he discourses upon the restoration of the Jews or the divisions of Noah's Ark. The pungent flavor of a bunch of fennel or caraway seed fails to prove an antidote to the unwonted atmosphere of rest. After a longer nod than usual, the sleeper arouses to look around with a look of innocence and renewed attention, and then the dear old head gives up the struggle and submits to the sway of Morpheus during the remainder of the sermon. Such a scene is enough to touch the springs of laughter and of tears.

Again, the effects of hard labor, with the narrowing of intelligent interest to a round of petty cares, have their full fruitage in the offspring of the farmer's wife. The child is often wronged and starved before it sees the light. Such instances are altogether too common.

And is there no remedy for this? There must be, or nature is at fault. With the isolated household there can and must be neighborhood co-operative industries in various important departments of household labor, which shall greatly relieve this overtasked sisterhood. Following these will doubtless be devised means for stated occasions of social, intellectual and moral culture.

—Hester M. Poole
The Continent, 1882

Yet, with everything, there runs a countercurrent of strength and quiet endurance. What had to be done was done.

GRANDMOTHER BROWN

"But, oh, one couldn't baby one's self long. There was so much to do all the time in the house and in the fields. I remember once, at harvest time, I suffered terribly with the toothache. But no one had time to hitch up and take me in to town to the dentist's. Besides, all the horses were needed for the work. In the daytime I didn't mind my aching tooth so much, but at night I could hardly stand it. So, one evening, I went out on the porch with the shears and an old looking-glass and just pried it out. I had cut my wisdom teeth when Willie cut his first ones. We were teething together. I was just beginning to get my senses about that time, I suppose. The tooth came out all good and smooth. I took it in the house and dangled it before Dan'l in the light. 'Why, Mother, how in the world *could* you do that?' he exclaimed. But it was *out!*"

—Harriet C. Brown
Grandmother Brown's Hundred Years
1929

THE HOMEMAKER
PROFESSIONALIZED

The American Woman's Home, written by Catherine E. Beecher and Harriet Beecher Stowe, was published in 1869 and was one of the most influential books of its time. Its aim was to reform and "professionalize" the occupation of homemaker. Accepting the "proper place of woman," the authors sought to free women from their burdens and to elevate their status by recognizing the dignity and importance of what they did and by training them for their profession just as men were trained for theirs. This, of course, was a reform much needed, but with whatever short- or long-range benefits it brought to the scientific management or environmental quality of the American home, that response stood directly in the way of any deeper or more inclusive considerations of women's rights.

The country girl learned housekeeping at home. If her mother was an indifferent or incompetent housekeeper, or if the girl lacked "natural aptitude," she had little recourse to useful instruction before the second half of the century. The books she found then were most often grim, dictatorial tracts that did little to motivate her or capture her imagination. This is why chatty, informative magazines like *The Household* and books such as *The American Woman's Home* were so important.

INTRODUCTION

The authors of this volume, while they sympathize with every honest effort to relieve the disabilities and sufferings of their sex, are confident that the chief cause of these evils is the fact that the honor and duties of the family state are not duly appreciated, that women are not trained for these duties as men are trained for their trades and professions, and that, as the consequence, family labor is poorly done, poorly paid, and regarded as menial and disgraceful.

To be the nurse of young children, a cook, or a housemaid, is regarded as the lowest and last resort of poverty, and one which no woman of culture and position can assume without loss of caste and respectability.

When the other sex are to be instructed in law, medicine, or divinity, they are favored with numerous institutions richly endowed, with teachers of the highest talents and acquirements, with extensive libraries, and abundant and costly apparatus. With such advantages they devote nearly ten of the best years of life to preparing themselves for their profession; and to secure the public from unqualified members of these professions, none can enter them until examined by a competent body, who certify to their due preparation for their duties.

Illustration on previous page: Library of Congress.

230

Woman's profession embraces the care and nursing of the body in the critical periods of infancy and sickness, the training of the human mind in the most impressible period of childhood, the instruction and control of servants, and most of the government and economies of the family state. These duties of woman are as sacred and important as any ordained to man; and yet no such advantages for preparation have been accorded to her, nor is there any qualified body to certify the public that a woman is duly prepared to give proper instruction in her profession.

—Catherine E. Beecher and Harriet Beecher Stowe
The American Woman's Home
1869

TEACH GIRLS TO BE HOUSEKEEPERS

No one expects a boy to become a physician just because he is put in charge of a physician's office, even though the books, surgical cases and furniture are just what they should be; but a girl is expected by two-thirds of the world to become a housekeeper when she is put in charge of a house. It is a compliment to the quick perceptions and wonderful intuitions of my sex, but it has led to so much unhappiness; so many wives, husbands and children suffer because of this accepted fallacy, that I am willing to waive the compliment, and beg of mothers to teach girls to be housekeepers by letting them keep house before their wedding day.

—Mary Willis
The Household
VOL . XXV, 1892

THE IMPORTANCE OF DOMESTIC EDUCATION

"Women act their parts
When they do make their ordered households know them."

Without saying one word in disparagement of those noble and humane efforts now being made to enlarge the sphere of woman, and open to her new avenues to self-support and independence, it is, nevertheless, a fixed fact that for a large majority of the female sex, *home* is the true field of labor and duty, with a view to which her training and education should be conducted. Not that she should never leave it to engage in those works of charity and benevolence for which woman is peculiarly and eminently fitted—

SEALINGWAX, RED, FOR BOTTLING MEDICINE

Rosin, 1 1/4 lbs.; tallow, lard, and beeswax, each, 1 oz. Melt together and add American vermilion, 1oz.

Remarks—Dip while hot. It is nice for druggists, who dip their vial corks, to have ready for use, or for bottles after the cork is cut off closely.

FAMILY SPRING BITTERS

Mandrake root one ounce,
dandelion root one ounce, burdock
root one ounce, yellow dock root
one ounce, prickly ash berries two
ounces, marsh mallow one ounce,
turkey rhubarb half an ounce,
gentian one ounce, English
camomile flowers one ounce, red
clover tops two ounces.

Wash the herbs and roots;
put them into an earthen vessel,
pour over two quarts of water that
has been boiled and cooled; let it
stand over night and soak; in the
morning set it on the back of the
stove, and steep it five hours; it
must not boil, but be nearly ready
to boil. Strain it through a cloth,
and add half a pint of good gin.
Keep it in a cool place. Half a wineglass taken as a dose twice a day.

This is better than all the
patent blood medicines that are in
the market—a superior blood
purifier, and will cure almost any
malignant sore, by taking
according to direction, and
washing the sore with a strong tea
of red raspberry leaves steeped, first
washing the sore with castile soap,
then drying with a soft cloth, and
washing it with the strong tea of
red raspberry leaves.

but everything outside of that charmed circle of which she is the center and the sun can present but minor claims upon her attention and her time.

The domestic economy of a household, with its many and various departments, may be likened to a machine. The guiding power of that machine is the wife and mother. She must understand every wheel and cog, and on occasion be able to turn the crank herself; but no matter how many hands there are to work it, without her watchful eye, it will soon go wrong. How important, then, that before assuming the duties of so responsible a position, she should have served an apprenticeship and become familiar with the details of her business. Would that mothers were more deeply impressed with a sense of their obligations to their daughters, in this respect, as well as to society at large; for the evils of an ill-ordered household do not cease with one generation, but are transmitted like hereditary diseases, from mother to daughter, down— down—till the aggregate of waste and wretchedness from one wrong beginning, would be fearful to contemplate.

What would be thought of a merchant who should place at the head of a mercantile establishment a son who had received no commercial education—who was a stranger to day-books and ledgers, and had never stood behind the counter? Or a sea-captain, who should give the command of his ship to a young man who had never studied navigation? Or a general, who was rash enough to permit one to lead a regiment into action who was utterly ignorant of military tactics? Yet a young girl with no training for the stern realities and actual duties of life—who knows nothing of cooking or housekeeping in general—whose stock of acquirements consists mostly of music, drawing and painting, which are seldom or never called for after marriage, assumes the fearfully responsible situation of head of a household. A more pitiable object scarcely exists. If she has servants she is destitute of the requisite knowledge to direct them; and ignorant and unprincipled as many of them are, she is wholly at their mercy, and cannot long retain their respect or her own. If obliged to do her own work, as is often the case, her trials are greater still, unused to labor, the unwonted hardships added to cares of which she had no previous conception crushes her to the earth. Perhaps she is among strangers, with no mother or sister or aunt to turn to in her troubles. How bitterly then she reproaches (mentally, if not in words) that fond, indulgent parent who wished her daughter to see only the sunny side of life—who would not press unwelcome offices upon her lest she might not have pleasant recollections of home—who could not have the delicacy of her hands marred by contact with household drudgery in any form—who shrank from inflicting on the gay, light-hearted young thing any lectures or lessons touching domestic economy. Mistaken love! Fatal error!

And the young husband—how is he affected by such a state of things? Perhaps his mother is a model housekeeper, and the contrast between her well-ordered establishment and his own home is painful indeed. The youthful wife, worn down by care and toil, mortified at the many mistakes which her want of skill and incapacity occasion, becomes low-spirited and unsocial. Irritated (though unreasonably,) by this want of cheerfulness in his once sprightly and chatty companion, as well as by the irregularity of his ill-cooked meals, and the general disorder and untidy appearance of the house, in an unguarded moment he says a bitter, reproachful word which he would fain recall a moment after,—but she retorts by reminding him that he used to remark before marriage that he did not wish *his* wife to know any thing of kitchen affairs (for it is true that there are young men weak and foolish enough to say such things).

> "And harsher words will then come in
> To spread the breach that words begin,
> And eyes forget the gentle ray
> They wore in courtship's sunny day,
> And voices lose the tones that shed
> A tenderness o'er all they said—
> Till fast declining one by one
> The sweetnesses of love are gone."

I might go on with the picture. I might speak of the accumulated cares and burdens which maternity brings,—but I forbear—hoping that some more able writer may take up the subject—a subject fraught with such vital interests that every mother in the land may ask, with fear and trembling, "Who is sufficient for these things?"

—A Mother
The Household
VOL. I, 1868

DOMESTIC TRAINING

If there is a need of Agricultural Colleges, where young men shall be taught the theory and practice of successful farming, surely there is an equal, if not greater need of similar institutions where young ladies may be taught the equally important theory and practice of housekeeping.

Without doubt, the best place for domestic training is home; the best teacher a judicious mother. But some mothers are incompetent, and many, from various causes, indisposed to give their daughters thorough instructions in the manifold duties of housekeeping. Some consider it too much trouble. They find it easier to go on and do up the work themselves than to have their girls "round in the way." Others are proud of the lily hands and attenuated waists of their daughters, and to preserve in them those excellent qualities, they are willing to make slaves of themselves. It would not be easy to compute the misery which results from this neglect. In whatever situation a lady may be placed, ignorance of domestic duties is a frightful source of annoyance. If she have servants, she is constantly at their mercy,—a servant of servants is she all the days of her life. If she does her own work, it is at the expense of a vast, and unnecessary account of mental and manual labor. Many a lady loses her health and grows prematurely old, from this cause alone. While the systematic housekeeper will do the work for a large family without hurry or confusion, the unskillful one will worry herself into illness over a much lighter task.

We would not be understood as decrying "book learning," or fashionable accomplishments. We believe that there is time enough, if it be properly improved, to learn music, drawing, etc., without encroaching upon the time necessary to acquire a thorough domestic education.

—*The Household*
VOL. I, 1868

EDUCATION IN HOUSEHOLD DUTIES

Mothers who are themselves genuinely interested in the proper management of their own households will find but little trouble if they would avail themselves of the natural *imitativeness* of children. The little ones like to be useful if they see others about them useful; they like to follow the mother about the house under pretense of helping, though often hindering her: they enjoy using their little hands about something that older people do:

SEALINGWAX FOR FRUIT JARS

Best orange (gum) shellac and beeswax, each 1 lb.; rosin, 4 lbs. Melt and dip or paint the corks with a brush. 'Tis a red shade, but may be colored more if desired, any color. [See No. 2 for a bright red.]
—Druggists' Circular

they like, in general, to *work* until false notions are instilled into their minds.

We know a little girl of six years—and there are many others in quiet homes all over the country who exhibit similar tastes—who already bids fair to be the nicest little housekeeper possible. Ever since she has been old enough to understand her *mission*—three years, at least!—she has been eager to do what she fancies is useful to others. She takes her tiny duster and flourishes over the chairs and sofas with positive results. After breakfast she demurely gathers up the teaspoons from the table, and thinks it very nice to wipe them on the soft cloth after they are washed; nothing suits her better than to make some miniature pies, and have them actually put upon the dinner table; with her little broom she forestalls the servant, and sweeps down the front-door steps before breakfast in the morning. She puts a particular room in order every day, and quite of her own accord has assumed so much the care of her father's wardrobe that her mother will gradually be supplanted in that duty. "Papa, you've put on the wrong *cravat*," she seriously says some morning; "*that's* your *best* one." She reminds him to put on a clean collar and wristbands; says, "Why, Papa! you haven't brushed your coat," and herself seizes his beaver and plies the brush. She seems to consider herself responsible for his neat personal appearance.

Almost all little girls delight to have some small household

Harper's Weekly, *April 17, 1875. Courtesy: Argosy Bookstore, N.Y.C.*

duty committed to their care; and if this disposition should be fostered, instead of being discouraged, as it often is, on the ground that they cannot do the thing so well as an older person, they would, with rare exceptions, grow up with sufficient knowledge of, and interest in, those home matters about which, nowadays, there is so much complaint that young ladies know little, and care less.

—E. X.
The Household
c. 1870

TO MODEL HOUSEWIVES

There goes the door bell! I wonder who it can be! I wish I knew! As I started to answer its call I picked up some half dozen (more or less) small articles and put them into my satchel; and passing through the sitting room I gathered together as many more larger ones, and piled them upon the sewing machine. Proceeding to the door I found Mr. Hunt awaiting admittance; a gentleman whose acquaintance I had but recently made and who but a few evenings previous had taken tea with us. In the evening the conversation drifted upon untidy and disorderly housewives. I can assure you that I congratulated myself upon the orderly appearance of things in general. Of course!—the lady on whom he bestows his name will be both orderly and tidy! I hope so!

I had just returned from town with sundry purchases preparatory to attending a large party, and in my haste to examine them, had thrown off my wrappings on the lounge, rubbers on the oilcloth, hat and gloves on the stand, and emptied the contents of my satchel on the table. Then I brought out the dress I was intending to wear, to compare with ribbon, laces, gloves, etc.

I began to unload myself in the sitting room, and continued the process along into the dining room, so that things were pretty evenly distributed in both rooms; the chairs, as well as lounge, table and stand were doing duty. I sat down surrounded by all my adornments and was admiring the blending of colors, and as I laid the rich lace in folds on my dress, I almost imagined myself in the gay throng when the door bell brought me to my surroundings. I can but confess my confusion and mortification at the disorderly state of my rooms, and gave myself a lecture while endeavoring to entertain my visitor, and also promised myself to try and prevent a repetition of a like scene.

THE FOLLOWING RECIPE for embroidery paste will prove very satisfactory. Mix three tablespoonfuls of flour and as much resin as will lie on a shilling with half a pint of water until smooth, pour into an iron saucepan, and stir till it boils. When it has boiled five minutes, turn it into a basin. As soon as it is quite cold, it is ready for use. Odd designs of birds and animals cut out of Turkey red cotton and applied to cream-colored material are effective for decorating splashers, night-dress cases, brush-and-comb cases, or shoebags.

I have been married; well, I'll not say how long, long enough to become a good housekeeper, but I'm not. I can account for my not being a model housekeeper (my mother was a superior one) only upon the fact that previous to my marriage I was a school teacher. For there is a proverb saying, "school teachers never make good housekeepers." I trust I am not doomed. I am a great admirer of order, and can stand only a certain degree of disorder without becoming—to use extravagant expression—almost frantic; and everything about the house must be cleanly. I have to work very hard to keep my house to please me. There must be an easier way, a secret which I do not possess.

Several months ago a request similar to this met my eye in THE HOUSEHOLD. I laid aside my pen and hunted it up. I thought I was not going to find it, but here it is, away back in last year's May number. "Will some correspondent or subscriber inform me what method to adopt to keep a well regulated house and always have things looking just so? and oblige Mrs. O. C." At the time I thought, this is a fine opening, suggestive of instructive saying to follow from one or more of our model housekeepers, something we can put into practical use. I shall now learn how to keep house! But each succeeding HOUSEHOLD has been searched in vain, and if the querist (as doubtless she has) has been as expectant a searcher as myself, with me she must begin to despair of receiving the much desired information.

I know of but one model housekeeper in our community. I shall call her Mrs. Mann. Go there when one will, seven o'clock in the morning, her work is never doing but always done. I have never been able to get any information as to how she manages. If I question her, as I very frequently do, she replies "I am no better housekeeper than you," when she knows she surpasses the whole neighborhood for blocks around. Could we have something from her pen it would be very valuable to those like myself who are aspiring to become such as she.

Model housewives, I add my request to that of Mrs. O. C. Will not some mother, aunt, or sister give me their secret of management? That is the word, management! I feel that is what I lack. Don't answer us by saying, "a place for everything and everything in its place," but tell me how to do it, whereby you will become a benefactress in helping more than one sister in need.

—Perplexity
The Household
APRIL 1874

FOR KICKING COWS

Take a short strap, and fasten the ends together. Next prepare a pin of some soft wood, about six or eight inches long, one and a half inches in diameter. Take the cow by the off fore-leg, and double it at the knee-joint close; pass the strap or loop over the knee, pressing it back until you can insert the pin between that and the knee-joint, and she cannot kick.

An important prerequisite to "professional status" was a heightened awareness of the scope and importance of woman's responsibilities. Ideally, this awareness would lead to the creation of conditions that would allow her to carry out her tasks with as much ease and efficiency as her husband carried out his. That woman's work merited a rational methodology was not easily understood or accepted by men or women.

How Many Wives Fade

When a man undertakes a business, he finds learned men ready to assist him; he knows what there is to do, and secures help accordingly. A young woman goes to housekeeping often without any help at all or perhaps one awkward girl.

There are three meals to get every day—that means cooking; and then comes the dishes to be washed after each meal. It would take about forty-five pieces for breakfast and supper, seventy for dinner for a family of five, one hundred and sixty-five pieces to be carried from the dining room to the kitchen every day, washed and carried back. If you have six rooms in your house, there is one room to be swept and cleaned daily, beside brushing up the others, making beds, bringing in wood and carrying water.

American Soap Company Advertisement.
Engraving. Library of Congress.

Twice a week there is bread making, twice a week yeast making, one day washing, one day ironing, all your pantries and safes to be washed out once a week, dairy work to be attended to, beside innumerable jobs in the way of preserving, jelly making, pickling, curing hams, putting down pigs' feet, looking over and nipping off your apples twice in winter, and making hogshead cheese, mince meat, a thorough house cleaning twice a year, then sewing on dresses, aprons, skirts, drawers, gowns, etc., by the dozen.

Then supposing the housekeeper has a baby; an average six months old baby that weighs about eighteen pounds. Suppose she has this child in her arms thirty times a day (a cross infant is taken up more frequently), and often she is obliged to work with the right arm, while carrying the burden of the baby about with the left.

Who says there is nothing in gymnastics equal to the endurance of a mother's arms? Even when the day's labor is accomplished and she goes to bed, she still holds her baby and does not sleep soundly for fear of rolling on it or its getting uncovered; she must attend to its wants several times in the night, and she must be in a constrained condition for fear of disturbing it.

I have heard women say that they would give almost anything for a night of undisturbed sleep, "with no care on the mind." Then in the morning up and at it again. Don't you see why women grow pale, and why they are some times a little cross, and how their husbands wonder that their wives don't look pretty and dress well, and entertain them as they did before they were married.

The wives don't reason on the matter; they think it is all the man's fault, and then they turn cross, and so things go at sixes and sevens, and this is the place woman's rights should be taken hold of. I don't think voting would help that very much; woman's labor should be made a study. In the first place men must realize that it is a great labor to keep house.

A great many women sink down under the weight and then everybody says: "Poor thing, she always was a good-for-nothing creature"; and the "poor thing" has been doing for the past ten years more than two women ought.

—*The Household*
VOL. III, 1870

TO KEEP MILK SWEET

Put into a panful a spoonful of grated horseradish, it will keep it sweet for days.

M iss Beecher and Mrs. Stowe make the ultimate case for system and order by attaching them to a somewhat more inclusive plan. One achieved efficiency and command and gained grace simultaneously.

HABITS OF SYSTEM AND ORDER

There is no one thing more necessary to a housekeeper in performing her varied duties, than *a habit of system and order;* and yet, the peculiarly desultory nature of women's pursuits, and the embarrassments resulting from the state of domestic service in this country, render it very difficult to form such a habit. But it is sometimes the case that women who could and would carry forward a systematic plan of domestic economy do not attempt it, simply from a want of knowledge of the various modes of introducing it. It is with reference to such, that various modes of securing systems and order, which the writer has seen adopted, will be pointed out.

A wise economy is nowhere more conspicuous, than in a systematic *apportionment of time* to different pursuits.

It is wise, therefore, for all persons to devise a systematic plan, which they will at least keep in view, and aim to accomplish; and by which a proper proportion of time shall be secured for all the duties of life.

In forming such a plan, every woman must accommodate herself to the peculiarities of her situation.

The Creator of all things is a Being of perfect system and order; and, to aid us in our duty in this respect, he has divided our time, by a regularly returning day of rest from worldly business. In following this example, the intervening six days may be subdivided to secure similar benefits. In doing this, a certain portion of time must be given to procure the means of livelihood, and for preparing food, raiment, and dwellings. To these objects, some must devote more, and others less, attention. The remainder of time not necessarily thus employed, might be divided somewhat in this manner: The leisure of two afternoons and evenings could be devoted to religious and benevolent objects, such as religious meetings, charitable associations, school visiting, and attention to the sick and poor. The leisure of two other days might be devoted to intellectual improvement, and the pursuits of taste. The leisure of another day might be devoted to social enjoyments, in making or receiving visits; and that of another, to miscellaneous domestic pursuits, not included in the other particulars.

It is probable that few persons could carry out such an arrangement very strictly; but every one can make a systematic apportionment of time, and at least *aim* at accomplishing it; and they can also compare with such a general outline, the time which

---

TESTING BUTTER

Melt some suspected butter; soak a wick in it; when cold, light it like a candle and then blow it out. If oleomargarine it will smell like a blown-out candle, if it is butter it will smell like butter.

---

they actually devote to these different objects, for the purpose of modifying any mistaken proportions.

Without attempting any such systematic employment of time, and carrying it out, so far as they can control circumstances, most women are rather driven along by the daily occurrences of life; so that, instead of being the intelligent regulators of their own time, they are the mere sport of circumstances. There is nothing which so distinctly marks the difference between weak and strong minds as the question, whether they control circumstances or circumstances control them.

Some persons endeavor to systematize their pursuits by apportioning them to particular hours of each day. For example, a certain period before breakfast, is given to devotional duties; after breakfast, certain hours are devoted to exercise and domestic employments; other hours to sewing, or reading, or visiting; and others, to benevolent duties. But in most cases, it is more difficult to systematize the hours of each day, than it is to secure some regular division of the week.

In regard to the minutiae of family work, the writer has known the following methods to be adopted. Monday, with some of the best housekeepers, is devoted to preparing for the labors of the week. Any extra cooking, the purchasing of articles to be used during the week, the assorting of clothes for the wash, and mending such as would otherwise be injured— these, and similar items, belong to this day. Tuesday is devoted to washing, and Wednesday to ironing. On Thursday, the ironing is finished off, the clothes are folded and put away, and all articles which need mending are put in the mending-basket, and attended to. Friday is devoted to sweeping and housecleaning. On Saturday, and especially the last Saturday of every month, every department is put in order; the casters and table furniture are regulated, the pantry and cellar inspected, the trunks, drawers, and closets arranged, and every thing about the house put in order for Sunday. By this regular recurrence of a particular time for inspecting every thing, nothing is forgotten till ruined by neglect.

—Catherine E. Beecher and Harriet Beecher Stowe
The American Woman's Home
1869

The idea of system and order extended particularly to a consideration of the environment in which women worked. At this time house planning in general and the workplaces of the house in particular were prodigies of inefficiency. Dreary, cramped, poorly constructed, poorly insulated, poorly ventilated, they worked as both prisons and torture chambers for many rural women. Home planning and improvement were, of course, the province of men, and many thoughtful architects or farm writers addressed the issue, but it was left again to Beecher and Stowe to perceive the real problems and develop the first truly functional and scientific approach to the design of the American home through a meticulous observation of the tasks to be done and the needs to be fulfilled. This concept of "the rational household" was something that most American architects did not begin to deal with seriously until well into the twentieth century.

The first thing to be considered in a plan for a kitchen is the saving of steps. Three times every day, and three hundred and sixty-five days each year, a house-keeper has meals to prepare, to arrange upon a table, and to clear away. Suppose, now, that in a well-arranged room, three hundred steps will, on an average, suffice to carry one through the routine of a dinner. If, as often happens, she is compelled to take six hundred, nearly one-half of her fatigue and consumption of time will be the direct consequence of unskillful and ill-advised planning. Thus, in the course of the year, a cause apparently so slight as the awkward collocation of the stove, pantry, closet, and sink may work an enormous difference in the amount of leisure and strength she may have to bestow on something better than mere household drudgery.

—Joseph P. Lyman
Philosophy of Housekeeping
1869

The Laborer's Kitchen

Let the kitchen be sufficiently large for a stove and a dinner-table, and space wide enough for a person to pass around the table at meal-time. There is little danger of making a kitchen too large. The whole country is full of houses with kitchens intolerably small.

The arrangement of the kitchen should be such, that one can go out of doors, down cellar, up stairs, and in the pantry from the kitchen. Always plan your kitchen first. Then make every other room in the house conform to the arrangements of the kitchen. If practicable, let the kitchen and dining-room be so arranged that they may be made, when necessary, as one room. The stairway, instead of having a cold out-door, should be central, and should receive the surplus heat, to temper the atmosphere of the upper rooms.

The old style of building, with a hall separating the principal rooms of the house, above and below, is as well contrived to make a cold house as anything can be. It makes one shudder to think of going into this open hall, or into the principal rooms opening into it. They are not much used now—the family room being in the rear, or in a wing, entered from without by a side door. The whole front has a dark, uninviting look in the evening; and it is not an economical way to build a dwelling-house.

The kitchen may be considered the great center of domestic operations. The frugal housewife must necessarily spend more of her time in the kitchen than in any other apartment of the dwelling. When the fire has been started and certain articles of food are cooking, she needs to have the sleeping and toilet-room as near the kitchen as it can consistently be located, so that she may step in for a few moments, and still be where she can supervise the operations of the kitchen. If her toilet and sleeping-room be up stairs, or beyond another apartment, the practice will be adopted of combing and dressing the hair in the kitchen, which neat housekeepers never will allow. Besides this, the main sleeping-room which is to be occupied by the head of the family, should open in the kitchen, or so near the kitchen as to be convenient of access in case of sickness. Then, in cold weather, the sleeping-room may be warmed, little or much, by the fire in the dining-room, or the fire of the kitchen. Besides this, the dining-room or the living-room should be contiguous to the parlor, without a broad hall between them; and the parlor and living-room should be so conveniently arranged, that guests may be introduced into either room from the front door, without passing through one of the other rooms. As the mistress of the kitchen must necessarily go frequently into the cellar, from the kitchen, to carry articles of food, and to return the same to the kitchen, it would be a very unsatisfactory arrangement to have the cellar door at the farther side of a room that joins the kitchen. Economical housekeepers often experience the inconveniences of such an arrangement of rooms. In many dwellings, the pantry cannot be reached from the kitchen without passing through some other room, which every intelligent housekeeper will acknowledge is an unsatisfactory arrangement. There should be also

TO INCREASE THE QUANTITY OF CREAM

Have ready two pans in boiling water; and on the new milk coming to the dairy, take the hot pans out of the water, put the milk into one of them, and cover it with the other. This will occasion great augmentation in the thickness and quality of the cream.

IN CHURNING

cream, add a lump of butter to the cream before commencing, and the butter will come in two-thirds the time it would without.

a back stairway, where those in the kitchen may reach the upper story, without passing through other rooms, and thence up the lobby or parlor stairs.

—Sereno E. Todd
Todd's Country Homes
1870

A CHRISTIAN HOUSE

Fig. 1 is an enlarged plan of the kitchen and stove-room. The chimney and stove-room are contrived to ventilate the whole house, by a mode exhibited in another chapter.

Between the two rooms glazed sliding-doors, passing each other, serve to shut out heat and smells from the kitchen. The sides of the stove-room must be lined with shelves; those on the side by the cellar stairs, to be one foot wide, and eighteen inches apart; on the other side, shelves may be narrower, eight inches wide and nine inches apart. Boxes with lids, to receive stove utensils, must be placed near the stove.

On these shelves, and in the closet and boxes, can be placed every material used for cooking, all the table and cooking utensils, and all the articles used in house work, and yet much spare

Fig. 1

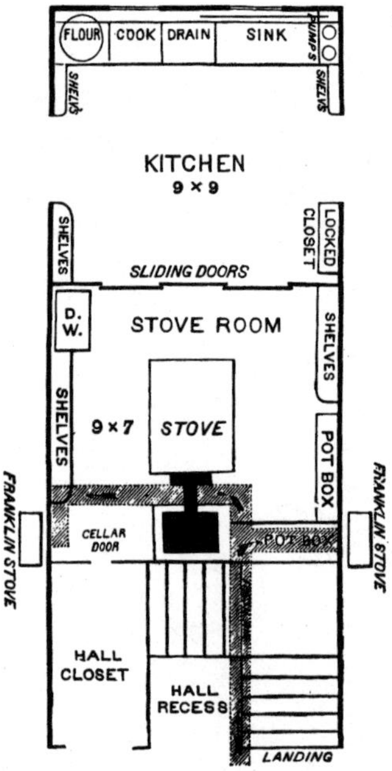

FLOUR | COOK | DRAIN | SINK

SHELVES   PUMPS

KITCHEN
9 × 9

SHELVES   LOCKED CLOSET

SLIDING DOORS

D.W. | **STOVE ROOM**   SHELVES

SHELVES

9 × 7 | **STOVE**   POT BOX

FRANKLIN STOVE

CELLAR DOOR | POT BOX | FRANKLIN STOVE

HALL CLOSET

HALL RECESS

LANDING

Fig. 2

room will be left. The cook's galley in a steamship has every article and utensil used in cooking for two hundred persons, in a space not larger than this stove-room, and so arranged that with one or two steps the cook can reach all he uses.

In contrast to this, in most large houses, the table furniture, the cooking materials and utensils, the sink, and the eating-room, are at such distances apart, that half the time and strength is employed in walking back and forth to collect and return the articles used.

Fig. 2 is an enlarged plan of the sink and cooking-form. Two windows make a better circulation of air in warm weather, by having one open at top and the other at the bottom, while the light is better adjusted for working, in case of weak eyes.

The flour-barrel just fills the closet, which has a door for admission, and a lid to raise when used. Beside it, is the form for cooking, with a moulding-board laid on it; one side used for preparing vegetables and meat, and the other for moulding bread. The sink has two pumps, for well and for rain-water—one having a forcing power to throw water into the reservoir in the garret, which supplies the water-closet and bath-room. On the other side of the sink is the dish-drainer, with a ledge on the edge next the sink, to hold the dishes, and grooves cut to let the water drain into the sink. It has hinges, so that it can either rest on the cook-form or be turned over and cover the sink. Under the sink are shelf-boxes placed on two shelves run into grooves, with other grooves above and below, so that one may move the shelves and increase or diminish the spaces between. The shelf-boxes can be used for scouring-materials, dish-towels, and dish-cloths; also to hold bowls for bits of butter, fats, etc. Under these two shelves is room for two pails, and a jar for soap-grease.

Under the cook-form are shelves and shelf-boxes for unbolted wheat, corn-meal, rye, etc. Beneath these, for white and brown sugar, are wooden can-pails, which are the best articles in which to keep these constant necessities. Beside them is the tin molasses-can with a tight, movable cover, and a cork in the spout. This is much better than a jug for molasses, and also for vinegar and oil, being easier to clean and to handle. Other articles and implements for cooking can be arranged on or under the shelves at the side and front. A small cooking-tray, holding pepper, salt, dredging-box, knife and spoon, should stand close at hand by the stove.

The articles used for setting tables are to be placed on the shelves at the front and side of the sink. Two tumbler-trays, made of pasteboard, covered with varnished fancy papers and divided by wires save many steps in setting and clearing the table. Similar trays, for knives and forks and spoons, serve the same purpose.

The sink should be three feet long and three inches deep, its width matching the cook-form.

—Catherine E. Beecher and Harriet Beecher Stowe
The American Woman's Home
1869

With the exaltation of system also came the problem of too much system with its oppressive effects on the family. Many eager housekeepers unintentionally over-reacted to the imperatives of efficient management; others, of course, embraced them joyfully.

TOO NEAT

I can't sit down in our best room,
It is so slick and spruce;
Fact is, 'most everything we've got's
Too good for common use.
Though next to godliness the Book
Puts cleanliness, I'm bound
To say Keturah's mighty apt
To run it in the ground.

—*The Household*
VOL. XV, 1892

SYSTEM IN HOUSEKEEPING

One must confess to a fellow feeling for the little girl who did not like to visit where they always had times for things, and yet that it is very desirable to have system in the household, goes without saying. But no wise housekeeper will make system a Moloch to which the comfort and convenience of the whole family must be sacrificed.

An experienced housekeeper knows that it is impossible to regulate household affairs by a set of fixed rules without seriously interfering with the freedom and pleasure of home life. The unexpected is always sure to happen, and a wise housewife will make her system so flexible as to be able to conform without serious friction to the unlooked-for emergencies of social life, and be prepared for frequent interruptions; else all the pleasure and sweetness of the little surprises of home and social life are spoiled by our inability to adapt ourselves to the exigencies of daily life. The ability of the housekeeper to conform easily and cheerfully to any little change in her household plans goes far to make or mar the comfort of the household.

It is a hard lesson for a systematic housekeeper to learn, this setting aside of our own plans, and entering heartily and cheerfully into others that rise up and confront one; but it must of necessity be learned if we desire to make our home all that a true home should be, and our home life pleasant and comfortable.

The wise housewife will make some provision for the unexpected, and have something in reserve for the requirements of hospitality. It is always well to be forehanded with our work and keep things done in advance as much as possible, for nothing so tends to make a housekeeper nervous and fretful as an accumulation of housework and unexpected interruptions.

While no one need be the slave of system, a little wise forethought in preparing for emergencies, will often save much care and perplexity.

—Lizzie Clark Hardy
Good Housekeeping
1895

The Lightning Peach-Parer.

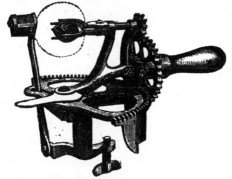

The only practical Peach-Parer made.
It pares Apples as well as the best Apple-Parers. Sold in all large markets.
D. H. GOODELL, Sole Manufacturer,
Antrim, N. H., and 99 Chambers-st., New York.
Also manufacturer of Improved Turn-Table Apple-Parers, Lightning Apple-Parers, Climax Corers and Slicers, Cahoon's Broadcast Seed-Sowers, etc.

CIDER MILLS.

American Agriculturalist.

MRS. RAYNOR'S SYSTEM

Mrs. Raynor's neatness was a proverb in the neighborhood in which she lived; her brother called her "painfully neat," and sometimes thought, when driven almost desperate by her "system," that he would buy a farm for himself, and never again take any of his brother-in-law's land on shares. But once when he spoke about it while haying in the field, Aaron seemed to feel so badly, that he promised not to make the change for some time, any how.

"Poor Aaron," thought Jack, when he saw how troubled was his brother-in-law's face, "he is worried at the bare idea that I might go off and leave him to that rigorous system of Emma's. For his sake I'll wait awhile; and I owe him some consideration, for if it hadn't been for me, he would never have met Emma.

Aaron Raynor was a very quiet man, and never had much to say on any subject; it was seldom, indeed, that he gave vent to his views on anything save the farm work, but he thought a great deal, and if Emma had only been able to read his thoughts, she would have been saddened, perhaps, by their desponding and regretful tendency. He was, however, a faithful, kind husband, who did all in his power to lighten his wife's burdens, and had he not lived in an atmosphere of fault-finding, would have been both genial and affectionate.

The unhappiness and regret which pervaded the atmosphere of the Raynor home had its rise in the system, that terrible system which was the one law which governed Emma's life. She ate, drank, and slept by it, and never guessed that she made the lives of her husband and brother unhappy by her strict adherence to it.

Every Monday morning the washing was done, rain or shine, and frequently on a rainy day, Jack and Aaron coming into the big kitchen wet and tired, and longing for seats by the fire, found the stove surrounded by chairs, all filled with damp clothes, from which a steam rose slowly, while across the room were stretched ropes on which hung the "small pieces." It wasn't very cheerful, certainly; but Aaron never complained, for it wasn't his way to complain about anything, and Emma never took any notice when Jack found fault.

On Tuesday the ironing was done, and well done, too. Every towel, no matter how old and worn, was faithfully smoothed, and folded evenly; the shirts were ironed on both sides, and the neighbors often remarked that the linen worn by Jack and Aaron would have done credit to a Chinese laundry.

LAMPBLACK—TO MAKE

Suspend over a lamp a funnel of tin plate, having above it a pipe to convey from the apartment the smoke which escapes from the lamp. Large mushrooms, of a very black, carbonaceous matter, and exceedingly light, will be formed at the summit of the cone. This carbonaceous part is carried to such a state of division as cannot be given to any other matter, by grinding it on a piece of prophyry.

This black goes a great way in every kind of painting. It may be rendered drier by calcination in close vessels.

The funnel ought to be united to the pipe which conveys off the smoke, by means of wire, because solder would be melted by the flame of the lamp.

Parson's House, Black River
Falls, Wisconsin, 1890. State
Historical Society of Wisconsin
(WHi (V24) 1911).

On Wednesday the baking and churning were done; on Thursday the house was thoroughly swept and cleaned from garret to cellar; on Friday the mending and little jobs were scrupulously attended to, and Saturday was devoted to baking and cleaning generally. Delicious bread, cakes and pies came forth from the capacious oven to be stored away on the pantry shelves, and the kitchen and hall floors were made marvelously white and clean by the vigorous use of soap and sand.

No matter what happened, the system went on as usual—nothing was allowed to interrupt that.

Aaron never thought of such a thing as coming into the house without first removing his boots in the little entry by the kitchen door, and putting on his slippers which were always in readiness in a neat bag; and he submitted to his wife's rule of retiring precisely at nine P.M., without a word of rebellion.

If Jack, in his careless indifference, sometimes crossed the white kitchen floor in his muddy boots, his sister, much to his annoyance, followed close behind him with a cloth in her hand, and carefully wiped up his tracks, with an expression on her face which spoke volumes, and distressed him more than a good round scolding would have done.

PRESERVE THE
COAL ASHES

which are usually thrown away as worthless. When you have a sufficient quantity, add to them an equal amount of small coal from your cellar, and then pour on a little water, and mix with a shovel. Use this compost for placing on the top or the back of the fire. It will burn brightly and pleasantly and only a little dust will remain unconsumed.

Emma was unaware that her system was rapidly destroying her good looks. She had been a pretty, pleasant girl in the days when Aaron had courted her; a little prim and precise, perhaps, but not given to lectures on neatness and order. She lived with two maiden aunts, who had taken pains with her bringing up, and thoroughly imbued her with their system of housekeeping.

Mrs. Raynor would not have a servant, for servants were so "slack and disorderly," and she preferred to see after her household affairs herself, unconscious that her voice was from much fault-finding becoming a fretful, querulous whine; that lines were marring the beauty of her white forehead, and crow's feet gathering around her eyes; that her elasticity and energy were less with every day, and that she was deteriorating both physically and intellectually.

"If I ever marry," said Jack, one evening, suddenly dropping on the floor the newspaper he had been reading by the center table, "I shall insist upon my wife's keeping a stout girl to help her. You don't seem to be aware of it, Emma, but you are working yourself into the grave."

Mrs. Raynor rose from her seat to pick up the newspaper, folded it neatly and laid it on the table. Then she took up her mending again, saying as she seated herself:

"I could not endure a hired girl in the house, Jack. They are all so slovenly and neglectful. Mary never could remember to rub off the kettle in the morning when she filled it; Bridget always forgot to hang up the broom, and Hannah used to spill things over the stove. I tried all three thoroughly, and decided never to have another girl."

"Well, those are only minor evils compared to your becoming a fretful invalid, or dying of overwork. Brooms are cheap, and what did it matter if the kettle was dusty occasionally."

"Jack!" Emma's tone was one of horrified disapproval, "it is the principle of the thing more than all else. I never could, if I tried fifty years, find a girl with any system about her."

Jack only smiled grimly in reply.

"And I will say this in my own praise," pursued Emma, "nobody could gather a teaspoonful of dust in my house after I have swept it, if they searched from garret to cellar."

"True," said Jack. "It would be a waste of time to try."

"If you ever do marry," said Emma, paying no attention to her brother's sarcastic tone, "I hope your wife will be orderly and neat. You have no system about you, and if she is no better, I pity the house you live in—it will always be at sixes and sevens."

"I would rather it would look like a pig-sty than that Fan—my wife—should overwork herself as you do in keeping it clean and neat. Aaron, you really ought to put a stop to Emma's perpetual trifling with her health and strength."

Jack had expected only a smile and a sigh from his brother-in-law in answer, but to his surprise Aaron spoke:

"I've talked to her about it often," he said, "but it will be necessary for her to have a severe lesson before she will learn common sense. I made up my mind a year ago that I would say no more to her on the subject."

"Common sense," said Emma, "I don't understand you. Would you have me sit with my hands in my lap and see the dirt rot the floors through, and the stove go to pieces with rust?"

"No," said Aaron, "but I would have you rest whenever you are tired. I would not have you polish the stove every Wednesday and Saturday, no matter how much else there is to attend to; and mop the kitchen and hall floors at regular intervals, even if suffering under a severe cold, which is liable to be increased by any imprudence."

"I never have had a severe illness, Aaron."

"That is no surety that you never will have one," said her husband.

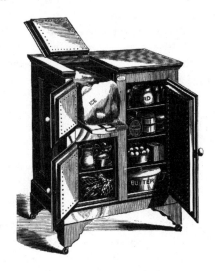

Household *magazine, 1884.*
Courtesy: Argosy Bookstore, N.Y.C.

"No; but I am well enough always. I've often felt under the weather, of course, but have always worked it off. There isn't a lazy bone in my body."

"If you were taken sick, the house would be handed over to the tender mercies of a servant. That fact, if no other, ought to make you prudent, and careful of your health," said Jack. "And another thing; when we come in at night, you are completely tired out, and consequently depressed and often fretful. Now, if you husbanded your strength, you would feel bright and cheerful every evening. Women who work as you do, wear out before they reach middle age, or else go insane. Farmers' wives help largely to keep the insane asylums full. And it makes such a difference to a man whether his wife is glum and cross, or—"

"It seems to me," interrupted Emma, "that Jack has a great deal to say lately about wives. I hope he won't bring home one of those Hopson girls and ask me to welcome her."

"And why not?" asked Jack, with a sudden flush.

"Your eyes ought to tell you why not," answered Emma, "their house is forever littered up with all sorts of trash. Books, newspapers, birds and plants scattered all around the parlor, and no attempt to systemize the work of the house."

"The family is very large," said Jack, "and of course the girls can't keep things in such apple-pie order as you do. But they are all amiable and full of fun—it's a treat to go there."

"Less fun and more work would be better for the house," said Emma. "I don't mean to say that I ever saw soiled curtains there, or rusty knives, but there seems to be no system about the work. Now I should have each girl perform certain duties on certain days—"

"In short, make herself into a patent machine to go by regular winding," interrupted Jack. "Well, Emma, perhaps it is as well to tell you now as any time that I am engaged to Fannie Hopson, and we are to be married in May."

It was all Emma could say, so shocked was she at this piece of news.

"Of course you pity me from the bottom of your heart," said Jack, "but no machine woman for me! I've had enough of systems, and I should hate Fannie if she followed me around to wipe up the tracks I made on the kitchen floor, or made a point of washing the windows at a certain hour on certain days of the week."

And with this parting shot Jack walked out of the room slamming the door behind him.

DEAFNESS—SIMPLE AND EFFECTUAL REMEDY

Garlic juice, expressed by mashing and pressing out through muslin, glycerine, and oil of sweet almonds, equal quantities of each, say, a teaspoonful. Shake together, in a phial, several times, or until there is only two portions of it, after standing—then shake when used—at first each of the 3 parts remain distinct. Put 3 or 4 drops into the affected ear, daily, until cured. I have found it very effectual. Possibly onion juice would have the same effect but I have not tried that.

The first thing Emma did when the door closed, was to set Jack's chair in its own particular place against the wall, the next to remark to her husband that she hoped Providence would interpose to save Jack from the certain misery which would be the result of a marriage with a girl who had no system about her work.

One Monday morning Aaron rose as usual at day-break, and went out to attend to the chores. He left his wife asleep, as he supposed, and was glad that she should have the rest, for she had complained of a severe headache the night before. He expected, however, to find her at work in the kitchen when he came in with the milk; but she was not there, and no preparations had been made for breakfast. Surprised and alarmed he went up stairs to the bed room.

"Are you sick, Emma?" he asked, going to the side of the bed.

She turned restlessly on her pillow, an anxious expression on her face.

"Don't throw away those soap suds," she said, "I want them to mop the floor when I get these clothes out."

Even in her delirium she knew the day of the week and washed as usual.

But the washings were done without her for many weeks to come. It was Fannie Hopson who took charge of the house, claiming it as her privilege to do so, and Jack and Aaron were only too glad to have her instead of an ignorant domestic. It is to be feared that the stove was not polished quite so often as it had been under Emma's reign, and the kitchen floor was not quite so white, but Jack and Aaron were made thoroughly comfortable in every way.

At last Mrs. Raynor was pronounced out of danger; but it was long before she was well. There were months of weary convalescence more trying than her dangerous illness had been; days when she could not hear a door closed without pain, and hour upon hour when she wept over the slightest jar to her quiet and calm. She had ample time to review her past, and recall to mind its mistakes and follies; more time than she needed to become convinced that she had acted without wisdom or discretion; time to think of the wreck she had become through carrying out the system she had so thoroughly believed in; time to learn to loathe that system, and to resolve to be a different woman and a better wife should she ever regain her health.

BREAKFAST

Farina Gruel
Stewed Sheep's Tongues
Oatmeal Bannocks
Chopped Potatoes
Fruit   Coffee   Tea

.

BREAKFAST

Baked Sweet Apples
Brain Fritters
Oatmeal Griddle Cakes
with Maple Syrup
Fruit   Coffee   Tea

SUMMER BREAKFAST

Green Corn Porridge
Deviled Kidneys
Mama's Muffins
Stewed Potatoes
Melons   Tea   Coffee

She learned to love Fannie, who, in May, had quietly married Jack, and continued her duties as if nothing had occurred, and had long talks with her young sister-in-law to whom she confided her most sacred thoughts and desires.

In midsummer Jack and Fannie moved to a home of their own, and again Emma took in her hands the reins of household government. But she had learned a lesson. Her long and expensive illness had taught her that she could not trifle with her health as she had done, and much thought during her convalescence had convinced her that she had no right to trifle with her husband's happiness either. Many things were now neglected, the performance of which had once been considered a sacred duty, and the servant whom Aaron had hired to help in the house was not dismissed for allowing the dust to gather occasionally on the kitchen mantel, or scolded roundly for inattention to the rain marks on the window panes.

In short the house on the old farm became truly a home to Aaron, and happiness reigned where once discontent had been king. No further lectures were needed from Jack; for Mrs. Raynor's system had taken wings to itself, and flown away forever.

—Florence H. Birney
The Household
c. 1870

RIGHTS &
REACTIONS

OLD MAIDS

—One of the best of women's rights is a right of exemption from man's duties.

—The Household
VOL. I, 1868

There is no class of people more maligned than those designated as "old maids." Why such a stigma should rest upon unmarried women who are over twenty-five years of age, I have never been able to determine. Why is a woman who chooses to remain in a state of "single blessedness," and blessedness it often is beside the lot which would have been hers had she married some quondam suitor, considered fair game for all the gibes, and shafts of contempt, which empty-pated people can hurl upon her? Many old maids are helpful, loveable and sweet-tempered, and fill their allotted niche as acceptably as do their married sisters. Many who are married would better have served mankind, God, and themselves, had they remained single, and there may be cases where some spinster might have been happier and done more good, had she married, but why should one class be blamed more than the other?

Is it not far more honorable to be single than to marry for a home, money, position, or anything except the most unbounded love? Our young ladies have erroneous ideas upon this subject. They feel almost disgraced, if they have arrived at a mature age, and are not yet able to write Mrs. before their names. Their whole ambition is to get a husband, by hook or by crook, but get him somehow they must. Now, a girl thinks she must marry, as that is the only way by which she can provide herself with a home, and necessary comforts, even though the one who offers, should not happen to be the one she most desires to call husband. But this man has proposed, the other never may. Now is her chance, and she accepts it as her fate.

I think the largely increased facilities for more equal advantages in education and business, will do much to ameliorate this feeling in the next generation. When woman, as well as man, has a chance to earn a living at a congenial occupation, and receives equal compensation for equal labor, there will be fewer girls who will marry for a home, and, as a consequence, fewer discouraged, unhappy wives and mothers, fewer disorderly, uninviting homes. When women can as coolly look over the circle of their masculine acquaintants, and as critically discuss their habits, characters, and the likelihood of their proving desirable life-partners, as the men now do, much of this wrong will right itself.

Marriage is almost always a help to a man. The advantages are greater for him than for woman, for unless the union be one

Photo on previous page: Women's Relief Corps, State Historical Society of Wisconsin (WHi (V2) 405).

of sentiment, thought, feeling and heart, and in all respects the most felicitous, it is her undoing.

Much is tolerated in man which is not allowed in woman, and we, my sisters, are much to blame for this unfair criticism of the world.

Meanwhile, as the millenium is not here, nor likely to come for some time, I wish to give a few words of consolation and advice to those girls who, though out of their teens, are not yet married. Get the best education possible, help about domestic affairs, and enter upon some trade or profession for which you have a taste and master it. Skilled labor is always well paid. Don't spend your time repining because you cannot see the coming man. If you never see him, you can live useful, happy lives. You think if you had a husband, you would have a strong arm on which to lean, a sharer of trouble and sorrow. Alas! many a slender woman has had not only to stand alone, but also serve as prop for children and husband, and very few wives find in their husbands all the sympathy and companionship they desire.

If you are good for anything you will not be hurt by remaining single, neither will you be elevated by becoming "John's wife." A good, true woman counts one in the world, no matter whether she is married or single. And though you should not entertain too gloomy views of married life, for the family is evidently a God-ordained institution, do not look upon marriage as a means of elevation, or as a sphere where you can do more good than as a single sister.

Do not be deceived; the men are not all Bayards, as many a hollow-eyed wife who built her hopes for happiness upon a graceful bow or a love of a moustache, could sorrowfully testify.

An old maid friend of mine, when rallied upon her lack of a masculine supporter (?) used to say that it was far better to be laughed at because you were not married than not to be able to laugh because you were. There is sound logic in that.

There are good and true men, men who are men. When such a one loves you, if your heart gives a responsive thrill, be as thoughtful, kind, womanly, loving, as you can, and treat him like a prince. You have found the white elephant.

—H. M .G.
The Household
VOL. XIV, 1881

This Woman's Rights Movement All Wrong

It is conducted chiefly by dissatisfied wives, or else by unmarried croakers, most of whom are in a grumbling *mood.* The very look and entire aspect of these "strong-minded" too plainly declare that their affections have been reversed, and that disappointed love has thoroughly soured them throughout. What one of them all is in a warm, gushing, genial, plastic, affectionate mood? Only those who are, have any "right" to say one word; yet those have no word to say. Waiting for such to move in these rights' movement would be like waiting for the water to stop running. At least, unmarried *novices,* though forty, are improper spokesmen. Only *laying* hens have any right to cackle. Let those speak who know something by *experience*—that best of teachers. This entire movement is directly calculated to breed conjugal disaffection.

One other absolutely determining question. Do men LOVE these women's rights women all the more, or the *less,* for their independent spirit? Do they admiringly flock around such with beseeching matrimonial proposals? A very few of these strong-minded bricks are indeed required in order to complete this great temple of humanity. A very few men, who are themselves two thirds feminine, require to marry these two thirds masculines; because opposite sexes must marry. Effeminate men naturally

The Age of Iron. *Library of Congress.*

take and propose to these strongly masculinized women, yet most vigorous human males "pass by" such women "on the other side"; because these commanding, independent, authoritative, positive women, who insist on overruling family affairs, must either marry tame, weak-minded, putty men, who are two thirds woman, and therefore willing to serve under them, or else create a conflict of jurisdiction. There are a few just such tame, meeching, automaton machines, just adapted to these arbitrary, driving, two thirds masculine, "strong-minded," "woman's rights" wives, who love to command, conduct business, lead off, and take the responsibility; while these easy, lazy, shiftless, inert husbands will endure to be "henpecked." This is a wise adaptation for both, because such men without such women would starve; and such women, with positive men, would "foment strife" perpetually. Yet men neither "take" to these positive women, nor many females to these negative "things." Arguing woman's rights is the surest way effectually to disgust all the others, or nine hundred and ninety-nine in every thousand, who FEEL all over,—

"Away with this eternal clatter about woman's rights. It nauseates me. I want no such thing for my wife. Let such support and enjoy their own independence for aught I care."

This test—whether men like or dislike this class of women most—is the *final* umpire; the supreme court of appeal. Young women, all women who value masculine appreciation, or desire marriage, take fair warning that this clamor drives men from you always, attracts them never. Beware, then, how you allow it to blast your matrimonial prospect—that sole end of the female creation, and only "sphere" in which you can ever be happy.

—O. S. Fowler
Sexual Science
1875

How to Manage a Man

Essay read at a Wisconsin Institute by
Mrs. A. M. Glenn, of Jonesville, in that state.

This being a farmers' institute it would be most natural to expect something along that line, but on thorough investigation I discover that more people are engaged in the business of matrimony

GROWING PAINS CURED

Following in our mother's footsteps, we have been routed night after night from our warm quarters, in the dead of winter, to kindle fires and fill frosty kettles from water-pails thickly crusted with ice, that we might get the writhing pedal extremities of our little heir into a tub of water as quickly as possible. But lately we have learned that all this work and exposure is needless. We simply wring a towel from salted water—a bowl of it standing in our sleeping room, ready for such an emergency—wrap the limb in it from the ankle to knee, without taking the child from his bed, and then swathe with dry flannels, thick and warm, tucking the blankets about him a little closer, and relief is sure.

than any other occupation, and it's the hardest way on earth for a woman to get a living unless she understands how to manage a man, and no woman should be married until she is thoroughly posted in this branch of her education.

After over thirty years of experience, it would be a dull scholar indeed that could not give some useful information.

IN COLD WEATHER
a leg of mutton improves by being hung three or four weeks.

When the meat is hanging, change its position frequently, to equally distribute the juices.

Helplessness of Man

In the very beginning it was decided by the highest possible authority that it was not good for man to be alone, and we don't wonder at it when we look about us and see how much some men expect of their wives. We read somewhere recently that "of all creatures in the world a man is the most helpless alone. A chicken two hours out of the shell can take better care of itself than a man can." Of course a woman wrote that, and the next conclusion is that that woman has washed her husband's neck and ears ever since she has had him and had made him just the helpless creature that he is.

Selecting a Husband

As a rule husbands are just what you make them (of course, it won't do to tell them this) and the better material you have to start on the better job you can perform with the same amount of labor. If you have a bump of cheerfulness developed in your nature, don't marry a tombstone. Altogether he is about as genial as an iceberg and you will go plodding through life with him to the dead march of his own leaden thoughts. You may be distant and dignified, you couldn't freeze him colder than he is; you may love and pet him, it's a waste of ammunition, he can't be thawed out. Above all things, don't marry a dude. He is a weakminded, contemptible apology for a man. God created him a man, therefore let him pass for one; but one good, honest, industrious young man is worth all the floating fops in the world. Unless they can choose wisely, or learn to manage a man, girls had better set their affections on cats and poodles and let matrimony alone.

The Family

The family is the oldest and most valuable institution on earth. It begins properly with the first offspring. In reality there is no family until the husband and wife can say to each other, "Two times one are two and one to carry makes three." And the little third party often brings the husband and wife nearer together than anything could possibly do.

Mutual Helpfulness

Every wife should be a helpmeet to her husband. For instance, if you have the pleasure of a large washing before you and he has the laborious task of going to the city, or taking a trip through the country, change work with him, let him help you wash in the forenoon and you help him ride in the afternoon. A good wife will deny herself to entertain her husband, especially on wash day. But some men will say, "When I come down to that I'll hire it done." We find no fault with hiring it done, but as to coming down to help a woman, my dear sir, who created you so far above a woman that you have to condescend to come down? I know the Bible says that "the husband shall be the head of the household," but it also says that "the wife shall be a crown to him," and you know the crown is a little higher and just above the head. Such being the case, come up, gentlemen, on a level with your wives and assist in the home whenever you can do so without infringing upon larger and more important duties.

Is Marriage a Failure?

The question is often asked. Is marriage a failure? We say, No, if you don't expect too much of it; but don't run the risk of trying to reform a man after marriage. In all probability you will be disappointed if you do. If your husband used tobacco when you married him, the Bible forbids all curtain lectures afterward, for it says, "he that is filthy, let him be filthy still." There is a bright side to everything, if you will only look till you find it. If your husband smokes, be thankful he doesn't chew; if he smokes and chews both, be thankful he doesn't drink; if he does all three, be thankful he won't live long.

It has been said that the best men are molded out of faults, but it is not every one who has the ingredients in her make-up to do the molding. The main difficulty is that people demand of marriage all of the universal virtues of a patent medicine, warranted to cure all infirmities. The marriage ceremony does not remove a woman's faults or a man's crooked disposition. They are exactly the same people they were before they were married, only a little more so. Do we not know this world? Haven't we measured

COCKROACHES AND CRICKETS

Cucumber peelings are said to destroy cockroaches. Strew the floor in that part of the house most infested with the vermin with the green peel cut pretty thick. Try it for several nights, and it will not fail to rid the house of them. OR, take a teacup of well bruised plaster of Paris, mixed with double the quantity of oatmeal, to which add a little sugar; then strew it on the floor or in the chinks where they frequent, and it will destroy them. Kitchens infested with cockroaches may be cleared by employing a hedgehog, which requires only bread and milk, and an occasional piece of raw meat or a dead bird.

it in the pint cup of our experience and found out many things which our youth and inexperience fondly disbelieved? Have you ever found perfection in literature, weather, climate, your friends, or anything in this world? Then why demand it of marriage more than of these other things? Behold the innocence of the young lady who told her father she was not particular in her choice of a husband, she only wanted one who used neither tobacco, strong drink nor profane language, who would spend his evenings at home and be wholly devoted to her. "My child," replied her father, "you're a stranger here, heaven is your home."

TO CLEAN STUFFED ANIMALS

First brush the specimen well with a clothes-brush. Then put some new bran into a pan and warm it, stirring it well to prevent it burning. Rub the warm bran well into the fur with your hand. Do this three or four times, and then brush the fur until all the bran is out.

The New Woman

We hear much about the new woman of today, and I am glad we have women who are not afraid to leave the beaten track of their grandmothers and step out on a new line for themselves. In former ages woman was little else than a cook and domestic of general housework, but she has added to these her personal liberty and higher education. It has taken the world eighteen hundred years to discover that a woman amounts to something, and perhaps in eighteen hundred more it will be willing to give her the same privilege it gives the ignorant foreigner who can't tell the English language from a porous plaster. Although women may not care to vote, it's just a little humiliating to know the only ones denied the ballot are the criminal, the lunatic, idiots—and women. Whatever the all-wise Creator gave woman ability and intelligence to do is positive proof to my mind that he intended she should do if she wanted to, and when a man has toiled step by step up the ladder of fame he will be sure to find a woman at the top. As a rule women are not so very anxious to vote, but they do want the men to admit that they have intelligence enough to do so.

—*Farm Journal*
MARCH 1903

FEMALE WOMEN

We respect, admire and love a female woman. We admire her in the beauty of her person, her moral presence and position; we respect her simple truthfulness and innocence, and we love her as the embodiment of the highest charms and sweetest attributes of humanity. But a male woman, who can bear! We cannot read of monster meetings, in which women perform the leading parts; of lectures on the subject of marriage to promiscuous audiences by female tongues, and of the perambulating female spouters who go about the country, without an involuntary emotion of disgust. Many of these women are mothers, who have families of tender age at home, and husbands who should have tender heads. Home duties forsaken, and the misguided mistresses go about teaching other people *their* duties! What comfortable wives they must be! What kind and assiduous mothers! How they must hallow a home that is too small to hold them! Gods of War! We would as soon live with a hyena or a steam engine. Don't come this way, we beg of you.

—*New England Farmer*
APRIL 1853

THE REASONS WHY

Somebody—a crusty old bachelor of course—inquires why, when Eve was manufactured of a spare rib, a servant wasn't made at the same time to wait on her? Somebody else—a woman, we imagine—replies in the following strain: "Because Adam never came whining to Eve with a ragged stocking to be darned, collar string to be sewed on, or a glove to mend 'right away—quick now!' Because he never read the newspaper until the sun got down behind the palm-trees, and he stretching out, yawned out, 'Isn't supper most ready, my dear?' Not he. He made the fire, and hung the kettle over it himself, we'll venture; and pulled the radishes, peeled the potatoes, and did everything else he ought to do. He milked the cows, fed the chickens, and looked after the pigs himself, and he never brought home half a dozen friends to dinner when Eve hadn't any fresh pomegranates. He never stayed out till 11 o'clock to a political meeting, hurrahing for an out-and-out candidate, and then scolding because poor Eve was sitting up and crying inside the gates. He never played billiards, rolled tenpins, and drove fast horses, nor choked Eve with cigar smoke. He never loafed around corner groceries while Eve was rocking little Cain's cradle at home. In short, he didn't think she was especially created for the purpose of waiting on him, and wasn't under the impression that it disgraced a man to lighten a new wife's cares a little. That's the reason that Eve did not need a hired girl, and with it was the reason that her fair descendants did."

—*The Household*
VOLS. XI, XII; 1878, 1879

CROUP—SIMPLE BUT EFFECTUAL REMEDY

Dutch Remedy—Goose oil, and urine, equal quantities. Dose— From a tea- to a table-spoon of the mixture, according to the age of the child. Repeat the dose every 15 minutes, if the [child] does not vomit in that time.

This remedy will be found valuable in mild cases, … and I know it to have saved a child when one of their best Doctors said it must die; … yet an old Dutch woman came in at the *eleventh* hour, from the next door neighbors' wash-tub, and raised the child with what she called "p—s and goose grease." I have used it with success.

WOMAN'S RIGHTS AND RESPONSIBILITIES

It is not here proposed to discuss woman's political rights or to assist her in making her way to the ballot-box. If that be a desideratum, woman's cause may safely be left in charge of the many able champions who have taken the field in her behalf. An attempt will here be made to survey the legitimate and undisputed sphere of woman, as marked out by Providence in the creation of the spheres; a sphere clearly indicated by the very frame-work of human society, and involving interests vital to man's existence, and essential to his happiness.

This sphere planned and sketched by unerring wisdom, undoubtedly embraces maternity as its central idea, together with the responsibilities and privileges which radiate from it and constitute a mother the natural guardian, and educator of her offspring.

This duty and privilege thus conferred and secured to the mother, should be considered a precious boon to be received with gratitude and its requirements faithfully discharged. It is nothing less than a sacred commission to train up immortal beings for everlasting happiness.

Will any pious mother repine at her destiny?—Will she not rather joyfully look forward to the great day of account, when she may be able to say, "Here am I, Lord, and the children which thou hast graciously given me." This sublime idea of woman's duty and destiny needs to be kept constantly in mind by the sex, to reconcile them to the labor and anxiety incident to the situation, as well as to inspire a confiding trust in that being who, in the ordinations of his providence, consults the highest good of his creatures.

—*The Household*
VOL. III, 1870

WOMAN'S INFLUENCE

It is impossible to discuss the subject of woman's influence, without encountering, at the very threshold, the question of her Rights. Within a few years a school has arisen, whose creed it is that the sexes are equal; that nature has endowed them with equal capacities for thought and action; and hence that in the arena of life, neither ought to be excluded from competing for any prize. Every kind of business, trade or profession should, they say, be open to both alike; and whatever state of society prevents this is to be deplored as imperfect and unjust.

It is not to be denied that woman does not possess all her rights, because she is not furnished with fair means for self-improvement or self-support. And on this account it is to be regretted that the cure for one evil has been sought by rushing into another.

While there is need enough for reform, society is too apt to take the first steps toward reformation very awkwardly. It conducts itself very much like a man who leaps into the open sea to avoid shipwreck. Pioneers in every enterprise are over-scrupulous; and, lest they should lose something, they make one great grasp for everything.

Before proceeding further, however, let us admit that we should look with leniency upon an error which is fortified with so many impregnable grounds of complaint. Throughout the past ages of the world, to a comparatively recent date, "woman's condition has been degrading, and demoralizing to her own sex, and dishonorable to the other"; and we are yet very far from doing her justice; for to insult her by petty, false adulation, is worse than to oppress her with physical wrongs; for while the latter pains and deforms the body at worst, the former stultifies the growth of those noble energies which constitute her glory.

Whatever lessens woman's capacity for enjoyment, or abates her opportunities for doing good, or withholds from her the means of self-support, is a denial of her rights; but the charms of her sex would be lost under a cumbrous load of masculine attainments.

We do not propose, however, to discuss those rights. We desire only to suggest that the question should be, whether she is beset with hindrances to the performance of any duty which devolves upon her by virtue of her refined social feelings, her acute perception, or her generosity; in all of which respects she is man's superior. Hers is a more glorious work to perform, that it is possible for him to accomplish; for only through the influence of a wise womanhood can the race be nursed into immortal strength, until it shall "stand erect and look on heaven."

Strictly speaking, neither sex is superior to the other. Totally unlike in their natures, they are yet alike. Woman's nature is man's once more refined. Her actions are prompted from the heart; his only by the head. Intuition leads her to conclusions which he can reach only by study. He is her superior in dealing out thunderbolts, but she works by a magnetic influence. He is her superior

BLACK BALL

Melt together, moderately, ten ounces of bayberry tallow, five ounces of beeswax, one ounce of mutton tallow. When melted, add lamp or ivory black to give it a good black color. Stir the whole well together, and add, when taken from the fire, half a glass of rum.

265

in works of devastation, but she rises above him, like an angel, in binding up wounds which he has made. Whatever is pure, noble and lovable is set forth in her character; and there are better things than majesty and muscle. It is better to entreat than to command. Fascination is more potent than logic.

To whatever country woman belongs, or in whatever condition there placed, she retains a distinctive character, possessed by her sex alone; and be this good or bad, by it is exerted an influence that man cannot withstand.

Great men usually owe their success more to a mother's early influence, than to all else combined. What child can resist her look of love, her tone of entreaty, her tear of regret?

Man constitutes the stone-work of society; woman is like a beautiful vine that clings to the wall, whose deformity it hides. Man builds a house, woman can decorate and adorn it better than he, because she has a more correct eye for what *constitutes* ornament. Her innate fickleness cannot be denied, but it is a physical, not a moral infirmity, and her constancy more than equals it. Her affection needs no such wretched support as the current fiction of the day. It may be insanity; but, pray, let her remain insane, for therein lies man's hope of salvation.

Young woman, you hold at your disposal an influence that cannot be withstood. Is that influence for good? You may think that *your* life is but a withered tree which bears no fruit; and that efforts—made perhaps in obscurity—are lost. This cannot be. There are sovereignties more royal than queens possess by mere virtue of their office, dynasties that shall never end. *Your* kingdom is the world, and angels wait to put your commands into execution.

—D. C. B.
The Household
1868

SWALLOW'S NEST

To prevent swallows building under the eaves, or in window corners, rub the places with oil or soft soap.

"WOMAN'S RIGHTS"

MR. EDITOR:—I saw in a late number of your excellent journal an article on "Woman's Influence," which I read with a good deal of interest (as I do *all* articles which I find in THE HOUSE-HOLD). The subject is one that I think very much upon; our country has been agitating the question of woman's rights so much of late that I have come to dwell upon the matter a good deal. I am an advocate for *woman's rights;* this I am desirous should be clearly understood by all. I contend that every woman, single or married, has rights which belong to her and that she should in no case give them to another.

You, my married friend, have the right of counseling and advising your husband in all his movements, and the exclusive right of so adorning his home and of giving him such entertainment while he is there that he will have no desire to seek the companionship of those that grow merry over the "jovial bowl." If you are a mother it is your right to superintend the education of your children, not the mental training alone, but the moral and physical as well. If there were more mothers in our country that claimed their rights we should have a society of a higher moral tone.

When the early training of children is trusted to ignorant and uncouth nurses—girls who have no high or noble aspirations—tell me how those girls can teach the children under their care to love those things which are pure and good. And if they are not taught those things when their minds are so susceptible of impression I contend that as *a rule* they are never.

You ladies that are so anxious to distinguish yourselves at the ballot box; the way is open for you, and you need not wait till your respective States have had some special legislation on the subject

Labor Employment Bureau, Library of Congress.

either; teach your sons to be thinking, honest men. In this way you can bring an influence to bear upon the ballot box far greater than if you were allowed to deposit your vote therein according to the custom of your brother man.

But I fear my single sisters will think they are to be left out in the cold; not so; you have rights—and rights in a certain sense mean influence. Your first grand right is to use every possible means for self-improvement. No matter what particular station in life you expect to occupy, be sure that you make of yourself all that circumstances will allow; then you can be instant in season and out of season to do acts of kindness and mercy—a word fitly spoken may do an untold amount of good—then you have the right of so conducting yourself that your brothers, and other gentlemen with whom you associate, will be led to respect and honor you, and through you the entire sex.

These, sir, are some of the rights that I am an advocate for and never while reason retains her throne will I ask any State legislator to extend those rights.

—Lily Dale
The Household
1868

SHALL WOMEN VOTE?

The Rev. Lyman Abbott opens the September *Atlantic* with an able and suggestive article on "Why Women Do Not Wish the Suffrage," an attitude which he claims results not from any inferiority of woman to man, but from her essential difference, bodily and mentally. His conclusions are:

"This much, then, seems clear to me, and I hope it is clear to the reader also:

"*First,* that the family is the basis of society, from which it grows.

"*Second,* that the basis of the family, and therefore of society, is the difference between the sexes—a difference which is inherent, temperamental, functional.

"*Third,* that the military function in all its forms and phases, belongs to man; that he has no right to thrust it upon woman or to ask her to share it with him; that it is his duty, and his exclusively, to do that battling with the elements which wrests livelihood from a reluctant or resisting nature, and which is therefore the prerequisite to all productive industry; and that battling with the enemies of society which compels them to respect its rights, and which is therefore the primary condition of government.

...The question, Shall women vote? is really, in the last analysis, the question, Ought woman to assume the responsibility for protecting person and property which has in the past been assumed by man as his duty alone? It is because women see, what some so-called reformers have not seen, that the first and fundamental function of government is the protection of person and property, and because women do not think that they ought to assume this duty any more than they ought to assume that police and militia service which is involved in every act of legislature, that they do not wish to have the ballot thrust upon them."

The Difference between the Sexes

We may be permitted to quote Doctor Abbott's statement of the difference between the sexes: "The first and most patent fact in the family is the difference in the sexes. Out of this difference the family is created; in this difference the family finds its sweet and sacred bond. This difference is not merely physical and incidental. It is also psychical and essential. It inheres in the temperament; it is inbred in the very fiber of the soul; it differentiates the functions; it determines the relation between man and woman; it fixes their mutual service and their mutual obligations. Man is not woman in a different case. Woman is not man inhabiting temporarily a different kind of body. Man is not a rough-and-tumble woman. Woman is not a feeble and pliable man. This essential difference in the sexes is the first and fundamental fact in the family; it is therefore the first and fundamental fact in society, which is but a large family. ...

Nature, Temperament, Function

"These twain are not identical. They do not duplicate each other. Man is not an inferior woman. Woman is not an inferior man. They are different in nature, in temperament, in function. We cannot destroy this difference if we would; we would not if we could. In preserving it lies the joy of the family; the peace, prosperity, and well-being of society. If man attempts woman's function, he will prove himself but an inferior woman. If woman attempts man's function she will prove herself but an inferior man. ..."

IN WINTER,

always set the handle of your pump as high as possible, before you go to bed. Except in very rigid weather, this keeps the handle from freezing. When there is reason to apprehend extreme cold, do not forget to throw a rug or horse-blanket over your pump; a frozen pump is a comfortless preparation for a winter's breakfast.

The Fundamental Fact

"This distinction between the sexes—inherent, temperamental, functional—is universal and perpetual. It underlies the family, which could not exist if this difference did not exist. It is to be taken account of in all social problems,—problems of industrial organization, religious organization, political organization. Should society ever forget it, it would forget the most fundamental fact in the social order, the fact on which is built the whole superstructure of society."

—*The Week's Progress*
SEPTEMBER 5, 1903

GIRLS, BE PRACTICAL

A girl who is confronted with the fact that she has to support herself, and possibly others of her family, ought to take into consideration the needs of humanity before she decides upon her work.

There are certain things that people must have—they must eat; they must be clothed.

There are some things that they need, and will obtain, if it is possible for them to do so, such as education and amusement.

Still again, there is a class of work—the purely artistic—which is not essential to humanity, which is merely a cultivation, the demand for which must necessarily be limited, more or less, to the wealthy.

And this is the class of work which usually appeals to girls of refined taste, who are not practical enough to know that the uncertainty attending it renders it too precarious to be even thought of.

It may be delightful to be an artist and paint pictures; but will they sell?—that is the question.

To go back to the absolute necessities of life—food and clothes—why is it that more of our girls who live in the country do not make use of the opportunities that lie at their door, instead of looking to the cities for an opening?

If will, brains and work are put into poultry-raising, the dairy, or the keeping of bees, there will be successful results. But one must be willing to work early and late themselves, giving to the business their whole time, as they would have to give if they accepted situations as stenographers, type-writers, book-keepers or saleswomen, and personally superintending any labor they might be obliged to hire in their undertaking, the same as a man would.

IN CHOOSING A COLOR
OF PAINT

or a papering for one's wall, it is well to remember that we have to live a long time with a house dressed in one sort of paint and paper. The papering which looks beautiful in a roll on the counter of the man who sells it may become terribly trying to you when you are obliged to see it by daylight and candle light for ten or twelve years; and if you are to have a fit of sickness or a period of weakness and nervous depression, it is well to think whether you could then endure it in a room which might be trying to your senses during days when you were shut in from out of doors.

A certain amount of preparation and education for these employments is as necessary as for any other work.

A good dressmaker can always find employment. A girl who has learned to cut and fit can find a way to use this knowledge in a country town or village at $1.00 per day, even when she first starts out.

Fashionable dressmakers in cities can command from three to four dollars per day, including dinners, suppers and carfare, and even then have her engagements in the busy seasons date six months in advance. A good, plain seamstress will command $1.50 per day.

The milliner's trade is easily learned by one who has taste in trimming her own hats and bonnets; and by beginning in a small way, among one's personal friends, and gradually advancing the price from 50 cents to $1.00 per hat, there will be many days in which one can make three and four dollars.

One of the best remunerative positions that a woman can obtain is that of forewoman in a large and fashionable millinery establishment. Her salary may range from $2,000 to $5,000, and in some cases she is the European buyer of the stock, and the firm pays her expenses to Europe twice a year.

Formerly, in most of these establishments, men did all the European buying, but it has been found that women are better calculated, because they understand the needs of the customers, and their judgment and taste in the selection is more to be depended upon.

Every girl who looks the question fairly in the face can decide for herself what she is by nature, education and circumstances best fitted for, and in what she will only show mediocre ability.

We often hear it said that a woman has a genius for her occupation, by which is inferred that she is blessed with some special talent for her work. She is; but the talent is open to us all. It is simply a power to do her work to the best of her ability, or, as Carlyle puts it, "Genius is the capacity for infinite painstaking."

—*The Household*
VOL. XXV, 1892

BURNT, OR BROWNED FLOUR COFFEE, FOR THE SICK

Take a pint of flour, and set it on the stove until it is perfectly dry; then roast it as you do coffee, until it is dark brown—stirring it all the time; put two tablespoonfuls into a pint of boiling water, and let it boil ten minutes; scald the milk in as you take it off; sweeten with best white or loaf sugar.—*Note.* This coffee will turn sickness when nothing else will.

WOMEN AS DECORATORS

"Women have intuitively an appreciation of graceful forms and accordant colors. They have shown that they can be successful painters and sculptors—that they can work well with dead stone

Dressmaker's School, 1900.
Photograph by permission of Minnesota
Historical Society.

or pigment. Equally well can they work with living forms of flowers. Let women in search of a living think on these things."

So wrote Mr. Samuel Parsons in commending to women the business of flower composition and decoration; and the woman who can work in a bower of flowers to win her daily bread, by means of artistic tastes and nimble figures, may count herself fortunate in having the lines fall to her in such a pleasant place.

The practical florist long ago took up the idea of employing flower-girls, and found that their skill and taste in the making up of designs largely increased his sales.

In our large cities there are several floral establishments owned and managed by women with noted success. Here the finest creations of woman's taste in flower-work may be found, and from these centres are sent out a corps of skilful and well-paid workers to decorate apartments for entertainments.

It is a worthy occupation for women, not over-done, full of pleasure as well as profit, and one for which they have been fitted by nature.

The women decorators of Paris have elicited universal praise. The least skilful of these decorators will compose for weddings symphonies in white which are very beautiful.

But not everyone who wishes can become a skilful decorator; certain talents and conditions are indispensable. The flower artiste

272

should possess an intuitive appreciation of color and beauty of form.

Training is as indispensable in this as in every other vocation, and experience is the best teacher. The girl who gives her whole heart to the making up of simple bouquets and baskets, clips and trims and stems flowers for her superior, and takes in with earnest, understanding eyes every detail of grouping, banking, wreathing and designing for spacious halls and reception-rooms, together with the brilliant effect of each, need not serve a long apprenticeship before taking a more important position. The length of this term will depend upon herself.

Not infrequently it happens that reverses of fortune leave some brilliant entertainer among society women to struggle with poverty. Some of them swiftly and skilfully take up the art which they have become accustomed to see beautifying their own reception-rooms, having little to learn save mechanical work, and this work is usually given to those who have no creative talent, but can only follow the plans and fill out the figures of designers.

The salary of decorators depends, as in other professions, entirely upon their skill. Beginners in the trade earn, usually, $8 to $10 per week, while workers of experience, taste and skill, who are sent out to decorate halls and reception-rooms, are paid by the piece from $25 to $50 and upward, according to the magnitude of the entertainment and the artiste's reputation for fine work.

—L. Greenlee
The Household
VOL. XXV, 1892

WOMEN AS STOCK FARMERS

That the women who are engaged in stock farming are exceptionally successful is significant. Ex-Governor Hoard of Wisconsin in speaking of women who devote themselves to this occupation said: "Of the many women I know who are engaged in stock farming on a scale more or less extensive, there is not one who has made a failure of it. I think that the reason for this is that they are more patient than are men; that they pay closer attention to detail and manage to get along better with the modest results which at first are all that can be confidently counted on. They invariably make their way carefully, and from one point of vantage proceed cautiously to another." He might also have added that, with scarcely an exception, they bring to their work a sympathetic insight which redeems it from drudgery and makes of it a recurring succession of delightful experiences. Indeed it is exceeding pleasant to record that these women, engaged in an occupation which until within a few years has been considered wholly impossible to them, are, as a class, touched more or less with that fine spirit of interpretation that renders nature, with which they are so continually and intimately in contact, endlessly and enthrallingly interesting.

A typical illustration of this touch of poetic insight among stock women is the following utterance of Mrs. Virginia C. Meredith, who is one of the most successful and well-known stock farmers in America. Mrs. Meredith says: "It lies within the province of the farmer to be an artist, as it is easily possible for him to create that which realizes an ideal. The farmer has constantly to do with life. He brings about the conditions for its creation and development both in the form of vegetable and of animal life. In the latter the law of variation opens to him a grand domain for the exercise of intelligence. He can mold into beauty and value the 'red, white, and roan,' the beautiful Jersey, or the thoroughbred. While the wheat of Pharoah's time was undoubtedly precisely like the wheat of the present day, the thoroughbred of today is by no means the horse known to the ancient Egyptians. Think you that the thoroughbred has that graceful pose, satin coat, clean bone, strong sinew, glorious courage, and docile temper by nature? Indeed, no! He is man's work. He is absolutely the realization of an ideal; as absolutely the result of intelligent thought, inspired patience, and loving enthusiasm as the canvas of Millet, the music of Wagner, or the drama of Shakespeare."

Mrs. Mary B. Clay of Whitehall, Kentucky, is an enthusiastic advocate of stock farming as an employment for women, and assumes that it is at once a pleasant, profitable, and fitting occupation. She is herself famed as one of the very best farmers in her part of the country. Finding herself, a number of years ago, possessed of a farm with no income and two children to support, although she had no knowledge of the business she determined to become a successful farmer, and succeeded, as a determined, capable woman usually does with whatever she undertakes. Mrs. Clay says that her experience leads her to the conclusion that the very best thing for a woman to do who has but small means and children dependent upon her is to buy a little farm, if it is only a few acres. It is, as she says, not only a safe investment but one which enables a woman to get a living and at the same time have her

BEDROOMS, VENTILATION OF

The importance of ventilating bedrooms is a fact in which everybody is vitally interested, and which few properly appreciate. If two men are to occupy a bedroom during a night, let them step upon weighing scales as they retire, and then again in the morning, and they will find that their actual weight is at least a pound less in the morning. Frequently there will be a loss of two or more pounds, and the average loss throughout the year will be more than one pound; that is, during the night there is a loss of a pound of matter which has gone off from their bodies, partly from the lungs, and partly through the pores of the skin. The escaped material is carbonic acid and decayed animal matter, or poisonous exhalations.

children with her and give them her personal attention. She further points out that the life is a particularly wholesome one for little folks.

It is a fact worthy of note that women stock farmers are uniformly enthusiastic in regard to their occupation and it would be difficult, if indeed not impossible, so far as I know, to induce a woman who has once engaged in it to give it up for any other employment or, for the matter of that, for elegant leisure.

—Antoinette Van Hoesen Wakenan
The Chautauguan
1892

MEDICINE

In no branch of woman's work has there been greater advancement than in the profession of medicine. In the face of opposition on all sides—in the face of derision from the opposite sex and condemnation from their own—a few brave souls have held fast, and, after advancing step by step to honor and renown, can look back upon their pathway and cry, "Excelsior."

To quote Dr. Mandana F. De Hart, in the *Business Women's Journal*: "They never doubted their ability and eminent fitness for the more arduous work of nursing. Women were trusted to carry out with accuracy, through the long and tedious nightwatch, the directions given by the doctor in his two-minute visit; but some insisted that no amount of study and experience could enable her to *give* those directions, or bear the strain of professional life.

Women Workers.
Photograph by permission of Minnesota Historical Society.

275

A PICKLE THAT WILL KEEP
FOR YEARS,

for hams, tongues, or beef, if boiled
and skimmed between each parcel
of them—To two gallons of spring
water put two pounds of coarse
sugar, two pounds of coarse and
two and a half pounds of common
salt, and half a pound of saltpetre,
in a deep earthen glazed pan that
will hold four gallons, and with a
cover that will fit close. Keep the
beef or hams as long as they will
bear before you put them into the
pickle; and sprinkle them with
coarse sugar in a pan, from which
they must drain. Rub the hams,
&c., well with the pickle; and pack
them in close, putting as much as
the pan will hold, so that the pickle
may cover them. The pickle is not
to be boiled at first. A small ham
may lie fourteen days; a large one
three weeks; a tongue twelve days;
and beef in proportion to its size.
They will eat well out of the pickle
without drying. When they are to
be dried, let each piece be drained
over the pan; and when it will drop
no longer, take a clean sponge and
dry it thoroughly. Six or eight
hours will smoke them; and there
should be only a little sawdust and
wet straw burnt to do this; but if
put into a baker's chimney, sew
them in a coarse cloth, and hang
them a week. Add two pounds of
common salt, and two pints of
water, every time you boil the
liquor.

Women were considered eminently unqualified for the much less difficult career of healthy and pleasant work. They were unquestionably born to be mothers, with all which that implies, of work, anxiety and agony, but lacking in the courage, endurance and strength necessary to assist others in labor so essentially feminine; as if it were not much easier to recommend and applaud heroism than to be a hero."

—*Queen of the Home*
1892

WOMAN'S KINGDOM

I see unrest, discontent, strife, and sin: I see girls—children in years—from whose cheek the first blush of innocence, from whose soul the last vestige of youth, have vanished; women sold to frivolity; women wasting most precious gifts; women whose ambition has no higher object than to mislead and triumph over men; men growing hard, selfish, and wicked, the slaves of their passions, going down to death, with no hand to save,—all for the lack of a *true home*. Then I remember that the home is the true kingdom of woman, where her rights can never be dethroned; that all pure love, all right thoughts, all religion, all governments, if you would have them live, must have their roots beneath its altar. This conviction impels me to say to every woman who has a home, Let home stand first, before all other things! No matter how high your ambition may transcend its duties, no matter how far your talents or your influence may reach beyond its doors, before everything else build up a true home! Be not its slave! Be its minister! Let it not be enough that it is swept and garnished, that its silver glistens, that its food is delicious. Feed the love in it. Feed the truth in it. Feed thought and aspiration, feed all charity and gentleness in it. Then from its walls shall come forth the true woman and the true man, who, *together*, shall rule and bless the land.

Is this an overwrought picture? We think not. What honor can be greater than to found such a home? What dignity higher than to reign its undisputed, honored mistress? What is the ability to speak on a public platform to large, intelligent audiences, or the wisdom that may command a seat on a judge's bench, compared to that which can insure and preside over a true home, with such skill that husband and children "rise up and call her blessed"? To be the guiding star, the ruling spirit, in such a position is higher honor than to rule an empire. *Woman's rights!* Has man any higher rights than these?

To be sure man often abuses his power, and brings sorrow and woe upon her who, trusting and loving him, should always be the mistress of his heart, an equal partner in all his possessions, his joys, and his sorrows. But are there no cases on record where "the woman Thou gavest me" has abused the power with which the marriage vow endowed her; destroying the peace, and making shipwreck of all that her husband holds most precious?

The law does not as yet secure to a wife such independence as will guard her against injustice and meanness from the hands of her husband; but what defence have they provided against the bitter sorrows that bad wives can bring down upon their husbands? Has any one ever ascertained the full statistics, or clearly estimated the average? It is well, no doubt, that this matter has been so widely agitated, as it all tends, we hope, to establish the rights of both man and woman on a firm foundation; but if, before this "revolution" is settled, man should make a full statement of his wrongs, there are those who could bring forward just cause of complaint in large measure. Ah! if husbands and wives would always remember that, with them, as in other associations, "union is strength"; that "united they stand, divided they fall"; that *together* they should walk through life, *together* share the joys, *together* bear the burdens and the crosses,—what a happy world this would be! If it is a united kingdom, the wife accepts the rough as well as the smooth of household rule, as her part of the administration. If able to govern without a "kitchen cabinet," a happy woman is she! But if not, she also takes the trials of the kitchen, the disagreeable details which must form a part of her home life, the vexation of spirit caused by the inefficiency of the servants of the present time, and this is the dreariest part,—all great and increasing hindrances to the perfection at which she should aim. But a good wife will endure these infelicities till a remedy is found, remembering that they are but a small part of home. The purest, sweetest, holiest elements that constitute a home, if recognized and administered in the right spirit, will enable her to forget these trials in the joy and peace that is set before her, and to which all may surely attain, if woman forgets not her high calling in a poor ambition.

Meanwhile the husband—the household king—accepts his part in the rule of this united kingdom. Are his cares any lighter than his wife's? Look at them. The dust and toil and strife, the battling with the great world outside, in whatever sphere his talents and duties call him, to provide necessities, luxuries, or honors, accordingly as he is prospered, for the family who are sheltered in his home.

We think the joys and the sorrows, the crosses and the crowns, in married life are about evenly balanced, and nothing will right all the wrongs, and bring order out of the confusion of these vexed questions, so surely as the shelter of a *true home, ruled by the true wife and mother.*

—Mrs. H. W. Beecher
Motherly Talks with Young Housekeepers
1873

AMERICAN HOUSEWIVES VERSUS SAVAGES

"I would rather be a good Sioux Indian than Most New England Housewives."

Thus, one of our most brilliant and scathing female writers ventilates herself—or rather, winds up a chapter upon the grievances of women by this heroic conclusion. Her idea is that woman's faculties are dwarfed by the narrow sphere of household labors which usually fall to her lot; that men consider her, in most cases, as merely a cooking, washing, mending, and baby-tending machine, and that the freer, less conventional, life of the savage is preferable to the increasing demands made upon the American housewife.

Now, while there are several grains of truth, mingled in the poisonous element of our text—which we may hereafter note—let us see how such sweeping assertions will be relished by readers of THE HOUSEHOLD, by housewives, to whom the work is especially dedicated, who may never have read our author's books. Here is one wearied, perhaps unusually, by the cares and labors of the day, but now sitting by her cheerful fireside and putting for a time her work-basket aside, enjoys a leisure hour in reading. As she glances at our heading, what thinks she of such a libel on the craft? Looking around her, upon the comforts of her household, which as a true help-meet she has helped her husband to obtain, upon loved children beautifying her home, but the proper care of which has cost her so much anxiety and toil, looking upon her own position, as a woman capable of ministering to the necessities of her household—not a mere toy on the one hand,

---

RAINY DAYS

Make the house look as bright as possible inside, have something good for tea, put on a pretty dress, light up early, romp with the children, tell them stories, and determine at least to have sunshine in the house, if you cannot have it outside.

---

nor a slave to man's lower instincts on the other—but a woman, who can make even labor ennobling, and can now for the moment forget her toils and cares, in the richness of life and the blessings of civilization. She may sometimes feel the burden of the day too heavy to be borne, and may have cravings for a more varied life—a desire for leisure and for self-improvement beyond her reach, yet these very desires and cravings will go far to overcome difficulties and make her life something more than a sordid or commonplace one. What thinks such a one of the compliment, paid by our author, to American housewives?

But here, THE HOUSEHOLD goes again—let us see—into a busy kitchen in the morning. There are but one pair of hands to do the work, and now all must be left just where it is, and baby taken for a while, though there are a dozen things that need doing at once. And with baby, the paper, just brought in, is taken up to be read, for the busy Mother has learned to make the most of every leisure moment. Her eye in time falls on our text, and she thinks: "Ah well-a-day, I do believe that is more than half true. Squaws do not have to see the children properly dressed and off to school in the morning—do not have the sweeping, and dusting, and house-arranging that we must do,—nor pies, puddings, cakes and preserves to make, besides a thousand other etceteras of civilization. And then, as for any time for improvement—well, I might about as well be a savage I verily believe, though after all, I can read some in snatches of time, and think while at work. And then it is better to wear out than rust out—better to live to some purpose than drift along in, either elegant uselessness, or thriftless, barren savageness. And perhaps, by and by my cares will be lightened and then I shall know how to prize a little respite." And so, even here, our satirist does not prevail, though her words have added a shade of discontent to the already burdened wife and mother.

Now, that there are very many of our housewives whose cares are greater and toils severer than the savages we are ready to acknowledge, but even with them life is not the barren, uncultivated waste of years as with their untutored sisters, for labor and the comforts it brings is what ennobles our material life. Neither does the fact that there are many, who in themselves are little elevated above the savage in mental culture, or in positive character call for such a sweeping assertion regarding housewives in general. Have you not known those, who with cares as thick as

A GOOD NIGHT KISS

Always send your child to bed happy. Whatever cares may trouble your mind, give the dear child a warm good night kiss as it goes to its pillow. The memory of this, in the stormy years which may be in store for the little one, will be like Bethlehem's star to the bewildered shepherds; and welling up in the heart will rise the thought; "My father, my mother—loved me!" Lips parched with fever will become dewy again at this thrill of useful memories. Kiss your little child before it goes to sleep.

FIRE KINDLERS

Take a quart of tar and 3 pounds of resin, melt them, bring to a cooling temperature, mix with as much sawdust, with a little charcoal added, as can be worked in; spread out while hot upon a board, when cold break up into lumps the size of a large hickory nut, and you have, at a small expense, kindling material enough for a household for one year. They will easily ignite from a match and burn with a strong blaze, long enough to start any wood that is fit to burn.

---

bees clustering around them, have yet amidst them all found, or taken, time for self-improvement—who have kept heart, and mind, and soul awake to the genial influences of something above their mere manual toil—who, with a will not readily overcome, make opportunities to indulge, to some extent, in such pleasures and pastimes as they most incline? In fact their toils only make more precious every available moment, spent in recreation, and enhance, the enjoyments as well as the dignity of life.

If such cases may be considered as isolated ones—as exceptions rather than the rule, there is yet a very large class of our housewives, who with no very decided abilities or positive character, in any one direction, are yet intelligent women as the world goes; who are capable of filling prominent positions creditably, and above all, know how to make a home neat and attractive to its inmates or guests. Neither above their lot, nor slaves to it, but adapting themselves to circumstances, they are none the less worthy or deserving than they would be were their position not that of a busy housewife. Left without such cares they might be mere women of the world and fashion, more ornamental perhaps, but less useful in their homes or society.

And now we come to cases such as, from our own standpoint, we consider our text—if so you please to call it— particularly applicable. It is those who consider work as the highest object of life, who weigh everything with a regard to utility and its money worth—who drudge, and save and narrow their very lives to the precincts of the kitchen—not in most cases because they *must* but because they *will,* and because they have no desire or taste for a broader, healthier, and more elevated life. They are practical machines and look upon every thing from a practical stand-point, while the true and beautiful, the sweeter, softer amenities of a more cultivated, enlarged existence is all unknown to them. They give mind, and heart, and soul ofttimes, as well as hands to household cares and sordid gains, and plod on in their narrow sphere unto the end. In many cases these same women could have help to relieve them of a share of their toils, but choose to slave themselves and save their pennies. And after all, such an one may as well drudge on, for with narrow views and tastes, what could she do with her leisure? She is no real companion for an intelligent person, be that person her husband or acquaintance, and unfitted to educate or truly elevate her children.

Such is the material, common-place, and unattractive life, of not a few in well-to-do situations—lives harder, and as we will readily agree, little preferable to that of a good Sioux Indian.

—Hortensia
The Household
VOL. 1, 1868

HER CIRCLE

"It is such a narrow circle in which to revolve," said one confined very much to the routine of every day home life, and its ofttimes homely duties, while her abilities, tastes, and culture, caused her to feel that life had, perhaps, broader paths in which, with more toward circumstances, she might aspire to walk.

"The cry of many a woman's heart," replied the dear, wise old friend, to whom the words were uttered, one who knew and sympathized with her tastes, and was himself a man of influence in the higher circles of society and intelligent action.

"But to think," said she in return, "How my time and limited strength is largely employed in these commonplace duties, my leisure needed for proper rest, and so little room is left for either improving or using the one, two, or five talents entrusted to my keeping. It is so different from that which I had planned, that my days seem being frittered away, as far as concerns the higher purposes of existence."

"You call this circle a narrow one," rejoined the friend, "and so it may appear as you now look upon it. But did you ever when a child amuse yourself by throwing pebbles into a sheet of water? And did you ever notice that however small the actual circle made where the pebble dropped, that its vibrations extended far beyond: one ripple beating against another, and that still onward to another and another, out into the broader waters? And from no sphere of life is the influence more significantly extended outwards than from this same narrow circle of a true woman's home, whether she labors with her heart, her head, her hands, or, as is wisest, with all together. And even one whose slender strength may not be equal to any long continued effort, has yet, if of persistent spirit to make the most of a little strength, and of broad, intelligent sympathies, a hold within her seemingly narrow circle, which may cause vibrations to extend far out into the sea of actual life. For her influence may be upon one and another from within her circle, and these, in turn, upon others,

OCTAGONAL PATCHWORK

Cut one hundred and twenty-seven squares of light print, each five inches by five inches, and one hundred and twenty-eight squares of the same size of a darker print, or, if one chooses, each one of the one hundred and twenty-eight pieces may be different. Then cut off the four corners of each dark square, so as, after allowing for a seam, to form an octagon.

Cut two hundred and fifty-six squares of the light print, two inches by two inches, and cut these across diagonally, making five hundred and twelve half-squares. The half-squares are to be sewed to the octagonal pieces in such a manner as to make them square again. For convenience, I sew the light half-squares on before cutting the corners off. The quilt is to be sewed with alternate squares of the plain and octagonal blocks, and will be seventeen blocks in length and fifteen blocks in width, with an octagonal block in each corner.

reaching out beyond the ken of mortal gaze into the far away realms of eternity."

These words of the elder friend to the younger were not forgotten, and henceforth her seemingly narrow circle was endowed with a new significance to her, as it may be to every thoughtful woman who will apply it to herself. And it is because the average woman does not sufficiently take thought of herself in the largest sense of the word, that her commonplace life so often seems to her a failure, and that her view of her sphere is such a narrow one.

—*The Household*
VOL. XIII, 1880

OUR DOMESTIC BEGGARS

I do not mean the man with the red nose and small bundle who wants a breakfast, nor the woman with two children who is trying to get to her relations. I mean your wife, my dear sir!

It happens, owing to the accumulation of wealth in this country, that there are many women who, by inheritance or otherwise, are possessed of money in their own right. But this is not the case with our country women in general. The majority of them are entirely dependent on either husband or father. It is for these that I wish to speak.

It is impossible not to be struck with the helplessness of woman in regard to money. I do not speak of those who might be expected to earn for themselves, but of the great number whose male friends intend and prefer to support them. Go into any ordinary town and call a meeting of ladies. Present a worthy cause to their consideration. You soon perceive that they are with you heart and soul. They flash, they melt, they are moved, and you can see that they are ready to do all they can.

Now send round the collection-box. Countenances fall immediately. The sum raised is in absurd contrast to the interest manifested. What is the matter? They cannot give, they have no money. A subscription paper only adds to their embarrassment. For how can they think of making a promise which their husbands may not see fit to fulfill? So both those devices utterly fail.

Try another plan: follow them to their homes; where of course there must be money for family use, and ask a small share of that. You will be surprised at the number who will say to you, "I would like to give, but I have no money in the house." Ask for a small subscription to be paid by and by. This also is declined after

---

HOW LADIES CAN MAKE THEIR OWN PERFUMES

If we spread fresh, unsalted butter upon the inside of two dessert-plates, and then fill one of the plates with gathered fragrant blossoms of clematis, covering them over with the second greased plate, we shall find that after twenty-four hours the grease has become fragrant. The blossoms, though separated from the parent stem, do not die for some time, but live to exhale odor, which is absorbed by the fat. To remove the odor from the fat, the fat must be scraped off the plates and put into alcohol; the odor then leaves the grease and enters into the spirit, which thus becomes "scent," and the grease again becomes colorless. The flower farmers of the Var follow precisely this method, on a very large scale, making but a little practical variation, with the following flowers: rose, orange, acacia, violet, jasmine, tube-rose, and jonquil.

some hesitation and with evident reluctance. To promise for the future she will not venture: to give now she cannot. The reason is obvious enough, though she does not mention it. The family treasury is not at home. It itinerates in her husband's pocket.

I have often thought that some husbands would be a little surprised, could they hear what is called a "Begging Committee" making a report to a caucus of ladies. It sounds something on this wise:

"Mrs. A.—Said she would ask her husband."

"Mrs. B.—Gave 15 cents and was sorry it was no more, but it was all she had in the house."

"Mrs. C.—Would send some money this afternoon."

"Mrs. D.—Could not give because her husband was out of town."

"Mrs. E.—Would let us know tomorrow."

"Mrs. F.—Would ask her husband."

"Mrs. G.—(A woman's rights woman) gave two dollars and would give more if we needed it."

"Mrs. H.—(Having money of her own) gave five dollars."

Some husbands got into the habit of disregarding their wives' request from the idea that they ask more than is necessary. With her knowledge of family details, she perceives that a few dollars spent now will save money by-and-by. He goes in and out and looks at home as a whole and finds it very comfortable, and so concludes that there is no such need as the one she has pointed out.

"Wife," said such a husband, laughing and good-naturedly, "you have got a *good want* and so l am going to let you keep it a while."

So the old stove waxed older and older and threatened daily to give out, but still by constant supervision from the wife, frequently burning her fingers as she arranged the flat-irons inside the oven to keep the top from falling in, daily suffering as she took the gas into lungs and eyes, and constant coaxing of the cook, the dinner came to the table well served and the husband rejoiced in his own superior discrimination.

"I tell you John that stove will surely fall in some day and ruin everything."

So one day John came home and announced that several gentlemen were coming out to dine with him. (They lived near the city and this is a true story.) He brought a fine quarter of lamb and various other edibles, the dinner was to be served at a certain hour and he wanted it very nicely done.

Now I do not say that what followed was justifiable, but I do say it was very natural. The wife was one of those high-spirited women of that particular type who hoped all things and endured all things up to the last moment, and then—the deluge. Her time had come. To cook all that dinner, with that stove! But she kept her own counsel. The cook was duly exhorted, the flat-irons arranged, the meat was duly prepared and the cooking went forward. Everything was nearly ready and the hour was at hand; the party had arrived and all that remained was to dish and serve. Watching her opportunity when the cook was elsewhere, the wife deftly slipped aside one of the flat-irons. Down came the inside of the stove and with it came an eruption of soot and smoke and ashes, covering the roast as Pompeii. The husband was called to view the catastrophe. "There John! didn't I tell you the top of that stove would fall in?" John took his guests to the hotel to dine, a wiser and a sadder man, and the next day there was a new stove in the house.

—Sarah Edwards Henshaw
The Household
c. 1880

The Sewing Machine Girl.
Wood Engraving, 1871.
Library of Congress.

MEN AND WOMEN

Among all the burdens that woman is called upon to bear, there is none that can be made so galling to her as the burden of dependence. Man is usually, in the life of the family, the bread-winner. However much he may be helped by woman in the economics of home life, he is usually the one who earns and carries the money on which the family subsists. Whatever money the woman wants comes to her from his hands, as a rule. Now, this money can be given into her hands in such a way that she can not only preserve her self-respect, but rejoice in her dependence; or it can be given to her in such a way that she will feel like a dog when she asks for it and when she receives it—in such a way that she will curse her dependence, and mourn over all the shame and humiliation it brings to her. We are sorry to believe that there are multitudes of wives and daughters and sisters, who wear fine clothing and who fare sumptuously every day, who would prefer to earn the money they spend to receiving it from the ungracious and inconsiderate hands upon which they depend.

If we had entitled this article "A Study of Husbands," it would have led us more directly, perhaps, to our main purpose; but the truth is that what we have to say has to do with dependent women in all the relations of life. It is natural for woman, as it is for man, to desire to spend money in her own way—to be free to choose, and free to economize, and free to spend whatever may be spent upon herself or her wardrobe. It is a delightful privilege to be free, and to have one's will with whatever expenditures may be made for one's own conveniences or necessities. A man who will interfere with this freedom, and who will deny this privilege to those who depend upon him, is either thoughtless or brutal. We know—and women all know—men who are very generous toward their dependents, but who insist on reserving to themselves the pleasure of purchasing whatever the women of their households may want, and then handing it over to them in the form of presents. The women are loaded with nice dresses and jewelry, and these are bestowed in the same way in which a Turk lavishes his favors upon the slaves of his harem. Now, it is undoubtedly very gratifying to these men to exercise their taste upon the necessities and fineries of their dependent women, and to feast themselves upon the surprises and the thanks of those receiving their favors; but it is a superlatively selfish performance. If these women could only have had in their hands the money which

CANDLES

Very hard and durable candles are made in the following manner: Melt together ten ounces of mutton tallow, a quarter of an ounce of camphor, four ounces of beeswax, and two ounces of alum. Candles made of these materials burn with a very clear light.

these gifts cost, they would have spent it better and they would have gratified their own tastes. A man may be generous enough to give to a woman the dresses and ornaments she wears, who is very far from being generous enough to give her money, that she may freely purchase what she wants, and have the great delight of choosing.

This is one side—not a very repulsive one—of man's selfishness in his dealings with women; but there is another side that is disgusting to contemplate. There are great multitudes of faithful wives, obedient daughters, and "left over" sisters, to whom there is never given a willing penny. The brute who occupies the head of the family never gives a dollar to the women dependent upon him without making them feel the yoke of their dependence, and tempting them to curse their lot, with all its terrible humiliations. Heaven pity the poor women who may be dependent upon him—women who never ask him for money when they can avoid it, and never get it until they have been made to feel as meanly humble as if they had robbed a hen-roost!

There is but one manly way in treating this relation of dependent women. If a man recognizes a woman as a dependent,—and he must do so, so far, at least, as his wife and daughters are concerned,—he acknowledges certain duties which he owes to them. His duty is to support them, and, so far as he can do it, to make them happy. He certainly cannot make them happy if, in all his treatment of them, he reminds them of their dependence upon him. We know of no better form into which he can put the recognition of his duty than that of an allowance, freely and promptly paid whenever it may be called for. If a man acknowledges to himself that he owes the duty of support to the women variously related to him in his household, let him generously determine how much money he has to spend upon each, and tell her just how much she is at liberty to call upon him for, *per annum.* Then it stands in the relation of a debt to the woman, which she is at liberty to call for and to spend according to her own judgment. We have watched the working of this plan, and it works well. We have watched the working of other plans, and they do not work well. We have watched, for instance, the working of the plan of the generous husband and father, who says: "Come to me for what you want, whenever you want it. I don't wish to limit you. Some years you will want more, and some less." This seems very generous; but, in truth, these women prefer to know about what the man thinks they ought to spend, or about what he regards as the

LOW SPIRITS

This is a state of mind generally associated with dyspepsia, in which all kind of imaginary evils are conjured up, and the slightest pain or unusual feeling is looked upon as the precursor of some dreadful malady. Persons so affected always fancy themselves on the verge of danger, and are fearful and irresolute in everything.

CAUSES—The causes are various. It may arise from intense study, some great stroke of affliction, indolence and inactivity, or excessive indulgence in venereal or other excesses, or deranged digestion.

TREATMENT—Change of scene, cheerful society, engaging the mind in some art or pursuit, which, although not too laborious, requires the use of the mental powers; exercise, tepid and shower baths, are among the remedial measures in this case. The bodily health must be carefully watched and preserved.

amount he can afford to have them spend. Having gained this knowledge by a voluntarily proffered allowance, they immediately adapt their expenditures to their means, and are perfectly content. It is a comfort to a dependent woman to look upon a definite sum as her own—as one that has been set aside for her exclusive use and behoof.

A great multitude of the discomforts that attach to a dependent woman's lot arise from the obtuseness and thoughtlessness of the men upon whom they depend. There are some men so coarsely made that they cannot appreciate a woman's sensitiveness in asking for money. They honestly intend to do their duty—even to deal generously—by the women dependent upon them, but they cannot understand why a woman should object to come to them for what they choose to give her. If they will ask their wives to tell them frankly how they can improve their position, these wives will answer that they can do it by putting into their hands, or placing within their call, all the money per annum which they think they can afford to allow them, and not to compel them to appeal to their husbands as suppliants for money whenever they may need a dollar or the quarter of one.

The absolutely brutal husband and father will hardly read this article, but we recall instances of cruelty and insult toward dependent women that would make any true man indignant in every fiber. A true woman may legitimately rejoice in her dependence upon a true man, because he will never make her feel it in any way; but a brute of a husband can make a true woman feel her humiliation as a dependent a hundred times a day, until her dependence is mourned over as an unmitigated curse.

—*Scribners*
VOL XXI, NO.1, DECEMBER 1880

HOW WOMAN CAN OBTAIN MORE THAN HER RIGHTS

Far be it from the author to hinder woman's obtaining double all her rights. He even claims to be an *apostle* of these as well as of all other rights. Woman, give your ear, while he tells you how to get twice as much as belongs to you.

Men will not be driven by men, much less by women; but woman can "coax" men into almost anything, as Delilah coaxed Samson. Get a man dead in love with you, and he will gladly allow you to do as you like with him and his purse. Nestle

yourself right into his affections, and he will let you pick his pockets every night, and work off his fingers to fill them the next day,
just for the pleasure of having his darling pet pick them again the
next night. Let this personal fact illustrate. A man bought a favorite horse; the seller expressing fear lest it might not be well cared for.
On learning afterwards that it had become a family pet, he said,—

"Now I am perfectly satisfied that the horse will be well used,
for I see you've made it a pet; and men always take good care of
whatever they pet."

Teaching man the true excellences of female character gives
woman not only all her rights, but all he can do for her besides.
Get him in love with the female *attributes* in general, and some
woman in particular, and "Othello's occupation's gone."

"Tack ship," you woman's rights advocates. Try flattering "these
men" in place of berating them. Make yourselves lovable, and they
will stand with cap in hand, perpetually saying, in action,—

"'Most cheerfully.' Can I do anything *else* for you? You do me
the greatest possible favor by allowing me to serve you."

Once get hold of a man's affections, by manifesting the genuine attributes of your sex, and he will redress all your wrongs, and
bestow all your rights; and then take real delight in loading you
down with every good and luxury within his power besides.

—O. S. Fowler
Sexual Science
1875

A Word to Mothers
on the Woman Question

Every newspaper at the present time has an article on the "woman
question," most of them written by men with the design of defin-
ing woman's position, and teaching her what she ought or ought
not to do. These articles are so various and contradictory that a
woman, looking to them for instruction, would be as much
puzzled as the traveler where three roads meet and no guide board.

One simple command of Scripture is worth them all: "Do
with thy might what thy hand findeth to do."

Good old Dr. Todd writes as if every woman had in possession or prospectively, a good husband, upon whom she could lean
in all difficulties, who would do her thinking, her voting, and who
would assume all her pecuniary responsibilities, while the happy
wife should bear children, mind the house, and be as amiable and

yielding as the tamed shrew, and for the reward of her conjugal devotion have inscribed upon her tombstone, if she ever dies a widow—"here lies the beloved relict, etc." Relict! A widow is nothing but a *relict—relinquo, relictus, relicta*—something left. Why always applied to a woman? Unfortunately for Dr. Todd's philosophy, there are many thousands who must rely upon themselves, who have neither husbands nor brothers to act for them, and thousands of others who are bound to sickly, weak, or bad men, whom they must support or they will become paupers.

In each State of our Union, there are from two hundred to a thousand prisoners whose labor is taken from their families and given to the State. Where are their wives, mothers and sisters?

The number of women who must maintain themselves, is large and constantly increasing. Some of them struggle on, holding to virtue as the sheet anchor of safety—others, less strong, fall in the contest, and after a brief life of shame, are carried forth to the Potter's field to fill nameless graves. The statistics of our great cities tell a fearful story of crime and suffering among women. Now, setting aside all question of woman's rights or wrongs, cannot mothers, foreseeing evil, prevent it?

There is no safe-guard like employment that is congenial and remunerative. The education of young ladies at present, in nine cases out of ten, is so superficial that they seldom aim higher than to become teachers of the common elementary studies which they have pursued at school, and such teachers are so numerous that the supply is greater than the demand.

Now, if mothers would study the tastes and proclivities of girls, as they do of boys, and allow them to pursue those employments which are congenial, might they not open to them avenues of enjoyment, and if need be, of wealth?

Has a girl a fine ear and voice for music? Cultivate it thoroughly. Give her as much time and as good a chance as you do your boy to learn a mechanical trade.

Has she a decided genius for drawing or modeling? Cultivate it, not by allowing her to spend a few hours under an incompetent teacher in making caricatures with which to deform your parlor, but make some sacrifice, if need be, to procure her admission to Schools of Design, where, if she cannot model like Canova, or sketch like Michael Angelo, she can at least make graceful designs for calico and delaine, or draft for the glassmaker and upholsterer.

HYDROPHOBIA

Take oyster-shells, wash them clean, put them upon a bed of live coals, and keep them there till they are thoroughly calcined, or burnt; then reduce them to fine powder, and sift it through a fine sieve. Take three tablespoonfuls of this powder, or lime, and add a sufficiency of egg to give it the consistency of soft dough,—fry it in a little fresh butter, or olive oil. Let the patient eat this cake in the morning, and abstain from food or drink at least six hours. This dose repeated for three mornings in succession, is, in all cases, sufficient.

A gentleman states that he is acquainted with six persons who were bitten, from eight to fifteen years ago, by dogs who were abundantly proved to be mad, from the fact that animals bitten, immediately after died with every symptom of hydrophobia; but by the use of this remedy, the six individuals are yet in perfect health.

TO MAKE A CANDLE BURN
ALL NIGHT

When as in the case of sickness, a
dull light is wished, put finely
powdered salt in the candle till it
reaches the black part of the wick.
In this way a mild and steady light
may be kept through the night by a
small piece of candle.

In the teeming population of our cities it is incompetence
that makes wretchedness. Skilled workwomen are scarce. How
few dressmakers understand their art! An accomplished one,
trained to business, who has an artistic taste and an eye for harmony in colors, can win a competence in ten years.

I know of one woman who has already made a fortune by her
culinary skill. Her pastry and cakes were wrought with great care
and nicety, and money flowed in upon her till she had enough to
retire and set up her carriage.

Mothers, do not be averse to any employment for which your
daughters have a taste. If they wish to be shoemakers allow them.
There is no harder work in making ladies' shoes, than in washing or
cheese-making. If they take to trade and understand arithmetic,
give them a little capital, if you can afford to do so, and let them
"set up a store." No matter if they can afford to live without labor.
Remember the old proverb—*"Labor ipse voluptas."* Labor itself is
pleasure.

Begin early and train them for some one business or profession. Let them look forward to this, and the beaux will be less in
their thoughts, but they will be better fitted for marriage when it
comes, and if it comes not, they have a resource from ennui and
poverty.

When men see that women can act as well as weep, that they
can do *well* what they undertake to do, they will lay aside their
pens and extremes will meet. Good Father Todd and Wendell
Phillips will rejoice together, for they both desire the elevation and
improvement of woman, but neither of them have gone further
than the A, B, C, of woman's needs and woman's power to do, if
all her faculties were cultivated in the way we propose.

—Mrs. A. E. Porter
The Household
VOL. I, 1868

A WIDOW WORTH HAVING *or* A SHORT CHAPTER ON FEMALE REPUTATION AND THE RIGHTS OF WOMEN

Some time last year, or in the year previous, there appeared first
in a Greenfield paper, Massachusetts, then in a Troy paper, N.Y.,
an article headed—"A Widow Worth Having." As usual with such
choice bits, it passed the circuit of the newspaper press, and became

a fragment of periodical literature. On its first appearance, the editor sanctioned it with the seal of authenticity, and furnished it with the above cognomen, indicative of the merits of the writer. The article was in the form of a letter addressed to him; and signed by the widow aforesaid—Marinda Hines. Extracts from the letter are as follow:—"I have five cows, and have sold, the past season, thirteen hundred pounds of butter, besides milk, cream, and butter for family use. Our family will average eight. I raised seven calves last Spring, and some late; two of them I got from my neighbors. I have fatted seven hundred and sixty-eight pounds of pork, mostly on sour milk. Now, let us leave one of the cows for family use, and set the credit to the other four: say thirteen hundred, divided by four, makes three hundred and twenty-five pounds, at sixteen and a half cents per pound—the price at which it sold—fifty-three dollars and sixty-two cents, to each cow. The calves were worth, say thirty dollars; twenty-five to four cows; and five hundred of the pork, at six dollars, will be thirty; and the twenty-five for the calves makes fifty-five dollars; and divided by four, leaves thirteen dollars and seventy-five cents to each cow; and this, added to what was received for the butter, will make sixty-seven dollars and thirty-seven cents of receipts for the produce of each cow; or two hundred and sixty-nine dollars and fifty cents for the produce of the four."

Mrs. Hines afterwards stated that her cows were of the native breed, and of medium size; that they have good pasture in summer, and good hay in winter; and no other feed, except a few apples, small potatoes, apple parings, and the like, in the winter, to Old Brindle, to make her milk hold out till some of the others came in. Thirty dollars is a large allowance for the feed of each of her cows. Now, suppose she were ambitious, and disposed to keep fifty cows instead of her present number, and there would be a clear profit of that number, of $1,868 75 cents annually. Who can say there is no profit in agriculture, under proper management? Such a widow would indeed make a wife, for a farmer, worth having. The dairy may, and should, properly, be under the direction of the female head of the family. Let all wives of farmers imitate the example of this widow, and there will be a new aspect in rural communities. All may do it, if they will. Mrs. Hines may be taken as a model agriculturalist. She has connected the improvement of the mind with the improvement of the farm. She has been accustomed to read the periodicals. The editor of the paper which introduced her to the public, said she had taken, and promptly paid him for, his journal, twenty successive years.

Of such instances of female talent our agricultural societies should take cognisance. The authors of them deserve publicity and tokens of public appreciation. The community at large would be stimulated by them. Hence we make record of them wherever found; and of the benefit that may be derived from that of Mrs. Hines we think so highly, we would cheerfully render her a more substantial tribute of regard. One thought we had was to procure her portrait for an illustration in the present volume. The difficulty of procuring it seemed to present an obstacle. Then it occurred to us, that instead of a kindness to the worthy widow, it might prove an evil to her. It can scarcely be supposed that a woman who can take care of herself and her farm as well as she can, needs a husband. And, if she were to try the experiment, and obtain one less competent for these duties than herself, she might naturally despise him. If so, the consequences would be the most inauspicious. Besides, it occurred to us, that if she were a handsome woman, she might be greatly annoyed from the crowds of rural widowers and old bachelors that would be thronging her from every part of the country where our book is read. And, on the other hand, it occurred to us, that possibly, notwithstanding her skill in the matters aforesaid, instead of being handsome, her features are coarse and repulsive. If so, she would by no means indulge a feeling of complacency in being paraded before the public. We happen to know that two of our most distinguished literary ladies have absolutely prohibited their publishers from prefixing their portraits to their published works, simply because they are notoriously ugly in their looks. We know not why a dairy woman may not have some pride in such a matter as well as a writer of prose or poetry.

—Rev. John L. Blake
The Farm and the Fireside
1855

• • •

Is the present discussion of the woman question calculated to make our sex happier or no? The present generation of women, I mean. That it will be for their good eventually, that it will open the doors of a fuller, larger life to those who may come after us, that it will tend to the righting of many wrongs, to the correction of many errors, and to the sweeping away of many sophisms, cannot be doubted, I think, even by those— and their name is legion—

who doubt the expediency of woman suffrage. The tendency of the movement is to make women think, to make them reason, to make them study cause and effect; and though they should never cast a ballot, practice law, or "make ship-carpenters of themselves," it will do them good, sooner or later. It will do men good, too, if they can be led to look at the matter calmly and dispassionately, through a glass undimmed by the mists of selfishness and prejudice. It will teach them—and thank God! many of them do not need to be taught—they know it already—that to crown the queen does the king no wrong. It will teach them that justice, like mercy, is "twice blessed; it blesses him that gives and him that takes."

But this is not what I started to say. What I *was* about to say is this. I doubt whether the effect of the movement *just now*, is to make women happier. Its tendency is to make them introspective. It leads them to tear the rose of life in pieces to see what it is made of, and how it is put together. It makes them search for thorns when they might be drinking in the rich perfume of the flower. And no human being ever yet deliberately hunted for thorns who did not find plenty of them. I strongly suspect that the young brides of the present day discover more of them than their mothers and grandmothers did.

Yet we need not worry about this. It will right itself in time. Neither need you and I, dear Rachel, if we do not happen to be in entire sympathy with the movement, be troubled by it. Nature is very strong; her laws are immutable. There is no more danger that woman will get permanently "out of her sphere," than that yonder planet will get out of its orbit. The logic of events may prove that her sphere is far wider than has been presumed. But one thing is certain. If by nature she is too gentle and tender to wrestle with opposing currents; if she shrinks from vulgar notoriety; if she is too timid to stand in public places, and too weak to lift life's heavy burdens; if the rude jostle and jar of political and business conflicts are at war with her finest instincts, we may rest assured that she will have none of them. No act of legislation will unsex her. The largest liberty will but leave her more free to listen to the voice of nature and of God. Woman will be woman, my friend, to the very end of the chapter.

And man will be man, as long as "grass grows and water runs." Consequently I do not fear that our moustached and

TO BLOW OUT A CANDLE

If a candle is blown out by an *upward* instead of a downward current of air, the wick will not smoulder down. Hold candle higher than the mouth in blowing it out.

bearded friends will devote their energies to baby-tending
and dish washing yet awhile. Do you?

—*The Household*
VOL. V, 1872

FARMER GREEN'S COMPLAINT

The men hev finished plowin', the seedin' just begun,
My wife is alwuz bizzy from sun around to sun.
The bread to bake, an' churnin'—great balls o' yaller gold—
The washin' an' the ironin'—the half on't can't be told.
The calves to feed, an' chickens, an' turkeys all to raise;
But she hez got a notion,—(they're swarmin' now-a-days).
Of one thing I am sartin'—a notion's like a weed,
That is forever sproutin' ef once ye drop the seed .

My wife is kind o' spindlin', but then she'd never shirk,
An' tho' she's full o' notions, a master hand to work.
We alwuz hev bin savin',—we started kind o' poor,—
An' now, we've got forehanded, we'd orter keep it, sure.
But she hez got an idee,—(an agent's work, I spoze)!
She wants machines fur washin' an' wringin' out the cloze!
A notion's just like pusley, the meanest kind o' weed,
Ye can't get red on't, nohow, ef once ye drop the seed.

Photographer.
State Historical Society
of Wisconsin
(WHi (V24) 1706).

She wants a lot of posies, that nobuddy kin eat;
She wants to take a paper! I tell ye, I wuz beat.
Now, all of my machinery is needed on the farm,
An' I hev heard that needles keep wimmen out o' harm.
There's Neighbor Jones's "eighty"—I've hankered fur so long—
He's got to sell—his hosses, too—I'll git 'em fur a song!
An' we must be more savin'—a notion's like a weed,
Ef once ye git it started, it's sure to scatter seed.

The wimmen's gittin' notions. They must be in the air,
Like grass in spring—none to be seen—an' then, it's everywhere.
They're doctorin' an' preachin', an' now they want to vote!
Of all the crazy ideas, that is the greatest note.
It's all cum of their readin'! That's why they are so smart
The only way's to squelch 'em, right at the very start.
Don't wait half through the summer, ef goin' to kill a weed;
To stop it's tarnal sproutin', jist go an' burn the seed.

Fur wimmen's pesky critters, git notions in their head.
They're bound to hev 'em, somehow, no matter what is said.
My wife keeps on a-teasin', fur them machines, I spose,
Fur washing', an' fur wringin', an' sewin' on her cloze!
She'd want some more to-morrer. Ye jist kin bet yer life,
She won't git any notions, not long ez she's my wife!
The surest way's to squelch it (a notion's like a weed),
An' keep the wimmen alwuz frum gittin' any seed!

—Margaret Stewart Sibley
The Household
VOL. XXV, 1892

Good for you, Uncle Frank! In behalf of wives generally I make you my best bow, with a hearty "Thank you sir." I did not look for a response in that direction, but it is better for coming from your side of the house. "John" will take it kindly from you, but if one of the wives had written it, perhaps he would turn up his nose and impatiently throw THE HOUSEHOLD on the table. I see you go in for "woman's rights"; well, so do I; not the kind of rights that some of our Amazons are prating about, but domestic, home, family, fireside rights. These political women who want to vote and get into office, and "rule the roost," are my especial horror. I would like to see them all at the wash-tub; the smell of soap-suds would do them good, I think. And it would not hurt my feelings much to see them cleaning stove funnels. If they don't get smutty and wish themselves clean from the whole affair before they get through with it, I am mistaken—Victoria C. Woodhull not excepted. Women have their rights, and they are sometimes woefully trampled upon, but in my opinion they do not extend into politics. I have no aspirations in that direction and would not thank Victoria, if she was President today, for an office. There are plenty of responsibilities down here in my low corner; all that I care to bear, and more, I fear, than I can well account for in the great settling day. ...

Your friend,

Olive Oldstyle
—*The Household*
VOL. V, 1872

WOMAN'S RIGHTS

"The rights of women," what are they?
The right to labor and to pray;
The right to watch while others sleep;
The right o'er others' woes to weep;
The right to succor in distress;
The right while others curse to bless;
The right to love when others scorn;
The right to comfort all that mourn;
The right to shed new joy on earth;
The right to feel the soul's high worth;
The right to lead the soul to God
Along the path her Saviour trod;
The path of weakness and of love;
The path of faith that leads above;
The path of patience under wrong;
The path in which the weak grow strong.
Such woman's rights our God will bless,
And crown their champions with success.

—*The Household*
APRIL 1874

And lastly, the expression of a clearer, more confident voice counterpointing the confusion, guilt, and uncertainty felt by so many country women. From a publication that did not, perhaps, measure the pulse of rural and small town America so closely, the article reflects quite another consciousness, not widely accepted in 1872, of course, but there, nevertheless—a utopian dream!

The District School Teacher.
Library of Congress.

THE COMING WOMAN

The main object in life for the Coming Woman will be not so much the mating as the making of herself. She will aim possibly at position, possibly at wealth—surely at independence. One thing she will never be content to remain, and that is the mere marital appendage of a man.

If progressiveness masculine as to ability, talent and influence shine, progressiveness feminine will aspire to light as brilliant a candle in her walk of life. She will repudiate shining altogether by reflected brilliancy.

The Coming Woman will protect herself. The "big brother" will be rid of his responsibility: he may go about his business. She is to be a markswoman: she will send the ball to its mark with the same unerring precision as now she does the end of a thread through the eye of a fine cambric needle. She will alone in the darkness safely traverse the highways and byways of the city. Bloody corpses of imprudently forward men, young and old, will occasionally be found in her track. The Coming Woman will be dangerous by night. It is time. Man to the single woman has been dangerous long enough. Not that we admire or endorse the female desperado, or "Girl of the Period," but there are still extant many masculine natures only to be coerced into a

---

IN BOILING PUDDINGS

mind that the cloth be perfectly clean. Dip it in hot water, and dredge it well with flour. If a bread-pudding, tie it loose; if a batter-pudding, tie it nearly close; apple and gooseberry puddings, etc., should be tied quite close. When you make a batter-pudding, first mix the flour well with milk, and stir in the other ingredients by degrees; you will then have it smooth, without lumps. The best way however, for a plain batter-pudding, is to strain it through a coarse hair-sieve, that it may have neither lumps nor the treadings of the eggs; and for all other puddings strain the eggs when they are beaten up. Be sure the water boils when you put your pudding in, and that it keeps boiling all the time, and that you keep it always covered with water; you should

proper respect for female honor and purity by fear of personal consequences.

She will not be deficient in nerve or weak in muscle. She will be a skillful driver, a daring rider, a hardy walker. Four miles per hour, up hill and down, will be her pace. Male adoration weak in the knees will do penance. The idea of woman as the weaker sex will become old-fashioned, and finally obsolete. Physical strength in the matter of agility and endurance is not for man alone. The South Sea Island women are better swimmers than the men. What woman ever tired of dancing? A washerwoman's daily toil might lay up a drygoods clerk for a week, and perhaps tire a ploughman. Male muscle may lift more pounds, but put that of the female in training, and it runs, leaps and climbs, as the female mind jumps at conclusions, as quickly as, if not quicker than, that of the male.

She will not spend her days cooped up in any house. At forty she intends being fair, healthy, vigorous, symmetrically adipose, and at the climax of life's attractiveness and enjoyment. At twenty she will be beautifully unfolding; at thirty, charming; at forty, magnificent. This because she puts sun, pure air and water to legitimate, plentiful and frequent use. No pent-up, hermetically-sealed, lathed-and-plastered, stove-heated cavern, its walls, its floors, its atmosphere permeated by the emanations of past generations, will be her den of life immurement.

Will she dress? Yes, and as women never dressed before. The fitting adornment of the body has its part in the mosaic of life with all other action and enjoyment. Nature has implanted the instinct and set the example. Since the world's birth, in the myriad forms of animal, bird, insect, plant and flower, has she beautified herself. It is she who changes the fashions. Are all birds of the same plumage? Are all flowers of the same hue and form, and are not through cultivation their colors deepened, varied, and their shape made more complicated? Would we that woman from year to year, from generation to generation, should attire herself in the garb of the Quakeress or the nun? Where, then, would be the sparkle of the promenade? In all things this inborn desire for change is the preventive to monotony. The principle extends to dress. Our Coming Woman will give to outward adornment its place. It is not to monopolize all her time and attention. She is to be fitted by that modiste still rare, Good Taste, and whoever shall run a muck through palatial dry-goods establishments and on the street make her appearance, having on her body whatever apparel happens thereunto to cling on such frantic passage, shall be shunned as a case of garmental leprosy.

She is to have her own house, her own hours, her own liberty, her own company. If she prefer female company to male, female company she will have. Possibly she may not. Couples were created male and female. He who desires to stand first in the heart of the Coming Woman, and is jealous, will lead a life of perturbation. For variety of association, male association—and attractive association at that—she will have. Not fops, not pretty men, nor military dandies, whose mission in this world is to ornament the front entrances of fashionable hotels. The Coming Woman will seek to cluster about her men distinguished in every department of intellect—literature, painting, poetry, sculpture, the drama, the platform— philosophers, inventors and discoverers. Aiming at culture of self, she will realize that personal association is the best of educators.

An able effort in any department of mind is well—the study of the man performing it is better. Her lunch-parties will comprise galaxies of intellect. We speak now of the Coming Woman single, with an establishment all her own—the poor author's home, the wearied poet's refuge, at all times open for them so long as with her they fall not too desperately in love; for that raving love, that all-absorbing passion, which leaves its victim no room nor power to think or treat aught else, she will deem a mania, a species of insanity. Her chosen love must be preceded by friendship. True friendship, like charity, suffereth long and is kind. True friendship is a plant of most delicate texture, and to maintain it in all its purity, to hold the substance and not the mere form, to so stand in the hearts of others that the thought of us when absent shall bring only gentle remembrance of past pleasure and a softened fragrance of past association, requires care, study, consideration, and often self-denial. Coming men and women will aim not to be burdensome to each other.

Her love will not be demanded or exacted by the Coming Man. Better than to-day will it be realized that love in birth and growth is spontaneous; that it is not a quality subject to will, that it may be given or withheld at pleasure; that exaction often causes the death of love, or turns the pure gold of affection into a base counterfeit.

All Nature is varied, and the maximum of variability belongs to feminine human nature. That Coming Woman the most

also move it about two or three times at first, or it may stick to the pot; dip the pudding into cold water immediately when you take it out, which prevents it sticking. If you boil your pudding in a dish or basin, butter the inside before putting the pudding in; the same should be done to the dish for a baked pudding or pie. The quality of pie-crust depends much on the baking. If the oven be too hot, the paste, besides being burned, will fall; if too slack, it will be soddened, and consequently heavy. Paste should be made on a cold, smooth substance, such as marble or slate, with a light, cool hand. It should be made quickly; much handling makes it heavy. Great nicety is required in wetting the paste; too little moisture rendering it dry and crumbly, while too much makes it tough and heavy; and in either case the paste cannot be easily worked. Practice alone can produce perfection in this art.

STEWED OX PALATES

Let four palates remain in a basin with warm water for half an hour; then wash them; simmer in a stewpan with water, until they can be easily skinned. Then take them out, skim them, and cut into square pieces; put them into a stewpan, with one pint of brown gravy, a spoonful of white wine, as much catsup and browning, an onion stuck with cloves, and a slice of lemon. Stew for half an hour (or until tender), take out the onion and lemon, thicken the sauce (as previously directed), serve with forcemeat balls, and garnish with sliced lemon. There are many ways of serving ox palates, but this is the best and simplest.

charming and piquant, may be subject to variability. Even perpetual sunshine becomes tiresome. Possibly the warm reception of to-day may be clouded by a shadow of frigidity tomorrow. This will not trouble the Coming Man. He will be wise enough and strong enough to accept the woman as Nature made her.

There will be in the Coming Woman that refined species of coquetry developing itself in the desire to please all. Such coquetry is the ever-renewed sparkle of the brilliant, and makes whosoever would wear it the more aspiring that he may deserve its wearing. The man will not be alarmed, remembering that the sense of justice, fitness and propriety is not exclusively a masculine inheritance, and that is not freedom which is enslaved in any bond of sin.

This, you may say, argues too much feminine independence. You dislike these independent women, ever shouting, "I am a free woman! I will be free! I will love whom I please, what I please, when I please and as often as I please! Will some tyrant tread on the skirt of *me* gown?" We are not surprised at this disgust. But there is a truer feminine independence, reposing under the veil of modesty, not appearing uncalled for, and this shall disarm your prejudice.

There is great use for man in the truest feminine independence. If our life is lived by that of an upright man or woman, we are more strongly influenced by such life than by all other admonition or precept. We may see but fragments of it, but we feel its whole. And not the outwardly manifested life merely, but the inward ideal of that man or woman concerning life acts on us from them like a strong, subtle, unseen yet powerful emanation, which controls and influences us without our knowing it.

And so association with the independent, self-contained woman, who resents our tyranny with indignation and our weaknesses with contempt, renders the man more independent and courageous in life's battle. It is the masculine instinct to delight in the display of its bravery in the presence of timorous and shrinking beauty; but when that beauty snatches the battle-flag and imperils its own life in the van of conflict, the masculine admiration and emulation force the cowards to become the heroes.

The Coming Man will hold congenial female association as the greatest help, the most refreshing rest, the highest enjoyment. But on this he will not allow his happiness, his internal peace, to be entirely dependent. On no means of happiness outside of himself will he lean exclusively, knowing well that by such act is lost half the pleasure and benefit such happiness may be capable of conferring. His life will emulate the mountain-chains of the Sierras, sustaining and rejoicing in their covering of verdure, but based only on their own granite foundation; rising perhaps to cold, stormy, barren heights of loneliness, only that they may shed more fertility, more water, more soil, to nourish the tender vines and flowers on the plain below.

All this, you may say, is very easy to preach, but quite another thing to practice. We agree. Doctors, and even preachers, are among the last to take their own medicines. But Progressiveness is inevitable for the Future, and Progressiveness means Strength.

The Coming Man will never imagine that he can permanently remain the idol of a woman, supposing that he become such. If at first she take him for china, he will hold himself in readiness for her to detect in him the more common clay of which brickbats are made. With such detection he knows he must fall in her estimation—for him a most painful tumble, unless previously anticipated. But from this fall he must rise equal to, and even above, the Coming Woman's aspiration.

Idolization often means worship. Humanity seems ever searching for a divinity among its own ranks. It imagines frequently it has found one, and is as frequently mistaken. Idolization frequently means the surrender of one side of individuality—the surrender on one side, and the reception on another, of heart, soul, body and intellect. The idolization is generally on one side, and is never at rest. In secret it is ever demanding the worship it gives. It is constantly bowing to an ideal which is constantly being defaced by the real.

And how does the little earthly god or goddess so adored receive this worship? You imagine, madame, that you have made a complete conquest of some man, or you, sir, of some poor woman. Now the human heart is deceitful above all things, and desperately mean. It is often a neglected house, with many unswept, untidy chambers. Roaming about this heart-house of yours, we will open some of these untidy apartments. You deem yourself to have made a conquest. Some man lives on your smiles, his happiness is all dependent on your association. What are your feelings for him? Look narrowly into those chambers. You find a little love, a good deal of exultation, pride and gratification, a little pity, and, if you will own it, a something else which hovers on the

CHEESE—FRESH

Sweeten two quarts of cream with sugar, and boil it thin; then put in some damask rosewater, and keep it stirred, that it may not burn. When it is thickened and turned, take it off the fire, wash the strainer and cheese-vat with rosewater, roll your curd backward and forward in the strainer, to drain the whey from it, put the curd into the vat as soon as it is cool, slip it into the cheese dish with some of the whey, and serve it.

POT CHEESE

Put about one-third buttermilk to two-thirds of sour milk, in a clean vessel over the fire; make it scalding hot; then take the curd from the whey with the skimmer, and put it into a muslin or linen bag, tie it up, and hang it to drain; after an hour or two, take it down, moisten it slightly with sweet cream; put a little salt to it, work the salt into it, and make it in balls the size of a teacup; press it close with the hands, lay a cloth on a dish to receive the cheese, cover it, then set it in a cool place.

confines of contempt. Now, neither Coming Men nor Coming Women will care to so involve themselves in another's estimation. They will shrink in terror and disgust from the possibility of being merely *endured.*

God means that we shall do exact justice to ourselves, as well as to others. If we do not, he punishes by making us see ourselves as prisoners dragged behind some male or female conqueror's chariot-wheels. He says, Love, but preserve your independence; love, but do not worship; love, but let all men and women recollect that they govern their own empire of soul, heart and intellect, and that in no excess of devotion is any portion of this empire's power and territory to be foolishly granted away.

The Coming Man will know, also, that he must earn love. It is the oak, not the sapling, among whose branches birds come to build their nests and make melody. Ere the sapling be favored with such company it must grow—it must have height, shade, strength and security to tempt the warblers.

There will also in his day be less complaint from struggling genius concerning the lack of appreciation and recognition; for he will to a certainty know that just so fast as in the cultivation of his talent he makes himself a power, just so fast will he attract to him whatever he needs. We reap not only as we sow, but the harvest is rich in proportion to the care with which we cultivate. We believe it a law that intellectual power and moral worth attract their own just as surely and certainly as the iron grains are drawn toward the magnet. If the magnet aspire to draw to itself a larger piece of metal, it must make itself sufficiently strong so to do.

It is common to symbolize the masculine element as the oak, the feminine as the vine. The comparison in actual life seems not always to hold good, for on looking around we find masculine vines and violets. The real backbone of the family is not always encased in a masculine envelope. There are men who seem born to be petted and cared for by women: you need not envy them. Which picture is most pleasing to the masculine aspiration—to be the protective oak or the delicate violet?

The Coming Woman will hold office. Through the spectacles of futurity I behold her installed the collectress of the port. She sits in her office. Her face is pleasing, her manner calm, dignified, self-possessed. She is surrounded by gentlemen on business, and business with the collectress is always interesting. She is attired in

---

SPRING FEVER

On rising, sponge the body lightly and quickly with cold water, briskly toweling after. It is not necessary that this be a long or laborious operation; the more rapidly the better, with sufficient friction to bring a glow to the skin. If you cannot secure time to go over the whole bodily surface, at least make it a point to daily sponge the trunk and arms. Rousing and stimulating the whole system, clearing and opening the pores, it imparts an indescribable freshness and exhilaration, amply repaying the effort. Rehabilitated, you are now ready for your morning bitters,

the female maritime costume of the period—dark blue blouse belted about the waist, wide, turn-over linen collar, jaunty glazed tarpaulin hat, moderately tilted in front, with a tasty length of black streamer behind, hair loose, and, thanks to her healthy, vigorous organization, luxuriant trowsers, similar in material to the blouse, and gathered at the ankle à la Bloomer. She has just returned from an early morning's trip outside the harbor in her private yacht. Being a practical sailor, she takes the helm herself on these excursions. She boasts that her vessel "lays nearer the wind" than any other owned by the club. The breeze and spray have freshened her complexion, for to her an occasional fillip of salt water in the face is only Neptune tossing his kiss to Juno.

But she is collectress of the port not in form merely, but in substance. She has executive capacity, and her eye is all vigilant, all supervising. Beauty and vigilance, grace and business, may go hand in hand.

As to-day, intrigue and cabal are at work to oust her. But she fights fire with fire. She wields a pungent, ready, logical pen, and her articles are read and known. Not a shrieker, she can still grace the platform, and is there in forensic tilt a ready, even a dangerous, combatant.

She is not to sink under varying and perhaps trying conditions of life. If her lot be poverty, she will accept and live it gracefully. If necessary, she will not hesitate to carry a broom newly purchased, or even a tin tea-kettle, through the streets. It is not so much what we do as our manner of doing it that tells. There is room for grace and beauty of action even in handling a broom.

But we accord not to the Coming Woman any elevation higher than man's. Perfect equality, perfect interdependence—woman's aspiration, man's strength: this is our platform of masculine and feminine union. God did not in his own image create man that he should stand below any other being. Between the masculine and the feminine the scales of moral and intellectual equality must be evenly balanced. Where is the beauty of their union if one is ever kicking the beam?

It is the woman that designs the model of a true manhood: it is the masculine will and strength which chisels such design from the rugged block. Both emulate and strive to be worthy of each other.

Will love be the episode or the life of the Coming Woman? Occupation will be given to her of an artistic kind. In this will she

namely, the clear juice of a fresh lemon in a wineglass of water, without sugar. This is a bomb straight at the enemy, for a more potent solvent of bile is not in the *materia medica*. Searching out rheumatic tendency, attacking those insidious foes which are storing up anguish against our later days—calculi—it pervades the system like a fine moral sense, rectifying incipient error. It is needful, perhaps, to begin with two lemons daily, the second at night just before retiring.

A primitive but most efficacious prescription, which corrected the physical reaction after a pork-eating winter for our ancestors.

BEESWAX

To obtain wax, boil the combs in a strong muslin bag, in a sauce pan, with water sufficient to keep the bag from burning, and while boiling, continue to press the bag with a wooden slice or spoon, to extract the whole, as you skim off the wax. Drop the wax into cold water, where it will swim on the surface. The wax thus obtained will still want refining, to effect which, place it in a sauce pan, and melt it over a slow fire. Then pour off the clear wax into proper vessels, and let it cool.

live, for Art is the first and greatest love with us all. It proves the strongest refuge when we are disappointed in any other. Other shrines may be beautiful, but they are inferior. To cultivate ourselves, to bring out the fullest expression of the divinity within us, seems the great aim of existence and the most fitting worship of the Infinite Spirit. This, actuated by the largest spirit of benevolence and good-will, proves the greatest source of pleasure to ourselves and our fellows. The genius that bases *all* aspiration and effort on the hope of winning some one exclusive human love, deserts the grand altar of the Infinite and bows to the inferior shrine of the Finite.

In the time of the Coming Woman more of her talent, power and capacity implanted by Nature will be known and used. To-day it is not alone the unfathomed caves of ocean in which are uselessly hidden all "gems of purest ray."

Will love then be the episode or the life? We answer, The life. But her first love will be for the gem of Art within, and the development of its brilliancy, the second for him who may best aid in such development.

Do we point toward a cold creature, all intellect, no heart— no wifely, no mother love? Not so. There will be heart enough, and an ounce of the Coming Woman's affection, controlled by wisdom, is worth a ton of that shadow love so common to-day— shadow love bought and accepted for dress, money, position, desire for something like a home, for female sympathy. Better the glance of affectionate regard once a month than a daily experience of indifference or passive endurance.

The Coming Woman will have much to do. External attraction in form, feature and adornment will not altogether answer. Behind these must be an intellect—a cultivated intellect, and an intellect ever increasing in cultivation. She will be much alone, that her knowledge, gathered from books and observation, from men and women, may in solitude be drilled to its place and use. Intellect, beauty, grace and tact combined form a power unequaled by any other. Such power will be her aspiration. Its possession in no degree detracts from the charm of true womanliness. Such womanliness is an armor wholly enveloping her, and most powerful to protect in all conditions and circumstances.

We essay no prediction of feminine perfection. It is not desirable. Perfection by either sex once attained, and nothing remaining to be improved, life would stagnate in monotony. No one desires to encounter a perfect man or woman. Such a presence would prove a constant irritation and reproach. The Coming Woman in private *shall* have her spurts of ebullition, as the man entrusted with her errands and not bringing home the exact shade of Berlin worsted will discover. Such "tantrums" are pleasant for variety's sake, and the woman entirely free from them is the lake without a breeze, the ocean without a gale.

She will grow old not only gracefully, but beautifully. Age for her will be mellowness, not decay. Our grandmothers of the future are not to be as forlorn, decayed, useless tenements, regarded half in pity, half in ridicule: rather as the Pyramids, grand still in their strength, interesting through association, imposing through antiquity.

—Prentice Mulford
Atlantic
1872

BIBLIOGRAPHY

Much of the background and the excerpted material for this book came from the periodicals of the time. There were an enormous number of magazines published all over the country before and during the period 1865–1900, and they seemed to communicate most directly and unself-consciously the problems and quality of life of the time. The magazines I used were mostly those related to farming, farm life, and domestic economy, although I did study a number that presented a range of popular culture and literature. It would be difficult (and interminable) to list all the articles, reports, essays, letters, poems, and stories separately by issue. I will let it suffice to list the magazines used. There were two, however, that seemed to be most useful, and to which I referred most frequently: *The Household* and *The American Agriculturist*.

The books I consulted, either for background and understanding of the period or for excerpt, fall into two categories. First were those books more or less contemporary with the period of this book, 1865–1890, which I considered primary sources of information about the time. And second were those books concerning the period 1865–1900, but clearly reflecting a different time or consciousness and providing historical perspective.

As for government publications, federal and state, The Annual Reports of the U.S. Patent Office from 1837–1862 included material on agriculture and farm life. From 1849–1861, separate volumes on agriculture were issued as Annual Reports, Agriculture. From 1862–1889, they became the Annual Reports of the Commissioner of Agriculture and after 1889 the Annual Reports of the Secretary of Agriculture.

These publications contained many articles of general interest on rural living and were very useful. In many states, state boards of agriculture issued annual reports containing their transactions and a wide range of articles, essays, and orations on farming and farm life. I have made use of many of these volumes from the states of New York, Massachusetts, Pennsylvania, Maine, Michigan, and Ohio.

GENERAL HISTORICAL BACKGROUND

Beale, Irene A. *Genessee Valley Women 1743–1985*. Geneseo, N.Y.: Chestnut Hill Press, 1985.
Blanc, Maclame (Marie Therese de Solms) (Th. Bentzon, pseud.). *The Condition of Woman in the United States*. 1895. Reprint, New York: Arno Press, 1972.

Boorstin, Daniel. *The Americans: The Colonial Experience*. New York: Random House, 1958.

_____. *The Americans: The Democratic Experience*. New York: Random House, 1973.

_____. *The Americans: The National Experience*. New York: Random House, 1965.

Brieger, G. *Medical America in the Nineteenth Century*. Baltimore: Johns Hopkins Press, 1971.

Brody, David, ed. *Essays on the Age of Enterprise: 1870–1900*. Hinsdale, Ill.: The Dryden Press, 1974.

Brown, Harriet Connor. *Grandmother Brown's Hundred Years: 1827–1927*. Boston: Little Brown, 1929.

Butterfield, Kenyon L. *Chapters in Rural Progress*. Chicago: University of Chicago, 1908.

Carruth, Gordon, ed. *The Encyclopedia of American Facts and Dates*. New York: T. Y. Crowell, 1956.

Carson, Gerald. *The Old Country Store*. New York: Oxford University Press, 1954.

Clinton, Catherine. *The Other Civil War: American Women in the Nineteenth Century*. American Century Series. New York: Hill & Wang, 1984.

Conrad, Susan P. *Perish the Thought: Intellectual Women in Romantic America 1830–1860*. New York: Carol Publishing Group, 1978.

Conway, Jill Ker. *The Female Experience in Eighteenth and Nineteenth Century America: A Guide to the History of Amercian Women*. Princeton: Princeton University Press, 1985.

Corti, Merle. *The Growth of American Thought*. New York: Harper & Row, 1964.

Davidson, Marshall. *Life in America*. Boston: Houghton Mifflin, 1951.

Diamond, Sigmund, ed. *The Nation Transformed*. New York: George Braziller, 1963.

Eighty Years of Progress. New York: New National Publishing House, 1864.

Eisenstein, Sarah. *Give Us Bread, but Give Us Roses: Working Women's Consciousness in the United States 1890 to the First World War*. New York: Routledge, 1983.

Farnham, Eliza W. *Life in Prairie Land*. 1846. Reprint, New York: Arno Press, 1972.

Fraisse, Genevieve, and Michelle Perrot. *Emerging Feminism from Revolution to World War: A History of Women*. Vol. IV. Cambridge, Mass.: Harvard University Press, Belknap Press, 1993.

Franklin, Peggy. *Private Lines: Intimate Diaries from Women from the 1880's to the Present*. New York: Ballantine, 1986.

Frost, John. *Pioneer Mothers of the West*. 1869. Reprint, New York: Arno Press, 1974.

Furnas, J. C. *A Social History of the United States: 1587–1914*. New York: Putnam, 1969.

Gabriel, Ralph Henry. *The Pageant of America: Toilers of Land and Sea*. New Haven: Yale University Press, 1926.

Garland, Hamlin. *Main Travelled Roads*. New York: Harper, 1891.

Gates, Paul W. *The Farmer's Age*. New York: Harper Torchbooks, 1960.

Giedion, Siegfried. *Mechanization Takes Command*. New York: Oxford University Press, 1948.

Ginger, Ray, ed. *The Nationalizing of American Life 1877–1900*. New York: The Free Press, 1965.

Gowans, Alan. *Images of American Living*. New York: J. P. Lippincott, 1964.

Hacker, Louis M., and Benjamin Kendrick. *The United States Since 1865*. New York: F. S. Crofts and Company, 1937.

Harveson, Mae Elizabeth. *Catherine Esther Beecher, Pioneer Educator*. 1932. Reprint, New York: Arno Press, 1969.

Hayter, Earl W. *Troubled Farmer: Rural Adjustment to Industrialism,1850–1900*. De Kalb: Northern Illinois University Press, 1968.

Hibbard, Benjamin Horace. *A History of the Public Land Policies*. Madison: University of Wisconsin Press, 1965.

Hofstadter, Richard. *The Age of Reform*. New York: Vintage Books, 1955.

Holbrook, Stewart H. *Dreamers of the American Dream*. Garden City, N.Y.: Doubleday, 1957.

The Yankee Exodus: An Account of Migration from New England. New York: The Macmillan Company, 1950.

Holmes, Kenneth L. *Covered Wagon Women: Diaries and Letters from the Western Trail, 1840–1890, Vol VI, 1853–54*. Covered Wagon Women Series. Spokane, Wash.: A. H. Clark, 1987.

Ingram, J. S. *The Centennial Exposition, Described and Illustrated*. Philadelphia: Hubbard Brothers, 1876.

Ise, John. *The Story of a Kansas Homestead*. New York: Wilson-Erickson, 1936.

Jackson, John Brinkerhoff. *American Space, the Centennial Years 1865–1876*. New York: W. W. Norton, 1972.

Jeffrey, Julia Roy. *Frontier Women: The Trans-Mississippi West 1840–1880*. New York: Hill & Wang, 1980.

Jones, Howard Mumford. *The Age of Energy: Varieties of American Experience 1865–1915*. New York: Viking Press, 1970.

307

____ .*Strange New World*. New York: Viking Press, 1964.

Jones, Jacqueline. *Labor of Love, Labor of Sorrow: Black Women, Work and the Family from Slavery to the Present*. New York: Basic Books, 1985.

Keir, Malcolm. *The Epic of Industry (The Epic of America)*. New Haven: Yale University Press, 1926.

Kelley, Mary, ed. *The Portable Margaret Fuller*. New York: Viking Press (Viking Portable Library), 1994.

Kouwenhoven, John A. *Made in America*. Garden City, N.Y.: Doubleday, 1962.

Larcom, Lucy. *A New England Girlhood*. Boston: Houghton Mifflin, 1892.

Larkin, Oliver W. *Art and Life in America*. New York: Holt, Rinehart & Winston, 1960.

Marshall, Josiah T. *The Farmer and Emigrants Handbook*. New York: Applegate and Company, 1857.

Mitchell, Edwin Valentine. *The Horse and Buggy Age in New England*. New York: Coward McCann, 1937.

____ .*It's an Old New England Custom*. New York: Bonanza Books, 1946.

Morison, Elting E. *From Know-How to Nowhere: The Development of American Technology*. New York: Basic Books, 1974.

Mumford, Lewis. *The Brown Decades*. New York: Harcourt Brace, 1931.

Needham, Walter (told to Barrows Mussey). *A Book of Country Things*. Brattleboro: Stephen Greene Press, 1965.

Nevins, Allan. *Emergence of Modern America, 1865–1878*. New York:1927. Reprint, Saint Clair Shores, Mich.: Scholarly Press, 1971.

Parrington, Vernon. *The Beginnings of Critical Realism in America*. New York: Harcourt Brace &World, 1930.

Randall, William Pierce. *Centennial: American Life in 1876*. Philadelphia: Chilton, 1969.

Riley, Glenda. *Frontierswomen: The Iowa Experience*. Ames: Iowa State University Press, 1981.

Roberts, Elizabeth. *Women's Work, 1840–1940*. Studies in Economic and Social History. New York: Macmillan, 1988.

Roberts, I. P. *Autobiography of a Farmboy*. Albany, N.Y.: J. B. Lyon, 1916.

Rolvaag, O. E. *Giants in the Earth*. New York: Harper & Row, 1927.

Rothman, Sheila. *Woman's Proper Place: A History of Changing Ideals and Practices, 1870 to the Present*. New York: Basic Books, 1978.

Schisgal, Lillian. *Women's Diaries of the Westward Journey*. New York: Schocken, 1982.

Schlesinger, Arthur M. *The Rise of the City, 1878–1898*. New York: The Macmillan Company, 1933.

Shannon, Fred A. *The Farmer's Last Frontier*. New York: Holt, Rinehart & Winston, 1945.

Stein, Roger B. *John Ruskin and Aesthetic Thought in America 1840–1900*. Cambridge: Harvard University Press, 1967.

Stratton, Joanna L. *Voices from the Kansas Frontier*. New York: Simon & Schuster, 1981.

Tarbell, Ida M. *The Nationalizing of Business 1878–1898*. New York: The Macmillan Company, 1936.

Taylor, C., et al. *Rural Life in the U.S.* New York: Alfred A. Knopf, 1949.

Taylor, Henry C. *Taroleywick: A Century of Iowa Farming*. Ames: Iowa State University Press, 1970.

Thompson, Holland. *The Age of Invention: The Chronicles of America*. New Haven: Yale University Press, 1921.

Tillson, Christiana Holmes. *A Woman's Story of Pioneer Illinois*. Chicago: R. R. Donnelley & Sons, 1919.

Trachtenberg, Alan, ed. *Democratic Vistas*. New York: George Braziller, 1970.

Twain, Mark, with Charles Dudley Warner. *The Gilded Age*. New York: Harper and Brothers, n.d.

Van Wagener, Jared Jr. *The Golden Age of Homespun*. New York: Hill & Wang, 1953 .

Weygandt, Cornelius. *A Passing America*. New York: Henry Holt, 1932.

Wilkman, Ruth. *Women, Work and Protest: A Century of American Women's Labor History*. London: RKP, 1985.

Williams, James Mickel. *The Expansion of Rural Life*. New York: Alfred A. Knopf, 1926.

Wilson, Forrest. *Crusader in Crinoline: The Life of Harriet Beecher Stowe*. Philadelphia: J. B. Lippincott, 1941.

Woloch, Nancy. *Women and the American Experience*. New York: McGraw-Hill, 1984.

Ziff, Larzer. *The American 1890s*. New York: Viking Press, 1966.

ISSUES AND IDEAS

Allen, Josiah (wife of). *My Opinions and Betsy Robert's*. Hartford: American Publishing Co., 1873 .

Baker, Elizabeth Faulkner. *Technology and Woman's Work*. New York: Columbia University Press, 1964.

Beecher, C. E. *Letters to the People on Health and Happiness.* New York: 1855. Reprint, New York: Arno Press, 1972.

Berg, Barbara J. *The Remembered Gate: Origins of American Feminism—the Woman and the City, 1800–1860.* Urban Life in America Series. New York: Oxford University Press, 1980.

Boys Own Book. New York: James Muller, 1881.

Carlier, Auguste. *Marriage in the United States.* Boston: 1867. Reprint, New York: Arno Press, 1972.

Clarke, Edward H. *Sex in Education.* Boston: 1873. Reprint, New York: Arno Press, 1971.

Cogan, Frances B. *All-American Girl: The Ideal of Real Womanhood in Mid-19th Century America.* Athens: University of Georgia Press, 1989.

Conwell, Russell H. *Acres of Diamonds or, How Men Get Rich Honestly.* Philadelphia: Temple Magazine Publishing Company, 1893.

Cott, Nancy F., ed. *Root of Bitterness.* New York: E. P. Dutton, 1972.

Crowe, Martha Foote. *The American Country Girl.* New York: Frederick A. Stokes, 1915.

Ditzion, Sidney. *Marriage, Morals and Sex in America.* New York: Octagon Books, 1970.

Drake, John, et al. *A Practical Book for Practical People.* Albany: Eagle Publishing Company, 1895.

Duffey, E. B. *The Relation of the Sexes.* 1876. Reprint, New York: Arno Press, 1974.

Flexner, Eleanor. *Century of Struggle: The Woman's Rights Movement in the United States.* New York: Atheneum, 1968.

Fraser, John. *Youth's Golden Cycle.* Philadelphia: William Patterson, 1885.

Howe, Julia Ward. *Sex and Education. A Reply to Dr. E. H. Clarke's "Sex in Education."* 1874. Reprint, New York: Arno Press, 1972.

King, William C. *Portraits and Principles.* Springfield, Mass.: King, Richardson and Company, 1894.

Lewis, Dio. *Our Girls.* 1871. Reprint, New York: Arno Press, 1974.

Lunardini, Christine. *What Every American Should Know about Women's History: Two Hundred Events That Shaped Our Destiny.* Holbrook, Mass.: Bob Adams, 1994.

MacDonald, Anne L. *Feminine Ingenuity: How Women Inventors Changed America.* New York: Ballantine Books, 1992.

Owen, Catherine. *Ten Dollars Enough.* Cambridge, Mass.: Houghton Mifflin, 1888.

Penny, Virginia. *How Women Can Make Money.* 1870. Reprint, New York: Arno Press, 1971.

Rayne, Mrs. M. L. *What Can a Woman Do.* Peterborough, N.Y.: Eagle Publishing Company, 1893.

Ryan, Mary P. *Womanhood in America.* New York: New Viewpoints-Franklin Watts, 1975.

Salmon, Lucy Maynard. *Domestic Service.* New York: 1897. Reprint, New York: Arno Press, 1972.

Scott, Anne Firor. *The American Woman: Who Was She.* Englewood Cliffs, N.J.: Prentice-Hall, 1971.

Sinclair, Andrew. *The Emancipation of the American Woman.* New York: Harper & Row, 1965.

Smith, Page. *Daughters of the Promised Land.* Boston: Little, Brown, 1970.

Smuts, Robert W. *Women and Work in America.* New York: Columbia University Press, 1959.

Thayer, William N. *Success: Oracle of the Age.* Boston: A. M. Thayer, 1892.

Welter, Barbara. "The Cult of True Womanhood—1820–1860." *American Quarterly* XVIII (1966).

ESSENTIAL FACTS

Balch, William. *Complete Compendium of Universal Knowledge.* N.J., Star Publishing Company, 1895.

Berg, Albert Ellery. *The Universal Self Instructor.* Thomas Kelly Publisher, 1883.

Blakelee, George E. *Blakelee's Industrial Cyclopedia.* New York: Baker and Taylor, 1884.

Chase, A. W. *Doctor Chase's Receipt Book.* Detroit: F. B. Dickerson Company, 1884.

Courtney, W. S. *The Farmer's and Mechanic's Manual.* New York: E. B. Treat and Company, 1868.

Ehrenreich, Barbara, and Deidre English. *For Her Own Good: One Hundred Fifty Years of Expert Advice to Women.* New York: Doubleday, 1989.

Felker, P. H. *The Grocer's Manual.* New York: American Grocer's Publishing Association, 1879.

Hamilton, Alexander V. *Daily Wants: The Household Cyclopedia of Practical Receipts.* Springfield, Mass.: W. J. Holland & Company, 1873.

Moore, R. *Everyday Wants.* New York: The World, 1884.

Northrup, Henry Davenport. *The Household Encyclopedia*. New York: n.p., 1881.

Pilkington, James. *Mechanic's Own Book*. Boston: Sanborn, Carter, Bazin and Company, 1857.

Ransom, D. *Ransom's Family Receipt Book*. Buffalo, N.Y.: D. Ransom and Son, 1902.

Robinson, Nugent, ed. *Colliers Cyclopedia of Social and Commercial Information*. New York: Peter Fenelon Collier Publisher, 1882.

Ruoff, Henry W. *The Century Book of Facts*. Springfield, Mass.: The King Richardson Co., 1902.

Yaggy, L. W. *How To Do*. Chicago: Powers Higley and Company, 1902.

Youman, A. E. *A Dictionary of Everyday Wants*. New York: Frank M. Reed, 1873.

FARMS, FARMING, AND FARM LIFE

Beecher, Henry Ward. *Fruits, Flowers and Farming*. New York: Derby and Jackson, 1859.

Blake, Reverend John L. *The Farm and Fireside*. New York: Alden Beardsley, 1855.

_____ . *The Farmer at Home*. N.p.: C. M. Saxton, 1852.

_____ . *The Farmer's Everyday Book*. Auburn, N.Y.: Derby and Miller, 1851.

Bunker, Timothy (William Clift). *Tim Bunker's Papers, or Yankee Farming*. New York: Orange Judd Company, 1868.

Commissioner of Patents. *Post Office Report*. Wash., D.C.: George W. Bauman, Printer, for the years 1849–1860.

Copeland, Morris R. *Country Life*. Cleveland: John P. Jewett and Company, 1859.

Dickerman, Charles W. *The Farmer's Book*. Philadelphia: Zeigler, McCurdy and Company, 1868.

Farm Conveniences. New York: Orange Judd and Company, 1884.

Flint, Charles L. *The American Farmer*. Hartford: Ralph H. Park and Company, 1884.

Greeley, Horace. *What I Know of Farming*. New York: G. W. Carlton and Company, 1871.

Henderson, Peter. *Garden and Farm Topics*. New York: Peter Henderson and Company, 1884.

_____ . *Gardening for Profit*. New York: Orange Judd Company, 1886.

Massachusetts Board of Agriculture. *Annual Report*. Boston: Wright and Potter Printing Company for the years 1870–1885.

Miller, James. *How To Get a Farm*. New York: n.p., 1864.

Mitchell, D. G. *My Farm of Edgewood*. New York: Scribners, 1863.

_____ . *Rural Studies*. New York: Scribners, 1866.

_____ . *Rural Studies, with Hints for Country Places*. New York: Scribners, 1867.

Roberts, Isaac P. *The Farmstead*. New York: Macmillan and Company, 1900.

Robinson, Solon. *Facts for Farmers*, vols. I and II. Cleveland: A. J. Johnson, 1866.

_____ . *How To Live*. New York: Fowler and Wells, 1860.

Thomas, J. J. *The American Fruit Culturist*. New York: William Wood and Company, 1871.

Thomas, Robert B. *The Old Farmer's Almanac*. Worcester, Mass.: Edward Whitney, 1893.

U.S. Department of Agriculture. *Report of the Commissioner of Agriculture*. Washington, D.C.: Government Printing Office, for the years 1863–1885.

THE HOME: PLANNING, DESIGN, DECORATION

Beecher, C. E., and H. B. Stowe. *The American Woman's Home*. New York: J. B. Ford and Company, 1869.

Chicago Daily Tribune, Home Department. *The Home Guide*. Elgin, Ill.: S. L. Taylor, 1877.

Cook, Clarence. *The House Beautiful*. New York: Scribners, 1881.

Downing, A. J. *The Architecture of Country Houses*. New York: D. Appleton and Company, 1850.

_____ . *Cottage Residences*. New York: John Wiley, 1853.

Eastlake, Charles L. *Hints on Household Taste in Furniture, Upholstery and Other Details*. Boston: James R. Osgood and Company, 1872.

Fitch, James Marston. *American Building: The Historical Forces that Shaped It*. Boston: Houghton Mifflin, 1966.

_____ . *Architecture and the Aesthetics of Plenty*. New York: Columbia University Press, 1961.

Fowler, O. S. *A Home for All*. New York: Fowler and Wells, 1853.

Gardner, E. G. *The House that Jill Built*. New York: Fords, Howard and Hulbert, 1882.

Lynes, Russell. *The Tastemakers*. New York: Harper, 1955.

Nelson, Lowry. *American Farm Life*. Cambridge: Harvard University Press, 1954.

Ryan, Mary P. *The Empire of the Mother: American Writings about Domesticity, 1830–1860*. Binghamton, N.Y.: Haworth Press, 1982.

Scully, Vincent. *American Architecture and Urbanism*. New York: Frederick A. Praeger, 1969.

Sloan, Samuel. *Sloan's Homestead Architecture*. Philadelphia: n.p., 1861.

Todd, Sereno Edwards. *Todd's Country Homes*. Hartford: Hartford Publishing Company, 1870.

Vaux, Calvert. *Villas and Cottages*. New York: Harpers, 1872.

Ware, John F. W. *Home Life*. Boston: William V. Spencer, 1870.

Waring, George E. *Book of the Farm*. Philadelphia: Porter and Coates, 1877.

____ . *Village Improvements and Farm Villages*. Boston: James R. Osgood and Company, 1877.

Wheeler, Gervase. *Rural Homes*. New York: G. E. Woodward, 1868.

Woodward, G. E. *Woodward's Suburban and Country Homes*. New York: Excelsior Publishing Company, 1873.

Woodward, G. E., and F. W. Woodward. *Woodward's Architecture, Landscape Gardening and Rural Art*. New York: G. E. and F. W. Woodward, 1866.

____ . *Woodward's Country Homes*. New York: G. E. and F. W. Woodward, 1865.

Wright, Lawrence. *Clean and Decent: The Unruffled History of the Bathroom and W.C*. New York: Viking, 1960.

____ . *Home Fires Burning: A History of Domestic Heating and Cooking*. London: Routledge and Kegan Paul, 1964.

HOME OCCUPATIONS: COOKING, MOTHERING, FASHION, HOMEMAKING

Abell, Mrs. L. G. *Ladies Guide, or Skillful Housewife*. New York: J. M. Fairchild and Company, 1852.

Barnard, Frederick, ed. *Johnson's New Universal Encyclopedia*. New York: Alvin Johnson & Son, 1876.

Bazar Book of Decorum, The. New York: Harper, 1877.

Beecher, Mrs. H. W. *Motherly Talks with Young Housekeepers*. New York: J. B. Ford and Company, 1873.

Benjamin, Park, ed. *Appleton's Cyclopedia of Applied Mechanics*. New York: D. Appleton and Company, 1881 .

Changing Year, Poems and Pictures of Life and Nature, The. New York: Cassell, Petter and Galpin and Company, 1883.

Child, Mrs. *The American Frugal Housewife*. New York: Samuel S. and William Wood, 1838.

Cornelius, Mrs. *The Young Housekeeper's Friend*. Boston: Brown, Taggard and Chase, 1859.

Croley, Mrs. J. C. *Jennie Jones's American Cookery Book*. New York: Excelsior Publishing, 1878.

Crowfield, Christopher (H. B. Stowe). *House and Home Papers*. Boston: Ticknor and Fields, n.d.

Edwards, Tryon. *Jewels for the Household*. Hartford: Cage, Lockwood and Company, 1857.

Ellet, Mrs. E. F. *The New Cyclopedia of Domestic Economy*. Norwich, Conn.: Henry Bill Publishing Company, 1872.

Ewing, Emma. *Cooking and Castle Building*. Boston: James R. Osgood and Company, 1880.

Finley Ruth E. *The Lady of Godey's*. Philadelphia: J. B. Lippincott, 1931.

Gillette, Mrs. F. L. *White House Cookbook*. New York: Saalfield Publishing Company, 1887.

Gregory, Mrs., and Friends. *Woman's Favorite Cookbook*. N.p., 1906.

Hall, Elizabeth M. *Breakfast, Luncheon and Tea*. New York: Scribner, Armstrong and Company, 1875.

____ . *Common Sense in the Household*. New York: Scribner, Armstrong and Company, 1874.

____ . *Practical Cookery and Domestic Economy*. New York: Saxton, Barker and Company, 1860.

Hewitt, Emma. *Queen of Home*. Philadelphia: International Publishing Company, 1892.

How To Keep House. New York: Frank Tousey Publisher, 1882.

Howland, Mrs. A. E. *The American Economical Housekeeper*. Worcester, Mass.: S. A. Howland, 1852.

Ladies Indispensable Assistant. New York: published at 128 Nassau Street, 1852.

Lewis, Jane, ed. *Labour and Love: Women's Experience of Home and Family 1850–1940*. Cambridge, Mass.: Basil Blackwell, 1986.

Lincoln, Mrs. D. A., and Maria Parlou. *New England Cook Book*. Boston: C. E. Brown and Company, 1887.

Logan, Mrs. John A. *The Home Manual*. Boston: A. M. Thayer and Company, 1889.

Lyman, Joseph P. *Philosophy of Housekeeping.* Hartford: S. M. Betts and Company, 1869.
McCoy, John M. *A Tribute of Flowers to the Memory of Mother.* Chicago and Philadelphia: Union Publishing House, 1882.
McLendy, Mary R. *The Perfect Woman.* N.p.: K. T. Boland, 1903.
New Practical Housekeeping, The. Minneapolis: Home Publishing Company, 1890.
Nichols, Mrs. J. C., and Anna Holverson. *The Household Guide.* Naperville, Ill.: J. L. Nicholas, 1893.
Northrup, Henry Davenport. *Crown Jewels, or Gems of Literature.* Boston: A. E. Wilson and Company, 1887.
Practical Housekeeping. Minneapolis: Buckeye Publishing Company, 1881.
Pulte, Mrs. J. H. *Domestic Cookery.* Cincinnati: George W. Smith, 1888.
Randall, Rona. *The Model Wife—19th Century Style.* Franklin, N.Y.: New Amsterdam Books, 1989.
Rutledge (Miss). *The Carolina Housewife.* Charleston: John Russell, 1855.
Sangster, Margaret E. *The Art of Homemaking.* New York: The Christian Herald Bible House, 1898.
Shapiro, Laura. *Perfection Salad: Women and Cooking at the Turn of the Century.* New York: Farrar, Straus & Giroux, 1986.
Shillaber, Lydia. *Mrs. Shillaber's Cook Book.* New York: Thomas Y. Crowell, 1887.
Smith, Mrs. Mary G. *The Temperance Cookbook.* Wellington: Houghton and Smith, 1877.
Successful Housekeeper, The. Detroit: M. W. Ellsworth and Company, 1883.
Trall, R. T. *The New Hydropathic Cookbook.* New York: Fowler and Wells, 1854.
Treasures Of Use and Beauty. Detroit: F. B. Dickerson and Company, 1883.
Tyson (Miss). *The Queen of the Kitchen.* Philadelphia: T. B. Peterson and Brothers, 1882.
Warner, C. D., et al. *The American Home Book.* New York: G. P. Putnam's Sons, 1872.
Wells, Richard A. *Manners, Culture and Dress.* Springfield, Mass.: King, Richardson and Company, 1890.
Wise Blackbird, The. *Household Notes and Queries.* Boston: D. Lathrop and Company, 1886.

HEALTH CARE AND MEDICINE

Beard, George. *American Nervousness.* New York, n.p., 1881.
Dunlop, Richard. *Doctors of the American Frontier.* Garden City, N.Y.: Doubleday, 1965.
Flexner, James T. *Doctors on Horseback.* New York: Garden City Publishing Company, 1939.
Foote, E. B. *Health and Disease.* Murray Hill Publishing Company, 1901.
Fowler, O. S. *Sexual Science.* Philadelphia: National Publishing Company, 1875.
Hertzler, Arthur E. *The Horse and Buggy Doctor.* Lincoln: University of Nebraska Press, 1970.
Home Advice. New York: Harper and Brothers, 1857.
Hoskins, Thomas H. *What We Eat.* Boston: T. O. H. P. Burnham, 1861.
Marti-Ibañez, F. *History of American Medicine.* New York: M. D. Publications, 1938.
Philbrook, H. B. *Cause and Cure of Disease.* New York: The office of "Problems of Nature," 1886.
Pickard, M. E., and R. C. Boly. *The Midwest Pioneer—His Ills, Cures and Doctors.* New York: Henry Schuman, 1946.
Pierce, R. V. *The People's Common Sense Medical Advisor.* Buffalo: World's Dispensary Printing Office, 1895.
Richardson, Joseph G. *Health and Longevity.* Philadelphia: Home Health Society, 1909.
Rothstein, William. *American Physicians in the 19th Century.* Baltimore: Johns Hopkins Press, 1971.
Shryock, Richard Harrison. *Medicine and Society in America.* Ithaca: Cornell University Press, 1962.
Smith, Edward. *Foods.* New York: D. Appleton and Company, 1837.
Storer, Horatio Robinson. *The Causation Course, and Treatment of Reflex Insanity in Woman.* Boston and New York: Arno Press, 1972.
Warren, Ira. *Warren's Household Physician.* Boston: A. I. Bradley Company, 1893.